KENTUCKY
Gardener's
Guide

The What, Where, When, How & Why
of Landscape Gardening in Kentucky

KENTUCKY
Gardener's
Guide

Denny McKeown

COOL
SPRINGS
PRESS

McKeown, Denny
    Kentucky gardener's guide: the what, where, when, how & why of landscape gardening in Kentucky /Denny McKeown.

    p.   cm.
    Includes bibliographical references (p.   ).
    ISBN 1-888608-17-X (pbk.)
    1. Landscape plants—Kentucky 2. Landscape gardening—Kentucky I. Title

SB407.M32 2000
635.9'09769—dc21

                                                                00-024018

Published by Cool Springs Press,
a division of Thomas Nelson, Inc.,
P.O. Box 141000, Nashville, Tennessee 37214

First printing 2000
Printed in the United States of America
10 9 8 7 6 5 4 3

On the cover (clockwise from top left): Cobbity Daisies, Lily-of-the-Valley, 'Knockout' Rose Tulips.

Horticulture Nomenclature Editor: Richard Feist

Visit the Thomas Nelson website at: wwwThomasNelson.com

DEDICATION

I would like to dedicate this book to my three children,
Molly, Christopher, and Jenny, who make me very
proud to be their father, and to Louis Hillenmeyer III who
comes from a great Kentucky nursery family, is
incoming president of the American Nursery and Landscape
Association, and personally does a terrific job of
promoting the nursery industry in Kentucky.

ACKNOWLEDGMENTS

A big thank you to all of my industry peers, both past and present, who have shared and continue to share their knowledge and expertise with me. This group certainly includes the University of Kentucky Extension Service, which continues to provide me with a vast amount of information.

I would also like to give a big thank you to Debbie Schneider and Marie Proffitt, who together took my handwritten "chicken scratch" and transformed it into this book you're about to read.

A thank you goes out to 55/KRC Clear Channel Communications for affording me the opportunity to spread the gardening word throughout Kentucky.

A big thank you to Roger Waynick, Hank McBride, Jan Keeling, Sara Anglin, and all the others at Cool Springs Press for publishing this book.

I would like to acknowledge Rick Frederick and his landscape supply company. He is always willing to share his plant expertise with me and all of his fellow Kentuckians.

A special thank you to my son, Chris, and a big hug to you for not only fulfilling your responsibilities as Vice President of our Garden Center, Landscape Division, and Farm, but for taking on many of my responsibilities to free up time for me to write this book.

A big thank you to Richard Feist for being my horticultural editor and teaching me lots of new information.

And last but certainly not least, to you, for having the confidence in me to have this book on hand to help you have the best landscape ever.

CONTENTS

*H*I! WELCOME TO the *Kentucky Gardener's Guide*. The purpose of this book is to help you expand your gardening and landscape knowledge.

First let me introduce myself. I've been a part of the nursery industry for nearly thirty-eight years. During that time, I've tried to serve the needs of the gardening public. I've worked in garden centers in both sales and management. I've been involved with landscape design and installation and have also been involved with the growing operation of nursery stock. Before you say, "Gee, Denny, you must have had a hard time keeping a job," let me explain.

My first twenty-nine years in the nursery industry were spent with one company, Natorp's, in southwestern Ohio. There I had the opportunity to learn and grow through working with the many professionals associated with the company. In 1992, I started my own Garden Center and Landscape Company that I operate with my son, Chris, who is the backbone of our operation. I've learned over the years that my success as a nurseryman depends solely on the success of the landscapes that belong to the customers I serve. This book contains over 175 plant varieties that I have worked with personally. Many of the plants are in my own home landscape, and others have been sold to customers and installed in their landscapes.

Personally, when it comes to outdoor plants of all types, I'm a low-maintenance, high-performance, high-color kind of guy. I like to enjoy a nice-looking landscape with my eyes and not my blood and sweat, and I believe that most homeowners feel the same way. Our busy schedules often don't allow the time needed to work in a landscape for hours a week all season long. This Kentucky book shares with you those plants that will give the best in landscape appearance with the least amount of maintenance. But those of you who enjoy yard work won't be disappointed either. Many of these plant varieties will do well without you, but they will do even better than you would ever expect if you provide some assistance. Successful gardening at any level needs you to do one important thing: "Use common sense."

BE HONEST WITH YOURSELF

Most of us go to buy plants at the garden store with the idea that *I'll buy what strikes my eye*, giving no consideration to the location in which that plant is expected to grow. We may tell ourselves and the nursery staff that we have the right location for a plant, hoping that our poor planting site will be the exception and not the rule. Canadian hemlock and rhododendron are perfect examples of plants that home-owners often fall in love with at first sight, but both of these plants need special growing conditions to thrive. Roses are another great example of plants that often wind up in too much shade because we have convinced ourselves that two hours of sun are as good as five. When buying plants, be willing to substitute a plant that will be happier in a particular planting site, and you will be a happier homeowner.

The USDA cold-hardiness zone map on page 256 will help you understand your growing environment a little better. A cold-hardiness zone is defined by the northernmost boundary in which plants can grow when the weather is at its coldest. Kentucky is located in cold-hardiness zone 6. It is useful to know the zone in which you garden.

TO AMEND OR NOT TO AMEND:
THAT'S THE QUESTION

The majority of us in Kentucky have clay soil of varying thickness. There are some pockets of good soil in western and eastern Kentucky, but again, most have clay soil of various thickness. For years, it was standard practice to tell homeowners installing new plants to amend the soil—by that

I mean to add peat moss, compost, manure, and all the above to the soil you dug out while digging the hole. Common sense is now convincing the industry to tell you that it is possible to *overamend* your soil. Think about it. What kind of soil is the plant going to grow in once the roots grow beyond the hole you dug? Overimproving the existing soil or, worse yet, replacing the old soil with nice fresh topsoil creates what I call "bathtubbing." When it rains, or when we water, the moisture goes through the overamended soil very quickly, hitting the hard clay bottom and filling up like a bathtub. Too much water equals a dead plant. I recommend using organic peat or pine bark chips to amend soil when needed, but do not add more than 30 percent amendments to mix with the existing soil. Always break up your clay soil so no particle is bigger than a golf ball.

How Big Will My Plant Grow?

Kentucky landscapes are full of sweetbay magnolias and Japanese weeping cherries that can grow up against the foundation of a home until the house looks like it was swallowed by the trees. Your only recourse is to trim the trees—but then it will look like they have a bad haircut. Such a situation is not all your fault. When you visited your favorite nursery store, the plant sign that identified the plants for sale probably said something like Magnolia 'Sweetbay', grows to 10 feet high and 6 feet wide. But no plant, with the exception of annuals, perennials, and ornamental grasses, ever stops growing until the day it dies. A cute little Alberta spruce that's considered a dwarf will grow a couple of inches a year. That growth adds up over a ten-year period. Find out how much growth you can expect from a particular tree, shrub, or evergreen every year, and how much trimming is going to be needed to maintain the plant at a finished size for you. This book will help you determine the growth rate, but your pruning shears will ultimately keep a particular plant within your bounds.

LET'S MULCH, IT'S SO PRETTY!

We hear that mulch discourages weeds. We hear that mulch retains moisture. And mulch gives our landscape beds that finished look. All of this is true, but more and more home-owners are unintentionally harming their landscape plants with mulch. First, what is mulch? It can be any organic material covering our soil, from newspaper to grass clippings to the ever-popular wood mulch. Wood mulches come two ways: actual bark that was either chipped or shredded, or hardwood that can be the wood of a tree or recycled lumber. The bark is best; it lasts longer, both in color and in quality.

Here's where common sense comes into play. Too much mulch can prevent air and water from getting to the plant's roots. And many plants mulch themselves with their own foliage spread. You don't want to put down more than 2 inches of mulch in any bed. You don't want to have any mulch up on the stems or trunks of any plants. If you say, "But I already have two inches of mulch on my planting beds from last year," I would say, "Either loosen the existing mulch to make it look better, or remove it completely before applying fresh mulch." Adding too much mulch to your plant beds will cause more harm than good.

FOLLOWING DIRECTIONS: IS MORE BETTER?

There are many products we can use that will help our plants grow happy and healthy, including fertilizer, selective weedkillers and other herbicides, pesticides, and fungicides. Companies that manufacture and package these products spend large sums of money to get each product approved by the Environmental Protection Agency and labeled. The label includes the very important *how much to use*, such as the amount to mix with water and how much area the mixture should cover. The label on granular material will tell you how much to use over so many square feet. All the labeled products will do the job that's required and remain environmentally friendly when used properly. Please do not expect any product to work faster by using more than the recommended rate. With pesticides and fungicides, the directions will also state what diseases and insects a particular product will control. Please be sure you are using a product that will treat your specific problem, and that you use it at the right time of day and month. Remember, common sense tells us to do only as the product label states.

THE GOOD, THE BAD, AND THE UGLY

Now we're talking about the creatures of the world, like insects (commonly called bugs) and other creatures like moles, rabbits, voles, deer, and anything else with four legs.

Let's start with insects. Fewer than 3 percent of insects are considered risks to our plants. Most harmful insects only attack plants that are already suffering from severe plant stress. Mother Nature succeeded for many years without the help of pesticides. That's why we have to be careful when treating for those bad bugs. We have a greater chance of killing the many more beneficial insects that are out there than we do of killing just the bad bugs. This is especially true if spraying for a bad bug at the wrong time of that insect's life cycle. Most insects have only a short lifespan anyway. A few holes in your maple leaves should not cause alarm. Try to fill up your spare time with other projects that don't allow you time to look for holes in your leaves.

Now, as for four-legged critters, a lot of us have to learn to coexist. Who was there first? I would say squirrels, raccoons, chipmunks, and mole ancestors were on your property way before the land was cleared for housing. Those of you who still have surrounding woods and open fields have natural breeding grounds for these critters. If you need controls, raccoons, foxes, and skunks can be trapped by a licensed exterminator (it's illegal for you to trap and relocate raccoons, foxes, and skunks). Chipmunks and squirrels can be captured in a Havahart trap and relocated. Moles are best eliminated by trapping and killing. There are products being sold to run the moles to your neighbors. These are safe products made up of castor oil and soap detergent mixed with water—but if you have a woods or open field near your home, forget it! Besides, moles only do aesthetic damage and no lawn damage. Voles can be trapped and eliminated, using baited (with peanut butter) mouse traps. Groundhogs can be discouraged by placing ammonia-treated rags in areas in which they're known to reside. Deer have become a major problem in many landscapes. There is a new product out now that is a combination of bitrex, a very bitter-tasting safe product, and a plant-friendly latex which allows the mix to remain on the plant for five to six months without being washed away. This product is sold under the name This-1-Works®, and it really does. With squirrels, make friends quickly. They are smarter than you, and if you get in the habit of feeding them, they'll allow you to keep your sanity and good nature.

The best answer is to learn to share with the critters. Remember, their family was there before yours.

KILLING WITH KINDNESS

I am sometimes asked by someone outside of our industry how we can afford to guarantee a living plant. They'll go on to say that anybody can buy a plant and not take care of it, and if it dies, we in the industry will have to replace it free of charge. While this scenario is possible, it's the exception, certainly not the rule. I have found over the years that, when it comes to planting, all homeowners want to be successful.

From annual flowers to shade trees, homeowners take tremendous pride in seeing their plants grow. If there is a problem getting new plants and plantings established, it's usually not from neglect but its opposite. I call it "killing with kindness." This comes about by trying too hard to assist Mother Nature. We overamend the backfill, placing soil around a plant's root clump that is too fine. We place too much fertilizer around the roots of freshly installed plants, causing their roots to burn. And the number one way plants are killed with kindness? Overwatering. Newly installed trees and shrubs, especially those planted in clay soil, get watered every day. During hot summers when our meteorologist on TV keeps telling us how hot and dry it is, we automatically go outside and water. Before watering, you should always check the soil around your plants with a garden trowel, checking down 3 to 5 inches to see if there's moisture. Water only when dry. All plants can sustain themselves much longer when kept on the dry side rather than too wet.

Is Cheapest Best?

Ever since gardening has become the number one hobby of the American public, more and more retail businesses have added plants to their inventory, especially in the spring. There has also been an increase in the population of landscape installers. Hey, it's America, the home of free enterprise.

But let's start with the garden center. In today's fast-paced world, we've gotten used to shopping by phone. Home-owners often call garden centers to find out the price of a 1-gallon barberry or a 3-gallon redbud. Then they'll call another nursery to get *their* price. Remember, you're buying the plant, not the pot it's growing in, and the plant's quality is difficult to judge over the phone. The best way to price-shop for any tree or shrub is to visit different garden centers to see just what you are buying. Would you buy a sofa over the phone? Probably not. And the right tree will outlast the best sofa . . .

A lot of the populace think that the only skill required to plant a tree is the strength to dig a hole. "Heck, anybody can dig a hole! Have you got a chain saw? Okay, then, you're an arborist." But tree arborists come in all sizes of qualifications. Some, and I really don't classify these as arborists, get a chain saw and a pickup truck and start knocking on doors. They usually do not have liability or workmen's compensation insurance. "So what?" you say. Well, if one of these "Today, we do windows" types causes property damage to you or your neighbor or, worse yet, gets hurt on your property, that chain-saw fellow could wind up owning your home. Then how much do you save? If you need some tree work, get a couple of estimates. If one looks too good to be true, it probably is.

If you need a landscape installation, be sure to find out how experienced the installers are. The often-heard expression "Why so much? Anybody can dig a hole!" is just not true. Good experienced installers have been trained over the years how to face the plant, how large to dig the hole, how to read plans, how to make good on-the-job changes to an installation, and how to work with others.

Buying living plants and landscape services is no different from any other consumer purchase: you get exactly what you pay for. Don't forget to figure quality and experience into the value column. This includes the handling of the trees, shrubs, and flowers before you buy them, and the ability to give you future advice and assistance. This type of operation may not be the cheapest in dollars alone, but don't forget to factor in all the other values when you are looking for the best deal.

Plants Are Like People

Yes, there are many similarities between people and plants. To begin with, both have a beginning and, unfortunately, both have an end. Both groups have the best chance of a long life when living in the best of environmental conditions. The healthier we keep ourselves, the less likely we are to catch a cold, contract the flu, or have heart and other problems. Plants are the same way: the better the planting site for any living plant, the better it will grow. Choosing poor to minimal planting sites can cause our plants to attract bad bugs, disease, and overall stress that will greatly reduce the plant's longevity.

This book will greatly increase your success in improving your home landscape if you follow the "likes and dislikes" of the many plants that are listed. Take the book with you as you shop for new trees, shrubs, perennials, and those summer-blooming flowers. It will help you decide what to buy and plant.

The Kentucky Nursery Association has developed a certification program for retailers and for landscape installers in our industry. Look for companies whose employees display their certificates. Feel free to seek out great gardening and landscape installation advice from highly skilled people.

Now, get set to read and discover some great plants that will add beauty and value to your landscape!

HAPPY GARDENING!

P.S. At times, I have included a section titled "Landscape Merit." This section appears within certain entries to indicate the exceptional, noteworthy qualities of a particular plant that may have application for your landscape.

PLANT CHARACTERISTICS AT A GLANCE

Each plant entry in this guide offers pertinent information about the plant such as its height, bloom time, flower color, and hardiness zone (the zone in which the plant is winter hardy). Each plant's light requirements (the amount of sunlight suitable for the plant's needs) are indicated by the following symbols:

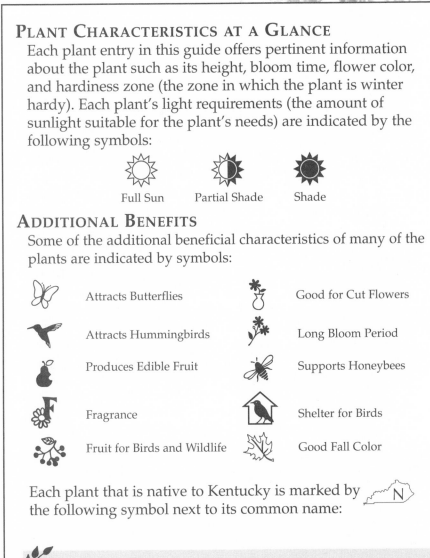

Full Sun Partial Shade Shade

ADDITIONAL BENEFITS

Some of the additional beneficial characteristics of many of the plants are indicated by symbols:

Attracts Butterflies		Good for Cut Flowers	
Attracts Hummingbirds		Long Bloom Period	
Produces Edible Fruit		Supports Honeybees	
Fragrance		Shelter for Birds	
Fruit for Birds and Wildlife		Good Fall Color	

Each plant that is native to Kentucky is marked by the following symbol next to its common name:

Did You Know?

Many plant entries end with a "Did You Know?" box that offers information about the plant's uses, nomenclature, history, or other information that is little known or just plain interesting.

CHAPTER ONE

Annuals

T HE DEFINITION OF "ANNUAL" is "a plant that grows, flowers, seeds, and then dies, all in one growing season." In this chapter you will find true annuals as well as tender perennials that are treated as annuals. Many of us are saddened when the first killing fall frost appears to take the lives of our annuals. Well, before you get out the hanky, remember that all annuals eventually go to seed and die even without a killing frost. Amusement parks in temperate areas, known for their masses of beautifully colored flowers, have to have annuals planted two to three times a year to keep the flowers looking great. Next time you visit Disneyland, be sure to appreciate what the groundskeepers have to do to keep the parks looking colorful. *Annuals bloom, get tired, and go away with or without cold weather.*

The Icing on the Cake

Annuals give the finishing touch to any landscape. Most of the varieties I have listed in this chapter require little to very little maintenance. I believe people should be able to visually enjoy their yards, and not always from behind a hoe or a hose. Annuals (and tender perennials used as annuals) make it easy to be successful with color combinations. These flowers have a way of enhancing all the other plantings and features in your yard, regardless of the variety or varieties that you choose.

Buy What Fits Your Landscape Conditions

Most of us make a trip to the greenhouse or nursery store in May, and we become like kids in a candy store. We want some of this and some of that, and we take it all home. Then we scratch our heads and say, "Now where am I going to plant all this stuff?"

Before you go and buy, take a walk around your landscape. Make notes about various areas, jotting down the type of soil, the amount

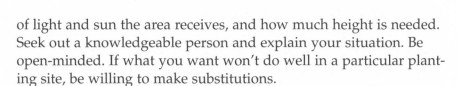

of light and sun the area receives, and how much height is needed.
Seek out a knowledgeable person and explain your situation. Be
open-minded. If what you want won't do well in a particular planting site, be willing to make substitutions.

What are Proven Winners®? Proven Winners (PW) are a select
group of plants that are copyrighted by a group of growers who
own the rights to those PW varieties. They are hybrids of popular
flowering plants, with undesirable qualities bred out, and desirable
qualities bred in. The seed is controlled, so it's not available to homeowners, but you can purchase the plants. These flowers have been
tried and tested, and all the descriptions about their benefits are true
as written. You will definitely have flowers that are new, colorful,
and exciting.

How to Buy Annuals

Homeowners that start their own seeds can save money (if they
don't spend too much time and money getting the seeds started, of
course). Most "seed-starter homeowners" begin seeds indoors too
soon, and the resulting plants grow very weak and "stretchy." Do
not start your seeds indoors any sooner than four to six weeks before
it's safe to plant seedlings outdoors. Most homeowners buy their
annuals already growing in pots and flats at the garden store or
greenhouse. The retailers that sell annual plants have to be experienced enough to take proper care of all those annual bedding plants
until they're sold. Poor watering and handling at the retail outlet can
have you buying summer-blooming flowers that have one foot in the
grave. Make sure all the annuals you buy look fresh and healthy—
remember, they won't get any better-looking on the drive home.

Pinching Off Early Flowers

I know, you're buying your annuals for the color, and it's the color on the annuals for sale that make you want to buy them in the first place. But early blooms on young annual plants slow down initial growth. By pinching off the early blooms, you will cause the plant to grow much quicker, giving you lots more bloom sooner. Keep the flowers pinched off your young transplants for the first couple of weeks after planting. It will hurt for a moment, but it will pay dividends for months. If my daughter Jenny can do it, so can you.

Final Tips on Watering

If you're planting impatiens in the sun, keep a hose handy. When you are planting impatiens in a bed with deciduous shrubs or ever-greens, you'll water the impatiens a lot more often than you will want to water those shrubs. This means you'll have to water the impatiens individually so the permanent plants don't get too much water. Many of the annuals listed in this chapter don't require a lot of water. Read about each variety carefully so you understand the needs of each summer-blooming flower.

I have listed some great petunia varieties. If water is needed, don't let a sprinkler ruin a lot of bloom color while getting the flowers wet. Keep the hose on the ground or leave a soaker hose in place.

Mulch with Common Sense

When adding bark mulch, be sure to keep the mulch away from your flower stems; you don't want any mulch piled up 2 to 3 inches on the stems. Many annuals "mulch themselves" with their spread-ing growth habit, which retains moisture and shades weed seeds, thus reducing weed production. If you do mulch, loosen the mulch monthly during the summer months so it won't become a hardened water barrier. A garden hook and a Garden Weasel® are two great tools for loosening your mulch. In fact, the Garden Weasel will cultivate the mulch very quickly, leaving the mulch looking like it was just freshly applied.

PLANT COMPATIBLE PLANTS

As you read this chapter, you will notice similarities in water and light needs of some of the different varieties. This is important to note when combining two or more varieties in the same planting bed. Select those that have the same common needs so when you water or the temperature gets hot, all will stay happy together with the same amount of maintenance from you.

YOU GET WHAT YOU PAY FOR

As with anything in life, cheapest is not necessarily best. Buy your summer-blooming annuals from nursery stores, garden centers, and greenhouses where knowledgeable people are on hand to answer all your questions and steer you in the right direction. Seasonal plant stores might have great prices, but if you buy all the wrong stuff, or the weather freezes, how much money have you really saved? *Now go out and make your landscape the most colorful ever.*

Ageratum

Ageratum houstonianum

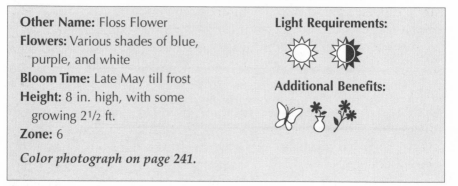

Other Name: Floss Flower

Flowers: Various shades of blue, purple, and white

Bloom Time: Late May till frost

Height: 8 in. high, with some growing 2½ ft.

Zone: 6

Color photograph on page 241.

Light Requirements:

Additional Benefits:

Ageratum has been available as a summer-blooming flower for many, many years. Many of you gave up on ageratum many hot summers ago, just as you did with a lot of other older varieties that bloomed well and kept attractive foliage only until the hot summer weather set in. When they collapsed in the heat, you may have vowed never to plant them again. But like a lot of old-name annuals, new ageratum varieties have come along, and you really should give this plant another try. It does well in sun to a half-day of shade and comes in dark blue, light blue, purple, and white. The plants are great for borders, growing only 8 inches tall while producing fuzzy, colorful blooms. Ageratum will grow in all types of soil with the exception of that heavy gumbo clay, and it is pretty drought tolerant as well. Plant it as a solid mass of color in a mounded bed or as a wonderful, low-growing, colorful border plant.

WHEN TO PLANT

If you want to start your ageratum from seed indoors, start it four to six weeks before it's safe to plant outdoors. I've found it best to plant ageratum already growing in pots or cell-packs. It is safe to plant outdoors after the danger of frost is over in your area of Kentucky.

WHERE TO PLANT

Ageratum is beautiful in its own bed or when used as a low border plant. Many gardeners use it in mixed pots and windowboxes with other upright and vining types of annuals that have similar light and water needs.

How to Plant

Loosen up your soil 6 to 8 inches deep. Dig a hole as deep as the soil clump and twice as wide. Loosen any roots that are wrapped around the soil clump. With young plants, pinch off any flowers that form for the first two to three weeks after planting. The results will be faster-growing plants that will give you much better bloom color quicker.

Care and Maintenance

Although drought tolerant, ageratum should be watered during hot, dry weather once a week. Fertilize your plants with a balanced fertilizer, following the instructions on the container.

Additional Information

A neat look to planting ageratum is alternating a light blue with a dark blue every other plant. A similar effect can be had by making the white-flowering ageratum the alternate color with a blue-flowering variety.

Additional Species, Cultivars, or Varieties

The 'Hawaii' Series grows to 8 inches and has flowers of light blue, deep blue, and an improved white. 'Pacific Plus' has the richest purple blooms of any ageratum, including 'Hawaii Royal' and 'Royal Delft'. 'Blue Horizon' is the height exception; this blue ageratum grows upright to 2$^{1}/_{2}$ feet.

Did You Know?

This will be hard to do, but it really works: When you bring home all those summer-blooming annuals from the nursery store or greenhouse, pinch off all the flowers. Now before you say, "Hey, Denny, I bought those for the color and you want me to take off the blooms?" remember that the blooms keep the plants from growing quicker and getting off to a fast start. Trust me on this one. Pinch off and keep off all your annual flowers for the first two to three weeks after planting, and by July 1, you'll have the biggest and prettiest flowers on your block.

Alyssum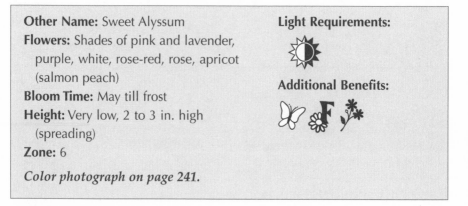

Lobularia maritima

Other Name: Sweet Alyssum

Flowers: Shades of pink and lavender, purple, white, rose-red, rose, apricot (salmon peach)

Bloom Time: May till frost

Height: Very low, 2 to 3 in. high (spreading)

Zone: 6

Color photograph on page 241.

Light Requirements:

Additional Benefits:

A lyssum is considered an annual ground cover. It grows flat on the ground, growing only 2 inches tall. Like many other annuals, it has been around for years. Many of the older varieties left homeowners with second thoughts about choosing them—some of the old boys stopped blooming when it got hot and just disappeared. Again, the hybridizers have come to our rescue, developing a vigorous hybrid for those of us who want a flat-growing, colorful annual that also looks great in rock gardens and hanging baskets. Alyssum does best in a half-day of sun or more. You have a bloom color choice of white, rose-red, pink, rose, salmon, purple, and apricot. The apricot is unusual, a light salmon peach that has the same heat tolerance of the newer blue alyssum varieties. This color tends to fade in hot sunny locations, so plant apricot in areas of morning sun only. All alyssum will provide you with low mounds of continuing summer color. Another great benefit of alyssum is its sweet fragrance: hence its common name "Sweet Alyssum."

WHEN TO PLANT

I wouldn't mess with starting alyssum from seed; start with plants already growing in pots or cell-packs. Plant in the ground anytime after the danger of frost is over in your part of Kentucky.

WHERE TO PLANT

Even the new varieties of alyssum can suffer heat stroke in late July and August. You will have greatest success with alyssum plants that are planted in all-morning or late-afternoon sun. It will grow in all types of soil. Just keep it out of gumbo heavy clay—like all annuals, alyssum wants good drainage.

How to Plant

Loosen your garden soil 6 to 8 inches deep. Dig a hole as deep and twice as wide as the soil clump, and loosen any roots wrapped around the soil clump. Backfill and water-in well to settle the soil. Don't worry about pinching off the early blooms individually; they're too small to pinch off.

Care and Maintenance

Don't overfertilize alyssum. I've found the best plant food is a once-a-season time-release fertilizer such as Osmocote® or Start-N-Gro®. Make sure your alyssum does not dry out during hot weather. Alyssum is an annual that "mulches itself," helping to retain moisture and shading weed seeds with its low-growing foliage. Leave the red or brown stuff in the bag.

Additional Information

Alyssum makes a beautiful, trailing flower for hanging baskets. It also works well in combination pots and windowboxes when used with compatible flowering and leafy annuals.

Additional Species, Cultivars, or Varieties

'Aphrodite Mix' comes in a combination of red, pink, purple, salmon, apricot, and white, with 1-inch-diameter flower heads. 'Easter Bonnet' Series is compact and very uniform in growth from plant to plant; colors include deep pink, deep rose, lavender, and violet. 'New Carpet of Snow' is an improved white-blooming variety that has great fragrance. 'Wonderland' Series, a very durable alyssum, provides blooms of deep rose, purple, or white.

Asparagus

Asparagus spp.

Other Name: Asparagus Fern	**Light Requirements:**
Flowers: None	
Bloom Time: Grown for foliage	
Height: 12 to 24 in.	**Additional Benefit:**
Zone: 6	
Color photograph on page 241.	

No, this is not about my most despised vegetable (I had to eat a lot of it from a can as a kid). I am talking about a group of plants that can be used for their fern-like foliage. No flowers here, but they add to a bed of blooming annuals what hot fudge does to vanilla ice cream. When we hear the word *fern,* we think of shade. Although not truly ferns, these plant varieties that I'm going to introduce to you grow in full sun to full shade. Now here's a plant with universal use. Speaking of use, the best uses I've seen for these ferns are in deck and patio pots, windowboxes, and mixed hanging baskets. *Asparagus sprengeri* is the most popular, because it's used the most by the pros. *A. sprengeri* has dark green, coarse needles on stems that will grow to 18 inches. *Asparagus setaceus* is commonly called *plumosus* or lace-veil fern. This one grows more in layers on multiple branches. Then there's *Asparagus densiflorus* that, from a distance, looks like a light-green cactus with its foxtail-like growth spikes. These plants look great by themselves in pots or mixed in with blooming annuals in any exposure.

WHEN TO PLANT

You will find asparagus in garden centers almost year-round. That's because they are really tender perennials, and some homeowners grow them year-round indoors. For those who want to treat them as annuals for seasonal outdoor use, you will find a great selection in May. Plant outdoors anytime after the danger of heavy frost is over.

WHERE TO PLANT

Asparagus species can be planted in flower beds, especially in shade, mixed in with shade-loving flowers. To add more variety and texture, plant solid in outdoor containers or mix in with dense-growing annuals like impatiens, browallia, periwinkle, or Million Bells® to add more bulk or height. Sprengeri, when planted on a container's edge, tends to weep over the side.

How to Plant

When planting asparagus in a new container, plant it like an annual in a soilless potting mix. When planting in flower beds, loosen the soil down 6 to 8 inches. It should really be good, loose garden soil. For planting in containers *or* in the ground, dig a hole as deep as the soil clump and twice as wide. The roots of asparagus varieties can really be wrapped around the soil clump; be sure to loosen all those wrapped roots so they're dangling freely. Backfill and water-in well to settle the soil.

Care and Maintenance

Asparagus is pretty drought tolerant. Do water during the hot, dry periods of summer, especially if it is planted in lots of sun. There are no bugs or diseases that bother this foliage plant. Occasionally a branch will yellow. This is normal; just prune it off. Speaking of pruning, prune off any unwanted growth anytime you want.

Additional Information

Asparagus varieties are very soft-looking, and when interspersed with blooming annuals can make an entire planting look like a picture out of a garden book.

Additional Species, Cultivars, or Varieties

Asparagus densiflorus has deep-green tapered needles on foxtail-like spikes. *Asparagus plumosa* has dark-green needles on layered branches. *Asparagus sprengeri* has dark-green, coarse needles that hang over the sides of pots, giving a weeping effect.

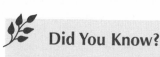

Did You Know?

You can dig up and pot any of the asparagus varieties in the fall before a frost. Bring indoors and that plant will grow all winter; put back outside in the spring if you like.

Blue Salvia

Salvia farinacea

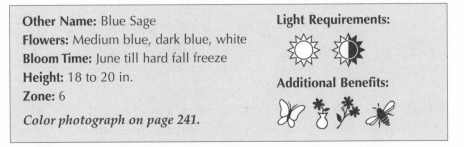

Other Name: Blue Sage
Flowers: Medium blue, dark blue, white
Bloom Time: June till hard fall freeze
Height: 18 to 20 in.
Zone: 6

Color photograph on page 241.

Light Requirements:

Additional Benefits:

I've been a fan of blue salvia since the mid-1980s. This annual grows 18 to 20 inches tall and has blue or white self-cleaning flower spikes that bloom all summer long. It's near the top of a list of summer-blooming flowers that I call "Denny's Heat Beaters." Give blue salvia some T.L.C. for a couple of weeks after planting and then release this plant to Mother Nature—it will tolerate all the hot sun and dry soil it is exposed to. It makes a great medium-growing border plant, or use it in masses in its own bed. A great combination bed, especially if you like blue and yellow together (you will), is melampodium to the front of the bed and blue salvia to the back. When you go to buy your blue salvia at the garden store or greenhouse in the spring, you won't see any bloom color on the plants; you'll see only the grayish-green leaves. Take my word for it, the flowers will come along shortly, and you'll soon agree with me that this is a low-maintenance flower with lots of color.

WHEN TO PLANT

Plant blue salvia in the spring after the danger of frost is over in your part of Kentucky. You will find it available in small pots and cell-packs in mid-May, and many nursery stores and greenhouses offer larger-growing plants in 1-gallon containers in late May to early June.

WHERE TO PLANT

Blue salvia will grow well in all types of soil as long as it has good drainage; it will grow in full-sun areas to areas receiving only four to five hours of sun.

How to Plant

Loosen the soil to a depth of 6 to 8 inches. Dig a hole as deep and twice as wide as the soil clump. Loosen any roots wrapped around the soil clump. Backfill and water-in well to settle the soil. Spread a 2-inch layer of mulch, remembering to keep it off the stems of the plants—it will help the blue salvia tolerate the hot, dry summer heat without additional irrigation.

Care and Maintenance

Blue salvia should be fed soon after planting with a time-release fertilizer like Osmocote® or Start-N-Gro®. Follow label instructions. Blue salvia is completely bug- and disease-free. There's no need to deadhead spent flowers, as this plant is self-cleaning.

Additional Information

Blue salvia is a great flower to cut and use in indoor arrangements. It is also an excellent flower for drying and using with other dried floral materials. Try planting a bed of blue-flowering and white-flowering blue salvia; the colors complement each other.

Additional Species, Cultivars, or Varieties

The 'Victoria' Series offers compact-growing 18- to 20-inch plants that produce medium-blue or silvery-white flowers.

Did You Know?

Mild winters will allow this "annual" to act as a perennial. The stems will die back to the ground, but the roots will not freeze, which permits those roots to put on new growth in the spring—just like a true perennial.

Browallia

Browallia speciosa

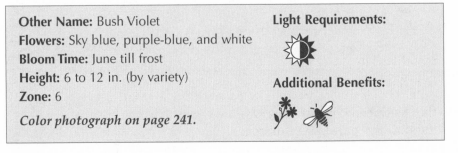

Other Name: Bush Violet
Flowers: Sky blue, purple-blue, and white
Bloom Time: June till frost
Height: 6 to 12 in. (by variety)
Zone: 6

Color photograph on page 241.

Light Requirements:

Additional Benefits:

Have a shade garden but tired of impatiens because of their constant need for moisture during dry periods? Browallia is a plant
whose flowers might remind you of impatiens, and that does well in
shady or semi-shady locations, but requires only a little moisture assistance during the hot, dry periods of summer. Although this annual has
been around for many years, it has not had much exposure until newer
varieties appeared during the last five years. It comes in bloom colors
of sky blue, purple-blue, and white. There is a cascading variety great
for hanging baskets that grows 10 to 12 inches tall, and there are dwarf
plants that grow only 6 inches tall. All browallia are spreading, and
when planted 12 inches apart will make a solid planting. Do not plant
in hot sun. *Great color and foliage on this one.*

WHEN TO PLANT
Plant browallia from small plants that will be available in pots
and cell-packs at your favorite garden center or greenhouse. Put the
plants out into the soil after any danger of frost is over in your area
of Kentucky.

WHERE TO PLANT
Plant browallia in shady areas or that part of the landscape that only
gets morning or evening sun. Plant in solid beds, or use it as a low
border plant. It is also a wonderful plant for a hanging basket where
you want hanging color in the shade, and it works well in deck pots
and flower boxes.

HOW TO PLANT
Plant browallia into soil that has been loosened 6 to 8 inches deep.
Dig a hole as deep as the soil clump and twice as wide. Loosen any

roots that are wrapped around the soil clump, place the plant in the hole, backfill, and water-in well to settle the soil.

CARE AND MAINTENANCE

Browallia does not want to be exposed to hot afternoon sun. Plant in shade with good sky light or in any area that gets either morning sun or late-afternoon sun. Fertilize with a balanced plant food, following the instructions on the container. Give browallia some water assistance during the hot, dry periods of summer.

ADDITIONAL INFORMATION

Some garden centers may not carry this wonderful plant— that's because they just don't know about it, and because you don't ask for it. If you want to see this flower before you buy, go to a greenhouse or nursery store that's known for its great selection of summer-blooming flowers.

ADDITIONAL SPECIES, CULTIVARS, OR VARIETIES

The 'Bell' Series offers cascading plants that grow 10 to 12 inches high and wide. It is available in dark blue, light blue, and white, and is great in hanging baskets. The 'Starlight' Series has dwarf plants that grow to only 6 inches. It makes a great low border with its sky blue, dark blue, or white flowers. 'Amethyst' is a dark-purple bloomer that grows to 12 inches and has 3/4-inch-wide flowers. This variety is the best for tolerating the summer heat; in fact, it is much more heat tolerant than are other browallia varieties.

Did You Know?

Many of these new varieties will be available for public viewing at local zoos, amusement parks, and other public areas known for their summer color.

Celosia

Celosia plumosa and *Celosia cristata*

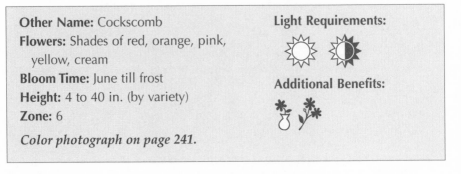

Other Name: Cockscomb
Flowers: Shades of red, orange, pink, yellow, cream
Bloom Time: June till frost
Height: 4 to 40 in. (by variety)
Zone: 6

Color photograph on page 241.

Light Requirements:

Additional Benefits:

This story is a tale of two varieties. *Celosia plumosa* has feathery, plume-type flowers that bloom in colors and shades of red, orange, pink, yellow, and cream. Total plant height ranges from 6 inches to 24 inches, depending on the variety, and the flower spikes extend from 4 inches to 8 inches. *Celosia cristata* is a cockscomb, rounded in shape, that with its crested, bunch-type flowers kind of resembles a brain. It is altogether different from *C. plumosa*. The *cristata* varieties grow from 4 to 40 inches tall and bloom in colors and shades of red, pink, yellow, and cream; flower size varies from 3 to 6 inches wide and high. All cockscomb grow best in full sun to a half-day of sun. For all the color cockscomb provides, it is a low-maintenance plant. Plant in beds or as a border plant; plant solid colors or mix them up. Stick to one type or the other (plumosa or cristata) when planting in a mass. Plumosa types are great for cut flowers, too, and they dry well for winter bouquets.

WHEN TO PLANT

You'll find the best and most popular varieties growing in pots or cell-packs at your garden center or greenhouse. Plant cockscomb in beds after the danger of frost is over in your part of Kentucky.

WHERE TO PLANT

Cockscomb will do well in average soil, and it wants good drainage and at least a half-day of sun. It makes for a beautiful container planting—be sure to use a soilless potting mix when planting in pots.

HOW TO PLANT

Loosen your garden soil down 6 to 8 inches. Dig a hole as deep and twice as wide as the soil clump. Loosen any wrapped roots, backfill the soil, and water-in well to settle the soil. Pinch off any flowers, and keep new flowers off your cockscomb for two to three weeks—this practice will make your plants much bigger much quicker.

CARE AND MAINTENANCE

Fertilize cockscomb as often as recommended on the container. If your plants are growing straight up, pinch off those branches to encourage more side shoots, encouraging more bloom. Give cockscomb an occasional drink of water during hot, dry periods.

ADDITIONAL INFORMATION

Plant shorter-growing varieties about 8 inches apart, especially if you want a tight, full border. Taller-growing varieties can be spaced 9 to 12 inches apart. Deadhead, or pinch off, all the spent flowers to encourage more blooms.

ADDITIONAL SPECIES, CULTIVARS, OR VARIETIES

Plumosa Types: The 'Sparkler' Series offers many bloom colors on plants that grow to 12 inches in bloom. 'Sparkler Wine' has bronze leaves. The 'Castle' Series offers many colors on plants that grow 12 to 14 inches high with 7-inch-high plumes. 'Forest Fire', the tallest of the plume types, is 2½ feet tall and has red flowers and red leaves. **Cristata Types:** 'Coral Garden', extra-dwarf, grows 6 inches high and has very large flowers in various colors. 'Chief' Series offers large flowers on plants that grow to 40 inches tall; they're great for cut flowers. 'Prestige Scarlet' is a 1997 All-America Selections winner, grows to 2 feet high, and has numerous large 3-inch blooms of scarlet red. 'Jewel Box' has very dwarf-growing plants (4 to 5 inches tall) available in many colors; it usually comes in mixed colors in cell-packs.

Did You Know?

Cristata *translates into "comblike" or "crested," describing the overall shape of this species' flowers.* Plumosa *translates into "plume-shaped," like the crest or comb on a rooster. Hence the common name "cockscomb."*

Cobbitty Daisies

Argyranthemum frutescens

Other Name: Marguerite Daisy

Flowers: White, yellow, and pink (by variety)

Bloom Time: Mid-May till frost

Height: 8 to 14 in. (by variety)

Zone: 6

Color photograph on page 241.

Light Requirements:

Additional Benefits:

A nother great new Proven Winner®, the botanical name ends in mum, and that may not be a coincidence. Two varieties, 'Sugar Bottoms' and 'Summer Melody', look like garden mums in bloom. This colorful annual comes to us straight from the University of Sidney, and offers colors and shapes you won't find anywhere else. Yes, these Marguerite daisies have come a long way, both in miles traveled and in bloom color (they used to come in only one bloom color: yellow). They are very easy to grow and maintain. Plant them in their own flower bed, or use them in patio pots and containers. They mix very well in pots combined with 'Summer Wave' petunias or 'Million Bells'. All Cobbitty daisies are very heat tolerant, almost desertlike. They grow 12 to 14 inches high and wide. Varieties such as 'Harvest Snow' and 'Sugar Baby' will remind you of the perennial Shasta daisy. 'Sugar Baby' is the dwarf of the family, growing only 8 to 10 inches high. A full bed of any of the Cobbitty colors will look awesome.

WHEN TO PLANT

Argyranthemum is not easy, if not impossible, to buy from seed. You will find lots of them at your garden center or greenhouse, growing in hanging baskets, pots of all sizes, and cell-packs. Plant outdoors after the danger of frost is over in your part of Kentucky.

WHERE TO PLANT

Cobbitty daisies love hot sun, but they will grow well in just a half-day of sun. Plant in average soil that has good drainage.

How to Plant

Plant your hanging baskets and patio pots using a good soilless potting mix. For planting in a bed, loosen your soil 6 to 8 inches deep. Dig a hole as deep and twice as wide as the soil clump. Loosen any roots that are wrapped around the soil clump. Backfill and water-in well.

Care and Maintenance

Cobbitty daisies are very low maintenance. Do not keep the soil moist—let the ground get dry between watering. Feed with a time-release fertilizer like Start-N-Gro® or Osmocote®. One feeding will take care of the whole growing season. Please read the instructions on the container. Pinch off the spent flowers every couple of weeks. There are no bugs or diseases that bother Cobbitty daisies.

Additional Information

I have not grown this one myself, but my son, Chris, has. His busy schedule does not allow him to pamper his flowers, but his Cobbitty daisies were fantastic. So don't take my word for it, take Chris's: these daisies look great when you mix them all together, using 'Sugar Baby' to border the bed and planting the others toward the back.

Additional Species, Cultivars, or Varieties

'Sugar Baby', which grows 8 to 10 inches, has white daisy flowers with yellow centers. 'Sugar Bottoms' has 2- to 3-inch-wide flowers that are white with a cream-colored center. 'Harvest Snow' has 3-inch white flowers with yellow centers. 'Butterfly' has bright 3-inch yellow flowers with golden yellow centers. 'Summer Melody' has deep pink, double, 3-inch, daisy-type flowers with yellow centers.

Did You Know?

Many varieties of summer-blooming flowers have been called daisies. None of the old-fashioned daisy types will ever match the hardiness and bloom color of Cobbitty daisies.

Coleus

Coleus × hybridus

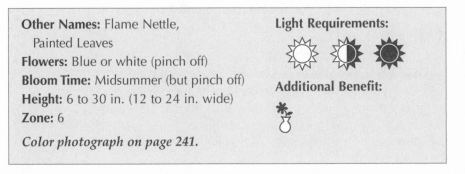

Other Names: Flame Nettle, Painted Leaves

Flowers: Blue or white (pinch off)

Bloom Time: Midsummer (but pinch off)

Height: 6 to 30 in. (12 to 24 in. wide)

Zone: 6

Color photograph on page 241.

Light Requirements:

Additional Benefit:

Coleus has blue or white flowers, but you don't want them. You see, if you let this plant have actual blooms, it will start to decline and then go downhill. Fortunately, you get enough color from the plant's leaves. Pinch off the flowers and you will have a very colorful, leafy plant that shows off in sun or shade. The color combinations of the leaves are many, and the leaves come in many shapes. Colors include combinations of white, green, red, purple, yellow, rose, or a mixture of all the above. The leaves of some varieties are heart-shaped, some are oval, and others are fringed and toothlike. Coleus makes a wonderful plant for that "hard-to-grow" area of the landscape. Very drought and shade tolerant, it is one of the best plants for low-maintenance containers. If you have pots or containers that are difficult to water, coleus should be your plant of choice. Control plant height by pinching back, keeping it full and bushy.

WHEN TO PLANT

Plant coleus from containers, either potted or in cell-packs, after the danger of a late spring frost is past. You can plant coleus well into summer as long as plants are available.

WHERE TO PLANT

Coleus will grow in any soil type as long as there is good drainage, and it's one of those tender perennials treated as an annual that will grow well in sun or shade.

HOW TO PLANT

Loosen the soil down 6 to 8 inches. Take your coleus out of its container and dig a hole as deep as the soil clump and twice as wide.

Loosen any roots that are wrapped around the soil clump. Place the root clump into the cultivated soil, backfill, and water-in well to settle the soil. For a full group planting of coleus, plant them 18 to 24 inches apart.

CARE AND MAINTENANCE

Coleus is a very low-maintenance plant. When planting in areas that are hard to water, mulch the soil with a 2-inch covering, keeping the mulch off the stems of the plants. Fertilize with a balanced plant food, following the directions on the container. There aren't any bug or disease problems that you'll have to worry about with coleus.

ADDITIONAL INFORMATION

Coleus will continue to grow and thrive under indoor conditions during the winter. When planted in pots, it can be brought indoors before a frost in the fall. Just place the pot in a room with good indoor sky light, and water only when dry. It will grow indoors for many years.

ADDITIONAL SPECIES, CULTIVARS, OR VARIETIES

Compact-growing 'Wizard' Series (to 16 inches) is available in a great mix of foliage colors. 'Carefree' Mix, which grows to 10 inches, has small, deeply lobed leaves in a multitude of colors. 'Rainbow' Mix offers very bushy plants that grow to 20 inches tall; leaves are predominantly red, yellow, copper, and pink.

 Did You Know?

You can take leaf cuttings from your coleus in early fall and place them in a glass of water to root. After roots form, place each rooted cutting in a 3-inch pot using a soilless potting mix. Grow them indoors and you will have great winter leaf color.

Cosmos

Cosmos bipinnatus

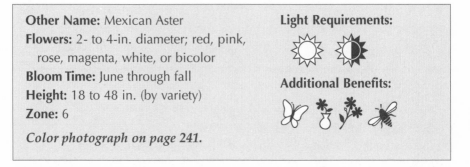

Other Name: Mexican Aster

Flowers: 2- to 4-in. diameter; red, pink, rose, magenta, white, or bicolor

Bloom Time: June through fall

Height: 18 to 48 in. (by variety)

Zone: 6

Color photograph on page 241.

Light Requirements:

Additional Benefits:

Where, oh, where has cosmos been? These daisylike blooming plants have been around for many years, but they have not been as colorful and bushy as the new varieties now entering the scene. Cosmos is easy to grow. Its bushy plant with fernlike foliage makes for a beautiful bedding plant that looks fantastic in a bed of its own. It also mixes well with other summer-blooming plants—but after you see it perform, you'll wish that you had planted more cosmos and less of the others. The flowers measure 3 to 4 inches, and the plants can grow to 4 to 5 feet tall. There are newer varieties that grow to only 20 to 24 inches but still bloom very freely, in various shades of red, pink, and white. You can also buy cosmos in mixed flats that have a beautiful mix of all the rainbow colors. Cosmos blooms best in full sun, although it will give very acceptable color when getting only a half-day of sun.

WHEN TO PLANT

You can start seedlings indoors around the middle of April. Plant in a seed tray filled with a soilless potting mix, and keep moist but not damp. My preferred way of planting cosmos is to use plants growing in pots or cell-packs. Plant outside in the landscape after the danger of frost is over in your area.

WHERE TO PLANT

Cosmos loves as much sun as it can get. The plants grow well in all types of well-drained soil. If mixing with other annuals and perennials, some cosmos get rather tall. Plant the taller-growing varieties toward the back of a mixed bed. The dwarfs look great as a border plant outlining a bed of taller-growing plants.

How to Plant

Plant your own seed starts or store-bought plants outside after the danger of frost is over in your area. With either type, loosen the garden soil 6 to 8 inches. Dig a hole twice as wide as the soil clump and place into the soil as deep as the soil clump. Backfill with existing soil. Water-in well to settle the soil. To allow the plant to grow bigger quicker, pinch off any early blooms. Do this for two weeks after planting, and then let the cosmos do their thing.

Care and Maintenance

Cosmos will grow in all types of well-draining soil. Give them a little sun and let the color begin. There are no bugs or diseases that attack cosmos. If the plants start to stretch and grow tall, pinch or prune halfway back to encourage more spread.

Additional Information

Both the bloom and the foliage make for a great bouquet. This is a blooming annual that's both beautiful outdoors or as a cut flower indoors when put in a vase on the dinner table. Cosmos is also known as a wildflower because of the plant's ability to reseed itself from year to year. Just space the volunteers the next spring so that each plant has room to grow.

Additional Species, Cultivars, or Varieties

The 'Sonata' Series, 20 to 24 inches, is June-flowering in many colors of red, pink, and pure white. The 'Versailles' mix is a taller-growing variety that blooms in rose, pink, red, and white, growing to 48 inches. The compact-growing 'Ladybird' Series blooms on young 12-inch plants bearing rose, pink, red, and white flowers.

 Did You Know?

Butterflies love this flower. If you want to have these flying beauties in your yard, plant cosmos.

Dianthus

Dianthus hybrids

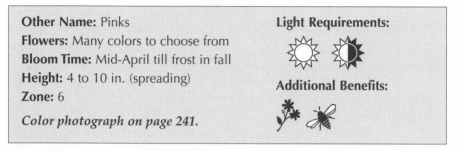

Other Name: Pinks
Flowers: Many colors to choose from
Bloom Time: Mid-April till frost in fall
Height: 4 to 10 in. (spreading)
Zone: 6

Color photograph on page 241.

Light Requirements:

Additional Benefits:

For many years dianthus was offered for sale during the cool weather of spring and fall. Technically a biennial, this plant would grow and bloom in the spring and then go to seed when it started getting hot in the summer (like pansies). Then came along the new hybrids. Dianthus hybrids come in many varieties and many colors. They are available to buy and plant in the spring or, if you miss that season, many growers have them available to plant in late summer and fall. You'll find fall dianthus alongside hardy mums and asters. Most hybrid dianthus grow 6 to 7 inches high and 9 inches wide. Most have 1¹/₂- to 2-inch-diameter flowers, many of them fringed on the edges. Many have flowers with dark-colored or bright-colored centers trimmed in white. Dianthus makes a spectacular full bed of color, and also a great plant to use as a border. It will tolerate summer heat as long as you assist with water during hot, dry periods.

WHEN TO PLANT

Hybrid dianthus is best planted from plants already growing in pots or cell-packs in the spring. Fall selections will all be potted. They also germinate very quickly from seed indoors. Start your seed around the first of April. Hybrid dianthus is cold hardy, and the plants can be set out and planted in mid-April.

WHERE TO PLANT

Dianthus hybrids can be planted in full-sun sites to those that get just a few hours of sun. Plant in their own bed, or line beds of other flowers with a border planting of dianthus. You can also use dianthus in containers of all types.

How to Plant

Loosen or cultivate your flower bed to a depth of 6 to 8 inches. Dig holes as deep as the soil clumps and twice as wide. Loosen any roots that are wrapped around the soil clump. Backfill and water-in well to settle the soil. Plant hybrid dianthus on 10-inch centers to make a full bed.

Care and Maintenance

Fertilize dianthus hybrids following the instructions on the container. Cut off spent flowers with scissors about every two to three weeks to encourage new bloom. Water during hot, dry periods. Don't worry about bugs and disease—no problem here.

Additional Information

Dianthus hybrids come in many single and bicolor flower varieties. They look great filling planter boxes. When using containers, be sure to plant your dianthus hybrids in a soil-less potting mix. Save a few dianthus to bring indoors in pots in early fall, before a frost. They'll continue to give you bloom indoors as the snow flies outdoors.

Additional Species, Cultivars, or Varieties

'Diamond' Series is a brand-new dianthus that comes in six colors and is very tolerant to heat and cold. 'Floral Lace' Series, named for lacy serrated flowers that are 1½ inches wide, is the largest of any hybrid; it grows 8 to 10 inches, is very heat tolerant, and is available in nine colors, including my favorite: 'Violet Picotee'. 'Ideal' Series grows 8 inches high and up to 15 inches wide. This variety is like going to the ice cream store—there are sixteen flavors to choose from, including raspberry. 'Telstar' Series, an early bloomer growing 8 inches high, offers 1⅓-inch-diameter flowers in abundance on very heat-tolerant plants.

Dusty Miller

Senecio cineraria

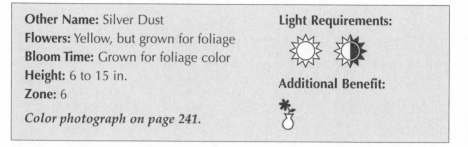

Other Name: Silver Dust
Flowers: Yellow, but grown for foliage
Bloom Time: Grown for foliage color
Height: 6 to 15 in.
Zone: 6

Color photograph on page 241.

Light Requirements:

Additional Benefit:

Dusty miller is a great summer addition to any landscape. What beautiful silver, dusty-looking leaves it has, just as its name implies! It is available in two different leaf styles. A lobed-leaf type that resembles a snowflake grows 10 to 12 inches high and wide; then there's a lacy-leaf type that has the same beautiful, silver-gray leaves, but the leaves are very serrated, and the plants grow 6 to 8 inches tall and 12 to 15 inches wide. Dusty miller is classified as an annual, but with a mild winter it has been known to stay around and start to grow again from the same roots the following spring. Not all plants have to bloom to be beautiful. Dusty miller is known as a "statement plant" that works well with other annuals. Picture a border with red-flowering wax-leaf begonias alternating with dusty miller. You can mix it with other border-type annuals for a real statement of class and color.

WHEN TO PLANT

Dusty miller is better planted from pots or cell-packs than from seed. Plant anytime the danger of frost is over. If you're lucky and the winter is mild, you can divide overwintering dusty miller in the spring as those wintered-over plants put on new growth.

WHERE TO PLANT

Plant dusty miller in full-sun areas to areas with only a few hours of sun. It grows well in all types of soil as long as the drainage is good.

HOW TO PLANT

Loosen the soil 6 to 8 inches deep. Dig a hole as deep and twice as wide as the soil clump. Remove the soil clump from the pot or cell-pack and loosen any existing roots growing around it so they're dangling freely. Place the soil clump into the ground, backfill, and water-in well to settle the soil. If your plants have long, lanky leaves, pinch the stems back halfway to make for a fuller plant.

CARE AND MAINTENANCE

Dusty miller is very hardy under all types of conditions. It will tolerate hot sun and dry soil. Like any plant, it would appreciate a good drink when Mom Nature is in a very dry mood. Don't overfertilize dusty miller. A time-release plant food like Ferti-lome's Start-N-Gro® will feed your dusty miller all season with just one application. Read the directions, guys!

ADDITIONAL INFORMATION

Dusty miller does not produce much of a flower of its own, but it will highlight the blooms of companion blooming plants.

ADDITIONAL SPECIES, CULTIVARS, OR VARIETIES

'Cirrus' has lobed silvery leaves that spread 10 to 12 inches. 'Silver Lace' has very fine, lacy leaves growing 6 to 8 inches tall. 'Silver Dust' produces bushy plants with somewhat lacy leaves.

Did You Know?

Most annual varieties come in cell-packs. These are like ice-cube trays that hold from two to twelve individual plants, and a flat contains anywhere from two to eighteen flower packs.

Flowering Tobacco

Nicotiana alata

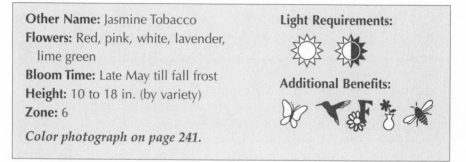

Other Name: Jasmine Tobacco

Flowers: Red, pink, white, lavender, lime green

Bloom Time: Late May till fall frost

Height: 10 to 18 in. (by variety)

Zone: 6

Color photograph on page 241.

Light Requirements:

Additional Benefits:

Now here is a tobacco product that is good for you. Flowering tobacco is a summer-blooming annual that really is not known by the majority of homeowners, but it's a great flower for sunny areas in a bed all by itself—from a distance, you might think the plants are petunias. Several varieties that deserve your consideration have been introduced in recent years. The 'Hummingbird' Series is exceptional in home or commercial landscapes. This dwarf-growing variety offers plants that grow 10 to 12 inches. Plant 10 inches apart, and within weeks enjoy a solid bed full of beautiful shades of lemon and lime and various shades of red, pink, or white. The individual trumpet-shaped flowers are 1 to 2 inches in diameter and up to 2 inches long. Oh, yeah! Did I mention that the flowers open at night, are very fragrant, and attract hummingbirds? Imagine, all these positives and you haven't heard of them. If you don't like to rush to try something new, just plant a few this year and form your own opinion.

WHEN TO PLANT

You can start nicotiana from seed indoors four to six weeks before it's safe to plant out in the landscape. Better yet, buy plants already growing in pots or cell-packs in mid- to late May after the danger of frost is over in your area of Kentucky.

WHERE TO PLANT

Plant flowering tobacco in its own bed to create a solid block of the same color, or mix up the colors. It also makes a fantastic short-growing color border. Plant in a sunny location that gets at least morning sun. Plant close to your deck or patio where you can enjoy the fragrance as well as watch the hummingbirds entertain.

How to Plant

When planting from seed, plant flowering tobacco indoors as you do any other annual seed. When using started plants, remove the soil clump from its container. Plant in pre-loosened average to good soil that is well drained. Dig a hole as deep and twice as wide as the soil clump. Backfill, and water-in well to settle the soil.

Care and Maintenance

Flowering tobacco responds well to water-soluble plant food like Miracle-Gro® or a time-release plant food like Start-N-Gro®. Follow the package instructions on how and when to use. Flowering tobacco is very heat and drought tolerant, but give these summer beauties an occasional drink during the hot days of summer.

Additional Information

Flowering tobacco grows together and forms a solid block of leaves and flowers. In essence, they mulch themselves with their own growth. The flowers are open at night and stay open the next day. To encourage quicker growth, deadhead or pinch off the spent flowers for the first two to three weeks after planting.

Additional Species, Cultivars, or Varieties

The compact-growing 'Hummingbird' Series has bloom colors that appear fluorescent. The 'Domino' Series, growing 12 to 14 inches tall with 2-inch flowers, is available in several colors, some with white eyes on pink or purple blooms. The 'Nicki' Series grows 16 to 18 inches tall and has fragrant 2-inch blooms of lime green, red, white, or bicolor.

Did You Know?

Hummingbirds are more naturally attracted to red or orange/red flowers. Stick to the darker colors of flowering tobacco, or at least mix some in with the lighter colors so you can enjoy those special birds.

Geranium

Pelargonium × hortorum

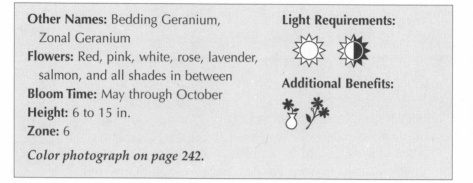

Other Names: Bedding Geranium, Zonal Geranium

Flowers: Red, pink, white, rose, lavender, salmon, and all shades in between

Bloom Time: May through October

Height: 6 to 15 in.

Zone: 6

Color photograph on page 242.

Light Requirements:

Additional Benefits:

The geranium is one of the most popular flowers planted by local municipalities to add low-maintenance color to public areas. In fact, geraniums are rated one of the top summer-blooming plants across the United States. They thrive in sunny, hot, dry areas, growing well in full sun to only four hours of sun. They don't require a lot of attention. Their flowers appear as a ball made up of hundreds of small individual flowers forming a total bloom from 5 to 7 inches in diameter. The flowers are borne on a stem of 8 to 10 inches, and each plant can have as many as eighteen flowerbuds at a time. Geraniums have been produced through stem cuttings for years, producing a type called a zonal geranium. Recently, a new type has been developed. These newer geraniums are called seed geraniums, and they also produce lots of bloom. Ivy or vining geraniums are another group; they grow as a ground cover or trail down in a hanging basket. Ivy geraniums do not want any hot afternoon sun.

WHEN TO PLANT

Geraniums are best planted from pots or cell-packs after the danger of a late frost has passed in your area of Kentucky. You can continue to plant geraniums into summer as long as the plants are available.

WHERE TO PLANT

Most geraniums, zonal and seed type, want lots of sun. They don't need excellent soil, just soil that has good drainage. They will produce good bloom in areas of the garden that only get a few hours of sun. Remember, ivy geraniums want shade to morning-only sun.

How to Plant

Always pre-loosen the soil where you plant any annual. With geraniums, loosen the soil to a depth of 8 to 10 inches. Dig a hole as deep as the soil clump and twice as wide. Loosen any wrapped roots. Place in the soil, backfill, and water-in well to settle the soil.

Care and Maintenance

Geraniums like to be on the dry side before you add more water. A geranium's worst nightmare is a wet growing season. Remove finished flower stems, especially for the first couple of months after they're planted. Fertilize with a balanced fertilizer, following the directions on the container. Geraniums can tolerate a light frost, which actually keeps them blooming later into fall. There are no bugs or disease that bother geraniums.

Additional Information

Seed-type geraniums do not hold their flower blooms in the rain as well as do the zonals. It won't be long, though, before more blossoms appear on the seed type.

Additional Species, Cultivars, or Varieties

The 'Pinto' Series offers many colors on compact-growing plants. 'Ringo' Series is an F1 Hybrid that grows 16- to 18-inch plants with three color choices. The early-flowering 'Glamour' Series brings lots of 4-inch blooms in many colors. 'Summer Showers' Series has cascading branches that produce 3- to 4-inch flowers in many colors; great for hanging baskets.

Did You Know?

Geraniums are not only showy when planted in the ground, but they make excellent flowering plants for patio and deck planters, windowboxes, and hanging baskets. The container-grown plants can be brought inside the home before a fall frost to extend their bloom.

Globe Amaranth

Gomphrena globosa

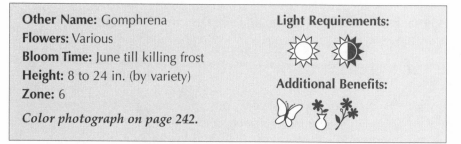

Other Name: Gomphrena
Flowers: Various
Bloom Time: June till killing frost
Height: 8 to 24 in. (by variety)
Zone: 6

Color photograph on page 242.

Light Requirements:

Additional Benefits:

So you want to dry your annual flowers. How about planting a flower that already looks dried when in bloom? I'm talking about globe amaranth. For many years, amaranth was only available in a reddish-purple. Now it's available in pink, purple, rose, red, and white. It generally grows to 12 inches high and 12 inches wide. It makes a great border plant that beautifully outlines any planting bed and attracts butterflies as well. This plant looks good whether planted all the same color or planted in alternating colors. You can cut off flower bunches and bring them indoors to place in a vase of water. Check out this unusual blooming annual when shopping for bedding plants in spring. You might find them more attractive "in person" than when you are trying to visualize them from a description in a book.

WHEN TO PLANT

Plant globe amaranth in the spring after the danger of frost is over in your part of Kentucky. You can start seeds indoors four to six weeks before planting outdoors.

WHERE TO PLANT

Plant globe amaranth in full sun to morning sun, in a bed all by itself or as a low border plant. It will grow well in all types of soil as long as the drainage is good.

HOW TO PLANT

Loosen the existing garden soil to a depth of 6 to 8 inches. Dig a hole as deep and twice as wide as the soil clump. Loosen any roots that are wrapped around the soil clump. Plant, backfill, and water-in well to settle the soil. Pinch off any flowers for the next couple of weeks—your plants will grow much faster, giving you more blooms than less. It's hard to pinch off those first flowers, but do it and it will pay dividends.

CARE AND MAINTENANCE

Globe amaranth is easy to care for. Give it an occasional drink of water during hot, dry periods. Fertilize following the instructions on the container. Globe amaranth is self-cleaning, so there's no work there. It is bug and disease free, too.

ADDITIONAL INFORMATION

For a full flower bed or border, plant globe amaranth on 10- to 12-inch centers. Globe amaranth's flowers look dried on the plant. Each flower is long lasting, up to ten days, and when planted in a mass is very, very colorful. The globosa types are much taller than the other types, reaching a plant size of 20 inches tall and wide.

ADDITIONAL SPECIES, CULTIVARS, OR VARIETIES

Globosa types grow to 20 inches tall and make excellent cut flowers. They bloom pink, purple, rose, and white, and are available mixed in cell-packs. 'Gnome' Series plants are dwarfs, growing only 8 to 12 inches high and 12 inches wide, in pink, purple, and white. 'Wood Creek' Series grows to 2 feet tall and has the biggest flowers, about 1$^{1}/_{2}$ inch in diameter; there are great bloomers in lavender or strawberry red.

Did You Know?

Do you want butterflies? Then plant globe amaranth. Not only does it provide nectar, but the butterflies are able to rest as they partake.

Hypoestes

Hypoestes phyllostachya

Other Name: Polka-Dot Plant
Flowers: Insignificant
Bloom Time: Grown for beautiful
  leaf color
Height: 8 to 24 in. (depending on variety)
Zone: 6

Color photograph on page 242.

Light Requirements:

Additional Benefit:

How do you even pronounce the name of this great annual? Well, it's easier to pronounce the names of its two varieties, 'Confetti' Series and 'Splash' Series. When you learn how to pronounce it (hy-po-ESS-teez), then you'll say, "Okay, but what is it?" Hypoestes is a tender perennial that is known not for a flower, but for striking foliage color. Even without flowers of its own, it makes quite a statement in the home landscape when planted as a border plant or when used among other low- to medium-growing annuals. 'Confetti' has leaves of burgundy, red, rose, and white, and it looks like an artist dabbled on a little green paint to break up those colors. 'Splash' has less color disruption on its leaves, which also come in pink, red, rose, and white. Both varieties grow rather low, and spread. 'Confetti' grows 18 to 24 inches tall, and 'Splash' grows a little shorter, only 8 to 10 inches tall. This plant offers another reason you should buy your summer flowers from a year-round nursery store: real nursery persons will have the plant available for you when you are ready to treat yourself and your landscape.

WHEN TO PLANT

Plant hypoestes from greenhouse-grown plants that will be available from your garden center or nursery store in May. Do not plant until the danger of a late frost in your area has passed.

WHERE TO PLANT

Hypoestes will grow in areas that have full sun to almost full shade. In shady areas, just make sure there is sky light so the colors in the leaves express themselves. Use hypoestes plants as a border with blooming plants behind them, and try in hanging baskets and patio pots.

How to Plant

Plant hypoestes in sun to almost all shade, from plants already growing in pots or cell-packs. (Trying to grow from seed, either indoors or directly into the ground outside, will not be very successful.) Remove the plants from their containers. Pre-loosen the soil and dig a hole twice as wide as the soil clump. Loosen any wrapped roots growing around the clump, then plant as deep as the clump. Water-in well to settle the backfilled soil.

Care and Maintenance

Keep hypoestes watered during hot, dry weather. If your plants get taller than you would like, pinch or prune them back to keep them in line. Fertilize with an all-purpose fertilizer, following the instructions on the label. These are definitely low-maintenance plants.

Additional Information

Mix many colors of the same variety of hypoestes to make a very colorful planting. They come in many leaf colors.

Additional Species, Cultivars, or Varieties

There are none known.

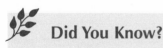 **Did You Know?**

Several plants are known and grown for their foliage color. Coleus and hypoestes are tender perennials—often used as annuals—that grow well in sun to shade. Caladium is a colorful bulbous plant that can be saved from year to year.

Impatiens

Impatiens wallerana

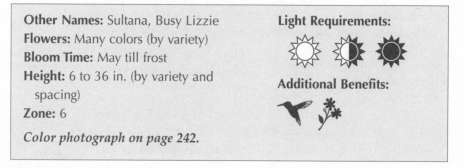

Other Names: Sultana, Busy Lizzie
Flowers: Many colors (by variety)
Bloom Time: May till frost
Height: 6 to 36 in. (by variety and spacing)
Zone: 6

Color photograph on page 242.

Light Requirements:

Additional Benefits:

Impatiens is a flower that I think that gets its name because of its impatience to bloom quickly and profusely. But for many, many years, homeowners were told by us in the industry that impatiens would only grow in shade—we've said this for the last twenty-five years. I've put an end to this rumor by growing lots of impatiens in my own yard in lots of sun, some in hot afternoon sun. Did they burn up? Heck no, but I have learned to hate them during hot, dry periods. I really love the color, but when grown in sun, they need to be watered daily. When I'm tired and just want to rest when coming home from work, I have to wait until after I water these sun-grown impatiens. Yes, impatiens will do very well in lots of shade, but they will also do well, with ample water, in sunny locations. Another myth is that various varieties come in different growing heights. Truth of the matter is, with impatiens, the closer you plant them, the taller they grow, and the farther apart you plant them, the shorter they grow.

WHEN TO PLANT

Impatiens seed *can* be planted directly into garden soil—but don't do it this way. The seeds are very small and hard to distribute. Buy plants already growing in pots or cell-packs from your favorite greenhouse or garden store in spring, after the danger of a late killing frost is over.

WHERE TO PLANT

Impatiens grow beautifully in shade to morning sun without much care. I don't know of any flower, however, that will give you as much bloom color as impatiens, so why restrict them only to shady sites? Do not plant water-loving plants like impatiens in beds that also have evergreen plants. Evergreens do not like to be watered daily, and the impatiens will require it in hot weather. You could wind up with beautiful impatiens and dead or weak evergreens. They do like good, loose garden soil and do extremely well in hanging baskets and patio pots.

How to Plant

Plant impatiens from plants already growing in pots or cell-packs. Loosen the soil 6 to 8 inches deep. Remove the plants from their containers and loosen any wrapped roots. Plant in a hole as deep as the root clump and twice as wide. Water-in well to settle the soil. If planting in 10- to 12-inch hanging baskets, plant in a soilless potting mix.

Care and Maintenance

Impatiens are over 90 percent water. They need to be watered on a regular basis, especially if planted in sunny locations. Fertilize with an all-purpose fertilizer, following the directions on the container.

Additional Information

Regardless of what the plant stake says, impatiens will grow to 3 feet if the individual plants are on 6- to 8-inch centers. These same plants will grow much shorter, 9 to 14 inches, when planted on 18-inch centers. You control the height of your impatiens by varying their spacing.

Additional Species, Cultivars, or Varieties

There are many great new varieties of hybrid impatiens. The 'Accent' Series offers twenty-four different shades of bloom that are not only very free-flowering, but also glow in the moonlight. The 'Blitz' Series comes in many colors with extra-large flowers. The 'Dazzler' Series offers twenty-one different shades including some bicolors. 'Super Elfin' Series is more compact-growing, blooming in twenty-three different flavors. The 'Swirl' Series plants have a unique Picotee pattern of bloom; the two-shaded blooms come in three colors. New Guinea impatiens are larger-growing plants with solid or multicolor leaves and large flowers, making wonderful bloomers for patio pots. 'Gemini' pink is my favorite.

Lobelia

Lobelia erinus

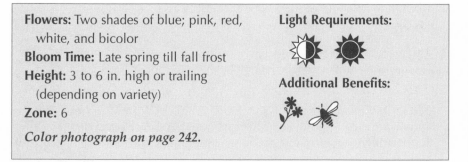

Flowers: Two shades of blue; pink, red, white, and bicolor
Bloom Time: Late spring till fall frost
Height: 3 to 6 in. high or trailing (depending on variety)
Zone: 6

Color photograph on page 242.

Light Requirements:

Additional Benefits:

Lobelia is a summer-blooming annual that really loves shade. Plant it on the north side of the house, or in areas of tree shade. It will do well in areas of morning sun, but please, no hot afternoon sun. It's available in a trailing form that's great for a very low ground cover or in a hanging basket, and it's also available in a form that is a little more upright and mounding, growing to 6 inches tall. All lobelia is spreading in its growth habit. It's available in two colors of blue, one dark, the other light blue. One dark-blue variety has light-bronze foliage, and there is a red bloomer with white eyes, also with bronze foliage. Lobelia flowers, as dainty and plentiful as they may be, are self-cleaning. They add a bright splash of color to any shady area.

WHEN TO PLANT
Lobelia is best planted from plants growing in pots or cell-packs purchased from garden centers or nursery stores. Plant anytime after the danger of a late frost is over.

WHERE TO PLANT
Plant in natural or tree shade (darker than natural shade). It will grow in areas of the garden that receive only morning sun. When planting around trees, plan to add water during the hot, dry periods of the growing season. For hanging baskets in shade, lobelia is great for both trailing growth and bloom color. Plant any of the colors of the 'Fountain' Series or the 'Regatta' Series—these varieties will drape down 2 feet or more by the end of the growing season.

HOW TO PLANT
Don't mess around with seed planting. The lobelia plants already growing are very inexpensive. Loosen the soil 6 to 8 inches. Take

your plants out of their container. Loosen any wrapped roots and place in the soil in a hole no deeper than the soil clump and twice as wide. Always use a soilless potting mix when planting in a 10- to 12-inch pot for a hanging basket.

CARE AND MAINTENANCE
Lobelia responds well to fertilizer; use any all-purpose fertilizer, following the directions on the package. Lobelia grows best in soil that is loose and loamy. Water this shade-loving plant during hot, dry weather, and keep out of hot afternoon sun.

ADDITIONAL INFORMATION
Lobelia makes a great hanging basket that blooms all summer long. It also makes a great flowering plant for a border or rock garden in shade to morning sun.

ADDITIONAL SPECIES, CULTIVARS, OR VARIETIES
Lobelia comes in two growing types, trailing and upright. Here are some of the best of both. **Trailing Lobelia:** 'Fountain' Series offers profusely blooming plants with a cascading growth habit, with blooms from blue to lilac to rose to white. 'Regatta' Series has many shades of blue and pink, and a pure white. **Upright Lobelia:** 'Palace' Series grows to 3 to 6 inches, blooming in all the favorite lobelia colors. 'Riviera' Series grows to 3 to 4 inches, and also blooms in many colors.

Did You Know?
A soilless potting mix often used for planting hanging baskets is made of Canadian peat moss, vermiculite, perlite, and some charcoal. It's the same mix most professional growers use to grow their baskets of lobelia.

Marigold

Tagetes spp. and hybrids

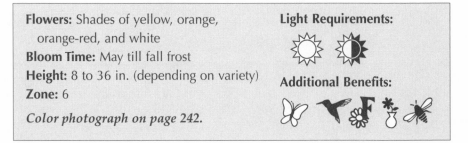

Flowers: Shades of yellow, orange, orange-red, and white
Bloom Time: May till fall frost
Height: 8 to 36 in. (depending on variety)
Zone: 6

Color photograph on page 242.

Light Requirements:

Additional Benefits:

They say if you can't grow marigolds, you should stay out of the garden. These flowers need very little maintenance, requiring little assistance from us or the hose during the summer. They offer many benefits to any home landscape, from growing in containers to forming a low-type barrier hedge. Marigolds have been around for many years. As is true for a lot of plants, major improvements have been made to these great summer bloomers. They are bred from three different families. There's the African, now called the American or Aztec (*Tagetes erecta*), the French, which are mostly low-growing dwarfs (*Tagetes patula*), and the Triploid, which are both dwarf and semidwarf and have large flowers (*Tagetes erecta × patula*) and serrated leaves that are known for their aroma. Some homeowners plant marigolds around vegetable gardens to ward off bug pests and four-legged, night-feeding creatures. Whether this actually works or not has never been scientifically proven . . . but there are those who do believe.

WHEN TO PLANT

You can plant marigolds very successfully from seed or store-bought plants. Plant the seeds directly into the soil in late May, or plant the already-growing plants in your landscape after the danger of a late spring frost passes.

WHERE TO PLANT

Marigolds are hardy and will grow in all types of soil. Although they will grow well in only four to five hours of sun, the more sun, the happier they will be.

HOW TO PLANT

Loosen the existing soil on the spot you are going to plant your marigolds. You can do this with a spade or shovel, down to 6 to

8 inches. When using seed, plant them 1/2 inch deep and as far apart as the seed packet suggests. With store-bought plants, take them out of the containers, loosen the roots, and plant as deep as the soil clump. Backfill and water-in well. To allow more growth and much more bloom sooner, pinch off any flowers that exist at planting time.

CARE AND MAINTENANCE

Marigolds really appreciate an occasional watering when it gets hot and dry. Although often listed as self-cleaning, deadhead spent flowers when they appear, especially when the plants are young in late spring. A 2-inch layer of mulch around the plants helps keep moisture in the ground. Keep the mulch off the marigold stems.

ADDITIONAL INFORMATION

Marigolds are relatively easy to grow. Some varieties have large 4-inch flowers on plants that grow to 18 inches tall. Staking with thin bamboo plant stakes may be necessary to keep the plants upright, especially during heavy rain and on windy planting sites.

ADDITIONAL SPECIES, CULTIVARS, OR VARIETIES

French Types: The 'Aurora' Series is compact growing, 10 to 12 inches tall; its orange, red, or yellow flowers are 2 1/2 inches in diameter. The free-flowering 'Disco' Series has 2- to 2 1/2-inch-diameter flowers in shades of yellow and orange, on plants that grow 10 to 12 inches tall.
American Types: 'Crush types F. Hybrid' plants are extra-dwarf varieties, growing up to 18 inches with yellow to orange flowers up to 4 inches in diameter. The 'Inca' Series is similar, though its large flowers can get up to 5 inches in diameter. **Triploid F1 Hybrids:** The 'Zenith' Series offers yellow to orange-red 3-inch-diameter flowers on plants that grow 24 inches tall.

Melampodium

Melampodium paludosum

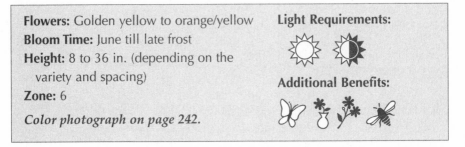

Flowers: Golden yellow to orange/yellow
Bloom Time: June till late frost
Height: 8 to 36 in. (depending on the
 variety and spacing)
Zone: 6

Color photograph on page 242.

Light Requirements:

Additional Benefits:

I first discovered this wonderful care-free plant while on a nursery tour in southern California back in 1987, when I saw a yellow-blooming plant growing along the interstate in unirrigated areas. I was told it was melampodium, a plant that blooms in Los Angeles year-round and doesn't need to be watered. I soon discovered that this flower would grow well in Kentucky as an annual. When I went home, I talked to several annual growers who said they had never heard of it. I convinced one of them to grow a hundred flats to try in the spring of '88. We sold them all, and since then, lots of homeowners have become hooked. They are like impatiens in that if you plant them close together, they stretch and grow to 30 inches. Space the plants on 18-inch centers and they only grow to 20 inches. There is a new variety (see below) that is a true dwarf, genetically developed to grow only to 8 to 10 inches.

WHEN TO PLANT

Melampodium plants are available from the garden center in May. Don't procrastinate—many garden stores carry only a few flats and pots, and if you wait till late May to buy, they might be all gone. Melampodium can handle a late-spring frost.

WHERE TO PLANT

Plant melampodium in any garden area that receives at least four hours of sun. If it gets a full day of sun, that's even better, although melampodium will be very showy in either type of exposure.

HOW TO PLANT

Melampodium will be available in cell-packs (you know, those "ice cube trays" of three, four, or six plants per pack) and in pots. Dig a hole as deep and twice as wide as the soil clump. Loosen any wrapped roots from around the clump and plant. Water-in well to settle the soil. Remember, the closer you plant melampodium, the taller it grows.

CARE AND MAINTENANCE

Melampodium truly fits the term "low-maintenance." Until they are established, water your plants when the soil is dry. You will notice after three to four weeks that the leaves have become twice as large, and that tells you to put the hose away. This plant is completely drought tolerant. Fertilize with any all-purpose fertilizer, following the instructions on the container.

ADDITIONAL INFORMATION

I hope you like yellow, because that's what you're going to get: thousands of yellow daisy-type flowers that never stop blooming until a hard freeze in fall. Melampodium can take 30-degree temperatures (Fahrenheit) and keep on growing. The flowers are also self-cleaning, which means you don't have to pinch or deadhead.

ADDITIONAL SPECIES, CULTIVARS, OR VARIETIES

'Derby' has orange/yellow flowers on lower-growing plants that average 14 to 16 inches tall. The brand-new variety 'Million Gold' has golden-yellow flowers and is truly a dwarf. It makes an excellent border plant, growing to only 8 to 10 inches.

 Did You Know?

There will be other flowers in this chapter that you might not know or have never even heard of. I have selected flowers that I know and personally have grown. The characteristic shared by all these flowers is their positive impact on or in the landscape.

Million Bells®

Calibrachoa hybrids

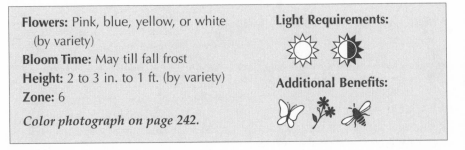

Flowers: Pink, blue, yellow, or white (by variety)
Bloom Time: May till fall frost
Height: 2 to 3 in. to 1 ft. (by variety)
Zone: 6

Color photograph on page 242.

Light Requirements:

Additional Benefits:

This Proven Winner® is a real proven winner! Million bells features hundreds of small, quarter-sized, petunia-like flowers that are available in six beautiful colors. The plant thrives in bright sun and heat. It is a fast-growing, hardy-blooming, and, most important, self-cleaning variety that blooms from spring through fall, has a low-growing, compact growth habit, and thrives in sun to a half-day of shade. Four of the varieties are low-growing, reaching a height of only 4 to 6 inches. Two other varieties grow a little higher, growing to 12 inches. Million bells makes an excellent bed planting all by itself, or a low border plant edging a bed of larger-blooming flowers. The low-growing trailing varieties make excellent mixed hanging baskets when combined with scaevola, browallia, or other colorful annuals. Million bells will naturally grow downward 5 to 6 feet when planted in a happy hanging basket. Many greenhouses and nursery stores will offer these mixed baskets available in mid-spring. Select the one or ones that suit your eye. Remember, million bells is easy to grow and oh, so beautiful!

WHEN TO PLANT

Plant million bells growing in pots, cell-packs, and hanging baskets in spring. It can tolerate some late-spring cool weather. Buy before the fourth week of May before the plants are gone.

WHERE TO PLANT

Plant million bells in its own flower bed. Raised beds are best to be able to view from a distance. Million bells also makes a beautiful, colorful border plant or can line a bed of shrubs, evergreens, or other taller-growing annuals. The plant is also great in a 10- or 12-inch hanging basket combined with other clump-type flowers that will fill the top and provide some height for the arrangement.

How to Plant

Buy already-growing plants from the greenhouse or nursery store. Loosen the existing soil to a depth of 6 to 8 inches. Dig a hole as deep as the soil clump and twice as wide. Backfill, and water-in well to settle the soil. If planting your own hanging basket, be sure to use a soilless potting mix, and loosen the roots wrapped around the soil clump before planting.

Care and Maintenance

Million bells not only looks like petunias, but the maintenance is a lot like that of petunias. The plants are heavy feeders, which means they must be fertilized often, following the instructions on how much to feed at one time. They are tolerant of dry soil, and the many flowers are self-cleaning. No bugs or disease with these either. In hanging baskets in full sun, check the watering needs daily in hot weather to keep them extra happy.

Additional Information

Million bells looks like miniature petunias the size of a quarter. They spread very quickly; keep them in-bounds by pruning away any excessive growth. Once you try these, you will always make room for them in the future.

Additional Species, Cultivars, or Varieties

Upright varieties include 'Terra Cotta' (a yellow bloomer) and 'Cherry Pink' (a bright-pink variety). Both grow to 12 inches tall, and they do spread. Flat-growing varieties great for a ground cover or a hanging basket include trailing blue, pink, white, or yellow. All of these grow flat on the ground or trail from hanging baskets.

Nemesia

Nemesia cultivars

Flowers: Blue or white (by variety)
Bloom Time: June through heavy frost
Height: 10 to 14 in.
Zone: 6

Color photograph on page 242.

Light Requirements:

Additional Benefits:

Well, Denny, here you go again! Writing about another summer-blooming flower that Kentucky gardeners may have never heard of. Well, it's not anyone's fault if they haven't heard of it—it's a new introduction to Kentucky and to the rest of the United States. It's a member of the Proven Winners®, a group of summer-blooming plants that are presenting us with many new annual flower opportunities. There are two varieties of *Nemesia,* both P.P.A.F. (plant patent applied for). That's an impressive statement to make for any plant, including annuals. Now why is nemesia P.P.A.F.? To begin with, they are cold hardy to 15 degrees Fahrenheit, yet tolerant of full sun into the 90s Fahrenheit (not a bad statement). The two varieties are 'Blue Bird', which has beautiful blue flowers with yellow centers, and 'Compact Innocence', which has pure-white flowers with bright-yellow centers. When in bloom, which is all summer, 'Compact Innocence' smells just like a lilac shrub in full bloom. I'll bet you'll remember it now!

WHEN TO PLANT

Plant nemesia from potted plants. You won't be able to mail-order the seed—only growers who pay a patent fee can order it. You will have to settle for potted plants, which I really feel is the way to go for best results. Plant in the soil after the danger of frost is over in your part of Kentucky.

WHERE TO PLANT

This relatively low-growing plant is best grown in full sun in pretty good, loose soil. If you don't have such soil and you still want to grow this beautiful annual, add 25 percent pine bark chips to existing clay soil to amend it. Nemesia will grow well in a half-day of sun. Don't forget to use it in hanging baskets and mixed planters with 'Summer Wave' torenia for a great combination of color in a container that will have blooms all summer long.

How to Plant

Loosen the soil to a depth of 6 to 8 inches. Remove the plant from the pot and loosen any wrapped roots. Dig a hole as deep and twice as wide as the soil clump. Backfill the hole after planting, and water-in well to settle the soil.

Care and Maintenance

Nemesia is no fluke. (You can't be a fluke and be considered for a P.P.A.F.) This plant is cold hardy to 15 degrees Fahrenheit (and that's cold) and very heat tolerant, continuing to bloom when temps are in the 90s. Fertilize with a complete plant food, following the instructions on the container. No bugs or disease bothers this great annual. Water nemesia during dry periods of the summer, but don't keep it wet. The flowers are plentiful and self-cleaning.

Additional Information

Nemesia is typical of the whole list of annuals known as Proven Winners. These varieties have gone through vigorous trial garden tests and have *proven* their worth. Nemesia does very well in mass plantings and as border plants, and is especially colorful in containers. You can mix nemesia with lots of other drought-tolerant flowers to make your patio pots look fantastic.

Additional Species, Cultivars, or Varieties

There are none known.

Did You Know?

Always plant flowers in pots with other plants that have the same "wants." Make sure the plants are sun- and water-compatible. If they are not, some will be happy and some very unhappy. Nothing looks worse than half-happy containers. Keep them compatible; the folks in the greenhouse can steer you in the Happy direction.

Ornamental Cabbage and Kale

Brassica oleracea

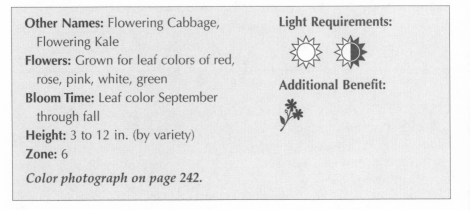

Other Names: Flowering Cabbage, Flowering Kale

Flowers: Grown for leaf colors of red, rose, pink, white, green

Bloom Time: Leaf color September through fall

Height: 3 to 12 in. (by variety)

Zone: 6

Color photograph on page 242.

Light Requirements:

Additional Benefit:

Ornamental cabbage and kale look just like their vegetable cousins in the spring and summer. As the weather cools down in September, all of a sudden the leaves of the ornamental cabbage and kale start to turn color. The cooler the weather becomes, the prettier the leaves turn, with shades of pink, or red, or rose, or white. These plants don't have a colored flower like those on blooming annuals. No, the whole leaf head of cabbage or kale turns into color, giving a flowering effect. Cabbage and kale make excellent border plants to use in prime planting places to replace those tired-looking summer-blooming annuals that aren't showing much. Ornamental cabbage and kale will last out in the fall landscape until the mercury dips to 20 degrees Fahrenheit. That means that in all of Kentucky, you can expect cabbage and kale color through Thanksgiving . . . even Christmas some years. Oh, yeah! What is the difference between cabbage and kale? Ornamental cabbage has round leaves, and ornamental kale has crinkly, wavy leaves.

WHEN TO PLANT

You can plant ornamental cabbage and kale from seed in late spring, if you like, and grow them on for the season. Remember, though, they are going to look like veggies until fall. I recommend that you buy potted plants in September and October. That way, you'll only have to care for them while they're pretty.

WHERE TO PLANT

Plant in average garden soil in part shade to full sun. The more sun, the more intense the fall leaf color will be.

How to Plant

If you want to start seeds indoors, do it in April and plant outdoors as soon as the seedlings reach 3 inches. Plant nursery-grown potted plants anytime they're available. Dig a hole as deep as the soil clump and twice as wide. Loosen any wrapped roots from the soil clump, backfill the soil, and water-in well to settle the soil.

Care and Maintenance

Fertilize with a water-soluble plant food as often as the label advises. When starting from seed in the spring, ornamental cabbage and kale are susceptible to green cabbage worms. Treat with a labeled pesticide. This is not a problem for plants that are installed in the fall.

Additional Information

Although true leafy vegetables, ornamental cabbage and kale do not taste as good as their edible cousins. Don't worry about eating the ornamental varieties. Just get ready to enjoy lots of fall landscape color. There are standard-sized plants growing 11- to 12-inch-diameter heads to dwarf types that grow 3- to 6-inch-diameter heads.

Additional Species, Cultivars, or Varieties

Ornamental Cabbage: Plants in the 'Dynasty' Series of the Osaka strain have tight, compact heads in pink, white, or red. Plants in the 'Pigeon' Series grow small, 4-inch leaves in red or white. **Ornamental Kale:** Plants in the 'Emperor' Series have 3- to 6-inch heavily fringed leaves of red, rose, or white. The 'Peacock' Series offers 10- to 12-inch heads of red, rose, or white. The 'Sparrow' Series of kale is even more dwarf than 'Emperor', and has ruffled leaves of red or white on very short plants.

Did You Know?

Ornamental cabbage and kale are used quite often in restaurants to display many foods on both buffet and table settings. Next time you eat out and see a rippled, colorful leaf on a plate at your table, you'll know what it is.

Pansy

Viola × wittrockiana

Other Name: Ladies Delight

Flowers: All the color combinations and solid colors you can imagine

Bloom Time: March through June, September through winter

Height: 6 to 10 in.

Zone: 6

Color photograph on page 242.

Light Requirements:

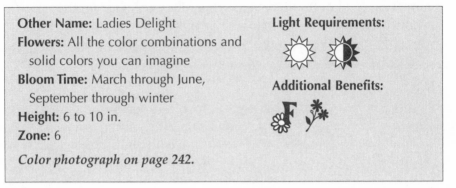

Additional Benefits:

Pansies have been around for many, many years. Early varieties weren't very cold hardy and also would stop blooming in late spring when there were seven straight days of temperatures in the low 80s Fahrenheit. They have been improved so much that now there are varieties that can be planted in the fall and overwinter quite well. In fact, the new, cold-hardy varieties will bloom during the winter on sunny days when the temp gets up to 40 degrees. Many of these same varieties will continue to bloom in late spring to early summer despite the warm weather. That's why I developed the expression: "Plant pansies in the fall and get six months of pleasure" (if you plant in the spring, you may get only six weeks). Yes, flowering pansies are tough. I will list some of my favorites below, but room doesn't allow for all. Check with your local garden center in the fall to see which ones they have that are best for your landscape.

WHEN TO PLANT

Plant pansies in early spring or early fall. Just a few years ago, pansies were only available in spring. My, how times have changed. Great cold-hardy varieties are available at your flower store during all fall months.

WHERE TO PLANT

Pansies grow best in full sun during the spring, fall, and winter. Some varieties are more heat and cold tolerant than others (listed below), and will tolerate a half-day of shade in the afternoon. That will keep all pansies blooming later into summer. You can plant all varieties in morning sun to extend their blooming period in late spring. Plant pansies in containers that can get spring sun and then be moved to summer shade to extend their bloom period. This type of planting will not overwinter—when containers are aboveground in winter, the roots will probably freeze.

HOW TO PLANT

Buy pansies in pots or cell-packs. Loosen the garden soil 6 to 8 inches. Dig a hole as deep and twice as wide as the soil clump. Loosen any wrapped roots, backfill, and water-in.

CARE AND MAINTENANCE

When planting pansies in fall, plant early in September to give the new plants more time to establish their roots in their new home. Fertilize with a high-phosphorus (middle number) fertilizer. Water if your area runs into a dry spell. Deadhead or remove spent flowers every couple of weeks.

ADDITIONAL INFORMATION

There are many varieties of pansies. Pansies will reseed themselves, keeping the color coming back year after year.

ADDITIONAL SPECIES, CULTIVARS, OR VARIETIES

'Bingo' Series is a high-rated pansy with short flower stems that hold a 3½-inch-diameter flower that faces up to look at you. 'Baby Bingo' Series is low growing, with loads of blooms in all colors, and it tolerates heat and cold better than most pansies (it's a great variety for overwintering). 'Crystal Bowl' Series, very heat tolerant, is compact growing and has flowers 1 to 2½ inches in diameter. 'Purple Rain F1' has large purple flowers on well-mounded plants. It's a free-flowering variety ideal for hanging baskets and ground cover plantings, and it overwinters well.

Did You Know?

Pansies are available by variety in at least twenty-five colors and combination of colors. Make sure the variety you want to plant is cold hardy so you can plant in fall for six months of enjoyment.

Pentas

Pentas lanceolata

Other Name: Star Cluster **Flowers:** Pink, red, violet **Bloom Time:** June till frost **Height:** 6 to 15 in. **Zone:** 6 *Color photograph on page 242.*	**Light Requirements:** **Additional Benefits:**

This new plant is another summer-blooming tender perennial (treated as an annual) you may not have heard of, but it's another one that you should not shy away from. You see, *Pentas lanceolata* is another terrific "Heat Beater"—by that I mean it has a flower that will perform well all summer in lots of heat and drought periods. Pentas grow to 12 to 15 inches high and wide. Their foliage is quite attractive, with dark green, somewhat glossy leaves. The pink, red, or violet flowers appear as clusters growing 4 to 5 inches wide. Each cluster is made up of many individual star-shaped flowers. I've only been able to plant these flowers in my yard two out of the last three years. Last year I waited too long to secure them and we ran out. Oh, well, at least my daughter Molly had them at her house, so I just enjoyed hers. Pentas make a wonderful display in a mass planting, or use them as Molly did in a border planting.

WHEN TO PLANT

You will probably find pentas only in 3- or 4-inch pots. They soon may be available in cell-packs. Secure your plants as soon as they're available and before the garden center or nursery store runs out. Do not plant outdoors until the danger of frost has passed in your area of Kentucky. Just keep them in their pots till it's safe to plant outside.

WHERE TO PLANT

Pentas will grow in full sun, in morning sun, or in afternoon sun. For best bloom results, make sure they get at least four hours of sun. They will grow in all types of soil as long as there is good drainage.

HOW TO PLANT

Loosen your garden soil to a depth of 6 to 8 inches. Dig a hole as deep and twice as wide as the soil clump. Loosen any wrapped roots, plant, backfill the soil, and water-in well.

CARE AND MAINTENANCE

There are no bugs or diseases that will bother your pentas. If your soil is heavy clay, add some soil amendments to it to loosen it. Never amend more than 25 to 30 percent. Pentas are very drought tolerant, but an occasional drink of water during drought periods would be appreciated—just don't keep them moist all the time. The flowers are self-cleaning.

ADDITIONAL INFORMATION

My pentas enjoyed being fed with a once-a-year time-release plant food. Start-N-Gro® and Osmocote® are two good ones. Read the instructions carefully (hey, guys, more is not better). All three colors of pentas are very fluorescent and will show off in the sun and also by moonlight. Plant them close to a viewing area from both inside and out.

ADDITIONAL SPECIES, CULTIVARS, OR VARIETIES

The 'New Look' Series offers star-shaped flowers in clusters that bloom all summer on plants that grow 6 to 12 inches. They bloom pink, red, or violet.

Did You Know?

Even though a plant may be listed with self-cleaning flowers, larger-blooming flowers (those having 2-inch-diameter or larger flowers or flower clusters) are better off when you remove spent flowers as often as you can. By doing this occasional flower cleaning, more strength will go toward leaves and new flowers, not into making seed.

Petunia

Petunia × *hybrida*

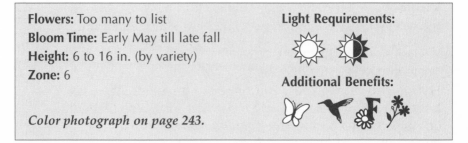

Flowers: Too many to list
Bloom Time: Early May till late fall
Height: 6 to 16 in. (by variety)
Zone: 6

Color photograph on page 243.

Light Requirements:

Additional Benefits:

To be honest, until five years ago I hated this annual. The older varieties had to be deadheaded, which meant getting your fingers painted green when removing all those spent flowers so the petunias would stay looking good until hot weather. When hot weather came along in mid-July to early August, forget it. Those flowers went away. But hey, this is the millennium, and new varieties have come to the rescue. 'Wave' petunias were introduced in the '90s with 'Purple Wave' and 'Pink Wave'. 'Purple Wave' was an All-America Selections winner. Two new waves were added in 1999, 'Misty Lilac Wave' and 'Rose Wave'. Then there were the Supertunias, a Proven Winner® with eight beautiful colors. Next came the Surfine Petunias, a great new family featuring eight colors and having a wonderful trailing habit for containers and hanging baskets. Finally, I want to introduce you to the Petuniafi, the grandiflora 'Hulahoop' Series, and the 'Picotee' Series. All of these petunia varieties have several great things in common: they're very colorful, love hot weather, are very drought tolerant, and are self-cleaning.

WHEN TO PLANT

Most of these new petunias are not available from seeds, but you shouldn't have any problem locating the plants in hanging baskets, pots of all sizes, and cell-packs. Petunias are cold hardy, and you can plant them as early as the first week of May.

WHERE TO PLANT

Petunia hybrids will grow in any type of soil that has good drainage. Give your petunia hybrids at least a half-day of sun; all-day sun is best. Petunias will also produce good color in areas of good sky light with little direct sun. Don't allow maple tree shade—that is much too dark.

How to Plant

When filling a hanging basket, plant your petunias in a soilless potting mix. For garden areas, loosen the soil 6 to 8 inches deep, and dig a hole as deep and twice as wide as the soil clump. Loosen any roots that are wrapped around it. Plant, backfill, and water-in well to settle the soil.

Care and Maintenance

Hybrid petunias are very cold hardy and will also tolerate lots of summer heat. They are heavy feeders. Keep them on a steady diet of fertilizer, following the instructions on the container. Hybrid petunias do not want frequent watering during the summer. Put the hose away and let Mother Nature take care of them. These new varieties are also self-cleaning—no green fingers here from pinching off spent flowers.

Additional Information

'Madness' is another floribunda petunia that has loads of 3-inch-diameter blooms in twenty-one beautiful colors.

Additional Species, Cultivars, or Varieties

Wave Petunias are easy to grow, have large 3-inch blooms, spread up to 4 feet a plant, and take hot and cold weather. Use in baskets, planters, or beds. Four colors to choose are 'Purple Wave', 'Pink Wave', 'Misty Lilac Wave', and 'Rose Wave'. 'Supertunia' has seven great single-flower varieties and new one, double-flowering 'Priscilla'. It is fast growing and self-branching, with a long trailing habit. Cold and heat tolerant, it loves full sun and plant food and has great curb appeal. The flowers are 3 inches in diameter. **'Surfina'** trailing petunia hybrid grows 8 to 10 inches high and has trailing branches. This variety is the best one for hanging baskets, planter boxes, or containers for the deck or patio. Large 3-inch blooms are available in eight colors. These are self-cleaning, hot and cold tolerant, and love plant food.

Portulaca

Portulaca grandiflora

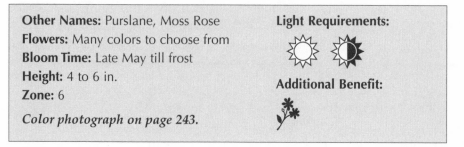

Other Names: Purslane, Moss Rose
Flowers: Many colors to choose from
Bloom Time: Late May till frost
Height: 4 to 6 in.
Zone: 6

Color photograph on page 243.

Light Requirements:

Additional Benefit:

"Would you lika portulaca?" My mom used to say this when I was seven years old and helped her plant our summer flowers. She always planted portulaca as a border plant across the front of our home. Maybe it's an old-fashioned flower. But it's low growing, has many blooms, and could be very new to a lot of you who have only been gardening a few years. New or old, this plant was destined to grow in the desert. It is a succulent-looking plant with leaves that look like evergreen needles and is very drought tolerant. It has a mature height of only 4 to 6 inches tall. The flowers come in many colors and are mostly double-flowering, and the blooms measure 1 1/2 to 2 inches in diameter. This is a wonderful annual to plant around the perennial creeping phlox, which tends to go away with summer heat. The hotter and drier the summer weather becomes, the prettier your portulaca will be. Now, I ask you again, "Would you lika portulaca?"

WHEN TO PLANT

Portulaca is very easy to start from seed. Start indoors four to six weeks before seedlings are safe to plant outdoors. You will also find lots of portulaca available from your nursery store or greenhouse in hanging baskets, pots, and cell-packs. Plant in mid- to late May after the danger of a late spring frost has passed.

WHERE TO PLANT

Portulaca is a good border plant, great for rock garden color, and does well in any hot, sunny spot where nothing else seems to want to grow. It grows well in all types of well-draining soil. It will grow okay in a half-day of sun, but remember, the more sun, the more flowers.

How to Plant

When planting, loosen the existing soil 6 to 8 inches. If planting directly into the soil, spread the tiny seeds as evenly as possible. With started plants in pots and cell-packs, dig a hole as deep and twice as wide as the soil clump. Loosen any roots that are wrapped around the clump, plant, backfill, and water-in well to settle the soil. Pinch off the early flowers on your freshly installed plants—this will allow for quicker growth and many more blooms sooner.

Care and Maintenance

No bugs or diseases to worry about with portulaca. Water when dry for the first month after planting, and then forget about the hose. Let Mother Nature take it from there. Start off your transplants with a little water-soluble plant food when you plant, and then put the fertilizer away.

Additional Information

Purslane makes a beautiful hanging basket for hot, sunny areas. Check out the varieties of 'Yubi', a light pink, and 'Duet', a red-on-yellow flower.

Additional Species, Cultivars, or Varieties

F1 Hybrid Portulaca: The 'Sundial' Series offers free-blooming, 1½- to 2-inch flowers that love the heat and bloom in ten different flavors. Be sure to check out 'Peppermint' and 'Mango'. **F2 Hybrid Portulaca:** 'Calypso Mix', another great heat beater, offers 1- to 2-inch double blooms in many colors.

Did You Know?

A first cousin of moss rose is the weedy purslane, Portulaca oleracea, *an obnoxious lawn and planting bed weed that's not known for a flower.*

Primrose

Primula × polyantha

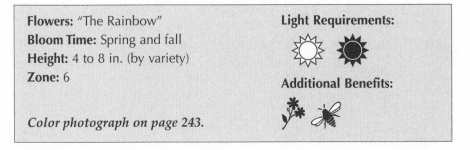

Flowers: "The Rainbow"
Bloom Time: Spring and fall
Height: 4 to 8 in. (by variety)
Zone: 6

Color photograph on page 243.

Light Requirements:

Additional Benefits:

This group of blooming plants goes into the same box with pansies and dianthus. Commonly called a biennial, the plants that are offered for sale will grow and bloom during the cool weather of spring and then stop producing flowers when the weather turns hot. These are short-lived perennials treated as annuals. Primrose comes in a multitude of colors, on 1- to 1½-inch blooms on very short plants that grow only 4 inches tall. As short as they are is as colorful as they are. There are up to twenty color combinations of bloom. Plant all this color in patio pots, windowboxes, or table pots, or mass in planting beds bordering a shrub or evergreen bed. There are other hybrid varieties as well—the Pacific Giants have 2-inch-diameter flowers on plants that grow 6 to 8 inches high and wide. All primrose varieties will stop blooming when it gets hot in the summer, but that beautiful color will return in the fall as the weather cools off. When planting in pots, leave them in a sunny location in the spring, then move them into shade when it gets hot in the summer so you can extend the blooming season.

WHEN TO PLANT

Although not readily available, seed can be planted indoors in mid-February. Potted plants will be available from garden centers and greenhouses by mid-March to early April. Go ahead and plant outdoors. Primrose is very cold hardy and provides lots of spring color in the landscape.

WHERE TO PLANT

Primrose does best in lots of spring sun. As weather warms in mid- to late May, the plants will stop producing flowers. Plant in pots or windowboxes so you can move primrose into a more shady area for late spring and summer, keeping it blooming longer.

How to Plant

Loosen your garden soil to a depth of 6 to 8 inches. Dig a hole as deep and twice as wide as the soil clump. Loosen any wrapped roots, plant, backfill, and water-in well to settle the soil.

Care and Maintenance

Primrose wants to be kept moist but not wet. When planting in containers, be sure the plants are allowed to go dry a little before adding water. Check the soil with your fingers to make sure the soil is dry before adding the H_2O. Fertilize following the instructions on the container. Slugs can eat holes in the leaves when planted in the garden; there are good slug baits available to control this problem. Follow the instructions on the box of slug bait.

Additional Information

I think primrose makes the best impression when you mix up the colors, and there are so many different colors to choose from. It's easy to mix them up. Remember, primrose will continue to bloom in summer shade. Plant some in containers that you can keep in sunny spring locations and then move into shade as the weather warms.

Additional Species, Cultivars, or Varieties

'Lovely' Series offers 3- to 4-inch-tall plants with flowers that average 1½ inches in diameter. The flower colors are shades of blue, apricot, pink, rose, scarlet, white, and yellow. 'Crayon' Series, vigorous and free flowering with large 2-inch-diameter flowers, comes in seven beautiful colors. 'Danova' Series has 1- to 1½-inch-diameter flowers. Choose from eighteen different colors blooming on 4- to 5-inch-high and -wide plants. 'Pacific Giant' Series has large 1½- to 2-inch-diameter blooms. The plants grow to 8 inches high and wide and have seven different bloom colors.

Salvia

Salvia splendens

Other Name: Scarlet Sage
Flowers: Lots of red in different shades,
   purple, rose, salmon, white,
   and bicolors
Bloom Time: June till frost
Height: 10 to 30 in. (by variety)
Zone: 6

Color photograph on page 243.

Light Requirements:

Additional Benefits:

Salvia is another old-timer in the summer-blooming annuals group. For many years salvia was available from seeds or plants as a red-blooming plant with just a few varieties, mostly of the tall 20- to 30-inch-high size. But plant breeders never sleep, and over the last twenty-five years many new varieties offering many more colors have been developed. One thing salvia plants, new and old, have in common is that they are very heat and drought tolerant. Many are still red, but now you also have a choice of a deep burgundy red to bright red, rose, salmon, white, light purple, deep purple, orchid, and bicolors of scarlet, salmon, and rose. Wow, what a choice! Depending on the variety, these terrific low-maintenance flowers look great mixed or planted in solid colors in large beds, as borders, or as background blooms. The foliage of all salvia is dark green and very attractive, making a wonderful contrast to the blooms. Finally, this plant attracts hummingbirds.

WHEN TO PLANT

You can start salvia seeds indoors four to six weeks before it's safe to plant outdoors. Plant garden center or greenhouse plants in mid- to late May after the danger of a late frost is over in your part of Kentucky.

WHERE TO PLANT

Full sun will give you the best flower count, although I've been very successful with my salvia that gets only a half-day of sun. Salvia will grow in all types of soil as long as there is good drainage. It does well in patio or deck pots as well as planter boxes. The plants are very drought tolerant, so if you forget to water them today, water tomorrow.

How to Plant
Loosen up your garden soil 6 to 8 inches. Dig a hole as deep as the soil clump and twice as wide. Loosen any wrapped roots around the clump and place in the hole. Backfill, and water-in well to settle the soil.

Care and Maintenance
Once a week, pinch off old, spent flowers as they appear. This is most important for the first four weeks after they're planted. Feed with an all-purpose fertilizer, following the instructions on the container. Even though salvia is drought tolerant, an occasional drink of water is appreciated during hot, dry weather. Taller-growing salvia might require staking when planted in windy areas.

Additional Information
Pinching off all the salvia flowers for the first couple of weeks will allow your plants to grow a lot more stems to give you a lot more bloom quicker.

Additional Species, Cultivars, or Varieties
The 'Empire' Series has uniform-growing plants (broadly growing to 12 to 15 inches high and wide) that are available in all the new colors. The 'Salsa' Series grows 12 to 15 inches high and wide and has all the new colors including bicolors. The 'Sizzler' Series offers early bloomers on 12-inch plants that produce lots of flowers in all the new colors. Late-blooming 'Splendens' offers tall 20- to 24-inch plants; all flowers are red. 'Early Bonfire' is an early bloomer that has plants growing 28 to 30 inches with large 10-inch red flower spikes.

Scaevola 'New Wonder'

Scaevola aemula

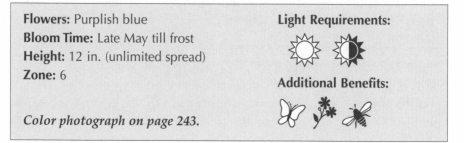

Flowers: Purplish blue
Bloom Time: Late May till frost
Height: 12 in. (unlimited spread)
Zone: 6

Color photograph on page 243.

Light Requirements:

Additional Benefits:

There is a relatively new group of summer-blooming flowers called Proven Winners® . This is a group of flowers, many of which you may not have heard of, that have been proven to be not only new, but beautiful and, in most cases, unusual when compared to what you are used to seeing. Many of these new varieties are listed in this chapter along with other new additions from other seed developers. Scaevola is a great one on this list. It is a weeping annual that trails over the soil like a ground cover or weeps and trails when planted in a hanging basket. The vigorous plant has small leaves on trailing stems with lots of medium-blue flowers appearing on the ends of the many branches. Plant it in full sun and it will require very little care. It is self-cleaning, so no spent flowers have to be pinched off. When checking out this one in the spring, look at the 10-inch hanging baskets, which will give you a good indication of how smaller plants for sale will look in only a few weeks.

WHEN TO PLANT

Plant scaevola from plants growing in pots, cell-packs, and hanging baskets in spring after the danger of frost has passed from your area. Be sure to buy yours before June, as this is one of the first flowers sold out in spring.

WHERE TO PLANT

Plant scaevola in full sun to half-day sun. It will grow in any garden soil as long as there's good drainage. Use a soilless potting mix when planting scaevola in a 10- to 12-inch hanging basket.

HOW TO PLANT

Loosen your garden soil 6 to 8 inches deep. Dig a hole as deep and twice as wide as the soil clump. Loosen any wrapped roots before placing in the hole. Backfill, and water-in well to settle the soil.

CARE AND MAINTENANCE
Scaevola is very low maintenance. I've had three in hanging baskets on my front porch facing south and the only work for me was to water every other day if they were dry. Fertilize with a time-release fertilizer like Osmocote® or Start-N-Gro®, which has to be applied just once for the entire growing season. If planting scaevola in the ground, water when extremely dry. Fertilize the same as above. Remember, scaevola is self-cleaning.

ADDITIONAL INFORMATION
You can mix scaevola and another Proven Winner, million bells, in the same hanging pot. It makes a beautiful combination that will have your basket very full on top and weeping down 4 to 5 feet. (See page 60, Million Bells®, to get the lowdown on another great flower).

ADDITIONAL SPECIES, CULTIVARS, OR VARIETIES
'New Wonder' is the best cultivar.

Did You Know?
Many of the new varieties of Proven Winners® don't last long at your favorite flower shop, for two reasons: shoppers who fall in love with them, and many store owners who aren't familiar with them don't buy enough. Buy them as soon as they become available in spring, but don't place them outside until the danger of frost is over in your part of Kentucky.

Snapdragon

Antirrhinum majus

Other Name: Snaps

Flowers: Red, pink, mauve, bronze rose, scarlet, white, yellow, orange, and many bicolors

Bloom Time: Mid-May to killing frost

Height: 6 to 36 in. (by variety)

Zone: 6

Color photograph on page 243.

Light Requirements:

Additional Benefits:

Snapdragons have been around for quite a few years. Like other short-lived perennials treated as annuals, the plants you buy at your favorite nursery, greenhouse, or garden store have been improved so that they are the best they can be. They come in many colors, with individual blooms consisting of two upper petals and three lower petals, forming a claw-type flower that looks as if it wants to pinch you. Regular varieties come in various blooming heights, from 12 inches to 36 inches. The tallest varieties make for great cutting flowers that you can bring indoors to enjoy. Snapdragons are very easy to maintain in the garden. The dwarf varieties make an excellent border plant that will outline any bed of other flowers, shrubs, or evergreens. The dwarfs also look great in their own bed. Snaps look great when planted with other summer bloomers in mixed patio pots and windowboxes. They are very cold hardy, producing blooms in the fall even after a few light frosts.

WHEN TO PLANT

Plant from seed indoors four to six weeks before it's safe to plant outdoors. You can cheat a little because of snapdragon's cold hardiness. Plant bedding plants around May 1 in zone 6, and mid-May in zone 5.

WHERE TO PLANT

Plant snapdragons in full sun to all-morning sun. Plant your snaps in areas of the landscape that usually have a breeze. They will grow in almost any type of soil, but they must have good drainage. Those of you who have gumbo clay should stick to melampodium (see page 58).

How to Plant

Loosen the soil in the planting area 6 to 8 inches deep. Dig a hole as deep as the soil clump and twice as wide. Plant, backfill, and water-in well. Plant dwarf snaps on 12-inch centers and taller-growing varieties on 15-inch centers. When planting in containers, use a soilless potting mix.

Care and Maintenance

It's best to keep the flowers pinched off for the first couple of weeks after planting. Fertilize with a balanced plant food, following container directions. For the first month, water the transplanted snaps when dry. With timely summer rains, that may be all the water you'll have to provide.

Additional Information

A few diseases can hamper snapdragons. To reduce the risk, follow my mulching instructions on page 20, and avoid overhead watering. Planting in a breezy area helps to dry the morning dew, helping ward off disease. Tall snaps might need some staking if the plants start to lean.

Additional Species, Cultivars, or Varieties

Dwarf Snapdragons: 'Floral Showers' Series is bushy, growing 6 to 8 inches tall; plants are very uniform growing and come in thirteen colors. 'Tahiti' Series offers loads of bloom color on plants growing 7 to 9 inches; it comes in fourteen different flavors. **Medium Snapdragons:** 'Ribbon Rose' Series is a strong grower; it grows 18 to 24 inches tall, is suitable for cut flowers, and is available in eight colors. 'Sonnet' Series is a great, strong grower with very bright bloom color; it grows 16 to 18 inches tall in eight flavors. **Tall Snapdragons:** 'Rocket' Series has plants growing 30 to 36 inches tall; it's great for cut flowers and might need staking.

Did You Know?

The flowers I remember most as a young child were snapdragons and nasturtiums. Get your children interested in gardening by giving them a small garden and helping them get started with flowers and vegetables like snapdragons and green beans.

Spider Plant

Cleome hasslerana

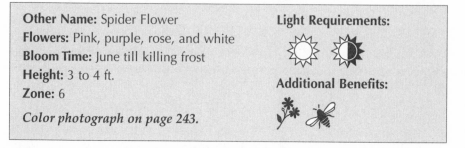

Other Name: Spider Flower
Flowers: Pink, purple, rose, and white
Bloom Time: June till killing frost
Height: 3 to 4 ft.
Zone: 6

Color photograph on page 243.

Light Requirements:

Additional Benefits:

Spider plant is a summer-blooming flower that's been around for many years. Like so many annuals that have the same name today that they did thirty years ago, spider plant has been improved by those wonderful people known as hybridizers. A variety known as 'Queen' is a series whose plants come in four colors, are strong all-summer bloomers, and are fragrant too. The flowers, which start appearing on the plant when it's 12 inches tall, continue to bloom on the top 25 percent of the stems, which grow until they reach a fall height of up to 4 feet. Spider plant gets its common name from its appearance; when in bloom, the flowers look like actual spiders weaving their webs of silken threads. If you are thinking about what happens the next growing season, spider plant offers some good news and some bad news. Spider plants produce a lot of seed, which volunteers quite readily the next season. If you want loads of free plants, you'll be happy. If you don't, and want to keep these plants from taking over your flower bed, be sure to use Preen®, a seed killer, in early April.

WHEN TO PLANT

Plant spider plants from plants already growing in pots or cell-packs, after the danger of frost is over in your part of Kentucky. You can start plants from seed if you can find it: start outdoors in late May, or start indoors around the middle of April.

WHERE TO PLANT

Spider plants make quite a statement when planted in their own bed. Plant on 12-inch centers in a sunny location. Spider plant is one of those summer-blooming annuals that will bloom in all types of Kentucky soil as long as there is good drainage. Plant in full sun to a half-day of shade and it will give you lots of color.

How to Plant

Loosen the soil 6 to 8 inches deep. Dig a hole as deep as the soil clump, and twice as wide. Loosen any roots that are wrapped around the clump. Plant, backfill, and water-in well to settle the soil. If any of your garden-store plants have blooms, pinch them off to allow for stronger growth, and keep the flowers pinched off for a couple of weeks after planting. If planting from seed, barely cover the seed with soil.

Care and Maintenance

Spider plants grow very well regardless of the care you give them. Fertilize spiders following the instructions on the containers. Pinch back the stems if they are growing tall and leggy. The longer into the season they grow, the more spider flowers you will have on your plants.

Additional Information

Unless you use Preen®, next year you may find spider plants growing from seed in beds you never planted them in. They also have prickly spines on the stems. Don't get stuck.

Additional Species, Cultivars, or Varieties

'Queen' Series plants grow 3 to 5 feet tall. They bloom all summer and produce very fragrant flowers, in colors of 'Cherry Rose', 'Rose Pink', 'Violet', and 'Helen Campbell' white. This is truly a care-free, low-maintenance group of summer-blooming flowers.

Did You Know?

Many summer-blooming annuals volunteer themselves from seed the next growing season. Among the most popular are spider plants, marigolds, impatiens, and melampodium. Be ready to replant and space these volunteers if you want to keep them. If not, use Preen® to kill the volunteer seed.

Sunflower

Helianthus hybrids and cultivars

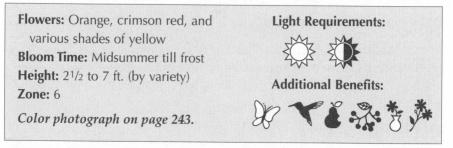

Flowers: Orange, crimson red, and various shades of yellow
Bloom Time: Midsummer till frost
Height: 2¹/₂ to 7 ft. (by variety)
Zone: 6

Color photograph on page 243.

Light Requirements:

Additional Benefits:

Who would have thought twenty years ago that we would ever talk about sunflowers as a summer-blooming flower for the home landscape? Back then they were judged by how high they grew. Can you imagine a 12-foot-high border plant? I don't think so. But flower hybridizers have really been busy with sunflowers. They have reduced those big, heavily seeded flowers on very tall plants to new varieties that in some cases only grow to 2¹/₂ feet. The flowers themselves have changed—many of the new varieties don't even expose their seeds. 'Prado Red' is a new hybrid that has crimson-red petals. The new varieties, many of which are All-America Selection (AAS) winners, have blooms from 3 to 7 inches in diameter. These new sunflowers can be used in containers of all sizes, planted in a mass in their own bed, grown for beautiful cut flowers, and used as a background planting. You will find many of the new varieties in bloom at your favorite garden center or greenhouse.

WHEN TO PLANT

Most of these new varieties are available only as plants, in pots of all sizes, and sometimes in cell-packs. The seeds are easy to plant directly in the soil where you want them to grow. Plant outdoors from plants or seeds after the danger of a late-spring frost is over.

WHERE TO PLANT

These plants do well in any type of Kentucky soil as long as the drainage is good. Sunflowers, as their name implies, want lots of sunshine, but they will grow and bloom well in morning-only sun.

HOW TO PLANT

Loosen your garden soil to a depth of 6 to 8 inches. Plant seeds directly into the soil ¹/₄ inch deep and 12 inches apart. For potted plants, dig a hole as deep and twice as wide as the soil clump. Loosen any wrapped roots, plant, backfill, and water-in well to settle the soil.

CARE AND MAINTENANCE

Sunflowers are big eaters. Be sure to fertilize as often as the container says to do so. Although drought tolerant, they would appreciate an occasional drink of water when it's hot and dry.

ADDITIONAL INFORMATION

All sunflowers produce seeds, and some varieties provide more than others. Redbirds love them all. Cut off and save the spent flowers. When they've completely dried, peel out the seeds to use in your birdfeeder during the winter.

ADDITIONAL SPECIES, CULTIVARS, OR VARIETIES

'Big Smile' has large, 6-inch-diameter, golden-yellow flowers on 2¹/₂-foot-high plants; it's great for containers. 'Sundance Kid' is a new variety that has several long-lasting 4- to 6-inch yellow flowers on the same stem; the plants grow 2¹/₂ feet and are great for bedding. 'Teddy Bear', a true double, has golden-yellow 3- to 5-inch flowers on a 2¹/₂- to 3-foot plant. 'Del Sol', an early bloomer, grows 3¹/₂ feet tall and has large 6-inch yellow flowers. 'Sonja' is a golden-orange sunflower with 4-inch flowers on plants that grow 3 to 4 feet tall. The 'Sun and Moon' Series grows large, 5¹/₂ to 7 feet; the flowers are 5 to 7 inches in diameter, and there are three colors to choose from: lemon yellow, golden yellow, and bright yellow. 'Sunrich' Series offers early-blooming hybrid sunflowers that have large 7-inch-diameter flowers of bright yellow and golden yellow; the plants grow to 6 feet.

Did You Know?

All the new hybrid sunflowers make great cutting flowers to enjoy in a vase. They will also provide excellent natural bird food for our feathered friends.

Torenia

Torenia fournieri

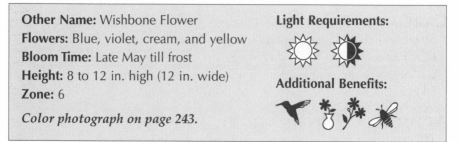

Other Name: Wishbone Flower
Flowers: Blue, violet, cream, and yellow
Bloom Time: Late May till frost
Height: 8 to 12 in. high (12 in. wide)
Zone: 6

Color photograph on page 243.

Light Requirements:

Additional Benefits:

When you first view this summer-blooming annual, you might think that it's a snapdragon gone bad. The flowers resemble snaps somewhat, but the flower opening is wider. This summer-blooming annual comes in several colors and bicolors and does best in full sun to a half-day of shade. Torenia is another old-time annual that was known as a shade-lover back in the sixties. Well, it will tolerate shade, but please, try giving it at least four hours or more of sun and you will see it bloom, and bloom, and bloom. It will grow in any kind of well-draining soil. The flowers are self-cleaning, which means you won't have to pinch off the old, spent flowers. The newer varieties, listed below, are compact-growing with lots of bloom color and attractive green leaves. The plant is not common, but that's good if you want to impress your neighbors. A new torenia called 'Summer Wave' is a Proven Winner®; its weeping habit makes it a great flowering plant for a hanging basket.

WHEN TO PLANT

Plant torenia from plants already growing in pots or cell-packs any-time after the danger of frost has passed. Start torenia in hanging baskets in early May, and bring them inside on cool to cold nights till the danger of frost has passed.

WHERE TO PLANT

Torenia does best in full sun to at least a half-day of sun.

HOW TO PLANT

Loosen your existing garden soil to a depth of 6 to 8 inches. Dig a hole as deep as the soil clump and twice as wide. Loosen any wrapped roots and place in the hole, spacing on 12-inch centers.

Backfill, and water-in well to settle the soil. Try planting torenia in a 10- to 12-inch hanging basket filled with a soil-less potting mix.

CARE AND MAINTENANCE
Torenia is not a heat beater—water when the soil is dry. Fertilize regularly, following the instructions on the fertilizer package. These plants grow very compact by themselves, so no additional foliage pinching will be necessary.

ADDITIONAL INFORMATION
This family makes an excellent 8- to 10-inch border plant, or mass torenia in its own bed. Use all the same color or mix them up. Either way, they are absolutely beautiful. If planting from seed, torenia will flower in six to eight weeks.

ADDITIONAL SPECIES, CULTIVARS, OR VARIETIES
The 'Panda' Series is very uniform growing, with short 8-inch-tall plants; flowers are bicolor, with two different shades of the same color on the same flower. The 'Clown' Series offers great performers on 10- to 12-inch plants that have many branches with flowers of blue, blue and white, white with pink, burgundy, plum, rose, and violet. 'Summer Wave' is a true Proven Winner® that will be covered with bicolor blue flowers that bloom all summer long. This torenia definitely thrives in heat and sun—try it in a hanging basket and enjoy.

Did You Know?
Proven Winners® are a group of summer-blooming annuals that are new to the majority of us and have excellent features. Take the word of this group from Rochester, Michigan. They wouldn't put their seal of approval on flowers that won't perform for you.

Verbena

Verbena × *hybrida*

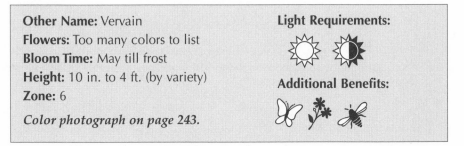

Other Name: Vervain
Flowers: Too many colors to list
Bloom Time: May till frost
Height: 10 in. to 4 ft. (by variety)
Zone: 6

Color photograph on page 243.

Light Requirements:

Additional Benefits:

Verbena is a summer-blooming plant that's been around for quite a few years. Older varieties are known to grow from 18 inches to 4 to 5 feet tall, are known for heat and drought tolerance, and come in colors of purple to pink. Then came along a new group called 'Temari', a variety that comes in many colors and is much lower growing, though still known for heat and drought tolerance. 'Temari' patio verbena is a prime choice for gardens as well as patio containers and hanging baskets. 'Temari' has become known for its bushy and somewhat upright growth habit. This group of plants literally blooms and blooms, and there are many new colors: bright red, bright pink, burgundy, cherry blossom pink, blue, and all other shades of pink. They grow close to the ground in sunny areas and are great for hanging baskets where you need color to really weep over the pots. All verbena are attractive to butterflies and bees, adding much more interest to the plantings.

WHEN TO PLANT

Verbena is best planted from bedding plants available from your greenhouse or garden center in spring. Install after the danger of frost has passed in your part of Kentucky.

WHERE TO PLANT

Old-fashioned verbena prefer decent soil in a sunny to a half-day-of-sun location. Just make sure that the area has good drainage. Many of the 'Temari' varieties do very well in hanging baskets and patio pots. Their low-growing growth habit makes them weep or trail. These plants stay fuller than their predecessors when planted in similar situations.

How to Plant

Plant verbena from pots or cell-packs. Pre-loosen the soil to a depth of 6 to 8 inches. Dig a hole as deep as the soil clump and twice as wide. Loosen any roots wrapped around the soil clump. Place the plant into the hole, back-fill, and water-in well to settle the soil. If planting the 'Temari' in a hanging basket, make sure the hanging basket is 10 to 12 inches in diameter, and use a soilless potting mix.

Care and Maintenance

Verbena likes to be fertilized on a regular basis. Choose your plant food and apply according to the instructions on the container. When planting verbena in a planting bed in the landscape, be sure to mulch to 2 inches with a bark mulch, keeping it off the stems.

Additional Information

Some verbena varieties are fragrant. Some bloom a solid color and have a white eye. Remember to shop early if you want to buy a 'Temari' Proven Winner®.

Additional Species, Cultivars, or Varieties

V. bonariensis grows to 4 to 5 feet and has pinkish-purple flowers with dark-green leaves; plant this one in a solid bed for great summer color. 'Peaches and Cream' is an All-America Selection that grows 8 to 10 inches high and 16 inches wide. 'Dwarf Jewels' grows to 10 inches high and blooms in many dark colors. 'Temari' is a new Proven Winner® that comes in red, burgundy, violet, blue, and many shades of pink to hot pink.

Vinca

Catharanthus roseus

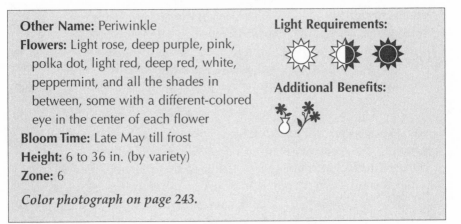

Other Name: Periwinkle

Flowers: Light rose, deep purple, pink, polka dot, light red, deep red, white, peppermint, and all the shades in between, some with a different-colored eye in the center of each flower

Bloom Time: Late May till frost

Height: 6 to 36 in. (by variety)

Zone: 6

Color photograph on page 243.

Light Requirements:

Additional Benefits:

To be or not to be, the real question is: "Is this plant called periwinkle?" Well, I usually go with vinca—that's how it's identified by seed companies like Ball Seed and Sakata. The confusion doesn't end with its name. When I first started working in a garden center in the early 1960s (child labor, of course), this plant was sold as a shade lover: "Don't give vinca any more than morning sun." People believed that until someone planted it in full sun and soon discovered that it was a tremendous heat beater, literally growing on its own with no outside help from water or shade. Vinca's worst nightmare is a cool rainy season or being planted in the grass zone of a sprinkler system. The original plants offered two choices: 2-inch purple-pink flowers with a red eye or white 2-inch flowers with a red eye. Boy, have new varieties come about, and now your choices of colors and growing styles are many. All vinca, old and new, have very glossy green leaves to add to their overall beauty. There's a lot to know about these plants, and it's going to be hard confining the information to these two pages. So whether you call it vinca or periwinkle, please read on.

WHEN TO PLANT

To be fair, I'll rotate the names. Periwinkle should be planted in the spring after the danger of frost has passed in your area of Kentucky. If growing from seed, start indoors six to eight weeks before it's safe to plant outdoors.

WHERE TO PLANT

As I said, sun or shade. But don't miss the opportunity to plant periwinkle's 1-foot-high-by-1-foot-wide plants in that hot spot, especially if the spot is difficult to water. The less summer water, the better these plants perform.

HOW TO PLANT

Pre-loosen your garden soil to a depth of 6 to 8 inches. Periwinkle is available in pots or cell-packs. Dig a hole as deep and twice as wide as the soil clump. Loosen any wrapped roots, place in the hole, and backfill. Water-in well to settle the soil. Plant all on 12-inch centers regardless of the plant size you start with.

CARE AND MAINTENANCE

I want to emphasize that vinca (its turn), with its glossy green leaves, many growth sizes, and beautiful 2-inch flowers of many colors, is very, very low-maintenance. No bugs, no disease, no water. In fact, too much water will result in stunted plants with yellow leaves.

ADDITIONAL INFORMATION

This great flower resembles impatiens in bloom. With its many new colors and all kinds of blooming forms, it is becoming my favorite. It is a great plant to dig up before a killing fall frost, pot up, and bring indoors to place by a sunny window for great indoor winter color.

ADDITIONAL SPECIES, CULTIVARS, OR VARIETIES

Vinca 'Little' Series is a new dwarf variety that grows and blooms on plants growing 6 to 8 inches tall; it's available in five different colors. 'Cooler' Series has large overlapping flower petals on upright, dark-green leaves; it grows 10 to 14 inches and blooms in ten different colors. 'Heat Wave' Series grows 10 to 12 inches; these bloomers are very drought tolerant in six different colors. 'Pacifica' Series has large, 2-inch flowers on plants growing 10 to 12 inches, and comes in six different flavors. Unique 'Apricot Delight' grows 10 to 12 inches high and wide and blooms in a soft apricot with red eyes. 'Sterling Star' is a lavender-blue variety that grows taller than most, each plant growing to 14 to 16 inches; it can spread as much as 2 to 3 feet.

Wax-Leaf Begonia

Begonia semperflorens-cultorum

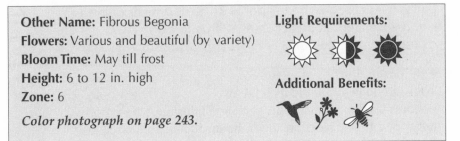

Other Name: Fibrous Begonia
Flowers: Various and beautiful (by variety)
Bloom Time: May till frost
Height: 6 to 12 in. high
Zone: 6

Color photograph on page 243.

Light Requirements:

Additional Benefits:

Wow, what a wonderful summer-blooming plant. Wax begonia is a flower for all occasions, blooming well in sun or shade and withstanding serious summer heat and drought. Best yet, it is just beautiful. Let's start with the leaves: there are varieties that have greenish-red leaves, narrow leaves, shiny-green leaves, or leaves that are green with a tinge of red on the edges. The flowers come in different shades of pink, white, white-edged pink, rose with a white center, and bright red. Salmon-and-white, edged with pink, also works its way into the color mix. Wax-leaf begonias make a great statement when planted in a solid bed and also make great border plants. My favorite way to use these plants is to alternate white-flowering ones with either pink or red ones—be sure you always use the same variety so you will have standard leaf color along with the alternating blooms.

WHEN TO PLANT

Don't mess around with trying to start your own plants from seed. You'll spend at least ten dollars and you might not end up with anything. Plant wax begonias from plants that were grown in pots or cell-packs; plant after the danger of frost has passed.

WHERE TO PLANT

Wax begonia will grow in sun or shade. When planting in sun, both green-leafed and red-leafed varieties will do. If you have mostly shaded areas, stick with the green-leafed varieties. Begonias do well in all types of soil as long as there's good drainage. Wax begonias also make excellent plants for hanging baskets and flower boxes.

How to Plant

Plant wax begonias in soil that's been pre-loosened down 6 to 8 inches. Buy plants already growing in pots or cell-packs. Dig a hole as deep and twice as wide as the begonia soil clump. Loosen any roots that are attached to the soil clump, place in the hole, and backfill. Water-in well to settle the soil.

Care and Maintenance

Begonias are very heat and drought tolerant. If you notice they are not as colorful during heat-stressed weather, give them a drink of water. There is no need to deadhead the old blooms, as these plants are self-cleaning. If the stems start to stretch in shady locations in August, cut them back halfway to encourage new, compact growth that will produce more blooms. Wax begonias are a great plant to dig up and pot in the fall, then bring inside to enjoy indoor blooms. Do this before a frost. Fertilize with a time-release plant food.

Additional Information

If your thumb doesn't feel green, plant begonias and you'll feel Irish.

Additional Species, Cultivars, or Varieties

'Cocktail' Series: hold the booze and plant these 8- to 10-inch bronze-leafed plants with flowers in light pink, rose, white edged with red, red, and white. Plants in the 'Super Olympia' Series are 8-inch-tall early bloomers with beautiful broad green leaves and large flowers that come in pink, red, rose, and white. The 'Encore' Series is a variety that has both green and bronze leaves and very large 1½-inch-diameter flowers; it offers many colors and is very bushy and upright, growing 10 to 12 inches.

Did You Know?

Plant wax-leaf begonias in areas that are hard to water during the hot periods of summer. They will grow in any landscape with very little work on your part.

Zinnia

Zinnia elegans

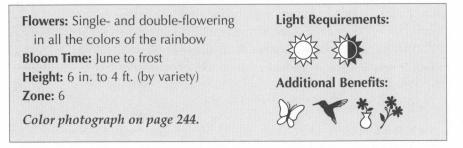

Flowers: Single- and double-flowering in all the colors of the rainbow
Bloom Time: June to frost
Height: 6 in. to 4 ft. (by variety)
Zone: 6

Color photograph on page 244.

Light Requirements:

Additional Benefits:

This new zinnia is a winner, a big prize winner. The 'Profusion' Series offers two colors. 'Profusion Cherry' was the 1999 All-America Selection Gold Medal winner and the 1999 Fleuroselect Gold Medal winner. The other variety is called 'Profusion Orange', and all it did was win the 1999 All-America Selection Gold Medal. Both these low-growing, compact zinnias are very easy to grow and bear multiple flowers on each stem, providing up to 24-inch-high mounds of wonderful color. They are very heat tolerant and resistant to disease all through the growing season. For you homeowners in Kentucky who swear you live in a summer desert, no need to worry about watering these plants when it's hot and dry: these zinnias are excellent for any landscape use in a sunny area. There are other great zinnia varieties, and they will be mentioned a little bit later. Some zinnia varieties only grow 12 inches, and others grow to 4 feet. But all have drought tolerance and beautiful color.

WHEN TO PLANT

Zinnias can be planted directly into the ground from seed. Do not plant the seeds outdoors until the soil temperature warms in mid- to late May. The seeds are large enough that you can place and space them without having to transplant later. Plant growing plants from the garden center or greenhouse after the danger of late frost is over.

WHERE TO PLANT

Zinnias do best in full sun. If that exposure is not available, choose a site that gets at least all-morning sun. This will reduce the risk of mildew to those varieties of zinnias that are susceptible. Remember, the 'Profusion' Series is very resistant to mildew.

How to Plant

When planting from seed, loosen up the soil first. Individually plant your seeds directly into the soil 1/4 inch deep and 12 to 24 inches apart, depending on the variety (your seed packet will give you more precise information). When planting zinnias that are already growing, take the root clump out of the container. Loosen the wrapped roots so they're dangling freely, and plant no deeper than the top of the soil clump. Water-in well to settle the soil.

Care and Maintenance

Water your young plants and seedlings when dry for the first three to four weeks. Then let Mother Nature take care of their moisture needs. Fertilize with an all-purpose plant food following the directions on the container. Pinch off old blooms for four to five weeks after planting—this will help your zinnias develop faster. If you grow giant or tall-growing zinnias, continue to deadhead all season.

Additional Information

Zinnias make excellent cut flowers for your enjoyment indoors. Do not cut the flowers until they are almost fully open. The blooms will still last about a week indoors.

Additional Species, Cultivars, or Varieties

'Star' Series, available in gold, orange, and classic white, is fade resistant and has 2-inch blooms on single stems; it grows 10 to 12 inches high. 'Peter Pan Hybrid' has large flowers on plants that grow 10 to 12 inches and is available in many colors. 'Thumbelina' mix offers 1 1/2- to 2-inch flowers on short plants growing 10 to 12 inches high. 'Zenith' hybrids, available in many colors, grow 30 inches tall with cactus-type flowers. *Z. angustifolia* 'Crystal White' is a 1997 All-America Selection winner and grows to 15 inches.

CHAPTER TWO

Bulbs

BULBS ARE A WHOLE GROUP OF PLANTS put on this earth to bring us color. When we hear the word "bulb," we most likely think of tulips and daffodils, which are true bulbs. But we can use the term to refer to a whole group of plants that include not only bulbs, but also such bulbous plants that come from corms, tubers, and rhizomes. Here is a breakdown of the various types of bulbs.

TRUE BULBS

A true bulb, like a daffodil, tulip, or hyacinth, is a complete plant wrapped in a skin. Inside the fleshy mass are the roots, stems, leaves, and flowers of the plant, which is very cold hardy and remains in the ground year-round. Most true bulbs have pointed tops. When buying, make sure the bulb is firm, with no mushy spots.

CORMS

Corms, such as gladiolus, are squatty, saucer-like bulbs whose tops are sometimes hard to distinguish from the bottoms. Most corms have one sunken side (that's the top) and one flat side (that's the bottom). Some corms are not cold hardy; they have to be dug up after a frost and stored indoors for the winter. Corms such as liatris and crocus are hardy corms that can remain in the ground.

TUBERS

Tubers are plant stems that grow underground. Some of the most popular tubers are dahlias and caladiums. The "eyes" on the tubers (potatoes are tubers too!) are the flowers and growth buds. Always buy tubers that have two or more eyes, and always plant with the eyes facing up. Tubers are not considered cold hardy and must be dug up in the fall and properly stored.

RHIZOMES

Rhizomes are fleshy stems that grow horizontally . . . under the ground. Canna is one of the more popular rhizomes. So are iris and lily-of-the-valley. Most rhizomes are also not considered cold hardy and must be dug and saved every fall. But that is not so with iris and lily-of-the-valley.

CARE

Bulbs are either cold hardy or not; if not, they are called "tender." Tender bulbs have to be dug up in the fall, stored inside the home for the winter, and replanted the following spring. Another option is to treat them as annuals and let them die in the ground. As for winter storage of your tender bulbs, wait until a killing frost has started to wilt the leaves. Then, using a spade or spading fork, loosen the tubers or rhizomes. Handpull the plants out of the ground, pulling on the stems to lift up the plants. Lay the entire plants, including roots and stems, on a piece of newspaper. Leave them there until the foliage and stems dry completely (this could take a week), and then remove the foliage and stems from the tubers or rhizomes. (If the temperature drops really low, take inside the house or garage to let dry.) Store the bulbs in an open container, packing them in moist but not wet peat moss. Store them in a dark, cool place for the winter. Try to remember to give them a little water monthly to keep the bulbs from drying out.

If growing cold-hardy bulbs like tulips, daffodils, and hyacinths, plant new bulbs in the fall. The best months to fall-plant are October and November. By this time, a lot of our seasonal color has dwindled and we don't feel bad pulling out annuals so we can plant our own spring-flowering bulbs. These months also provide a better chance of soil moisture from rain, making our digging easier. All spring-flowering bulbs want sunny locations. Remember, early-flowering bulbs like snowdrops, crocus, daffodils, and early tulips bloom before the leaves come out on the trees. That means that you can plant these and other early-flowering bulbs under shade trees, which will allow these bulbs to grow and bloom before any shade sets in.

PIGGYBACK THE PLANTING OF YOUR BULBS

Bulbs can be planted in rows like soldiers or planted five to seven bulbs to a hole, which is called bouquet planting. I prefer the latter. To me, it looks more natural, and you will have space in-between the clusters for planting other plants that will help camouflage the leaves of the bulbs after they finish blooming. Most tulips, daffodils, and other bulbs bloom from one to two weeks. You can double the bloom time of each variety by digging your hole as deep as the variety should be and adding 2 inches. Plant four of your bulbs in the bottom of the hole. Add 2 inches of soil and plant three more. The shallower bulbs will bloom first, and the deeper ones will bloom through the others a week later. This type of piggyback planting will double your bloom time, and you can use different colors. It will drive your neighbors nuts when they think your daffodils were white one week and yellow the next.

DIVIDING YOUR BULBS

The best time to divide your cold-hardy bulbs is in the spring as the leaves start to dwindle, approximately six weeks after flowering. The spent leaves will have matured after blooming. Carefully dig down around the outside of the buried bulbs with a shovel or gardening fork. Lift up the bulbs. Remove any dried leaves that are still attached. Remove any smaller attached bulbs (called bulblets). You can now relocate the freshly dug bulbs and, if you like, plant the smaller bulblets in the new growing area you've assigned them. The smaller bulblets will probably not bloom the next two years, but eventually they will. Some gardeners will tell you to wait until fall to replant your dug-up bulbs, but don't listen to them—you'll wind up forgetting about them after football starts in August and finally find them next spring while you are looking for that misplaced paintbrush.

Your tender bulbs, rhizomes, and tubers can be divided in spring when you're ready to replant. You can divide your tubers and rhizomes with a sharp knife, leaving at least two eyes on each divided tuber. Leave the divided tubers and rhizomes in the open air for forty-eight hours or longer after dividing before planting into your garden soil.

FORCING COLD-HARDY BULBS INDOORS

Nothing can be more spring-inspiring than a pot of blooming tulips or daffodils on a coffee table in the dead of winter. Sound difficult? Not really. You can force narcissus, tulips, hyacinths, and crocus to bloom indoors. Purchase the bulbs in the fall along with some bulb pots and loamy potting soil. Pot up crocus, leaving the bulbs 1 inch below the soil surface in the pot. With tulips, narcissus, and hyacinths, leave the pointed top out of the soil 1/2 inch. All these bulbs need at least twelve weeks of cool to cold temperatures; add three additional weeks for tulips. The best way to give them this is to plant the potted bulbs outdoors in the soil and cover the buried pots with 4 inches of bark mulch. Anytime after the required weeks of cooling, start bringing the buried pots indoors. Place them in indirect light in a room with temps around 65 to 70 degrees Fahrenheit. Water the pots as often as the soil feels dry. In two to three weeks you'll have flowers.

Allium

Allium spp.

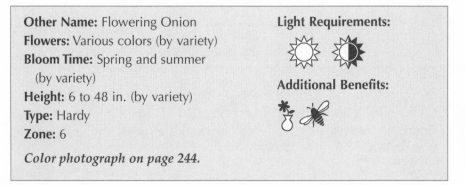

Other Name: Flowering Onion
Flowers: Various colors (by variety)
Bloom Time: Spring and summer
  (by variety)
Height: 6 to 48 in. (by variety)
Type: Hardy
Zone: 6

Color photograph on page 244.

Light Requirements:

Additional Benefits:

There are over 400 species of the allium family. Some are classified as herbs, some as veggies, and some as ornamental plants. Included in this family are such well-known players as onion, garlic, leek, chives, and shallots. Makes one hungry just to think about it. There are lots of colorful ones as well. *Allium giganteum,* also known as giant onion, is a beautiful late-spring bloomer with a flower spike that grows 3 to 4 feet tall. The round, 5- to 6-inch-diameter flower that appears on the end of that tall flower stem is like a purple-lavender burst of fireworks—a real garden stopper. On the other side of the bloom height spectrum is *Allium cyanecium,* which grows just 6 to 12 inches high and has 1/4-inch-wide, bell-shaped, purplish-blue flowers that bloom in late spring to summer. See other varieties on the next page. Don't be afraid to add allium varieties to your perennial beds or other beds where they can grow and be enjoyed.

WHEN TO PLANT
Plant alliums in the fall from mid-September till early November or later, but before the ground freezes.

WHERE TO PLANT
Alliums will grow in full sun to all-morning sun. They will grow in any type of soil as long as the drainage is decent.

HOW TO PLANT
As a general rule, plant allium two to three times deeper than the thickness of the bulb. Plant smaller bulbs like *cyanecium* 4 to 6 inches apart, and larger bulbs like *giganteum* 12 inches apart. After

planting, always water-in your bulbs well. No extra water should be necessary through winter.

CARE AND MAINTENANCE

The most important thing you can do for all bulbs is to fertilize them in spring as they start to grow. Use a fertilizer high in the middle number (for example, a 5-10-5 analysis), and follow the instructions on the container that tell how much to use. When the flowers have finished, cut off the spent flower heads and allow the leaves to remain. The leaves rebuild the bulbs with the food they make so they will bloom again next year. When the leaves yellow naturally, you can cut them back to the ground.

ADDITIONAL INFORMATION

When buying your bulbs in the fall, read about each variety before making your choices. Because alliums are a big family, there are many growing heights. You will need this information in advance so you will know where to plant them.

ADDITIONAL SPECIES, CULTIVARS, OR VARIETIES

A. giganteum has 3- to 4-foot flower stalks with purple flowers up to 6 inches wide. *A. flavum* has yellow 1/8-inch flowers on 12- to 16-inch stems. *A. cyanecium* has purple/blue flowers on 6- to 10-inch stems. *A. roseum* has 1/2-inch pinkish-white flowers on 2-foot stems. *A. senescens* has rose-purple flowers on 2-foot stems.

Did You Know?

When buying bulbs, look for the information tabs that should be located near the bulbs' containers. These tabs will have all your planting info.

Bearded Iris

Iris germanica hybrids

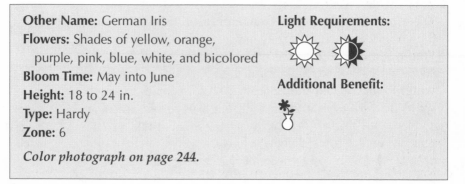

Other Name: German Iris
Flowers: Shades of yellow, orange, purple, pink, blue, white, and bicolored
Bloom Time: May into June
Height: 18 to 24 in.
Type: Hardy
Zone: 6

Color photograph on page 244.

Light Requirements:

Additional Benefit:

Iris might be considered one of the prettiest flowers of spring. A common expression heard when people view an iris flower is, "It almost looks artificial." I guess some people think manufacturers can make something more beautiful than Mother Nature. I don't think so. The light-green leaves of bearded iris resemble swords, and they can grow to a height of 18 to 24 inches. The flower stems grow from the base and produce outstanding flowers that resemble orchid blooms. Each flower has six petals. Three of these petals are called "standards." Three droop downward and are referred to as "falls." Iris rhizomes continue to expand, giving you more and more blooms over time. The one negative I find with this plant is the unattractive foliage once the iris finishes blooming. The iris clump looks better in the landscape during the summer if surrounded by daylilies and other summer-blooming plants that can help conceal all those light-green, pointed leaves.

WHEN TO PLANT
Plant bare-root rhizomes in August to early September so the new plants have time to establish before winter. Bearded iris are also available potted in the spring. You can plant potted ones anytime the potted iris are available.

WHERE TO PLANT
All hardy bulbs want good drainage, although they will grow in clay soil as long as that soil does not stay wet. You can add some organic material to clay soil to help drainage. Iris prefer full sun but will bloom in areas of all-morning sun. In mixed flower beds, your iris

might be one of the taller plants when they bloom. When mixing, keep the iris to the back of the bed.

How to Plant

When planting bare-root rhizomes, loosen the soil 6 to 8 inches deep. Dig a hole as deep as the rhizome is thick. Water-in well. With potted iris, dig a hole as deep and twice as wide as the soil clump. Backfill the soil and water-in well. (Make sure the top of the rhizome is even with the top of the soil!)

Care and Maintenance

Feed your iris in the spring with an all-purpose fertilizer. Read the instructions to learn how much to use. Cut off the spent flowers as they finish blooming. Most summers will find your iris leaves looking a little sick. This is normal, but they can become an eyesore. Wait until late August and cut back all the leaves to 2 to 3 inches from the ground. Iris rhizomes need to be thinned or separated every four or five years. Do this in August: dig up the rhizomes, separate, throw away any soft ones, and replant right away.

Additional Information

Iris borer is the only serious problem you may have. The borer enters the tops of the young leaves in the spring and eats through the center of the leaf, going in a downward direction toward the rhizomes. You have to look for what appears to be a lighter green line that gets longer by the week. Soil-drenching pesticides like Cygon® will eliminate the problem. Read the label before using. If the borer goes undetected, you will finally see the damage when you discover in the ground rotten rhizomes that the borer has entered and eaten.

Additional Species, Cultivars, or Varieties

Bearded iris come in every color of the rainbow. It has cousins that are also bulbous. Dutch iris is easily planted and provides low-growing, early-spring-flowering plants that bloom in March to April.

Caladium

Caladium × *hortulanum*

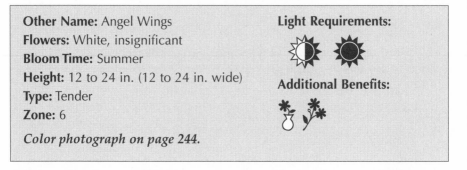

Other Name: Angel Wings
Flowers: White, insignificant
Bloom Time: Summer
Height: 12 to 24 in. (12 to 24 in. wide)
Type: Tender
Zone: 6

Color photograph on page 244.

Light Requirements:

Additional Benefits:

Now here is an underused tender bulb that produces great shade color. Caladium does have a flower, but it's pretty insignificant compared to the beautiful color mixes provided by the leaves. The leaves come in every possible color combination and they grow in shade, yes, even tree shade.

WHEN TO PLANT

Buy caladium bulbs in the spring (in April), and pre-start them by putting each one in a 5-inch pot filled with a soilless potting mix. Plant outdoors after the danger of frost is over in your corner of Kentucky. Or you can wait until May to buy caladiums already growing in pots from a garden center or greenhouse.

WHERE TO PLANT

Caladiums are shade lovers. They will tolerate morning sun but no hot afternoon sun. They like decent soil that's kept moist but not wet.

HOW TO PLANT

When planting from a pot, plant as deep in your soil as the caladium was growing in the pot. If starting the bulbs in April, plant each bulb in a 5-inch pot filled with soilless potting mix. Plant the bulb 1 inch below the surface of the pre-moistened mix. Place in a warm, bright room, but not in a window receiving direct sun. Keep the soil moist but not wet. Don't cheat! You can buy your caladium bulbs as early as March, but don't start them in pots until mid-April. Leave them in the bag till then, but don't forget where you left the bag.

CARE AND MAINTENANCE

When planted in outdoor soil, keep the plants moist but not wet. Planting under trees will have your caladiums competing with soil moisture with those tree roots. Check them every few days, especially during hot weather. Caladiums appreciate fertilizer. Use water-soluble types like Miracle Gro™. Following the instructions will keep them big and beautiful.

ADDITIONAL INFORMATION

Remember, caladiums are not winter hardy. If you have them planted in the ground, you'll have to dig them up and store them indoors to be able to replant next spring. In the fall after a killing frost has burned the leaves, dig up the bulbs, let them dry out in the sun, and store them over winter in a cool, dark place with moist but not wet peat moss placed over the bulbs in an open container.

ADDITIONAL SPECIES, CULTIVARS, OR VARIETIES

There are none known.

✿ Did You Know?

If you leave your individual caladiums potted all summer, you can bring them indoors in September and treat them as an indoor plant all winter. Don't overwater while indoors or the leaves may decline. Keep the plants away from any cool drafts.

Canna

Canna × generalis

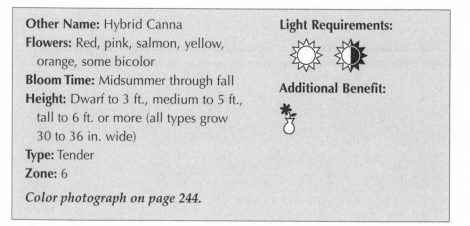

Other Name: Hybrid Canna
Flowers: Red, pink, salmon, yellow, orange, some bicolor
Bloom Time: Midsummer through fall
Height: Dwarf to 3 ft., medium to 5 ft., tall to 6 ft. or more (all types grow 30 to 36 in. wide)
Type: Tender
Zone: 6

Color photograph on page 244.

Light Requirements:

Additional Benefit:

Hey, what's that blooming in the park with the impressive leaves and super-big red, yellow, or pink flowers? Those flowers are cannas, tropical-looking plants that grow from tuberous rootstocks. Their leaves are very big, stately, and sometimes colored. There are nearly forty species, but most are not known for their uniformity—there are only a handful of species that are true to form. They will give you great color if you have the bed space. Cannas show off best when planted in a bed all to themselves, making quite a statement whether that bed is a formal one or just out in the middle of a big yard. They are available in plastic bags as rhizomes that you can plant directly into the soil in late May, or you can buy them already growing in containers from your favorite nursery. The rhizomes must be dug up and stored after a killing frost in the fall. Dig them up, store in the sun for a couple of days, and separate the old leaves from the roots; then store the rhizome roots in open containers surrounded with moist peat until they can be replanted in the spring. Check on your stored rhizomes monthly, and if the peat feels dry, add a little water. Cannas come in various growing heights from 1 1/2 to over 6 feet tall.

WHEN TO PLANT

Plant the rhizome rootstocks directly into the soil in late spring. Canna rhizomes need a soil temperature of at least 65 degrees Fahrenheit, which means late-May planting in zone 6 and mid-June in zone 5. You can pre-start cannas in pots indoors in late April.

Already-growing potted plants will also be available at some garden stores in mid-May.

WHERE TO PLANT
Give cannas their own bed. If planting different varieties, make sure the taller-growing ones go toward the center or back of the bed.

HOW TO PLANT
Loosen the soil in the bed down 6 to 8 inches. Make sure each rhizome has at least one but not more than two eyes (the pointed swellings on what looks like a root). Plant so the eyes are 3 to 4 inches deep in the soil; plant on 18-inch centers to allow room for each rhizome to grow.

CARE AND MAINTENANCE
Cannas need lots of hot sun, and they want some water during the dry periods of summer. When fall frosts first appear, dig up your plants with the rhizomes attached. Lay them out on a newspaper in the sun and let the leaves and stems dry. Store the rhizomes like dahlias: separate the stems and dried leaves from the rhizomes, and store the rhizomes in a dark, cool place over the winter. Lightly cover the canna rhizomes in moist, but not wet peat. Check monthly so they don't dry out.

ADDITIONAL INFORMATION
There's not much of a problem with bugs or diseases with cannas. Select healthy rhizomes.

ADDITIONAL SPECIES, CULTIVARS, OR VARIETIES
There are none known.

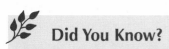 **Did You Know?**

This is a one-member plant family—it has no cousins. Its closest relatives are in the ginger family (gingers, bananas, birds-of-paradise), which includes cannas.

Crocus

Crocus vernus

Other Name: Dutch Crocus

Flowers: White, blue, purple, yellow, bronze, and striped

Bloom Time: March to April

Height: 5 to 6 in. (spreading)

Type: Hardy

Zone: 6

Color photograph on page 244.

Light Requirements:

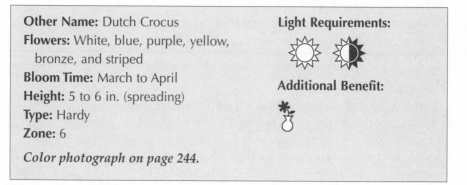

Additional Benefit:

Crocus is considered a hardy, minor bulb. It is actually a true corm, very winter hardy, whose bloom is often considered the first sign of spring. (There are other minor bulbs that bloom earlier, but those are considered late-winter-flowering bulbs.) These corms are planted just 3 to 4 inches deep, but they are not bothered by chipmunks, squirrels, or other begging critters. The leaves of crocus are grasslike, and the rainbow of flowers offers blooms that are all about 2 to 3 inches wide. Year after year, crocus will continue to spread, becoming more showy over time. There are many other species of crocus—some bloom earlier, and a relative that blooms in the fall and goes by the name colchicum can bloom indoors on a tray of pebbles. Because crocus blooms early and wants at least a half-day of sun, the bulbs can be planted under any deciduous tree as the blooms will appear before any tree puts on its leaves. Dutch crocus come in blooms of white, purple, lavender, yellow, and striped flowers.

WHEN TO PLANT

Buy your crocus corms as early in the fall as possible. This will allow sufficient time for your crocus to develop its roots.

WHERE TO PLANT

Plant crocus corms in sunny locations. They will grow well among competing tree roots. Just make sure there's good soil drainage. Always plant in groups of at least ten bulbs per planting hole to make a first-year statement. And remember, they will spread.

How to Plant

Plant crocus bulbs 4 inches deep in a hole that is large enough to accommodate at least ten bulbs; place the bulbs 4 inches apart as well. Backfill and water-in well. No water other than natural rain should be needed over winter.

Care and Maintenance

Fertilize your crocus bulbs as new growth appears in the spring. If you decide to plant some crocus in lawn areas, don't mow the crocus leaves until at least four weeks after they finish blooming.

Additional Information

Crocus can be forced in pots for late-winter bloom indoors. Refer to the "how to" on forcing in other parts of this chapter. Do not plant crocus in areas where you plan on planting summer-blooming flowers that will need summer watering. Crocus bulbs want to stay dry during their summer resting period.

Additional Species, Cultivars, or Varieties

Scotch crocus, great for rock gardens, offers 4-inch-wide flowers that come in many colors. 'Etruscan' has very narrow leaves with a white band on each, and 4-inch-wide flowers of purple or lilac. Versicolor, the parent of many other crocus varieties, has 3$^{1}/_{2}$- to 5-inch-wide flowers of white, yellow, lilac, or purple. *C. crysanthus* is a very early bloomer. Cultivars include 'Blue Bird', 'Blue Pearl', 'Cream Beauty', and 'Ladykiller'.

Did You Know?

Kentucky in spring can be warm, cold, and then warm again. When changeable weather occurs, bulbs can start poking leaves out of the ground early. We have a natural, caring tendency to go out and cover those green leaves. Don't—the bulbs know what they are doing. And what to do when daffodils or tulips show bloom color just before a night freeze? Nothing. Spring-flowering bulbs can take a lot of cold weather. More damage can occur when trying to cover the flowers than the cold air would ever do.

Crown Imperial

Fritillaria imperialis

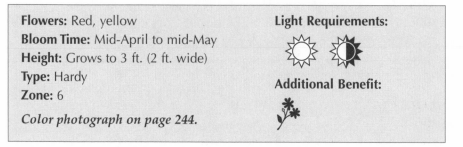

Flowers: Red, yellow
Bloom Time: Mid-April to mid-May
Height: Grows to 3 ft. (2 ft. wide)
Type: Hardy
Zone: 6

Color photograph on page 244.

Light Requirements:

Additional Benefit:

O h, boy, when you buy this bulb and place it in a warm car for the drive home, you'll ask yourself, "What is that smell?" Crown imperial is a bad-smelling bulb. But the flower is beautiful. *Fritillaria* is a group of fine old-fashioned garden flowers, one of over one hundred known species developed in the northern part of the United States. The flower stem grows about 3 feet tall before it starts to bloom, with either red or yellow trumpet-shaped flowers that bloom toward the ground. It looks truly tropical with these flower heads and a tuft of green foliage on top. Crown imperial is one of the larger bulbs, and you plant it 6 inches deep in the ground. It blooms best in full sun to a half-day of sun. Each individual flower in the cluster is 2 inches in diameter. These bulbs bloom in mid- to late April in zone 6, early to mid-May in northern Kentucky. These are specialty flowers that should be planted where their true beauty can be appreciated and observed.

WHEN TO PLANT

Plant crown imperial in the fall as soon as the bulbs are available. Be sure to plant before the soil freezes.

WHERE TO PLANT

Plant *Fritillaria* in well-draining, fairly decent soil. Remember, crown imperial blooms on stems of 36 inches. They don't take up a lot of foliage room, but if you're planting with other plants, place toward the rear of the planting bed. *Fritillaria* wants a sunny location with good drainage. Don't cheat, or you'll be very disappointed.

HOW TO PLANT

Dig a hole 12 inches wide and 8 inches deep. Place the bulb pointed end up in the hole and backfill with the existing soil, first breaking up all soil particles to the size of golf balls. Water-in well.

CARE AND MAINTENANCE

Crown imperial is very care-free. Select a planting site that has some sun and good drainage. There are no bugs or diseases that bother this plant. Fertilize it in the spring as the new foliage starts growing out of the soil, using an all-purpose fertilizer. Follow the instructions that will tell you how much to use. Be sure to supply ample moisture if dry during spring and early summer.

ADDITIONAL INFORMATION

It's best to buy locally so you can see if you're buying firm, healthy bulbs. Remember, don't judge a bulb by its smell. Plant as soon as you can in the fall, as they can dry out while waiting to be bought and planted.

ADDITIONAL SPECIES, CULTIVARS, OR VARIETIES

F. lanceolata, commonly called checker lily because of its foliage markings, is very sensitive to wet soil. *F. pudica,* a yellow bloomer, grows 9 inches tall and has flowers 3/4 inch in diameter. *F. meleagris,* called snake's head, grows to 8 inches tall and has small pendants of flowers in a pattern like a checkerboard.

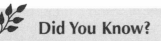

Did You Know?

Fritillaria *comes from the Latin word for dice-box, which refers to the foliage markings on some varieties. This plant is native to the Himalayas.*

Daffodil

Narcissus species and cultivars

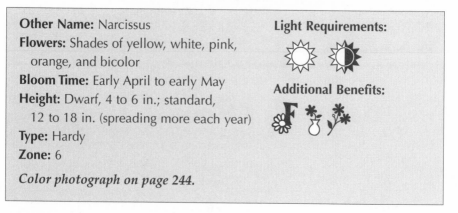

Other Name: Narcissus

Flowers: Shades of yellow, white, pink, orange, and bicolor

Bloom Time: Early April to early May

Height: Dwarf, 4 to 6 in.; standard, 12 to 18 in. (spreading more each year)

Type: Hardy

Zone: 6

Color photograph on page 244.

Light Requirements:

Additional Benefits:

What a neat family of hardy bulbs. To begin with, they are bothered by no rodents. They are also considered very perennial—even when planted in bed areas in which you've planted other summer-blooming flowers, they won't rebel and refuse to bloom again the following year. They always do! There are many varieties of daffodil: all daffodils are narcissi, but not all narcissi are daffodils. Daffs are known for their elongated trumpet, while narcissi are flowers with short trumpets. In the *Narcissus* family there are not only daffodils, but jonquils and paper-white narcissi. Daffodils bloom early enough that the blooms are not affected by warm days. The average narcissus or daffodil blooms for about two weeks. How much room do you provide for daffodils? Plenty, because they are dependable bloomers for many years.

WHEN TO PLANT

Plant these bulbs as early in the fall as possible. To allow for good root development, plant daffodils and other narcissi at least six weeks before your ground normally freezes. This would be by 15 November in northern Kentucky, 15 December in the rest of the state.

WHERE TO PLANT

Daffodils and other narcissi like full sun to at least a half-day of sun. They tolerate any type of soil as long as it drains well. Remember, daffodils bloom before the leaves come on the trees, so they can be planted in what's considered summer shade under large trees, and they will be finished blooming and curing before the tree leaves develop.

How to Plant

I prefer daffodils, and other spring-flowering bulbs, to be planted bouquet-style. That means digging a hole 6 to 8 inches deep and wide enough to accommodate three to five bulbs. Since the individual bulbs will need to be planted 6 inches apart, be sure to dig the hole wide enough to accommodate them. Backfill with the soil you dug out, and water-in well.

Care and Maintenance

Cut off the spent flower stems and leave the leaves on until they naturally turn yellow and brown. Feed your daffodils when the foliage first appears in spring. Use a fertilizer higher in the middle number (for example, a 5-10-5), and follow the instructions on the fertilizer container.

Additional Information

Daffodils make excellent bulbs for early forcing indoors during late winter. Refer to the beginning of this chapter (page 99) for forcing information. Daffodil blooms are easy to gather: simply cut off the flowers for use indoors and put in a bud vase. They are also great for naturalizing out in the landscape where the foliage will not be in the way of lawn grass. A great companion plant in a daffodil bed is daylilies. Daylilies are just getting perky as the narcissus and daffodils are starting to fade, and the daylily leaves will hide your bulb leaves after bloom.

Additional Species, Cultivars, or Varieties

There are some great varieties to consider, from 'Tête-à-Tete', which grows only 6 inches tall, to many of the taller-growing common ones that give you great color, yellow to white, and some that bloom in both colors. Some are very aromatic as well.

Did You Know?

Those bulb planters sold at the garden center are what I call "wrist breakers." Use a spade or shovel to plant all your bulbs. It's a lot easier and goes a lot faster.

Dahlia

Dahlia spp.

Flowers: Yellow, orange, red, purple, pink, white, or bicolor
Bloom Time: Mid-June till frost
Height: Medium growers, 1 to 2 ft.; tall growers, 3 to 8 ft.
Type: Tender
Zone: 6

Color photograph on page 244.

Light Requirements:

Additional Benefits:

Dahlias are tuberous roots that you plant in the spring. They are available from your garden center or greenhouse in packages. Many greenhouse growers start them from seed. These seed dahlias are the smaller-blooming plants that grow to 16 inches high and stay very bushy. The tubers you buy in packages are usually the giant-growing varieties that have blooms up to 14 inches wide on plants that grow to 6 feet high. The larger-growing dahlia varieties should be staked when first planted to keep these tall, heavy plants from falling over. Dwarf-growing dahlias make excellent border plants, while their larger cousins are excellent for hedging or for making a tall statement in any sunny landscape situation.

WHEN TO PLANT

These tubers go into your garden soil in late May after the soil temperature reaches 65 degrees Fahrenheit. If you buy the tubers early, keep them moist, but not wet, until the soil is ready. You can pre-start your dahlias indoors in mid-April (see Additional Information on facing page).

WHERE TO PLANT

Plant dahlias in lots of sun. They do best in soil that is well drained, loamy, and high in phosphorus, potash, and organic matter. Now this won't be the natural soil for many of you, so you can add a fertilizer high in the last two numbers (for example, 5-10-10) and mix pine bark chips or organic peat into the existing soil. Just make sure the now amended soil drains well.

How to Plant

After adding the above fertilizer and soil conditioners to the existing soil, place the plants at least 4 feet apart in all directions. Place a stake next to all the tall-growing types. Dahlias do best when planted in full sun to part shade. After they start to grow, feed each plant with a mixture of bonemeal and muriate of potash, placed within about 8 inches of each plant.

Care and Maintenance

Dahlias will bloom more freely if you remove some of the growth. This will allow better light and air circulation. Keep half the buds pinched off so the remaining buds can enlarge and give larger blooms. Keep spent flower heads pinched off as they appear. Let a killing frost kill the tops of your dahlia plants. Carefully dig up the roots, removing any soil that's attached. Allow the roots to dry for several days in the sun. Cut away the stems and leaves and store the roots in an open container, covering them with moist but not wet sphagnum peat. Store in a cool, barely moist place around 40 to 45 degrees Fahrenheit.

Additional Information

You can pre-start your dahlias in containers in mid-spring. Using garden soil, pot up your dahlia tubers in 1-gallon containers in April. Keep in a room with good sky light, and water only when dry.

Additional Species, Cultivars, or Varieties

There are many varieties of dahlias grown, both from tubers and from seed. Read all the information about the dahlia you're about to buy so it matches the growing size you wish for your landscape. Common-name varieties that dahlias go by are cactus, peony, pom-pom, and anemone.

🌿 Did You Know?

Dahlias make excellent cut flowers you can enjoy inside. Their blooms last about ten days to two weeks.

Gladiolus

Gladiolus × hortulanus

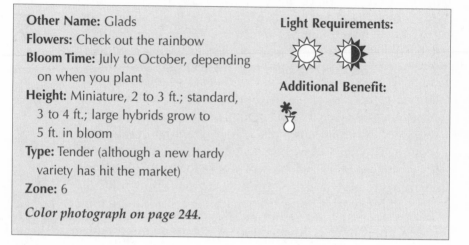

Other Name: Glads

Flowers: Check out the rainbow

Bloom Time: July to October, depending on when you plant

Height: Miniature, 2 to 3 ft.; standard, 3 to 4 ft.; large hybrids grow to 5 ft. in bloom

Type: Tender (although a new hardy variety has hit the market)

Zone: 6

Color photograph on page 244.

Light Requirements:

Additional Benefit:

Want to have some great blooms to show off in your yard and in a bud vase? The solution is easy: plant some gladiolus. Commonly called glads, these bulbous plants are available in miniature, growing just 2 to 3 feet tall with flower spikes just 2¹/₂ inches wide, to giant glads that grow 3 to 5 feet tall and have flower spikes 5¹/₂ inches wide. Glads are considered tender bulbs called corms. A new, cold-hardy group of glads have come along, but recent mild Kentucky winters have not been cold enough to really test these new ones. So for Kentucky, the jury is still out. Glads have one flower spike per bulb. To extend the blooming period, buy three times as many as you think you need, and plant one-third in early June, one-third in late June, and one-third in mid-July. That way you'll assure yourself of glad color most of the summer. Tender bulbs should be recovered after a killing frost in the fall. Dig up the corms, dry in the sun, and store over winter in a dark, cool place in your home.

WHEN TO PLANT

Plant glads in mid- to late spring after you've planted your summer-blooming annuals. You can expect flowers eight weeks after planting.

WHERE TO PLANT

Glads, like all other bulbs, need good drainage. Avoid areas of heavy gumbo clay. Glads would love sun all day, but if that's not possible, give them at least all of the morning sun. Plant your glads 6 to 12 inches apart.

How to Plant

Glads can become very top-heavy when in bloom. There are two important things to do. First, plant your corms deep. This will allow the soil to help support those top-heavy blooms. For corms like the minis, plant the 1/2-inch corm 3 inches deep. For medium corms (1/2 to 1 inch), plant 4 to 5 inches deep. If you have large corms (1¼ inches or larger), plant 6 to 8 inches deep. For insurance, place a bamboo stake along each flower spike and tie off for added support during heavy rainstorms or high winds.

Care and Maintenance

You can dig up and remove the old leaves and corms six weeks after they've finished blooming—you don't have to wait until fall. This is important if you want to use their space in the garden for fall-blooming plants. Remember to take care when storing your corms for winter. If you are trying the new, cold-hardy glads, wait the six weeks after bloom to remove the leaves, then just leave the corms in the ground.

Additional Information

When cutting a glad bloom, cut the spike when the first flowers open at the bottom of the flower stem. Place the cut flower stem in water in a cool room for the first twenty-four hours. Then go ahead and use the blooms as desired. (Remember, when cutting off the flower, leave all the other leaves on the plant.)

Additional Species, Cultivars, or Varieties

There are many different gladiolus hybrids. When buying, get all the information on the types you select. They come in all colors.

Grape Hyacinth

Muscari spp.

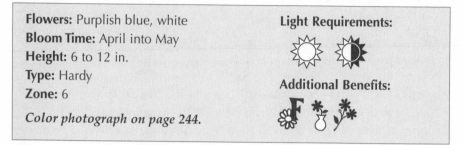

Flowers: Purplish blue, white
Bloom Time: April into May
Height: 6 to 12 in.
Type: Hardy
Zone: 6

Color photograph on page 244.

Light Requirements:

Additional Benefits:

G rape hyacinths are not closely related to the hyacinth family that we know, but both are cousins of the same lily family. These low-growing flowers bloom on stems 6 to 12 inches high. The bloom colors are light blue, a dark purplish-blue, or a white. The leaves are grasslike, 4 to 6 inches long. The flowers grow on stems from the soil, growing through the foliage. Grape hyacinths look best in the landscape when planted in large masses of twenty-five to fifty bulbs. Over time, they will continue to spread their amount of bloom in early spring. They grow best in sunny areas in loose, rich, somewhat sandy soil. That's what they want—but I've seen grape hyacinths bloom and thrive in soil conditions that include clay. They also do well when planted around tree trunks, competing with those tree roots. They are a wonderful contrast when planted in-between low-growing species tulips and various varieties of narcissus. Oh, yeah!—they have a very pleasant fragrance, too. These are enjoyable to behold and trouble-free to grow.

WHEN TO PLANT
Plant in mid- to late fall before the ground freezes. Since they are best planted in large numbers, buy in late fall and there's a good chance they'll be on sale. That's because people who haven't bought this book won't know them, and most garden centers will have lots of them yet to sell late into the fall season.

WHERE TO PLANT
Grape hyacinths would like to have good, loamy, somewhat sandy soil. They will tolerate light clay. Just make sure that the area you've selected has good drainage. Grape hyacinths do well in full sun to a half-day of sun. In fact, afternoon shade will extend their blooming time.

How to Plant

Grape hyacinths are small bulbs less than 2 inches in diameter. Dig up and loosen the soil 6 to 8 inches where you want to plant. Plant grape hyacinths 3 inches deep and 4 inches apart. Plant plenty, twenty-five to fifty to an area, to make a great showing the first spring. Cover the bulbs with soil and water-in well.

Care and Maintenance

No pest or disease problems here. After grape hyacinths bloom, allow the leaves to remain until they turn brown on their own. Fertilize the plants in early spring as the bulbs start to grow. Use a fertilizer with a high middle number. Read label instructions to learn how much fertilizer to apply.

Additional Information

Grape hyacinths belong to a bulb category known as "minor bulbs." This means the bulbs are a lot smaller than their larger counterparts, like tulips, daffodils, and others. Just because they're called minor, don't think they won't have a major color impact on your landscape if you plant them in large numbers.

Additional Species, Cultivars, or Varieties

Muscari comes in several varieties of fragrant blue flowers (and one white) under the name of *Muscari azureum* 'Album'.

Did You Know?

How did a bulb called Muscari *come up with the common name grape hyacinth? Take a look at each individual flower cluster on the flower stalk; it looks just like a bunch of purple or white grapes.*

Hyacinth

Hyacinthus orientalis

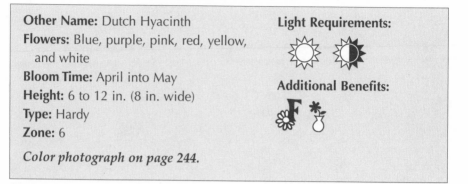

Other Name: Dutch Hyacinth
Flowers: Blue, purple, pink, red, yellow,
   and white
Bloom Time: April into May
Height: 6 to 12 in. (8 in. wide)
Type: Hardy
Zone: 6

Color photograph on page 244.

Light Requirements:

Additional Benefits:

Talk about a great aromatic flower! You have to be talking about hyacinth. Those fragrant flowers are a series of hundreds of small, bell-shaped flowers growing and producing on the same stem. Plant hyacinths near entryways to the house, where the aroma can filter in when the door is open. Hyacinths make a great statement when planted in clusters of several bulbs. They make a great border planting, lining a bed with all of the same or mixed colors. They come in shades of blue, purple, white, yellow, pink, and red, and they also force well in pots. (This process is explained at the beginning of this chapter, page 99). They also can be grown pre-cooled in water in a hyacinth glass. Make sure the hyacinth bulb was "pre-cooled" at the nursery. Then place the bulb in water in a special glass made for this purpose; place the glass in the dark, and allow it to stay there until the bottom of the glass is filled with white roots. Then place the glass in a bright room where the hyacinth will bloom indoors. It's great fun for a young child to watch the bulb grow and bloom.

WHEN TO PLANT

Hyacinths should be planted as early in the fall as possible. They make all their root growth, necessary for a healthy plant, within six weeks after planting.

WHERE TO PLANT

Hyacinths, like all hardy bulbs, want to be planted in a well-drained soil. Avoid heavy clay that tends to stay wet during rainy periods. They also do best in lots of sun, at least a half-day.

How to Plant

Hyacinths should be planted 6 to 8 inches apart and deep. I prefer to plant hyacinths in groups of five bulbs to a hole, spacing the clumps 2 feet apart. Backfill the hole and water-in well. They can also be planted in rows like soldiers. Use a spade to plant this way as well (if you've ever used a bulb planter, either short- or long-handled, you know that this tool will only make more work for the project).

Care and Maintenance

Fertilize hyacinths with an all-purpose fertilizer in the spring as the new growth starts. Follow the instructions and apply the recommended amount to the soil. Cut away the spent flowers when they finish. Leave the leaves on until they naturally brown off. Plant hyacinths in a bed where you won't plant summer-blooming annuals on top later in the spring season. Hyacinths, like all spring-flowering bulbs, want to stay dry during their summer sleeping season.

Additional Information

Hyacinth bulbs are cultivated to produce a large bloom the first year they flower. Chances are they will not bloom as large the following year. Fertilize as mentioned above and they should produce large flowers again their third year.

Additional Species, Cultivars, or Varieties

There are many variety colors. Just be sure to buy nice, firm bulbs when you select your hyacinths. *Muscari*, commonly called grape hyacinths, is a different genus that bloom in the spring and are listed elsewhere in this chapter.

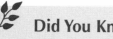 **Did You Know?**

Do not use your hands a lot to handle hyacinth bulbs. Hyacinths have a dust on them that can cause irritation to your skin. Wash your hands with soap and water after you handle the bulbs.

Lily

Lilium spp.

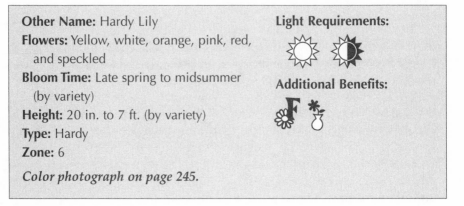

Other Name: Hardy Lily

Flowers: Yellow, white, orange, pink, red, and speckled

Bloom Time: Late spring to midsummer (by variety)

Height: 20 in. to 7 ft. (by variety)

Type: Hardy

Zone: 6

Color photograph on page 245.

Light Requirements:

Additional Benefits:

These beautiful flowers—including the beautiful Easter lily—are all cold hardy, and grow very well in Kentucky. The lily hybrid flowers are extremely showy, very erect growing, and very easy to manage. Their funnel or trumpet-shaped flower comes in many colors, some solid, some speckled. These hybrids are divided into several classes. The American hybrids have large 4- to 6-inch-wide flowers on 4- to 6-foot-tall plants, and bloom during the summer. The Asiatic hybrids grow 2 to 5 feet tall and produce flowers that are 4 to 6 inches wide. Some of these varieties have speckled blossoms, and all Asiatic lilies bloom during the early part of summer. Aurelian hybrid lilies flower 6 to 7 inches wide. The summer-blooming candidum hybrid is a 4- to 5-inch-wide white-flowering lily growing on stems 3 to 4 feet high. Candidum hybrid lilies are the exception to the overall rule for planting depth: plant them 1 inch deep for every inch of bulb height. The Oriental hybrids produce many colors, blooming in the summer with fragrant flowers that range from 2½ to 10 inches wide on stems that grow from 2½ to 7 feet tall.

WHEN TO PLANT

Hybrid lilies can be planted from bulbs in the fall or spring. The bulbs are most widely available in the fall, and potted lilies are most plentiful in the spring.

WHERE TO PLANT

Plant hybrid lilies in lots of sun, at least all-morning sun. They want decent garden soil, and it helps to load the soil with organic material.

You'll need good drainage as well. Hybrid lilies also like to have their roots shaded; there are many ground covers and low-growing perennials in this book that will fill that bill.

How to Plant

Dig up and loosen the garden soil 10 to 12 inches deep. Incorporate organic material like pine bark chips into the existing soil. Plant lily bulbs pointed side up into the ground at a depth that is three times the height of your lily bulb (example: if your lily bulb is 2 inches high, plant the bulb 6 inches deep). Fertilize each spring with an all-purpose granular fertilizer as new growth starts to appear. Keep your garden soil moist, but not wet, until they finish flowering, then cut back the water and allow your lily to dry out. Do not remove the leaves until they naturally brown.

Care and Maintenance

When planted in a happy home, lilies require very little maintenance. Have some bamboo plant stakes handy, and watch to see if the lily stems start to lean as the flowers open. If they do, give them a staking hand.

Additional Information

Cut off the yellowish pollen-laden anthers as they form inside the flower. This will keep the trumpet-shaped flowers, especially the white ones, from getting stained.

Additional Species, Cultivars, or Varieties

Most lilies mentioned can grow from 3 to 6 feet tall. A new dwarf hybrid lily was developed in the mid-'80s. This hybrid group is called pixie hybrids, which grow to 20 inches.

🌿 Did You Know?

The Easter lily commonly given to a loved one at Easter is a hardy lily, too. The proper name is Lilium longiflorum, *and when planted in a good lily spot in your landscape, it will grow to 3 feet tall. If you receive an Easter lily, let it bloom and leave it in the pot until the leaves die. Then remove the bulb from the pot and plant three times deeper than the height of the bulb.*

Scilla

Scilla sibirica

Other Names: Squill, Blue Bells
Flowers: Dark blue, white
Bloom Time: February to March
Height: 4 to 6 in.
Type: Hardy
Zone: 6

Color photograph on page 245.

Light Requirements:

Additional Benefit:

This is a great little hardy bulb that produces a small, very-early-blooming flower. Did I say flower? I meant to say lots of flowers, in February or early March. The blue bell–shaped flowers are 1/2 inch in diameter and bloom on flower stems only 5 to 6 inches from the ground. Their leaves always remind me of miniature hyacinth leaves. This is another bulb you'll want to use in masses. Scillas are very inexpensive to buy and look best in groups of twenty-five to fifty. Before you say, "Hey, I'm not digging all those holes!" remember, these bulbs can be planted in a large shallow-dug hole, and each bulb can be placed inches from the others and then covered all at one time. This is a bulb that gives you great late-winter bloom, is not bothered by the cold, and is out of the way before your spring color arrives. This last point makes *Scilla sibirica* ideal for planting in lawn areas—everything will be gone from the bulb before the lawn needs to be mowed. They will also reseed themselves, and that's good. They are not invasive, and you get even more blue or white color for free.

WHEN TO PLANT
Plant scillas in the fall. Try to have them planted by mid-October to give them ample time to root. Remember, scillas are early risers.

WHERE TO PLANT
Scilla sibirica prefers full sun to part shade. When planting around shrubs that you want to get bigger, be sure to plant them far enough away so the scillas won't be blooming underneath the shrubs someday. Remember, all bulbs want to stay on the dry side after bloom. Do not plant them in lawn areas if you have an irrigation system.

How to Plant

Plant scillas 3 inches deep in well-drained soil. These are small bulbs producing small flowers—let's make a show. Dig a hole 18 inches wide. Place twenty-five scilla bulbs in the hole, 2 inches apart. Move over 4 to 5 feet and repeat. Talk about a show of color! You can also plant smaller clumps, but make each clump a minimum of five bulbs. Water-in well after backfilling the soil.

Care and Maintenance

Feed your scillas along with all your other spring-flowering bulbs as the leaves start to grow in February. Use an all-purpose plant food following the application instructions on the container. Don't worry about the foliage after bloom; it goes away before your other landscape plants start growing.

Additional Information

Low-growing *Scilla sibirica* should be planted in good soil. In exchange for that, they will increase in numbers naturally over the next few years. Just be sure to plant them in sunny areas.

Additional Species, Cultivars, or Varieties

There is a *Scilla sibirica* called 'Alba', a white-flowering variety. I'm not sure how I feel about white, low-growing flowering bulbs that bloom white in the infrequent snows of February.

Did You Know?

Why won't my bulbs bloom a second year? Tulips and daffodils—actually all bulbs—thrive when planted in their own area, away from the summer-blooming flowers that we tend to water all summer. After cold-hardy bulbs finish blooming in the spring and their leaves turn brown, the bulbs remaining in the ground don't want to be watered or fertilized from above. Plant your cold-hardy bulbs in areas that you don't tend to during the summer.

Snowdrops

Galanthus nivalis

Other Name: Candlemas Bells
Flowers: White
Bloom Time: Mid- to late February
Height: 4 to 11 in. (by variety)
Type: Hardy
Zone: 6

Color photograph on page 245.

Light Requirements:

Additional Benefit:

Wonder how this bulb got its name? Could it be that it blooms in Kentucky in mid- to late February? I think so. Snowdrops are among the earliest spring bulb flowers to appear, producing a lot of white color in late winter to early spring. Plant them in a sunny location, especially in the midst of ground cover, and they'll bloom in mid-February. If you plant them in a half-day of shade, chances are they'll wait to bloom until late February. These plants bloom close to the ground, growing only 4 to 6 inches. Considered a minor bulb, snowdrops should be planted in masses of twenty-five to fifty bulbs to a planting site. They also mix well when planted among other early minor bulbs such as winter aconite and *Scilla sibirica*. They are great bulbs for naturalizing under deciduous shrubs and trees, and, when planted in rich garden soil, will continue to spread in large numbers through the years.

WHEN TO PLANT

Plant these small bulbs anytime during the fall before the soil freezes. Try to plant before mid-October to give snowdrops time to root-in before winter.

WHERE TO PLANT

Snowdrops want decent soil. It can be clay, but not the heavy gumbo clay. Plant in areas of the landscape where you can view them from inside the house—remember that they'll bloom when the snow is coming down. They bloom early enough that their foliage is not in the way of other spring-growing plants.

HOW TO PLANT

Plant these minor bulbs in groups of twenty-five to fifty. Dig a hole 3 inches deep and 18 inches wide. Place the snowdrops in the hole,

126

spacing the bulbs 2 to 3 inches apart. Backfill and water-in well. Space the large clumps at least 4 to 5 feet apart to allow them to spread each year by themselves.

CARE AND MAINTENANCE

Fertilize the snowdrops as new growth starts to appear in late winter. Use an all-purpose fertilizer according to the instructions on the container. Let the leaves dry naturally after the flowers have finished blooming. The old leaves will be gone before most of your landscape wakes up.

ADDITIONAL INFORMATION

Plant snowdrops where you won't be doing any future cultivation. Remember, you've planted them only 3 inches deep. Don't be disappointed in their size when you buy snowdrops or other minor bulbs. All these bulbs are very small, but the pleasure from the blooms can be large.

ADDITIONAL SPECIES, CULTIVARS, OR VARIETIES

Galanthus nivalis 'Flore Pleno' is a double-blooming white variety that grows 4 to 6 inches tall and blooms very early. 'Elwesii' leaves grow to 8 inches tall; the flower stalks grow to 11 inches and produce white flowers.

 Did You Know?

Another type of indoor forcing uses pre-cooled hyacinths and narcissus that you can buy in the fall. They will grow and bloom in a saucer filled with pebbles and water. Simply place the bulbs on the pebbles with water that is not so deep as to touch the bottom of the bulbs. Place in a dark closet until roots start to grow and the tips start showing new growth. Bring out into a room with good daylight and enjoy the bloom. Continue to add water to the pebbles as needed. To keep paperwhites' leaves short and stocky, add a teaspoon of gin to a quart of water, and use this mixture to keep water in the saucer. It works!

Tuberous Begonia

Begonia × tuberhybrida

Flowers: Various colors; pink, orange, red, yellow, white, picotee
Bloom Time: Summer
Height: 12 to 16 in.
  (12 to 16 in. wide, too)
Type: Tender
Zone: 6

Color photograph on page 245.

Light Requirements:

Additional Benefits:

Tuberous begonias are a group of tender-blooming bulbs so spectacular that when you first see them for sale in the spring at your favorite garden store or greenhouse, you will undoubtedly say to yourself: "I've got to have that flower in my yard!" These are the large, up-to-4-inch-wide tissue-paper-type blooms. They are absolutely beautiful. The flowers resemble double peonies or camellias, and their color range is the rainbow. But the biggest mistake a homeowner makes is not realizing that these plants are shade lovers. They'll be okay in morning sun, but no, absolutely no hot sun. Regardless of which way you go, begonias are a beautiful summer-blooming plant that I'll bet you can find some room for.

WHEN TO PLANT

They are available in pots or hanging baskets in May. They are also available in early spring as tender bulbs, which is the most economical and may be the best way to buy them—even though you will have to care for them for awhile indoors before placing outside.

WHERE TO PLANT

Tuberous begonias are best planted in light shade to morning sun. They also like to be in an airy planting site that helps dry the dew off the plants as soon as possible each morning. They like fairly good soil to grow in, as they have a very fine root system.

HOW TO PLANT

Tuberous begonias transplant very easily from containers into your soil. If you buy them in hanging baskets, you will have instant results. When starting from purchased bulbs, place each one in a 5-inch pot in mid-April in a soilless potting mix. Plant each bulb in a pot 1 inch below the soil line. (Always make the soil line 1 inch below the top of the pot so you will have a water reservoir.) Keep the pots moist but not wet until it is safe to plant the newly grown plants outside in mid- to late May.

CARE AND MAINTENANCE

Tuberous begonias prefer decent soil that stays moist, not wet, and no hot sun. They can be tricky to water, especially in containers like hanging baskets, because it's easy to overwater begonias. Always check the soil and be sure it feels dry down a couple of inches. If you feel moisture, wait to water. If you want to recover and save the bulbs for next year, dig them up after a killing frost and store the bulbs in a cool, dry place for the winter, covered with moist but not wet peat moss.

ADDITIONAL INFORMATION

Do not water your ground-planted begonias with overhead irrigation—this could lead to mildew on the leaves. Water directly on the soil (even though the same risk is there if you don't plant your begonias in an area that gets lots of natural wind).

ADDITIONAL SPECIES, CULTIVARS, OR VARIETIES

There are many colors of tuberous begonias that are very upright in growing habit. There are solid colors as well as a strain called 'Picotee Lace', which has a different color around the flower's outer edge. There are also vining begonias that will spread over the ground or weep downward in a hanging basket.

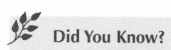 **Did You Know?**

The tuberous begonias in this entry are sometimes called 'Non-Stop'. They don't seem to stop blooming.

Tulip

Tulipa spp.

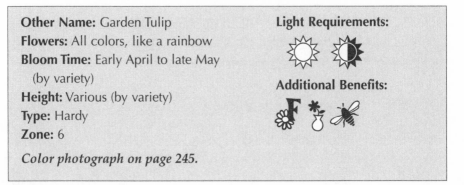

Other Name: Garden Tulip
Flowers: All colors, like a rainbow
Bloom Time: Early April to late May
  (by variety)
Height: Various (by variety)
Type: Hardy
Zone: 6

Color photograph on page 245.

Light Requirements:

Additional Benefits:

Tulips, a great bulb family that produces flowers of different shapes and plants growing to different heights, often have a common problem: great blooms the first year and then few if any the following years. There are some reasons for this. Let me begin by saying many of us plant tulips in bed areas in which we later plant summer-blooming flowers. What do we primarily do with summer-blooming flowers? We water them—and tulips, even more than most other bulbs, are very intolerant of moisture during their summer rest period. There are also some tulips that are more naturally perennial than others. Darwin hybrids and species tulips are among the best repeat-bloomers.

WHEN TO PLANT

Plant tulips in the fall, but don't rush to plant. You can buy them in early fall, but refrigerate and plant in October after the soil has started to cool down.

WHERE TO PLANT

Plant tulips where they will get at least a half-day of sun. In fact, if you're planting late-spring-flowering tulips, plant them in morning sun, as hot afternoon sun will cause the tulips to bloom out too quickly. Tulips have to be planted in well-draining soil, and please, no heavy clay.

HOW TO PLANT

Throw away the bulb planter and get out the spade or shovel. Dig your hole 8 inches deep and 12 inches or more in diameter. Place three to five bulbs in the hole. Break up all soil particles to the size of golf balls and backfill. Water-in well. Remember, the pointed end goes up. If you have Alvin and his chipmunk buddies, dust the bulbs with sulfur to discourage their good taste.

CARE AND MAINTENANCE

Tulips can be a great dessert for deer. Instead of fencing, use Fertilome's This 1 Works®, and spray the flower petals as they start to open. Fertilize your tulip and all other spring-flowering bulbs with an all-purpose fertilizer as the leaves poke their heads out of the soil in spring.

ADDITIONAL INFORMATION

Tulip foliage has to remain after the flowers finish. You can cut off the spent flower heads to prevent the tulips from forming seedheads. The leaves, however, have to resupply food so the bulbs will bloom again. That's why I suggest bouquet-planting your tulips so you have space in-between the clumps for drought-tolerant annuals like periwinkle to be planted. Remember that tulips don't want a lot of irrigation for the entire summer after they flower.

ADDITIONAL SPECIES, CULTIVARS, OR VARIETIES

Darwin hybrids have large flowers in May on tall, 1¹/₂- to 2-foot flower stems; flowers are 3 to 4 inches in diameter. Fosterianas are early spring-flowering on short stems 12 to 18 inches high, with large flowers up to 3 ¹/₂ inches in diameter that bloom in early spring. Single early hybrids are April-blooming flowers 2 to 4 inches in diameter blooming on 14- to 16-inch stems. Greigii hybrid tulips have striped leaves and flowers to 3 inches in diameter on short stems of 6 to 9 inches.

Did You Know?

A lot of tulip bulbs are in a weakened condition when you buy them. They need a good, airy, cool storage area before planting, and they do best where they are kept cool until they are sold in the fall. Ask the staff at your nursery how the bulbs were stored before you buy.

Winter Aconite

Eranthis hyemalis

Other Name: Buttercup
Flowers: Yellow
Bloom Time: Late winter, early spring
Height: Up to 6 in.
Type: Hardy
Zone: 6

Color photograph on page 245.

Light Requirements:

Additional Benefit:

Do you want to feel like spring in February? Well, shrug off the winter blahs with a covering of lovely, bright, deep-yellow flowers. Winter aconite blooms about the same time that white snowdrops, Dutch iris, and even some early crocus bloom. Talk about a color show just when you think winter will never end! The yellow flowers are single and cup-shaped. Each flower is 1 inch in diameter, but you get several flowers from each tiny minor tuber. Winter aconite is in the buttercup family, and that's just what the flowers look like, a butter cup. The very cold-hardy leaves are rounded with lobed edges. This plant is an example of why you shouldn't try to assist Mother Nature when it comes to green leaves and bloom color. Don't try to cover any spring-flowering bulb plant or flower when the weather turns cold. Your covering of plastic (never use) or cloth will do more damage to spring-flowering bulbs than the cold weather could ever do.

WHEN TO PLANT

Plant in the fall, preferably before the end of October. Winter aconite needs two months to get established before it starts to grow and bloom.

WHERE TO PLANT

Winter aconite prefers loose, loamy soil. If that's not what you have, plant in soil that drains well and is not considered gumbo clay. Plant in open areas around trees and shrubs that you can see from inside your home.

How to Plant

Winter aconite, like so many of the small minor tubers, makes a much bigger statement when planted in clusters of at least twenty to twenty-five tubers. Dig a hole 3 inches deep and 18 inches wide. Place the winter aconite tubers in the hole, spacing them 2 inches apart. Backfill with the existing soil, and water-in well.

Care and Maintenance

Winter aconite tubers are free of bugs and disease. Fertilize as the new growth starts to appear in late winter. Use an all-purpose granular fertilizer and follow instructions. Leave the leaves on until they naturally go brown. Remember, the leaves build the tubers back up after bloom so they will bloom again next season.

Additional Information

Purchase your tubers at garden centers where you have the opportunity to check them first. When buying through the mail, don't be surprised when you see the winter aconite tubers, as is true of all minor tubers, are very small.

Additional Species, Cultivars, or Varieties

There are no known other varieties.

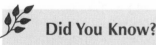 **Did You Know?**

Eranthis *is a Greek word for "flower of spring." Winter aconite reseeds itself freely, which means you are going to get lots of free new flowers each year.*

CHAPTER THREE

Ground Covers

GROUND COVER PLANTS are, by definition, any group of plants that cover the ground. So what's the number one ground cover in our landscape? *Guess what, it's grass.* Yes, grass is the ground cover that greens up most of the landscape. It is also the easiest ground cover to maintain—even if the lawn is full of weeds and some grass, just mow it and the lawn looks good again.

But what about those areas of our landscape where grass (and sometimes even weeds) won't grow? Is there a group of low-growing plants to fill those areas? Indeed there is. A low-growing ground cover beautifies a landscape and can provide many of the benefits of mulch as well. You might consider using a low-growing ground cover *instead* of a bagged mulch—mulch the bed with leaves rather than wood chips. Ground covers can highlight and add beauty to an existing landscape.

CONTAINING YOUR GROUND COVER

No ground cover stops growing during the season until fall. This means to contain its height and spread, you are going to have to discipline it. You can use the lawn mower, string trimmer, hedge shears, or any other means to keep it in *your* bounds. You're the boss—you control your ground cover space. Study this chapter. Some ground covers travel lower and slower than others. Some grow taller and need more trimming. Pick the one that's right for you.

THE WEED PROBLEM

One of the biggest headaches in a nice planting of ground cover is weeds. Now remember, if you have weeds in turfgrass, you just mow and they're gone for now. You can't do that with other ground covers. What to do? Well, there's a wonderful product out there called Preen®. Preen is a weed seed germination preventer. You say,

"Okay, so what?" The fact is, 60 to 70 percent of the weeds you get in your planting beds—including ground covers—come each year from wind-blown or bird-carried seed from last year's weeds. Preen kills the weed seed as it tries to germinate. Because different weed seeds germinate at different soil temperatures, apply Preen in mid-March and again in mid-May. If you experience a very wet spring, apply Preen again in mid-June. You can try another product, Roundup®, which can be sprayed on English ivy or purple wintercreeper, but be careful—this product can damage or kill new ground cover growth as well as weeds. If you select other ground covers, you'll have to either pull out the weeds (hoping to get the entire root), or you can use the wick system to apply the Roundup. The wick system works like this:

1. Put a plastic surgical glove on your right hand and place a cotton glove over the plastic glove.

2. Follow mixing instructions on the Roundup package to combine Roundup and water in a bucket.

3. Place your gloved hand in the solution, pull out your hand, squeeze out the excess solution, and carefully wipe the weeds with your gloved hand.

PERENNIALS AS GROUND COVERS

I have listed my favorites in this chapter, but there are even more to choose from. Check the Perennials chapter (pages 172–239) for perennials that give you great low-growing, blooming plants that come back year after year and cover lots of ground.

Ajuga

Ajuga reptans

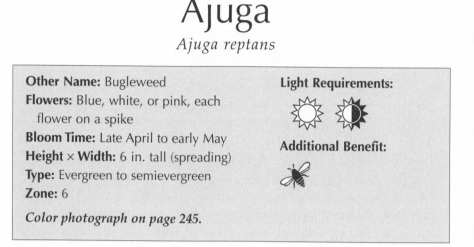

Other Name: Bugleweed

Flowers: Blue, white, or pink, each flower on a spike

Bloom Time: Late April to early May

Height × Width: 6 in. tall (spreading)

Type: Evergreen to semievergreen

Zone: 6

Color photograph on page 245.

Light Requirements:

Additional Benefit:

Ajuga is a low and colorful ground cover. Depending on the variety, its leaves can be purplish-bronze, green, pink-and-white, or green-and-white. It's one of a very few plants that offer a bronze-leaf variety that keeps its leaf color even when grown in shade. Ajuga also offers color in spring blooms of blue, white, or pink, which last for a couple of weeks in late April to early May. All ajuga does best in a fairly shady location, which means shade to morning sun. Ajuga also needs good soil to spread and thrive. It makes its new growth by spreading new plants through the soil. This is important to remember, because many homeowners use ajuga as a ground cover to fill in underneath large existing shade trees. But the spread of ajuga and tree roots do not go well together. The tree roots win the contest of "I was here first," and so the ajuga grows spotty. Plant ajuga where you can grow a ground cover without fighting with competing tree roots.

WHEN TO PLANT

Most ajuga is available in spring from your garden center or nursery. You can plant beginning in the spring, as soon as the frost is out of the ground, up to mid-August. Don't plant any later in the season, or the new planting might not have enough time to establish itself before the winter.

WHERE TO PLANT

Ajuga wants good to decent soil that is well drained. If you don't have that type of soil, look for other ground cover options in this chapter. Stay away from competing tree roots.

How to Plant

Use a rototiller or spade to loosen the soil in the area you wish to plant. To amend light clay soil, add pine bark chips. Plant ajuga on 12-inch centers, using a trowel to dig the hole no deeper than but twice as wide as its soil-root clump.

Care and Maintenance

Be sure to plant your ajuga in well-drained soil; wet spring seasons can cause crown rot and browning of the leaves. Aside from this, there should be no significant problems when growing ajuga, except for its tendency to become aggressive in its growth and move into areas where you might not want it. It is important to plant ajuga where it can be contained by a concrete sidewalk or edging.

Landscape Merit

Ajuga grows low and full, forming a carpet of foliage. It's one of the best ground covers for shade and offers lots of color in both blooms and foliage.

Additional Information

After your ajuga has been in the ground for two or more years, you can spread the wealth by taking a spade, digging up clumps of existing ajuga, and transplanting them to other areas of the landscape. Do this in mid-May.

Additional Species, Cultivars, or Varieties

'Burgundy Glow' has blue flowers and offers shades of purple, cream, pink, and green on the same leaf. 'Alba' has large leaves and white flowers. 'Gaiety', with its dark-purple leaves and blue flowers, is the most popular ajuga. 'Pink Beauty' is more upright, growing to 12 inches high, and, as its name suggests, it blooms in light pink.

Did You Know?

Most ground covers are sold in flats. Some contain solid plants and soil, holding up to one hundred plants per flat. Others are sold in flats containing cell-packs of four to six plants per pack. All flat-planted ground covers should be planted by mid-August.

Chameleon Plant

Houttuynia cordata

Flowers: Insignificant
Bloom Time: Spring
Height × Width: Up to 15 in. high;
  prune to control spread
Type: Deciduous vine
Zone: 6

Color photograph on page 245.

Light Requirements:

Additional Benefit:

Chameleon is a plant with tricolor leaves of green, white, and reddish/orange. This is a ground cover that definitely covers the ground—if left uncontrolled, it can become invasive, and that's not good. So why do I include it? Because chameleon will grow in places other ground covers won't, as in low-lying, wet areas. It can be controlled in other planting sites by using it in areas where sidewalks or the house wall itself will keep it in bounds. You can also contain this plant with a spade, cutting off excess growth whenever it appears, or with a nonselective herbicide like Finale® to spray the newest growth. Chameleon is very colorful during the growing season, although it does drop its leaves in the fall.

WHEN TO PLANT

Chameleon plants are available for planting all season long; plant anytime the ground is not frozen.

WHERE TO PLANT

Chameleon plant does well in any type of soil, even heavy clay that drains poorly. I've seen it growing along the roadside during a very hot, dry summer with no additional help from the homeowner.

HOW TO PLANT

Chameleon plant is available from garden centers in 3-inch, 4-inch, and 1-gallon containers. Dig a hole as deep as the soil clump and twice as wide. Loosen any roots wrapped around the soil clump. In wet areas, plant chameleon on the high side, leaving about 25 percent of the soil clump out of the ground, mounding the plant above grade level. With good drainage, plant at grade level, backfill using existing soil (first breaking up all soil particles to the size of golf balls), and water-in to settle that soil.

CARE AND MAINTENANCE
This plant responds well to water-soluble plant food. Fertilize biweekly in the spring and early summer. Keep fall shade-tree leaves off the bare stems in late fall by using a leaf blower. This plant grows so thick that weeds are not usually a problem.

LANDSCAPE MERIT
Chameleon plant is fast-growing and tolerates all types of soil. It has colorful leaves during the growing season.

ADDITIONAL INFORMATION
Chameleon grown in 1-gallon containers can be planted on 3-foot centers. If you install plants in smaller containers, plant on 12- to 18-inch centers, depending on pot size.

ADDITIONAL SPECIES, CULTIVARS, OR VARIETIES
There are none known at this time.

Did You Know?

This plant can become a weed itself if not contained. Plant only in areas in which other ground covers will not grow well. But if you have a hillside or other site that you can't maintain, plant it and enjoy the leaf color and the ground covering it will provide you.

Creeping Juniper

Juniperus spp.

Other Name: Groundcover Juniper
Flowers: Inconspicuous
Bloom Time: Spring
Height × Width: Various (by variety)
Type: Evergreen
Zone: 6

Color photograph on page 245.

Light Requirements:

Creeping or low-growing junipers are among the best and quickest-growing ground covers you can plant. This family of ground cover plants will do well in any type of soil as long as that soil has good drainage. Some of us may hear the name juniper and think of sticky, prickly evergreens; the newer varieties I have listed are soft to the touch and grow into each other, forming a wonderful evergreen ground cover. Junipers make a good accent planting under high-branched trees, whether they are in the lawn area or the foundation planting. Best of all, junipers perform quite well in conditions of heat, drought, and not-so-great soil. Some varieties have good foliage color as well. Junipers have a lot to offer in places where you need an ever-green that stays low and colorful. There are many varieties from which to choose; I've listed my favorites.

WHEN TO PLANT

Junipers are available in 1-, 2-, 3-, and 5-gallon containers and B&B. You can plant any juniper anytime the ground is not frozen.

WHERE TO PLANT

Plant junipers in any soil type in a location that's good for the variety you're planting. Just make sure it has good drainage. Junipers are drought tolerant—for most of them, the more sun, the better they grow.

HOW TO PLANT

Since most junipers come in containers, remove the soil clump from the pot and loosen any roots that are wrapped around it. Dig a hole no deeper than the soil clump and twice its width. Chop up existing soil to the size of golf balls, and backfill with this soil. Water-in well to settle the soil.

CARE AND MAINTENANCE

No plant stops growing until the day it dies. With junipers, tip-prune any unwanted or overgrown growth as it appears. Use handpruners, not hedge shears, to do this task, and the result will be junipers that look loose and fresh for many years. The newer varieties of juniper ground covers do not attract insects or disease.

LANDSCAPE MERIT

Creeping juniper is a low-growing plant that does well in difficult soil. It has great needle color.

ADDITIONAL INFORMATION

Very wet spring seasons can cause junipers to brown out on their newest growth. You can't control the weather, but you can trim off any brown or dead tips when they appear.

ADDITIONAL SPECIES, CULTIVARS, OR VARIETIES

Though most of the varieties listed here do best in full sun to a half-day of sun, 'Blue Pacific' does best in light to medium shade; it has very soft, silver-blue needles and will grow to 6 inches high. 'Silver Mist' has wonderful needle color, as its name suggests; the more sun it receives, the prettier it will be. 'Blue Chip' is very low-growing and its needles have a great blue color; it does best in the sun, growing to 6 inches. *J. procumbens* 'Nana' is a Japanese garden juniper that grows to 18 inches tall with a mounding effect and produces green foliage.

Did You Know?

New low-growing juniper varieties are being introduced every year. You might want to wait a couple of years before planting one of the new varieties over a large area; first see how well it grows in Kentucky.

Creeping Phlox

Phlox subulata

Other Name: Moss Phlox
Flowers: Pink, reddish-purple, blue, white, and bicolor
Bloom Time: April into May
Height × Width: 2 to 3 in. tall; spreads as much as allowed
Type: Semievergreen
Zone: 6

Color photograph on page 245.

Light Requirements:

Additional Benefit:

Talk about a ground cover that makes a spring bloom statement—creeping phlox blooms either reddish-purple, pink, blue, white, or bicolor. It grows very flat, its foliage like a mat—thick, fine textured, and controlled. The flowers, which appear in late April to May, bloom for an average of ten days to two weeks. The warmer the weather, the shorter the bloom period. The foliage stays perkier if the phlox stays out of hot afternoon sun in the summer. Creeping phlox works well in rock gardens, on top of stone walls, or anywhere else you can take advantage of its low, creeping growth habit. Phlox is considered an evergreen perennial, but don't be disappointed if the foliage hides during cold winters. Remember, it's a perennial—it should be back.

WHEN TO PLANT

Creeping phlox will be most often available from garden centers in the spring. You can plant it before it blooms or while in bloom. If you want to wait until after it blooms to purchase, you may be disappointed to discover it has all been sold.

WHERE TO PLANT

Plant creeping phlox in partial sun. You can plant it in full sun, but it's likely to cook in the summer Kentucky sun. Keep it away from shade, or you'll be disappointed in the amount of bloom.

HOW TO PLANT

Creeping phlox is available in 3- to 6-inch pots or in large clumps sold in baskets. You can divide the clumps into several plants. Dig a hole as deep as the soil clump and half again as wide. Backfill and water-in well.

CARE AND MAINTENANCE
Prune or remove any unwanted growth. Creeping phlox is free of bugs and diseases. If you've planted phlox where it gets hot summer sun, water when the soil gets dry.

LANDSCAPE MERIT
Phlox is very low growing, and colorful when in bloom. It's a great plant for walls or rock gardens, and is available in the spring in pots of all sizes and in half and full flats.

ADDITIONAL INFORMATION
Don't be disappointed if your phlox goes away during the hot summer weather; it will be back when cooler weather returns. Phlox makes a beautiful appearance when planted between steppingstones. Always plant it in an area large enough to allow for summer-blooming annuals to fill in when the phlox stops blooming.

ADDITIONAL SPECIES, CULTIVARS, OR VARIETIES
There are many varieties of creeping phlox, providing color ranging from pink, blue, reddish-purple, or white to a pink-and-white-striped bicolor called 'Candy Stripe'. They all grow low to the ground and bloom in the spring.

English Ivy

Hedera helix

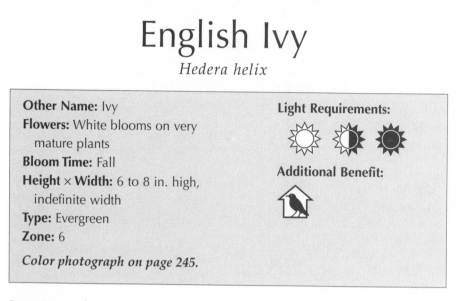

Other Name: Ivy

Flowers: White blooms on very mature plants

Bloom Time: Fall

Height × Width: 6 to 8 in. high, indefinite width

Type: Evergreen

Zone: 6

Color photograph on page 245.

Light Requirements:

Additional Benefit:

Ivy may make some of us think of ivy-covered walls, but in my opinion, ivy makes one of the best ground covers. Not only is it evergreen, covering the ground with foliage year-round, it will grow well in many different areas and will even tolerate more year-round sun than most people think. It does not like summer shade from trees that drop their leaves in the fall, exposing the shade-grown ivy leaves to winter sun and causing a lot of leafburn in late winter to early spring. English ivy will not compete with trees and shrubs in the landscape; it just makes a fresh, green covering of the planting bed. Remember that ivy functions much as mulch does: both cover the roots of our plants to keep weeds out and moisture in. And both do another most important thing for landscape beds: they simply look good.

WHEN TO PLANT

English ivy is available in the spring in three forms: potted plants, cell-packs, and rooted cuttings. Rooted cuttings and cell-pack–grown ivy is best planted in the spring and summer, no later than mid-August. Larger potted plants, especially those grown in 1-gallon containers, can be planted anytime the ground is not frozen.

WHERE TO PLANT

Ivy grows great in full shade, partial sun, and even full sun if the sun is present year-round. Sun-grown ivy can result in some leafburn damage after severe winters, in which case ivy beds might look a little empty until the new leaves grow in the spring.

How to Plant

Ivy will grow in all types of soil as long as it has good drainage. Amend heavy clay soil with a soil conditioner to help root development. Dig a hole as deep as the root or soil clump and a little wider. Mulch the area after planting to help retain soil moisture until the ivy fills in.

Care and Maintenance

Trim anytime to keep the ivy contained and as short as you would like. I personally like to see ivy kept at 6 to 8 inches. Weeds are easy to contain in English ivy beds—you can spray Roundup® at the normal rate without any fear of damage to the ivy. Just don't spray when the ivy is producing new, young leaves, or they could burn.

Landscape Merit

English ivy is a fast-growing ground cover with attractive, glossy green leaves.

Additional Information

English ivy is a great ground cover to choose when planting underneath trees with competing tree roots. Ivy, unlike some of its cousins, has a central root system that allows it to get along with tree roots. You can plant ivy roots between the tree roots, and the vine will grow and cover them.

Additional Species, Cultivars, or Varieties

Common English ivy has large glossy green leaves. 'Baltic' has blue-green leaves and is winter hardy. 'Thorndale' is similar to 'Baltic', is quite hardy as well, and has leaves with creamy veins.

Did You Know?

Plant rooted cuttings, cell-packs, or small potted ivy on 12-inch centers. Larger, 1-gallon plants can be planted on 3-foot centers. Either type will fill in an area by the end of its second year after installation.

Lily-of-the-Valley

Convallaria majalis

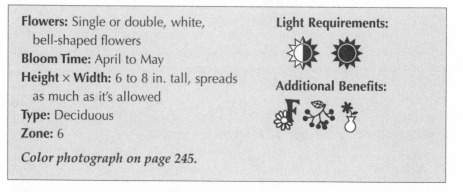

Flowers: Single or double, white, bell-shaped flowers

Bloom Time: April to May

Height × Width: 6 to 8 in. tall, spreads as much as it's allowed

Type: Deciduous

Zone: 6

Light Requirements:

Additional Benefits:

Color photograph on page 245.

Lily-of-the-valley is an old-time favorite that's becoming new again. A grandmother can get teary-eyed thinking back to her childhood and this beauty that graced her parents' home. It remained popular until the seventies, then for some reason nobody seemed to want to plant it anymore. Because of the drop in popular demand, garden centers quit stocking it. With the millennium, its popularity is coming back, and homeowners are rediscovering it as a great, shade-loving ground cover. Lily-of-the-valley has attractive leaves that form each spring and then share the spotlight with fragrant, white, bell-shaped flowers that appear in May. In late summer, you might find orange berries where the flowers once were. The leaves die and drop in the fall, to return again in spring. The plant loves shade, especially natural shade on the north side of a house.

WHEN TO PLANT
You can buy lily-of-the-valley in the spring as pips, which are bulb-like stems; plant these by the end of April. Pots of lily-of-the-valley can be planted anytime the ground is not frozen.

WHERE TO PLANT
Plant in natural shade, or tree shade. Lily-of-the-valley does not compete well when planted in the root areas of shallow-rooted shade trees, but it will grow in beds shaded by those trees; it grows best in its own bed, away from other plants.

How to Plant

When planting from pips, loosen the entire soil area to a depth of 6 to 8 inches. Plant each pip 1 inch deep and space 6 inches apart. Water-in to settle the soil. For potted or container-grown plants, dig a hole as deep as the container and twice as wide. Loosen any wrapped roots, and backfill with existing soil. Water-in well.

Care and Maintenance

Lily-of-the-valley is low-maintenance. Except for an occasional drink of water during hot, dry summers, this ground cover is on its own. It is resistant to bugs and disease. Keep it contained by pruning or cutting away any excess with a spade.

Landscape Merit

Lily-of-the-valley grows well in dense shade and is low-maintenance. Its leaves and fragrant white flowers are ideal for cutting and look great indoors in a vase.

Additional Information

Lily-of-the-valley can be described as invasive under certain conditions. To keep it controlled, plant it in those narrow shady areas between the sidewalk and a wall. Other good places for this ground cover are those areas of the landscape where grass won't grow, especially near the house.

Additional Species, Cultivars, or Varieties

'Flore Pleno' has beautiful foliage and large double flowers. 'Fortin's Giant' has healthy, large leaves and beautiful, large, fragrant flowers with many blooms on each stem.

Did You Know?

Many florists use both lily-of-the-valley leaves and blooms in their wedding arrangements.

Lily Turf

Liriope muscari

Other Name: Monkey Grass
Flowers: Blue, violet, or white by variety
Bloom Time: August through September
Height × Width: 12 in. high, spreading
 to desired size
Type: Evergreen
Zone: 6

Color photograph on page 246.

Light Requirements:

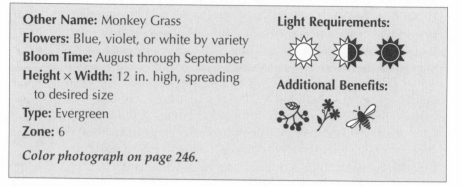

Additional Benefits:

L ily turf, or liriope (which is how I will refer to it), comes from a wonderful family of plants. However, it is not your typical ground cover. It does not spread by creeping aboveground growth or by underground stems. Instead, it grows in clump form, with those clumps getting a little larger each year. There are two great varieties of *Liriope muscari*. One is named 'Majestic' and has dark-green, grasslike, evergreen leaves. The other is 'Majestic Beauty', which has beautiful green leaves edged in yellow. The leaves of both varieties are slender, about 1 inch wide and 8 to 10 inches long. Liriope has blue, grape-hyacinth-type flowers from mid-August through September. From the flower comes black fruit, which is borne on the old flower stems. Considered evergreen, liriope's leaves will be windburned back toward the ground during very cold winters. It makes a beautiful accent plant, can border a planting bed line, and makes a fine understory planting for larger trees.

WHEN TO PLANT
Plant liriope anytime the ground is not frozen. Liriope is mostly available in 1-gallon containers, although some garden stores sell it in 2¼-inch pots.

WHERE TO PLANT
If you have good drainage, plant liriope in sun to shade. The plant will adapt to heavy clay soil but will spread faster in rich, fertile soil. This plant has many options in your home landscape.

How to Plant

Dig a hole as deep as the soil clump and twice as wide. Remove the liriope from its pot and loosen any attached roots. Backfill with the existing soil (first breaking up all soil particles to the size of golf balls). Water-in well.

Care and Maintenance

There are no bugs or diseases that bother liriope. This plant is also drought tolerant, but give it a drink occasionally during hot, dry weather. After a cold winter, some of its leaves will be windburned back toward the ground. Leave these damaged leaves if you want new growth to grow more quickly from the center. If they are too unsightly for you, prune them back anytime.

Landscape Merit

The gorgeous liriope grows no taller than 12 inches and is easily controlled even though it is a spreading type. It complements any other plant growing in its vicinity.

Additional Information

Liriope does not have to be so thick that it completely covers a bed area. If it does, that's great, but if there's space in-between plants, that looks good too.

Additional Species, Cultivars, or Varieties

'Majestic Beauty' has green leaves edged in gold trim, and spiked blue flowers in late summer. 'Majestic' has dark-green leaves with blue flowers that bloom beginning in August and into September. 'Silver Queen' has green leaves with silvery-white vertical stripes and white berries; it does well in shade.

Myrtle

Vinca minor

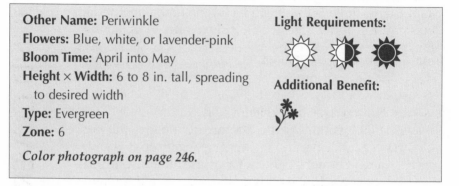

Other Name: Periwinkle
Flowers: Blue, white, or lavender-pink
Bloom Time: April into May
Height × Width: 6 to 8 in. tall, spreading to desired width
Type: Evergreen
Zone: 6

Color photograph on page 246.

Light Requirements:

Additional Benefit:

In recent years, the name vinca makes us think of that wonderful, summer-blooming annual: periwinkle. But way before anyone heard of periwinkle, *Vinca minor*, or "myrtle," was leading the pack of popular ground covers. Myrtle is a broadleaf, evergreen ground cover that has waxy, dark-green leaves. The two most popular varieties are 'Bowles' Blue' myrtle with dark-blue flowers in the spring and 'Alba', which also blooms in the spring but has white flowers. The flowers will last about a month if the weather stays cool. When myrtle is blooming in the landscape, neighbors are sure to want some in their own yards. It grows best in shade to morning sun. It does not grow well under trees that have a lot of surface roots, or under trees whose leaves fall, leaving the myrtle in the harsh, afternoon winter sun. Myrtle will seldom grow more than 8 inches tall. It gives an excellent small evergreen effect in winter when planted around deciduous shrubs.

WHEN TO PLANT
Plant bare roots or flats of myrtle in spring to early summer. Larger, 1-gallon-size plants can be planted anytime the ground is not frozen.

WHERE TO PLANT
Plant myrtle in average to good soil in an area that gets morning sun to total shade. The shadier the location, the more bluish-green the leaves will be. Make sure the planting site is well drained.

HOW TO PLANT

Loosen the soil bed 6 to 8 inches deep, being careful not to damage other plant roots in the area. Dig the holes as deep as the roots or soil clumps and a little wider. Backfill with existing soil, and water-in well. If you plan on mulching, mulch first, then plant the myrtle through the mulch into the soil below. Be careful not to leave any mulch touching the myrtle stems.

CARE AND MAINTENANCE

Water newly planted myrtle during any hot, dry periods the first year. During wet springs, especially in clay soil, myrtle can get crown rot, which causes some leaves and stems to turn black. This is not fatal, but good drainage will help prevent this unsightly problem.

LANDSCAPE MERIT

Myrtle grows fast after it has been in place for two years and does well in lots of shade. It boasts beautiful blooms on top of waxy green leaves.

ADDITIONAL INFORMATION

Be sure to apply the weed seed germination preventer, Preen®, in mid-March and again in mid-May. It's one great way to keep down weed counts. If you have weeds, the only way to remove them is by pulling (please get the entire root) or by using the wick method mentioned in the beginning of this chapter (page 135). Plant small myrtle plants on 12-inch centers. Larger, container-grown plants can be spaced at 3 feet.

ADDITIONAL SPECIES, CULTIVARS, OR VARIETIES

'Bowles' Blue' has dark-blue flowers and is a heavy bloomer. For a great color combination, try mixing it with 'Alba,' which blooms in white. 'Atropururea' has deep lavender-pink flowers.

GROUND COVERS

Pachysandra

Pachysandra terminalis

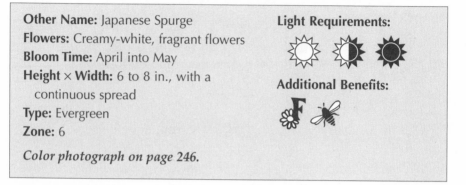

Other Name: Japanese Spurge
Flowers: Creamy-white, fragrant flowers
Bloom Time: April into May
Height × Width: 6 to 8 in., with a continuous spread
Type: Evergreen
Zone: 6

Color photograph on page 246.

Light Requirements:

Additional Benefits:

Pachysandra is considered a low-maintenance ground cover if it's growing in fairly decent soil in the landscape. It is evergreen, grows to a constant height of 6 to 8 inches, and can easily be contained in a particular area of the landscape. Pachysandra does not compete well with tree roots when planted beneath shallow-rooted shade trees. It makes all its new plants by growing underground stems that pop up new growth, so it does best in a soil area that it can call its own. It also prefers well-drained soil and an exposure that protects its evergreen leaves from the prevailing winter winds. Cold winters can produce yellowish leaves if the plant is in an unprotected location. Don't worry, though, because pachysandra recovers just fine. It also produces fragrant, white, spiked flowers in the spring, adding much to its beauty.

WHEN TO PLANT

Plant pachysandra from small pots, cell-packs, or rooted cuttings in spring to early summer. Don't plant in late summer to fall or the plant might not have enough growing time to establish itself before winter. Plant pachysandra from 1-gallon containers anytime the ground is not frozen.

WHERE TO PLANT

Pachysandra prefers shade with some good natural light or areas of morning sun. It will grow with more sun, but expect some winter-burn on the leaves. Pachysandra makes a great "living mulch" when planted under flowering trees and shrubs.

How to Plant

Loosen the soil to a depth of 6 inches. If you are going to mulch the planting area, do it now. Then plant the rooted cutting or soil clump through the mulch into a hole as deep as the roots and a little wider. Keep the mulch off the stems of the pachysandra, and water-in well after backfilling with existing soil.

Care and Maintenance

Pachysandra can become weak and thin during wet springs, which is why it's important to plant it in well-drained soil. If your pachysandra becomes weak-looking or grows too tall for you, shear it back to the desired height and appearance. Keep leaves from trees off the pachysandra leaves in the fall; a leaf blower will do this best.

Landscape Merit

Pachysandra is a fairly fast-growing ground cover with attractive foliage and fragrant white flowers.

Additional Information

If your pachysandra gets too tall and thin, set the rotary lawn mower to 3 inches and mow in mid- to late April. Collect and remove the cut-off foliage. This is especially true if your pachysandra has suffered winterburn. Be sure to use Preen®, the weed seed preventer, in mid-March and again in mid-May. Weeds don't look pretty in a bed of pachysandra, but remember, the thicker pachysandra grows, the fewer weeds you'll have.

Additional Species, Cultivars, or Varieties

'Green Carpet', the most popular cultivar, has dark-green leaves. 'Green Sheen' has glossy green leaves. 'Silver Edge' has green-and-white leaves—it is not as winter hardy and requires protection in parts of zone 6.

Wintercreeper

Euonymus fortunei 'Coloratus'

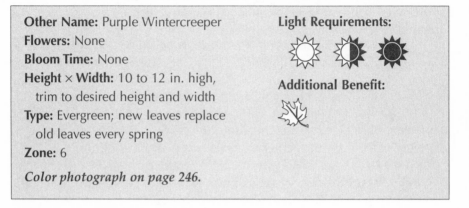

Other Name: Purple Wintercreeper

Flowers: None

Bloom Time: None

Height × Width: 10 to 12 in. high, trim to desired height and width

Type: Evergreen; new leaves replace old leaves every spring

Zone: 6

Color photograph on page 246.

Light Requirements:

Additional Benefit:

There are many varieties of the low-growing *Euonymus fortunei* group, and 'Coloratus' is especially hardy and attractive. 'Coloratus' is commonly referred to as purple wintercreeper because of its beautiful purple-red leaf color in the fall that remains on the plant during most, if not all, of the winter. It is a vigorous-growing ground cover that has deep-green, glossy leaves (1 to 2 inches long) during the growing season. By the following spring, all the old purple-red leaves fall to the ground and are replaced by shiny, new green ones. This ground cover does well in all types of soil that drain, and, like English ivy, grows well in shade to full sun. It is great for steep banks that are difficult to mow, competes successfully with tree roots, and fills in quickly.

WHEN TO PLANT

Plant young plants in cell-packs or rooted cuttings in the spring to early summer to allow enough time for the roots to get well established before their first winter. If you wait until fall to plant, there's a chance the young plants could heave out of the ground during freeze-and-thaw periods. Plants grown in 1-gallon containers can be planted anytime the ground is not frozen.

WHERE TO PLANT

You can plant wintercreeper in loamy soil, sandy soil, or clay soil—as long as the drainage is good, it will grow. Summer tree shade that gives way to harsh sun in the winter does not bother wintercreeper as it does ivy. 'Coloratus' can really solve a vegetation problem on steep slopes that are dangerous to mow.

How to Plant

When planting rooted cuttings or cell-pack–grown winter-creeper, dig a hole as deep as the clump or root, make it a little wider than the clump, backfill, and water-in well. For plants in 1-gallon containers, dig a hole no deeper than the soil clump but twice as wide. Loosen any wrapped roots, backfill, and water.

Care and Maintenance

Unlike other varieties of *Euonymus fortunei*, 'Coloratus' is not likely to get the scale insect. If your wintercreeper grows taller than you want or is not filling in enough, set your rotary lawn mower at a 3-inch cutting height, and mow the ground cover in April for fast, effective pruning. You can also prune with a grass string-trimmer.

Landscape Merit

In addition to being heat- and drought-tolerant and very low-maintenance, wintercreeper is attractive and fast-growing. It is a real standout during the winter with its purple-red leaf color.

Additional Information

Deer can grow fond of wintercreeper. To deter deer, use a Fertilome® product called This 1 Works®—because it does, and it lasts six months. Another way to keep deer away is with a roll of Erosionette®, used for holding grass seed on hillsides. Just roll it out on top of the wintercreeper and pin it to the ground in several places so the mat stays in place; the deer stay away because they don't like to walk on it. You can also spray for weeds in wintercreeper with the herbicide Roundup®, which will kill weeds without harming the wintercreeper—but not while the plant is putting on new growth.

Additional Species, Cultivars, or Varieties

The 'Emerald' Series is made of low-growing evergreens that have colorful leaves during the growing season; some are gold, and some are white with green leaves. 'Moonshadow' and 'Sunspot' are two winter-hardy varieties that grow a little larger and have beautiful leaf color.

CHAPTER FOUR

Ornamental Grasses

*I*N 1979 I JOINED A FELLOW ARBORIST on a learning mission to help determine why Scotch pines were declining. While examining the pines on a golf course, I noticed an unusual plant growing in a sand trap. Knowing my colleague played golf back home, I asked, "What do you suppose happens if you hit your golf ball into a sand trap and it lands in that six-foot-high grass?"

"I don't know," he laughed, "but I'm thankful we don't have that problem on the golf courses back home."

Well, that was my introduction to ornamental grasses. I headed home thinking about the interesting landscaping plant I'd "discovered" growing on a golf course. If it grew in a sand trap, it must be very hardy! I wanted to learn all I could when I got back home—but to my dismay, none of my fellow gardeners was familiar with this beautiful tall grass, and only one or two local nurseries had varieties for sale at that time.

ABOUT ORNAMENTAL GRASSES

Ornamental grasses come in all colors and sizes. There are grasses like blue fescue that grow to only 6 inches high and other grasses that grow to 8 feet high. There are ornamental grasses that have green blades, some with green-and-white blades, some with green blades with yellow blotches, and some that have purple blades all season long. There are even some with red blades.

When you go to buy your ornamental grass in the spring, take this book with you to help you select the one you want. All will look the same, green grass blades just starting to grow; they don't reach their mature height until mid-August. It won't make any difference if the final growing height is 6 inches or 6 feet, they'll all look the same height in the pot in the spring. When they finally reach mature height, they will start to develop their seedheads, which adds to their ornamental beauty and lasts until a wet snow breaks down the blades and the seedheads.

Landscape Value

The plants in this family can solve aesthetic problems or be beautiful by themselves. Two of the biggest eyesores in an "outdoor living room" are those cable boxes and electrical transformers. Ornamental grasses do a beautiful camouflage job. Talk about a fast-growing yearly screen to hide the side of a garage or nasty neighbor view! Ornamental grass will fit that bill. And picture your mailbox appearing to grow out of a clump of ornamental grass. The medium-growing grasses also look great planted by themselves out in the lawn, looking like a green fountain softly gracing the lawn area.

How Did It Get Started?

The most-often-asked questions by homeowners looking for ornamental grasses are "Is this pampas grass?" and "Do you sell pampas grass?" I don't know how it started, but a lot of homeowners not familiar with ornamental grass varieties think that all ornamental grass is "pampas grass." Pampas grass is one specific ornamental grass variety. It is not hardy in Kentucky. However, there is a species, *Erianthus ravennae*, commonly called "hardy pampas grass," that is suitable for Kentucky.

Ornamental Grass Maintenance

The only work is removing the old blades and seedheads in late winter. The easiest way to do this is by tying up your medium-to-tall grass in three different places. Tie it up tight! Cut off the bundle as close to the ground as possible, cutting the brown blades with a chain saw or a trimmer. The old grass will tumble over in a bundle like an old tree stump. Always do this before next year's grass starts to grow.

Blue Fescue

Festuca ovina 'Glauca'

Other Name: Turf Fescue

Flowers: Tan

Bloom Time: Late June until fall

Height × Width: 8 to 12 in. by
  8 to 12 in.

Type: Deciduous

Zone: 6

Color photograph on page 246.

Light Requirements:

Blue fescue is a cute plant. I don't usually refer to plants that way, but this one is a very small tuft of grass that has great color. It stays in mounds about 12 inches in diameter and has a blade height of 8 to 12 inches. The seedheads form in late June to July and grow about 16 to 18 inches above the foliage. The foliage color is icy-blue during the growing season, turning a copper-tan for winter. It works well as a low-growing border plant. You can even use it in a mass planting as you would another ground cover. Blue fescue is relatively fast-growing. If you want to reduce its size, do so by root division in spring. Always replant the divisions at the depth at which they were growing before being divided.

WHEN TO PLANT

Plant blue fescue anytime the ground is not frozen. The best selections will be in spring and early summer. Remember, if you buy blue fescue in the early spring, it won't look as pretty as it does when it has new blades. But soon it will!

WHERE TO PLANT

Blue fescue is an ornamental grass that likes good drainage. It prefers nice, loamy soil but will tolerate some clay. In heavy clay, add an organic material such as pine bark chips to the existing soil. Blue fescue grows best where it is shaded from hot afternoon sun in summer, especially in zone 6.

How to Plant

Blue fescue is available in 4-inch pots and 1- and 2-gallon containers. Dig a hole no deeper than the soil clump. Loosen any roots that wrap around the root clump, and dig your hole twice as wide as the clump. Break up the dug-out soil to the size of golf balls. Backfill and water-in well to settle the soil.

Care and Maintenance

Coming out of winter, your blue fescue will be brown, not blue. Cut back the old brown blades to within 2 to 3 inches of the ground. Do this before April 1. If you want to divide any of your blue fescue, do it as new growth appears in spring. As far as bugs and diseases go, leave the sprayer in the garage—blue fescue is trouble-free.

Landscape Merit

Blue fescue is a great ornamental grass with a unique appearance. It has silver-blue foliage and long-lasting seedheads.

Additional Information

Blue fescue makes a neat specimen plant, can be used as a border, or can be mixed with other colorful, low-growing plants like coral bells, 'Purple Palace', or any other such perennial with red leaf color.

Additional Species, Cultivars, or Varieties

'Elijah Blue' grows 8 to 12 inches high and has ice-blue, fine-textured blades. It grows fast but stays very compact.

Did You Know?

Blue fescue is the shortest-growing ornamental grass. It can be used as a ground cover on hard-to-mow slopes. Plant on 2-foot centers and it will be solid in three to four years.

Feather Reed Grass

Calamagrostis acutiflora 'Overdam'

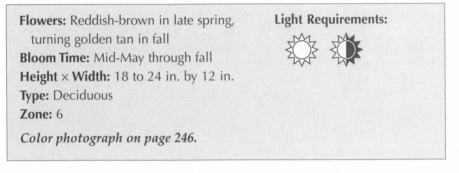

Flowers: Reddish-brown in late spring, turning golden tan in fall
Bloom Time: Mid-May through fall
Height × Width: 18 to 24 in. by 12 in.
Type: Deciduous
Zone: 6

Color photograph on page 246.

Light Requirements:

Some ornamental grasses are very tall and have modest seedheads . . . and then there is feather reed grass. Feather reed grass has foliage that grows only 18 to 24 inches tall, but its seedheads grow an additional 4 feet, blooming out at 6 feet. The blades have yellow margins in spring, maturing to pinkish-white margins in summer. The flower spikes are upright and have feathery flowers that emerge reddish-brown in June, turning to a golden color in fall. 'Overdam' is vertical in its growing habit, allowing it to be used in many unique landscape situations. Use it as a group planting or as a narrow, low screen—use your imagination! Feather reed grass is best planted in a sunny location, although it will tolerate a half-day of shade. As you do with all grasses, cut back and remove all the old blades in late winter. They grow back new each spring from the remaining clump.

When to Plant

Plant feather reed grass anytime the ground is not frozen. You might want to wait until late spring so you can view the plant before you buy and see if its unique growing habit fits your taste. I'll bet it will.

Where to Plant

All ornamental grasses will tolerate heavy clay soil. For feather reed grass, make sure there's good drainage. It prefers full sun but will tolerate a half-day of shade (it may cost you a few blooms, but the plant will still be attractive). Its slender, upright growth habit makes it desirable to plant several together in the same bed—then watch the wind work those beautiful flower heads all summer long.

How to Plant
Feather reed grass will be available from the garden store in 1-, 2-, 3-, and 5-gallon containers. Choose your size, and dig the hole as deep as the soil clump and twice as wide. Take the soil clump out of the container and loosen any wrapped roots. Backfill with your existing soil, leaving no particles larger than a golf ball. Water-in well to settle the soil.

Care and Maintenance
All ornamental grasses are considered low-maintenance. Once established, they are drought-tolerant too. Cut back all foliage and seedheads in late winter. Do your pruning before new blades begin to appear in spring.

Landscape Merit
Although it is a short plant, feather reed grass blooms early into tall flower spikes that are graceful in the wind.

Additional Information
Feather reed grass is the ornamental grass that is earliest to flower.

Additional Species, Cultivars, or Varieties
'Stricta' has purplish-bronze flowers in late spring that turn tan in fall. It grows 3 to 5 feet high and has 6-foot flower heads.

Fountain Grass

Pennisetum alopecuroides 'Hameln'

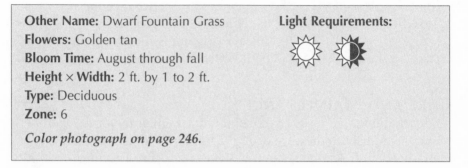

Other Name: Dwarf Fountain Grass
Flowers: Golden tan
Bloom Time: August through fall
Height × Width: 2 ft. by 1 to 2 ft.
Type: Deciduous
Zone: 6

Color photograph on page 246.

Light Requirements:

I would have to say, fountain grass is probably the most popular ornamental grass to date. One big reason for its popularity is the fact that it is easy to use in landscape designs—many landscape professionals love it and make sure it is incorporated in their designs. 'Hameln', which grows best in full sun, grows to only 2 feet high and 1 to 2 feet wide. It is highlighted by fluffy tan-colored plumes that grow just a few inches above the foliage. Each plant looks like a little round, fuzzy pillow. The plants work well in combination with other shrubs or as a backdrop to a perennial bed. Because of its short size, even heavy winter snow does not disfigure this plant that turns tan in fall. Cut all the foliage and seedheads back to within 3 inches of the ground in late winter to early spring. Prune back before new growth begins.

WHEN TO PLANT

You can plant fountain grass anytime the ground is not frozen. It transplants easily (as do all ornamental grasses). Remember, when you buy grasses in early spring before they have grown much, they all look about the same. If you want to make sure you get this low-growing, fuzzy one—remember its name.

WHERE TO PLANT

Fountain grass will grow and flower in full sun to a half-day of shade. It will grow in all types of soil but will grow best where the drainage is average to good. It can fit into the landscape in many places. Try using it for underplanting larger trees and shrubs; its special winter appearance makes it a valuable year-round ornamental.

How to Plant

Fountain grass is available in containers of various sizes. Plant whatever size fits your budget, knowing that it will grow. Dig a hole as deep as the soil clump. Remove the plant from the pot and loosen any wrapped roots. Dig the hole twice as wide as the soil clump, break up all soil particles to the size of golf balls, and backfill. Water-in well to settle the soil.

Care and Maintenance

Fountain grass is maintenance-free—no bugs or diseases will bother it. Be sure to cut back all the old foliage and seedheads in late winter or early spring before new foliage starts growing.

Landscape Merit

Fountain grass is a great-looking plant for any landscape situation. You can plant one or many of these easy-to-care-for plants.

Additional Information

Ornamental grasses are in the same family as turfgrass. The difference is that the ornamentals grow larger, some of them a lot larger.

Additional Species, Cultivars, or Varieties

'Little Bunny' is the smallest of all the fountain grasses, growing only 10 to 12 inches high. 'Moudry' is a black-flowering fountain grass that grows 2 feet tall and 3 feet wide.

ORNAMENTAL GRASSES

Did You Know?

Just like ornamental grasses, turfgrass would have flower heads of various heights if we did not mow it.

Hardy Pampas Grass

Erianthus ravennae

Other Name: Ravenna Grass

Flowers/Foliage: Silvery-white plumes; green blades

Bloom Time: Midsummer through fall

Height: 10 to 15 ft. plus 2-ft.-tall flower plumes

Type: Deciduous

Zone: 6

Color photograph on page 246.

Light Requirements:

Additional Benefits:

No other family of plants has risen so rapidly in popularity as the ornamental grass family—and for all the right reasons. Ornamental grasses come in many growing sizes, do well in sun to medium shade, and require little maintenance. When different varieties were first introduced, most homeowners called all varieties pampas grass. The original pampas grass (*Cortaderia selloana*) is not winter hardy in Kentucky, but hardy pampas grass (*Erianthus*) is totally winter hardy. This plant does best in full sun, and it can reach a height of 10 to 15 feet. Though tall growing, the stalks of this grass are strong enough to withstand moderate winds without damage. Hardy pampas grass produces very showy 2-foot-long silvery-white plumes in August that provide gorgeous fall coloring. The flower plumes appear above the blades. Plant this grass as a specimen, a border, or a screen. Take advantage of the flowers for cutting or drying, and bring them indoors for fall and winter enjoyment. Hardy pampas grass is easy to grow and even easier to enjoy.

WHEN TO PLANT

The best selection of hardy pampas grass will be available in the spring. All ornamental grasses start off each spring with all new growth coming from the soil in the pot. In April and May different varieties will look similar in growing height, so make sure you find out the mature growing size of your favorite before purchasing it. Plant ornamental grasses of all varieties anytime the ground is not frozen.

WHERE TO PLANT

Plant hardy pampas grass in a sunny location with at least a half-day of sun. This plant will grow in all types of well-drained soil and is pH adaptable. Don't worry about the summer heat and drought; hardy pampas grass, like all ornamental grasses, is very drought tolerant.

HOW TO PLANT

The nursery or garden center will sell all ornamental grasses growing in containers. Dig a hole as deep as and twice as wide as the soil clump. Loosen any roots that are wrapped around the outside of the soil clump. Break up all soil particles to the size of golf balls, backfill, and water-in well to settle the soil.

CARE AND MAINTENANCE

All ornamental grasses die back to the ground every late fall and winter. Bundle and cut off your hardy pampas grass as close to the ground as possible in late winter to early spring. Definitely cut it back before new growth starts to appear in the spring.

ADDITIONAL INFORMATION

After the hardy pampas grass has been in your landscape for three to four years, you can divide and replant clumps of it. Do this in early April as the new blades start to grow, and replant to the same depth that it was growing. Use this plant in many ways in a home landscape. An extra benefit is that it attracts birds and provides food for them.

ADDITIONAL SPECIES, CULTIVARS, OR VARIETIES

There are none known at this time.

Japanese Blood Grass

Imperata cylindrica var. *rubra*

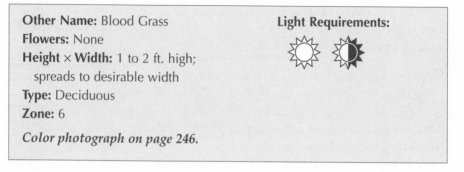

Other Name: Blood Grass
Flowers: None
Height × Width: 1 to 2 ft. high;
  spreads to desirable width
Type: Deciduous
Zone: 6

Color photograph on page 246.

Light Requirements:

Plant this ornamental grass in full sun, and red foliage you shall have. Japanese blood grass is low-growing, only 1 to 2 feet tall. It spreads itself by means of underground stems, but it is certainly not aggressive in its growth habit. Most of the red foliage growth will be on the tips, greening out toward the ground. Plant blood grass in mass plantings and you will have a beautiful sight in spring, summer, fall, and even into winter. After a hard freeze in fall, the foliage turns a brownish copper and stays that way until you trim it back in late winter. To trim this one back, you might mow off the foliage at 3 inches with a rotary power mower. Use blood grass in rock gardens, around water ponds, or anywhere in the landscape you can use some great foliage color. Blood grass does not flower, so don't expect those flower heads that other ornamental grasses display.

WHEN TO PLANT

You can plant Japanese blood grass anytime the ground is not frozen. If you look at the blood grass in early to mid-spring, you'll swear you're buying a pot full of soil and nothing else. If you want to see it growing in the pot, view it at your garden center in May.

WHERE TO PLANT

For best foliage color, plant Japanese blood grass in full sun. I have it planted in my yard in an area that gets only four hours of afternoon sun, and it still looks great. Any type of soil will do for this one. Blood grass will even tolerate a little soil moisture. Plant it in areas where you can view it from both outside and inside the house.

How to Plant

Japanese blood grass is available in containers. Dig a hole as deep as the soil clump and twice as wide. Remove the plant from the pot and loosen any wrapped roots. Use the existing soil to backfill, breaking up the soil particles to the size of golf balls. Water-in well.

Care and Maintenance

Japanese blood grass is low in maintenance. The most you'll do is cut it back to within 3 inches of the ground in late winter. If you want to spread the wealth, divide and transplant blood grass in spring before the new blades grow taller than 8 inches.

Landscape Merit

Japanese blood grass is a low-growing plant with great foliage color. Plant several in open areas where you can make a beautiful landscape statement.

Additional Information

Many Kentucky nurseries and garden centers buy their ornamental grasses from West Coast nurseries in spring. Those grasses coming out of southern California will have as much growth on them when they are shipped here in April as our natural-growing Kentucky grasses will have in June.

Additional Species, Cultivars, or Varieties

'Red Baron' is an excellent cultivar.

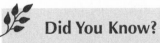

Did You Know?

Even though blood grass gives you no flowers, it more than makes up for it with its beautiful red foliage.

Maiden Grass

Miscanthus sinensis 'Gracillimus'

Other Name: Silver Grass
Flowers: Silvery-white plumes
Bloom Time: July through fall
Height × Width: 5 to 7 ft. by 3 to 5 ft.
Type: Deciduous
Zone: 6

Color photograph on page 246.

Light Requirements:

Maiden grass is sometimes referred to as "silver grass" because its thin, fine-textured blades are silver-and-green and it has silvery-white, plume-type flowers in late summer and fall. (The silver-green blades turn golden brown after a killing frost.) The plant grows 5 to 7 feet tall and 3 to 5 feet wide, with flower plumes that grow about a foot taller than the foliage. It makes an excellent screen or a good background plant for other lower-growing grasses or ornamental plants. Maiden grass has several other colorful members in its family. One variegated cultivar called 'Variegatus' has a creamy white stripe along its dark-green blades. Others are listed on the next page.

WHEN TO PLANT

You can plant maiden grass anytime the ground is not frozen. When you shop in early spring, maiden grass will look a lot like other ornamental grasses. The best selection of maiden grass and other ornamental grasses will be in spring to early summer.

WHERE TO PLANT

Maiden grass grows best in full sun to half-day shade. This plant can really spread, so plant it in an area that gives it room to grow wide. It's not invasive and can be reduced in size by transplanting some of it after it's been in the ground for several years. Maiden grass grows well in all types of soil. Use group plantings to screen unsightly views, or for an individual landscape place it out in the lawn.

How to Plant

Maiden grass is sold growing in containers of various sizes. Dig a hole no deeper than the soil clump and twice as wide. Take the soil clump out of the pot and loosen any wrapped roots around the soil clump. Backfill with the soil, breaking it into pieces no larger than a golf ball. Water-in well to settle the soil.

Care and Maintenance

Maiden grass, like all other ornamental grass, is low-maintenance. It's easy to care for because all you have to do is enjoy it and prune it back to 3 inches from the ground in late winter to early spring, before the new growth appears.

Landscape Merit

This maiden grass variety makes a good screen, a grassy hedge, or just a good-looking lawn specimen.

Additional Information

There are many great varieties of maiden grass. This plant really makes a statement in any home landscape. If you want to divide this plant to spread the wealth in either your yard or others, transplant in spring when new growth begins. Use a spade and remove a few spadefuls to another location.

Additional Species, Cultivars, or Varieties

'Morning Light' has variegated green-and-white blades that grow in a clump 5 feet tall by 3 feet wide; it has reddish-bronze flower plumes in late summer. 'Variegatus' has silvery-white flowers on blades that are highlighted with a large, creamy-white stripe. 'Strictus' (commonly called porcupine grass) is vase-shaped and has green blades highlighted with golden horizontal bands. 'Yaka Jima' is a true dwarf maiden grass, growing to only 3 to 4 feet; it has silvery-white blooms.

Ribbon Grass

Phalaris arundinacea var. *picta*

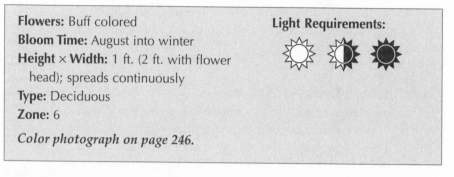

Flowers: Buff colored
Bloom Time: August into winter
Height × Width: 1 ft. (2 ft. with flower head); spreads continuously
Type: Deciduous
Zone: 6

Light Requirements:

Color photograph on page 246.

Ribbon grass is an ornamental grass that makes a quick statement. Its green blades with white stripes grow about 1 foot high. It grows well in full sun but will also tolerate a lot of shade. It is quite aggressive, which could be an asset when you plant it on hillsides to control erosion, or on the banks of creeks or lakes. But when you use ribbon grass in the general landscape, be prepared to control its growth. Limit it to a desired area by cutting away the excess. Ribbon grass has buff-colored flower spikes that appear in late summer and last into winter. Use it in shadier areas where its beautiful green-and-white blades will brighten up the site, and plant it around deck and patio areas where you sit at night. Moonlight will illuminate the ribbon grass, giving a beautiful nighttime appearance to the surrounding landscape.

WHEN TO PLANT

Plant ribbon grass anytime the ground is not frozen. The best selections of ribbon grass and other ornamental grasses will be during the spring. To make sure you like the appearance of ribbon grass, wait until the new blades are growing in the pot around the middle of May before you buy.

WHERE TO PLANT

Ribbon grass does extremely well in hot, sunny locations and in shaded areas of the landscape, and it does well in all types of soil. It provides a great solution for an erosion problem on a hillside. It appreciates good drainage but will tolerate some moisture.

How to Plant

Dig a hole as deep as the soil clump and twice as wide. Loosen any roots that are wrapped around the soil clump when you remove it from its container. Break up all soil particles so that none is bigger than a golf ball. Backfill and water-in well to settle the soil.

Care and Maintenance

Ribbon grass, like all ornamental grass, is low-maintenance and resistant to bugs and disease. When planted in hot, sunny, sloped areas, an occasional drink of water during dry spells will be appreciated. Use your lawn mower to mow down the brown blades of last year's growth; do this in late winter or early spring, before new growth begins in April.

Landscape Merit

Ribbon grass is fast-growing and will tolerate shade. It is great for planting on steep slopes and other hard-to-mow areas.

Additional Information

Ribbon grass can be aggressive. Be prepared to prune away all unwanted growth with a spade. It transplants easily, so if you have a large area to fill, start with a few plants and continue to divide and fill in the other areas with your own transplants. Do this anytime during the growing season.

Additional Species, Cultivars, or Varieties

There are none known at this time.

Did You Know?

Unwanted growth can be controlled by spraying with the nonselective herbicide called Finale®. This herbicide will kill just those individual leaves that are sprayed.

CHAPTER FIVE

Perennials

HERBACEOUS PERENNIALS are soft-stemmed plants that come back year after year. They die back to the ground after a killing frost or two, but the roots stay alive over winter, and each spring gives you new leaf growth and flowers. They will keep coming back every year if they have a happy growing space and, in some cases, cooperative winter weather both from temperature and moisture conditions. Extreme cold-weather temperatures following a dry fall can make the roots of many perennials vulnerable to freezing, thus failing to survive. If you experience a dry fall, be sure to water in late fall to reduce the risk of root failure.

MOISTURE AND EXPOSURE

As you read this chapter, you will notice that the great majority of perennials require good soil drainage. I've listed some varieties that will tolerate all kinds of Kentucky soil, but they will still want good drainage. If perennials are constantly exposed to wet soil, the roots rot and the plants die. This can happen during the growing season or in the winter in areas that have large snow coverings that thaw, puddling water around the sleeping perennial roots, eventually rotting them.

SUN OR SHADE

This book and many other garden books describe a lot of plants that do best in full sun. Now think for a moment. The only exposure we have for full sun is south. If you insisted on full sun for all the sun-loving plants, that would mean that 75 percent of your plants would be located on the south side of your house, away from any shade or ornamental trees. Let's use common sense. In a perfect world, we could do this, but it's not perfect. Pay close attention to the minimum amounts of sun the sun lovers will tolerate so you will be happy with the outcome. I have personally grown many of these sun lovers in areas of my yard that get less than six hours of sun. They did great and so will yours.

TO CUT BACK OR NOT TO CUT BACK

All herbaceous perennials as opposed to woody perennials die back to the ground every late fall. Most of the perennials in this chapter can be pruned back to the ground in late fall or early spring. Some homeowners like to watch football and say, *The heck with the perennial plants. I'll deal with them in the spring.* Others want a tidy look to their winter landscape and prune off the past year's twigs in late fall. The choice is yours. So what do I personally do? *Excuse me, what's the score?*

WHAT PERENNIALS ARE BEST?

Beauty is in the eye of the beholder. There are many varieties of perennials to choose from. I've listed my favorites. Heck, it's my book! They may or may not be yours.

Do not be afraid to try many of the other perennials that you'll find at your favorite nursery store or greenhouse. There are loads of qualified nursery persons and certified Kentucky Nursery Technicians to assist you with their experience and advice. Don't get locked into saying "but Denny says." There are too many perennials out there to limit yourself to mine alone. Just be sure to follow the basic rules for the best planting sites, care, and maintenance.

One thing you'll notice about the listings in this chapter—they are very rewarding to grow because of their good color and their low maintenance requirements.

Aster

Aster novi-belgii, Aster novae-angliae

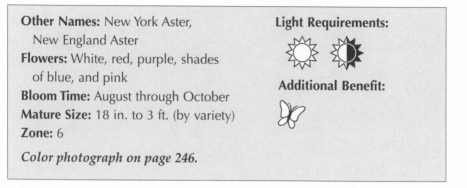

Other Names: New York Aster,
New England Aster
Flowers: White, red, purple, shades
of blue, and pink
Bloom Time: August through October
Mature Size: 18 in. to 3 ft. (by variety)
Zone: 6

Color photograph on page 246.

Light Requirements:

Additional Benefit:

Fall is a season of mixed emotions. Summer-flowering annuals are coming to an end, leaves are starting to fall from their plants . . . *and what's that gorgeous color starting to bloom in the garden?* Well, it could be mums, but if the colors are various shades of pink or blue and other colors, all looking like daisies, those plants, ladies and gentlemen, are fall asters. They start coming into bloom in late August and bloom into October. They come in blue, lilac, white, pink, rose, and red, and many have yellow centers. They do best in full sun to light shade and grow well in average soil that's moist but drains well. There are over six hundred species of asters in the world, and many are native to the United States. The two species on these pages do well in Kentucky. The best selection of hardy asters is at the nursery store in late summer to fall; they will be in bloom so you can see exactly which ones appeal to you. But please, save a spot in your landscape for at least a few of these to pick up the flower scene in your yard in the fall.

WHEN TO PLANT

Transplant existing asters when they first start greening up in the spring. Plant new-boughts whenever they're available. You will find them in 3- to 4-inch pots in the spring and 4-, 6-, and 8-inch potted ones in late summer. Plant in the fall before they finish blooming to allow the roots time to get established.

WHERE TO PLANT

Asters do best in full sun. Light shade will also produce lots of satisfying color. They will grow in all types of soil as long as you keep that soil moist and well drained.

How to Plant

Replant existing asters at the same depth they were growing previously. When planting new, loosen the existing soil to a depth of 6 to 8 inches. Remove the plant from its pot, loosen any wrapped roots, and dig a hole as deep as the soil clump and twice as wide. Backfill, and water-in well to settle the soil.

Care and Maintenance

As your asters grow from spring into summer, pinch back stems to about the height you want them to bloom. This will cause your asters to spread more. If they get too wide, trim back the sides as well. By pinching you will also double and triple your blooms. Stop pinching and trimming by mid-July. Transplant and divide asters in the spring, making each division at least 6 inches in diameter. There are no insect or disease problems with asters. Just keep them moist in hot, dry weather, but not wet.

Additional Information

'Alma Potschke Aster' is one variety that needs no pinching to maintain loads of flowers. This variety grows to 3 feet tall and wide. Plant in open, airy locations. Asters can mildew in really humid summer heat. Don't crowd them into areas too small for them—they should be able to receive a good breeze to help deter the mildew.

Additional Species, Cultivars, or Varieties

Novi-Belgii varieties: 'New York Aster' blooms in white, blue-violet, or pink flowers with yellow centers. It grows 24 to 36 inches. Pinch back growth in June to keep it bushy and colorful. 'Alert Aster' grows to 24 inches tall and wide and has deep-red flowers with yellow centers. 'Professor Kippenberg Aster' has semidouble lavender-blue flowers on a plant growing to 24 inches tall and wide. **Novae-Angliae varieties:** 'Alma Potschke Aster' is my favorite. It has pink flowers with yellow centers. This one doesn't need pinching. It grows very compact, 3 feet tall and wide, and has gray-green leaves. 'Red Star Aster' has pinkish-red flowers on a short plant (it grows to 18 inches tall and wide).

Astilbe

Astilbe × arendsii

Other Name: False Spirea
Flowers: White, pink, shades of red, lavender, peach, and pink
Bloom Time: Late June to early August (by variety)
Mature Size: 12 to 36 in. (by variety)
Zone: 6

Color photograph on page 247.

Light Requirements:

Additional Benefit:

What a great summer-blooming perennial for light shade to morning sun. Astilbe has very attractive, dark-green, glossy leaves. That in itself makes it a great plant. Add to that beautiful flowers and you've got a terrific summer plant that comes back year after year. Some varieties of astilbe have bronze-green leaves. All the leaves of astilbe are fernlike, and serrated. It has dense plume-type flowers made up of small florets at the tips of the flower branches. Considered a woodland plant, astilbe grows best where it is protected from direct sun but gets good natural light. It blooms in colors of white, pink, red, peach, and lavender. Astilbe makes a great mass planting of all the same color, or use as a border planting. Not only does it look great when in bloom, but it is also a nice glossy green plant that defines any bed line well. Plant hostas nearby to make a great combo. Water this plant when it gets hot and dry.

WHEN TO PLANT

Transplant existing plants in the spring as new growth appears. Make each transplanted clump at least 6 inches in diameter. Plant nursery-grown astilbe available in 3- and 4-inch pots in April and May. You can plant larger 1- and 2-gallon potted astilbe anytime the ground is not frozen.

WHERE TO PLANT

Astilbe prefers moist but not wet soil that's loose and loamy. It prefers shady areas that have good sky light (not underneath sugar maples). Morning sun is all right, too.

HOW TO PLANT

The key to success with astilbe is the soil it has to grow in. If you have average soil, work organic peat or pine bark chips in with the existing soil to a depth of 6 to 8 inches. Replant transplants at the same depth they were growing in their old home. If you are making new installations, dig a hole in the loosened or amended soil as deep and twice as wide as the soil clump. Loosen any roots that are wrapped around the soil clump. Backfill, and water-in well to settle the soil.

CARE AND MAINTENANCE

Astilbe wants to be kept moist during hot, dry weather. Remove finished flowers as they appear. Fertilize astilbe in the spring with a time-release fertilizer like Osmocote®. Apply a thin 1- to 2-inch layer of bark mulch around their roots but not on their stems. Divide the clumps every four to five years to keep your astilbe providing lots of bloom.

ADDITIONAL SPECIES, CULTIVARS, OR VARIETIES

'Erica' grows 28 to 36 inches tall and has long flower panicles producing pink flowers. 'Bridal Veil', 18 to 24 inches tall, has glossy foliage producing cream-colored flower spikes. 'Fanal' has deep-red flowers and blooms earlier than other astilbe; it grows to 24 inches tall. 'Peach Blossom' offers beautiful salmon-pink flowers on a plant with fernlike foliage; it grows to 24 inches tall. *A. simplicifolia* 'Sprite', Perennial Plant of the Year in 1994, grows to only 12 inches tall and has shell-pink flowers that last up to six weeks.

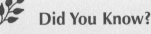

Did You Know?

Astilbe makes an excellent cut flower. Be sure to cut the flower stems when the flowers are no more than half open.

'Autumn Joy' Sedum

Sedum 'Autumn Joy'

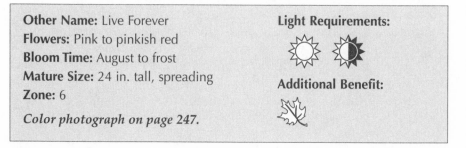

Other Name: Live Forever
Flowers: Pink to pinkish red
Bloom Time: August to frost
Mature Size: 24 in. tall, spreading
Zone: 6

Color photograph on page 247.

Light Requirements:

Additional Benefit:

Talk about an easy perennial to grow! One of the common names of *Sedum* 'Autumn Joy' is live forever, and it does that. 'Autumn Joy' grows all by itself in the hot, dry soils that Kentucky is famous for; indeed, it grows in all types of well-draining soil. 'Autumn Joy' grows to 24 inches tall and continues to spread each year. You control the width of this perennial by making soil divisions in early spring. The leaves are very thick and fleshy, resembling a succulent. The flower heads first start to form in mid- to late August, then the color change of the flowers begins. At first the flower heads appear to be white. As we move into September, those many flower heads change color and become a warm pink. Wait two weeks and these same flowers deepen to a pinkish red. By October they turn to a rust color, and finally to brown after several hard freezes. These dried-looking flowers will add winter interest to the garden, looking like a dried arrangement. Mix 'Autumn Joy' with dwarf fountain grass, hydrangeas, and other plants that provide winter interest.

WHEN TO PLANT

Transplant 'Autumn Joy' in early spring as it first starts to green up again. Install new plants anytime they are available from your favorite garden center, greenhouse, or nursery store. You will find them available in early spring in 3- and 4-inch pots. Larger 1-gallon sizes should be available all summer and into fall.

WHERE TO PLANT

'Autumn Joy' will grow in just about any type of garden soil. It actually prefers heavy clay soil that is well drained and never stays wet after a rain. This sedum grows best in full sun but will grow very well in only four to five hours of sun. It displays best when planted in a group of at least five to seven plants.

How to Plant

Replant transplants at the same depth they were growing in their last home. With new plantings, pre-loosen the existing soil 6 to 8 inches deep. Loosen any wrapped roots and dig a hole as deep and twice as wide as the soil clump. Backfill, and water-in well to settle the soil.

Care and Maintenance

Although 'Autumn Joy' will grow in partial shade, this might lead to very tall stems that tend to bend over when in bloom; if this occurs, staking might be necessary. Do not overfertilize. Follow the instructions on the container. There are no bugs or diseases to worry about. During the winter, your sedum will have bare stems with dried flowers on top. Some homeowners call this winter interest; others think it looks yuck. If you think it's yuck, prune off the bare stems in late fall to within 3 inches of the ground.

Additional Information

'Autumn Joy', like fall mums and fall asters, provides lots of great color to your September landscape. Be sure to locate your fall bloomers where they can be enjoyed from both outside and inside your home. You can start new 'Autumn Joy' plants by stem cuttings. Cut 4 to 6 inches off each stem and place 1 inch deep in damp, coarse sand. They'll root in about ten days.

Additional Species, Cultivars, or Varieties

'Ruby Glow' grows 12 to 14 inches and has deep, pinkish-red flowers beginning in late summer. 'Vera Jameson' is a low-growing sedum that has large purple flowers on short stems. 'Stardust' grows up to 18 inches tall and has deep-pink flowers.

Did You Know?

'Autumn Joy' and the other varieties of fall sedum are very good flower producers. If you want to double the fall bloom, prune back all the stems halfway when they reach 10 inches in June. This will produce twice the stems, thus twice the flowers.

Baby's Breath

Gypsophila paniculata 'Bristol Fairy'

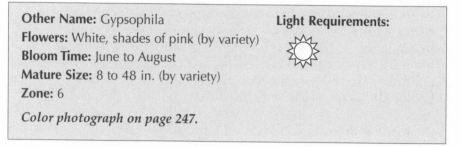

Other Name: Gypsophila
Flowers: White, shades of pink (by variety)
Bloom Time: June to August
Mature Size: 8 to 48 in. (by variety)
Zone: 6

Color photograph on page 247.

Light Requirements:

I s this a shrub or a true perennial? This question is asked by many who first see baby's breath growing in someone else's yard. That's because it has dainty white flowers that bloom from June into August—but the plant itself can be as large as 3 feet tall and 4 feet wide. The individual leaves of this plant are rather insignificant, yet the total plant can look like a large shrub. The flowers are certainly abundant and very showy. Individual flowers are 1/4 inch in size, double like a rose, and pure white, appearing all over the plant. Baby's breath grows best in well-drained, average soil with a high pH. That's why it grows so well in Kentucky with all its alkaline clay soil. This plant needs lots of room to grow. When planting baby's breath with other perennials, give it lots of room to grow on its own.

WHEN TO PLANT

Baby's breath is not a plant that you can divide, because it has a single-stem growth habit. Thus, you have to buy plants that are growing in pots at your favorite garden center. Plant new installs in the spring, summer, or fall. In other words, plant anytime baby's breath is available.

WHERE TO PLANT

Baby's breath prefers alkaline soil, which is good news for those of you who have limestone clay soil (that's a lot of you). When planting in clay, add some soil amendments to loosen that soil. Baby's breath grows best in full sun. Remember, this is a wide-spreading plant, so locate it in a bed with some room.

How to Plant

Baby's breath grows with a single taproot. Don't try to transplant it after it gets established; it doesn't like having its root cut and disturbed. With new plantings, loosen the existing soil to a depth of 8 to 10 inches. Add soil amendments if you have clay soil. Dig a hole as deep and twice as wide as the soil clump. Loosen any wrapped roots, backfill, and water-in well to settle the soil. When planting several baby's breath, plant on 24-inch centers.

Care and Maintenance

There are no bugs or diseases that bother baby's breath. When planting in acidic soil, add a handful of ground limestone to the soil as you backfill. Cut back the stems to 12 inches after a killing frost. There is no need to mulch, as it mulches itself with its foliage spread. Baby's breath is drought-tolerant, but water during hot, dry weather.

Additional Information

You can dry baby's breath by cutting off stems with the flowers still attached. Hang the cut branches in a dark, dry room. When the branches are easy to break, it's dried, and looks almost as nice as when it was fresh. Baby's breath cannot be divided. You can, however, plant from seed or by taking stem cuttings in the spring.

Additional Species, Cultivars, or Varieties

'Pink Fairy' is a pink-flowering version of 'Bristol Fairy'. 'Perfecta' has white-blooming double flower blooms on plants growing to 48 inches. White-flowering *G. repens* is dwarf, growing to 6 inches tall and 18 inches wide. 'Flamingo' has large mauve-pink flowers on plants growing to 36 inches. 'Bodgeri', a cultivar of *repens*, grows 8 to 12 inches tall and has light-pink flowers.

Did You Know?

Florists are among the biggest users of baby's breath stems and flowers. You will find some cut baby's breath in about 65 percent of florists' mixed arrangements.

Balloon Flower

Platycodon grandiflorus

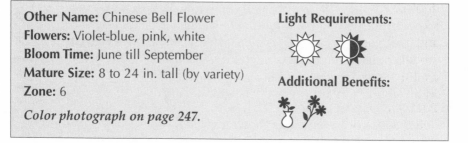

Other Name: Chinese Bell Flower
Flowers: Violet-blue, pink, white
Bloom Time: June till September
Mature Size: 8 to 24 in. tall (by variety)
Zone: 6

Color photograph on page 247.

Light Requirements:

Additional Benefits:

Another of my favorite low-maintenance plants, balloon flower is up near the top of the list. It is an absolutely care-free perennial that's very easy to grow. There are no pest or disease problems to contend with, it is a dependable bloomer for several months, and the plants last many years. Balloon flower grows to 24 inches tall and wide. The flowers are violet-blue, pink, and white, and somewhat star-shaped, with a 2-inch-diameter bloom. It will grow in full sun to partial shade, and grows well in average soil with good drainage. This perennial starts to grow from the soil a little later than some of its cousins. Be patient. The stems will grow straight up, producing silvery, dark-green leaves. The first bloom buds appear at the top of the stems in early June. Each flower then opens with five broad, pointed petals that form a somewhat fat, blue star. Balloon flower continues to spread and produce flowers into September. Balloon flowers mix well with other flowering perennials, especially white, pink, and yellow ones. Plant balloon flower where you can view those fluorescent blue flowers in the moonlight.

WHEN TO PLANT

Transplant and divide existing balloon flowers as they start to grow in mid-spring. Take clumps at least 6 inches across when dividing. Plant new nursery-grown balloon flowers that were grown in 3- to 4-inch pots or 1-gallon containers in spring to summer. Your best selection of 3- and 4-inch-potted balloon flowers will be in April and May. One-gallon containers can be planted anytime the ground is not frozen.

WHERE TO PLANT

Balloon flower will grow and prosper in almost any soil. Just be sure there is good drainage. Plant in full sun to half-day sun.

How to Plant

Transplant existing balloon flower plants by digging up clumps at least 6 inches in diameter. Replant at the same depth they were growing previously. For new installations, loosen the existing soil 6 to 8 inches. Dig a hole as deep and twice as wide as the soil clump. Loosen any roots that are wrapped around the soil clump. Backfill, and water-in well to settle the soil.

Care and Maintenance

Remove the old blooms as they fade. This will keep your plants looking healthier and blooming more. Fertilize in the spring as they start to grow, using a balanced plant food and following the instructions on the container. Give balloon flower an occasional drink during hot, dry weather.

Additional Information

Great perennial companions for balloon flower are lady's mantle, yellow loosestrife, white baby's breath, and any of the tall summer phlox. You should divide balloon flower every five to six years.

Additional Species, Cultivars, or Varieties

'Apoyama' is dwarf-growing, only 8 inches tall, and has purple-blue flowers. 'Mariesii' has purple-blue flowers on compact 12- to 16-inch stems. 'Mother of Pearl' and 'Shell Pink' both have light-pink flowers. 'Fuji' is available in pink, white, or blue flowers that are great as cut flowers in a vase and grow to 24 inches tall.

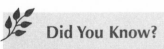 **Did You Know?**

When cutting balloon flower stems to bring indoors and place in a vase, use a match to singe the cut end of the flower stem. This will stop the flow of milky sap out of the stem, giving your cut balloon flowers much longer bloom time in the vase.

Beebalm

Monarda didyma

Other Name: Oswego Tea
Flowers: Pink, bright red, wine red, purple, and white
Bloom Time: July to September (by variety)
Mature Size: 30 to 42 in. (by variety)
Zone: 6

Color photograph on page 247.

Light Requirements:

Additional Benefits:

This is truly a story about the birds and the bees. Beebalm gets its common name from its flowers' ability to attract honeybees. But don't tell that to the hummingbirds! Plant beebalm in an area near a porch or window where you can enjoy the entertainment provided by the hummingbirds it attracts. Beebalm is available in the pink-flowering 'Marshal's Delight', a new bright-red variety named 'Jacob Cline', a wine-red variety named 'Raspberry Wine', and a new violet-purple variety called 'Scorpio'. Beebalm grows 30 to 42 inches tall and 36 inches wide. It prefers loose, moist, loamy soil but will tolerate soil of a lower quality. It will grow in full sun to morning sun. Some varieties are susceptible to mildew while others are quite resistant. Overall, beebalm is trouble-free and easy to grow. It spreads through underground roots that push up new stems. It's not considered invasive, but you may need to thin out new shoots to keep it contained in your allowable space. It is considered drought tolerant, but giving it timely moisture during dry weather will prevent water stress, which means it will be less susceptible to mildew.

WHEN TO PLANT

Transplant existing beebalm in the spring as the new growth appears. Take divisions that are at least 4 to 6 inches in diameter. Install new plants anytime the plants are available during the growing season.

WHERE TO PLANT

Plant beebalm in full sun to morning sun. It will grow in all types of soil as long as the drainage is good. Plant in groups of three or more in an area that is large enough for the plants to spread. Beebalm also makes a great planting along fence rows and areas set aside for that wildflower look.

HOW TO PLANT

Replant your beebalm transplants at the same depth they were growing in their previous location. For new plants, loosen the soil 6 to 8 inches deep. Dig a hole as deep and twice as wide as the soil clump. Loosen any roots that are wrapped around the soil clump, backfill your soil, and water-in well to settle the soil.

CARE AND MAINTENANCE

Beebalm is considered very low-maintenance. Water when the soil is dry to keep the plants from stressing. Prune away any spent flowers on a weekly basis. This will keep the beebalm looking neater and will also encourage later, additional bloom. Thin out and replant your beebalm every four to five years. Discard the old centers and space your replants on 12-inch centers. There's no need to fertilize beebalm, as the plant food could cause your plant stems to get too long and require staking.

ADDITIONAL INFORMATION

Beebalm makes great cut flowers to enjoy in a vase. It will really attract hummingbirds as well as the hummingbird moth, which a lot of homeowners confuse with true hummingbirds.

ADDITIONAL SPECIES, CULTIVARS, OR VARIETIES

'Snow Queen' is a white, free-flowering beebalm that grows best in morning-only sun. It grows to 36 inches tall and is very resistant to mildew.

Did You Know?

Honeybees are very friendly and do not attack people. Of course if you step on one with your bare feet, a sting could happen, but who wouldn't fight back if someone had a size-ten foot on his forehead? Bees are the biggest pollinators we have for fruits and berries. A landscape with lots of bees is a healthy landscape.

Black-Eyed Susan

Rudbeckia fulgida var. *sullivantii* 'Goldsturm'

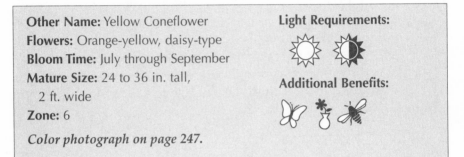

Other Name: Yellow Coneflower

Flowers: Orange-yellow, daisy-type

Bloom Time: July through September

Mature Size: 24 to 36 in. tall, 2 ft. wide

Zone: 6

Color photograph on page 247.

Light Requirements:

Additional Benefits:

Without a doubt, this is the most impressive perennial in my home landscape. It's very hardy, gives many weeks of colorful bloom, and simply needs no help from me. 'Goldsturm' black-eyed susans are sensational. They start blooming in mid- to late July, continuing through August. Prune off spent flowers and they will bloom until frost. Each 'Goldsturm' flower has many ray-like flower petals and a black center—the black eye. Regardless of the weather, black-eyed susans will flower, and flower, and flower. Each orange-yellow flower is 3 to 4 inches wide. The flowers all appear on the top of each branch, which makes black-eyed susans great for cut flowers. The leaves are dark green and fuzzy. This plant multiplies rapidly, making it a great perennial plant that if given enough bed space will produce twice the number of last-year's flowers every year. There are other perennials that mix in well to give you that wildflower look. Check out coneflower (page 198) for starters.

WHEN TO PLANT

You can divide existing black-eyed susans as the plants start to grow in early spring. Transplant clumps at least 6 inches in diameter and replant at the same depth. Plant nursery-grown susans anytime in the spring, summer, or fall. You will find *Rudbeckia* available in several pot sizes.

WHERE TO PLANT

'Goldsturm' will grow in just about any garden soil as long as there is good drainage. Black-eyed susans love it best in full sun, although I grow mine in just-morning sun, and I get lots of blooms. It grows 30 to 36 inches tall, so don't plant it in front of lower-growing plants.

How to Plant

If transplanting existing plants that have been in the ground a year or more, dig a clump at least 6 inches in diameter. Replant it at the same depth it was growing. For nursery-bought plants, dig a hole as deep and twice as wide as the soil clump. Loosen any wrapped roots and place in the hole. Backfill, and water-in well to settle the soil.

Care and Maintenance

Fertilize *Rudbeckia* when it first starts to grow in the spring. Use a time-release fertilizer that you only have to use once. Deadhead or pinch off the flowers as they finish blooming. When all the flowers have finished around the middle of August, prune the entire plant back to 10 inches from the ground. Wait a couple of weeks and your susans will be blooming again. There are no bugs or diseases that bother this plant.

Additional Information

Black-eyed susan's beautiful orange-yellow flowers blend in well with other flowers in the same bed. Start with *Rudbeckia*, add a little blue salvia, some nicotiana, and a border of wax begonias, and you have an annual and perennial bed that will need little care and even less water.

Additional Species, Cultivars, or Varieties

Rudbeckia laciniata is a cutleaf variety of coneflower; it has slender yellow petals on plants that grow to 6 feet. *Rudbeckia nitida* grows in a way similar to 'Goldsturm', with plants growing 2 to 3 feet with droopy petals.

Did You Know?

Even the blackest thumb can look like a horticultural genius when planting black-eyed susans. Just give them average soil, lots of sun, and good drainage. Schedule your lawn party for early August so your susans will make you look good.

Blanket Flower

Gaillardia × grandiflora 'Goblin'

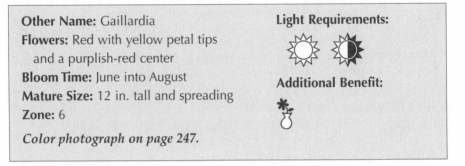

Other Name: Gaillardia
Flowers: Red with yellow petal tips
and a purplish-red center
Bloom Time: June into August
Mature Size: 12 in. tall and spreading
Zone: 6

Color photograph on page 247.

Light Requirements:

Additional Benefit:

B lanket flower is another of my favorite summer-blooming perennials. In fact, these 3- to 4-inch-wide flowers are described by perennial experts as bearing similarities to Native American blankets—hence the name blanket flower. They can survive in hot, dry, poor soil. The large showy flowers, which are maroon in the center with rays of red petals tipped with golden yellow, begin blooming in June and continue blooming into August. Blanket flower grows to 12 inches tall and 12 to 18 inches wide. 'Goblin' can live for many years in happy planting locations or as little as two years in so-so situations. Every yard has room for some of these summer-blooming, very colorful perennials. Plant 'Goblin' in full sun to a half-day of sun; plant in a mass to make a spectacular blooming summer site. The beautiful colors of the flowers make 'Goblin' a showpiece for any landscape. They also work well when mixed with other perennials such as lavender, coreopsis, coneflower, and black-eyed susans. 'Goblin' makes a beautiful cut flower in a mixed arrangement.

WHEN TO PLANT

Divide and transplant blanket flower in the spring as soon as the new growth starts to appear. Plant new store-bought plants in the spring or early summer. Plants will be available in 3-, 4-, and 6-inch pots and 1-gallon containers.

WHERE TO PLANT

Blanket flower will grow in all types of soil as long as the planting site has good drainage. It will even grow in bad soil that has good drainage. Choose a planting site that's hot and dry, one that other perennials will not grow in. Gaillardias will do just fine. Blanket flower looks great as a border for taller-growing annuals and perennials.

How to Plant

Plant your transplants at the same depth they were growing previously. Space and plant them on 12-inch centers. For new installs, loosen the existing soil 6 to 8 inches. Dig a hole as deep and twice as wide as the soil clump. Loosen any wrapped roots, backfill, and water-in well to settle the soil.

Care and Maintenance

There are no bugs or diseases to bother blanket flower. Give your plants some fertilizer in the spring as they start to grow. Use a balanced fertilizer, following the instructions on the container. When planted in rich garden soil, they may flop a little, though they will still be colorful. This plant stays more compact in average to poor soil (just make sure there's good drainage). Cut off spent flowers weekly as they appear to keep new blooms coming.

Additional Information

For a plant that only grows to 12 inches, it will provide tons of color when planted in large or small masses as well as borders. Some of the other varieties of gaillardia listed below might require staking.

Additional Species, Cultivars, or Varieties

'Baby Cole' is dwarf, growing only 6 to 8 inches, and has red daisylike flowers with yellow tips on the petals. 'Burgundy' has wine-red flowers and reaches a height of 24 to 36 inches; this one blooms into September. 'Dazzler' is a tall-growing variety with large yellow flowers that have red centers; it appears very showy from anywhere in the landscape.

Bleeding Heart

Dicentra formosa 'Luxuriant'

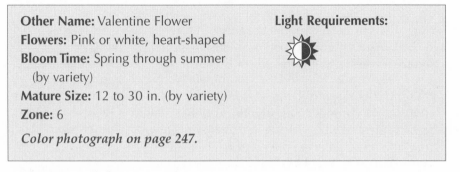

Other Name: Valentine Flower
Flowers: Pink or white, heart-shaped
Bloom Time: Spring through summer
  (by variety)
Mature Size: 12 to 30 in. (by variety)
Zone: 6

Color photograph on page 247.

Light Requirements:

*D*icentra spectabilis is the Japanese bleeding heart, graceful and beautiful in bloom. The problem with *D. spectabilis* is its bloom period. It blooms only for a month in spring. 'Luxuriant' is not quite as graceful, but it will bloom on arching 15-inch sprays of reddish-pink heart-shaped flowers from June until October. 'Luxuriant' grows 12 to 18 inches tall. Its attractive foliage is deeply serrated, bluish-green in color, and more finely textured than that of *D. spectabilis*. All varieties of bleeding hearts want to put on their display of foliage and color in a lightly shaded woodland atmosphere with dark-green shrubs and evergreens as background. Bleeding hearts will tolerate some morning sun and will grow best in rich, moist, well-drained soil. Make sure the drainage is good, as no varieties of bleeding heart will tolerate wet feet. Have a heart and plant one or many if you have the right location.

WHEN TO PLANT

Transplant and divide existing bleeding hearts in early spring as the new growth appears. Plant new, nursery-grown bleeding hearts from 3- to 4-inch or 1-gallon containers from mid-March until fall. Smaller potted sizes will be most plentiful in April and May. You can plant larger, 2-gallon plants all summer long. They'll look like they've been in your garden for a couple of years.

WHERE TO PLANT

Bleeding hearts want to be planted in good, humusy soil that has good drainage, and they want to be planted in the shade with good natural light. They will tolerate morning sun, but no afternoon sun. Bleeding hearts look best when planted in groups among evergreens and flowering shrubs.

How to Plant

When transplanting existing clumps of bleeding hearts, take a clump at least 6 inches in diameter, and replant at the same depth it was growing. Plant nursery-grown plants in a hole as deep as the bleeding heart was growing in the pots. Dig your hole twice as wide, backfill, and water-in well to settle the soil.

Care and Maintenance

There are no bugs or diseases that bother bleeding hearts. Fertilize with a time-release fertilizer in the spring, following the instructions on the container. Keep bleeding hearts watered during the hot, dry days of summer, especially if they're planted among competing tree roots.

Additional Information

If the summer is hot enough, some bleeding hearts will go dormant and disappear until next spring. That's why it's a good idea to plant bleeding heart with hostas, ferns, and other shade lovers that will fill the void of disappearing bleeding heart leaves.

Additional Species, Cultivars, or Varieties

Dicentra spectabilis is the original common bleeding heart that has pink heart-shaped flowers in mid-spring. This variety grows 24 to 30 inches tall and 18 to 24 inches wide; it has beautiful bluish-green foliage that dies back to the ground after blooming. *Dicentra spectabilis* 'Alba' is the same as the common bleeding heart, except it has white heart-shaped flowers and it goes to bed in early July for the season as the weather gets hot.

Did You Know?

Bleeding hearts reseed themselves for additional plants the following spring.

Candytuft

Iberis sempervirens 'Snowflake'

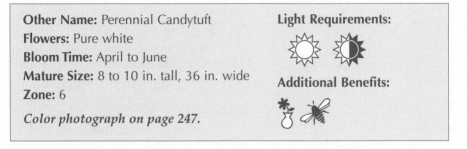

Other Name: Perennial Candytuft
Flowers: Pure white
Bloom Time: April to June
Mature Size: 8 to 10 in. tall, 36 in. wide
Zone: 6

Color photograph on page 247.

Light Requirements:

Additional Benefits:

Candytuft is a very hardy perennial. In fact, candytuft is so hardy that most winters it hangs onto its green needlelike leaves; in many parts of Kentucky, candytuft is considered an evergreen. It's low-growing and very spreading. The flower clusters are pure white, measuring 2 to 3 inches across. Each flower is made up of tiny flat-bladed petals forming a circular whirl. Candytuft does best in average to good soil that is well drained. It will grow in a half-day of shade but will bloom better and stay evergreen better if planted in full sun. Most candytuft is available in small sizes in the spring. Don't be discouraged—even when started out small, candytuft will continue to grow and will form a 30- to 36-inch clump in a couple of years. Candytuft performs well as a low border plant, planted in a rock garden, or weeping over a landscape wall. Plant it in and around other colorful annuals and perennials to allow the snow-white color to bring out those other plant colors. Another great combination is made by planting candytuft on top of tulip and hyacinth bulbs.

WHEN TO PLANT

You can divide your existing candytuft in spring before it starts to bloom or in the summer after the flowering has finished. Plant new store-boughts anytime the plants are available from your greenhouse or nursery store. Most will be available in 3- and 4-inch pots. One-gallon containers are usually available by mid-May.

WHERE TO PLANT

Candytuft prefers full sun; this exposure will give you the most bloom and better evergreen staying power. In zone 6, you can cheat and plant in a half-day of sun for that good, evergreen appearance.

Candytuft prefers good, loose soil that's well drained. Always plant it to the front of your planting or flower beds.

How to Plant

When transplanting your own divisions, replant at the same depth that those 6-inch clumps were growing. With new-bought plants, loosen the existing soil to a depth of 6 to 8 inches. Dig a hole as deep and twice as wide as the soil clump. Loosen any wrapped roots, backfill, and water-in well to settle the soil.

Care and Maintenance

After your candytuft has finished blooming, take a pair of hand-held hedge shears and prune back all the leaves and stems to 4 inches from the ground. This practice will promote new growth that will keep your candytuft looking fresh until next year's bloom time. Fertilize with a balanced plant food following the instructions on the container. Candytuft is bug- and disease-proof. Give your plants an occasional drink of water during hot, dry weather.

Additional Information

Candytuft is a low, evergreen, spreading plant. If yours starts to take up too much room, either dig up the excess and transplant or simply prune away the growth that you don't want. When transplanting several divisions, replant on 12-inch centers.

Additional Species, Cultivars, or Varieties

'Alexander's White' is early blooming, as early as late March. Its mounds of leaves and flowers grow to 8 inches. It does not bloom as long as 'Snowflake', but it has the same 2- to 3-inch-diameter white flowers. 'Pygmaea' is dwarf, growing only to 4 inches tall; it is very spreading and has white flowers. 'Autumn Beauty' and 'Autumn Snow' both grow 8 to 10 inches tall and spread to 24 to 36 inches. Both of these cultivars bloom for four weeks in the spring and another four weeks in the fall.

Cardinal Flower

Lobelia cardinalis

Other Name: Indian Pink

Flowers: Brilliant red, lavender, white, and pink

Bloom Time: July into September

Mature Size: 36 to 40 in. tall, spreading

Zone: 6

Color photograph on page 247.

Light Requirements:

Additional Benefit:

This is one perennial that's not suited for every landscape, but every landscape would love to have it. Cardinal flower can be seen from a quarter of a mile away. The brilliant red flowers are borne on single, tall, sturdy stems reaching up 36 to 40 inches. There is also a lavender bloomer that goes by the name of 'Vedrariensis'. Both varieties bloom from July to late September, and they have reddish-green leaves to add to their overall beauty. Unfortunately, cardinal flower is not suited for every home landscape. Let's see if yours qualifies: cardinal flower prefers to grow in partial shade but will tolerate full sun if it's planted in great soil, or if it's growing in eastern Kentucky where the summers are cooler than in central and western Kentucky. And here's good news for all. This plant readily reseeds itself, so even when planted in an unhappy location, it could come back from its own seed to bloom again the next season . . . be unhappy . . . and reseed itself again. The red color and size of its flowers may taunt you into trying some soon. One last tease. Cardinal flower is a real attraction for hummingbirds. So even if you don't have a good spot for cardinal flower to live over winter, you can treat it like an annual and enjoy for a single growing season.

WHEN TO PLANT

Divide existing cardinal flower in the early spring or early fall. Discard the old center of the plant. Plant nursery-bought plants in the spring. You will find cardinal flower available in 3-, 4-, and 6-inch pots.

WHERE TO PLANT

For most of Kentucky, plant in a semi-shaded area.
Morning sun will do just fine. Remember, cardinal flower
spreads when happy, and it will need some room to spread.
Most of us don't have the loamy soil that this plant wants,
but you can amend your existing soil by adding humus,
compost, and pine bark chips to make a happier home for
your cardinal flower.

HOW TO PLANT

Replant your transplants at the same depth they were
growing. For new plants, loosen and amend your existing
soil to a depth of 8 to 10 inches. Dig a hole as deep and
twice as wide as the soil clump. Loosen any wrapped
roots, backfill, and water-in well to settle the soil.

CARE AND MAINTENANCE

Cardinal flower prefers moist soil. Add water to the soil
when Mom Nature gets skimpy with her rainfall. There are
no known bugs or diseases that will bother these plants.
Fertilize with a balanced plant food once as the plants start
to grow in the spring. Read the instructions on the container to learn how much to use. This is the only fertilizer
necessary for the growing season.

ADDITIONAL INFORMATION

Don't be afraid to try two or three of these cardinal flowers. Select the most fertile soil in your landscape for
planting. The beautiful blooms are worth the effort. You
could also plant these in containers, making sure the soil is
good and the exposure works. Place the container in an
unheated garage for the winter. Be sure to water the container in the garage once a month. Go ahead, try it.

ADDITIONAL SPECIES, CULTIVARS, OR VARIETIES

'Compliment Scarlet' is a beautiful shade of red of this
native cardinal flower. It's considered wild, but you won't
think so with those large flowers. It blooms from July
through September on plants growing to 40 inches tall.
'Vedrariensis' is a hybrid with beautiful purple spikes that
bloom from July into late September. Great for cut flowers,
this one grows to 36 inches.

Columbine

Aquilegia

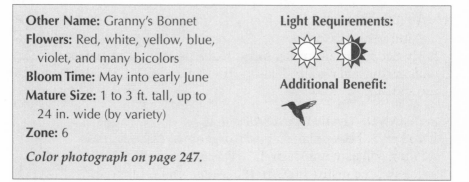

Other Name: Granny's Bonnet
Flowers: Red, white, yellow, blue, violet, and many bicolors
Bloom Time: May into early June
Mature Size: 1 to 3 ft. tall, up to 24 in. wide (by variety)
Zone: 6

Color photograph on page 247.

Light Requirements:

Additional Benefit:

Columbine hybrids are graceful flowers in spring, presenting beautiful colors in any perennial bed. These hybrids grow best in well-drained, ordinary garden soil. Some growers say that columbine wants full sun, while others say columbine blooms best in light shade. Both opinions could be correct, depending on whether you're thinking about color quality or length of bloom period. The best color will come from columbine growing in lots of sun, but those plants will disappear when that sunny location gets too hot; columbine plants growing in part shade will stay around into late summer. All columbine plants live for only two to three years, but don't despair—they reseed themselves, giving you more perennial bloom with sometimes different hybrid color combinations. It can be very exciting to see what new free color combinations you will get in May to early June. Columbine hybrids all grow 18 to 24 inches tall and 18 to 24 inches wide. The bloom color can be many different color combinations, with some flowers having solid colors. All are great attractions to hummingbirds. Check out the picture of columbine in this book to get a better appreciation of this great spring-blooming perennial.

WHEN TO PLANT

Columbine hybrids will be available from your garden center in spring in 3- and 4-inch pots. Larger, 1-gallon-container-sized plants will be available in late May, many of which will be in bloom.

WHERE TO PLANT

Columbines like full sun and well-drained soil. The soil does not have to be extremely good. Bloom time will be longer if the hybrids get a little shade. Plant columbine in groups of five together or planted close to other perennials whose leaves will shade the columbine roots.

How to Plant
Columbine has a taproot, so pre-loosen your garden soil fairly deep, 8 to 10 inches. Dig a hole as deep and twice as wide as the soil clump. Loosen any wrapped roots, backfill the soil, and water-in well.

Care and Maintenance
If you have heavy clay soil, add organic material to the existing soil as you loosen it. Fertilize in the spring, following the instructions on the container. Lightly mulch around the roots of your columbine to help keep them cool during the summer. Do not use a weed seed preventive in your beds that have columbine in early spring; it will kill your columbine's free seed that was deposited from last year's plants.

Additional Information
Hybrid columbines do not like to be divided or transplanted. Don't fret, you'll get lots of new ones from their seeds. These new plants will also give you bloom colors that, in some cases, you've never had before. The seedlings that develop from last year's flowers will be different from their parents, but like children, they will be very lovable. Columbine hybrids look great when mixed in a bed of other spring- and summer-blooming perennials.

Additional Species, Cultivars, or Varieties
'McKana Giant' hybrids are large blooms of pastel mixed flowers that last five to six weeks. The plants grow to 3 feet; plant on 18-inch centers. 'Music Series' hybrids are bicolor blooms of lavender, red, yellow, and white on plants that grow to 24 inches tall and wide. The flowers last five to six weeks if given a little shade. They grow extremely well in average soil. 'Biedermeier' has multicolored blooms on low-growing plants of 12 to 15 inches. The bloom colors include pink, blue, red, and yellow, with tips of white. It reseeds itself very easily.

Coneflower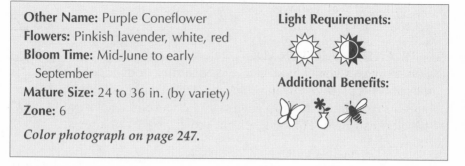

Echinacea purpurea

Other Name: Purple Coneflower
Flowers: Pinkish lavender, white, red
Bloom Time: Mid-June to early
   September
Mature Size: 24 to 36 in. (by variety)
Zone: 6

Color photograph on page 247.

Light Requirements:

Additional Benefits:

This perennial comes in two colors, pinkish-purple ('Magnus') and white ('White Swan'); the leaves are dark green and toothed on a plant that produces flowers from mid-June until fall. This perennial grows best in part to full sun, in average garden soil that is well drained. It makes a colorful statement in a large garden bed or a border planting. Coneflower is great for cut flowers brought indoors and placed in a vase. The cultivar called 'Magnus' blooms with pinkish-purple flowers. The white varieties include 'White Swan', which blooms on plants growing 2 to 3 feet, and another called 'White Luster', which blooms on stems of 3 feet. Coneflowers are very easy to grow, and require a half-day of sun or more. Plant this perennial in a group, or mix it with other perennials like black-eyed susan, Shasta daisy, yarrow, and gayfeather.

WHEN TO PLANT

Divide and transplant coneflower in the spring as new growth from the soil appears. Plant nursery-grown container plants from mid-March until the garden store runs out. The best selection of 3- and 4-inch potted plants will be from mid-March until mid-May. One-gallon containers should be available all spring and summer.

WHERE TO PLANT

Plant coneflower in full sun to part shade; it will do well in average and well-drained soil. Originally a prairie flower, this perennial can be planted in masses for that wildflower look. Mix with black-eyed susans and low-growing ornamental grasses.

HOW TO PLANT

When dividing existing clumps of coneflower, take clumps at least 6 inches in diameter. Plant the clumps in their new home no deeper than they were growing in their old. Container-grown plants should be planted at the same depth they were growing in their pots, but dig the hole twice as wide. Backfill, and water-in well to settle the soil. And don't forget to loosen the roots.

CARE AND MAINTENANCE
Coneflower is very low-maintenance and very drought-tolerant. Fertilize according to the instructions on the container. Prune back the flower stems 12 or more inches after the blooms finish. This will encourage more bloom later in the season.

ADDITIONAL INFORMATION
Coneflowers make perfect cut flowers that will last a couple of weeks in a vase. All coneflowers have a dark, almost brown center in every flower. These dark centers remain showy after the petals fall, and they make a great addition to any dried arrangement.

ADDITIONAL SPECIES, CULTIVARS, OR VARIETIES
'White Swan' offers white flowers on a plant growing to 36 inches. For mass planting, plant on 2- to 3-foot centers. This one is great for shade. 'Magnus' has large (4-inch-diameter) pinkish-purple flowers on a plant that grows to 36 inches. Space plants 18 to 24 inches apart. 'Crimson Star' has large, 4-inch, rich pink flowers on plants that grow 24 to 30 inches tall and 24 to 36 inches wide; it's a great one for cut flowers.

Did You Know?
Coneflower grew in and among the native grasses and other prairie plants. We've now discovered that coneflowers are wonderful in the home landscape.

Coral Bells

Heuchera 'Palace Purple'

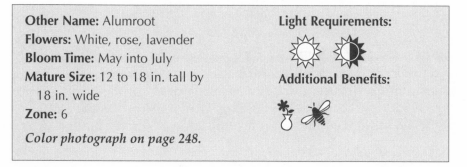

Other Name: Alumroot
Flowers: White, rose, lavender
Bloom Time: May into July
Mature Size: 12 to 18 in. tall by
  18 in. wide
Zone: 6

Color photograph on page 248.

Light Requirements:

Additional Benefits:

The perennial coral bells has been around for many years. *H. sanguinea* is an old-time species that was well known for its clumps of green leaves and for producing small red flowers on 12-inch stems, blooming in May into June. Then came 'Palace Purple' coral bells. Perennial growers and experts thought so much of this new one that 'Palace Purple' was pronounced the 1991 Perennial Plant Association Plant of the Year. This gorgeous plant grows 12 to 18 inches tall and up to 18 inches wide. The leaves are metallic and dark purple, and white flowers on 18-inch stems are produced from May into July. The reddish-purple leaves keep this plant very desirable in the landscape all season long, even after its bloom period. The leaves are 4 inches wide and resemble a maple leaf. They hold their dark-green color when planted in full sun, but you can expect great leaf color in morning-only sun. When grown in lots of shade, the leaf color will be a greenish-maroon. 'Palace Purple' looks great when mixed in with other green-leafed perennials. Use it as an underplanting for larger-growing shrubs or as a very showy border plant.

WHEN TO PLANT

Transplant existing coral bells in the early spring as the new growth starts to appear. Take divisions at least 3 to 4 inches in diameter. Plant new ones from your greenhouse or nursery store in spring and summer. You will find 'Palace Purple' available in 3- and 4-inch pots and 1-gallon containers.

WHERE TO PLANT

All coral bells want to be planted in average to good soil that is well drained. Coral bells prefer full sun, but you will find 'Palace Purple'

keeping its best summer leaf color where it gets relief from the hot afternoon summer sun.

How to Plant

Replant transplanted coral bells at the same depth and exposure that they enjoyed in their previous home. With new plantings, loosen the existing soil down to a depth of 6 to 8 inches. Dig a hole as deep and twice as wide as the soil clump. With clay soil, add a small amount of organic material to the soil you've dug up. Backfill, and water-in well to settle the soil.

Care and Maintenance

There are no pests or diseases to bother 'Palace Purple'.  Supply additional moisture to the roots during hot, dry weather; do not keep them wet. Coral bells tend to grow upward on a woody plant center above the soil every few years. Raise these elevated clumps every three years and remove the old growth. Replant the young plants that are growing on their own roots. When planting coral bells in hot sun, apply a 2-inch layer of a good bark mulch around their roots, keeping the mulch off the plant stems.

Additional Information

Two great companion plants for 'Palace Purple' are *Artemisia* 'Silver Mound' and hostas. They also make a great landscape appearance when planted in clusters among foundation-type shrubs and evergreens. Remember, the leaves will get a lot larger after planting than they appear in the garden store.

Additional Species, Cultivars, or Varieties

'Bressingham' hybrids have shiny leaves that resemble those of geraniums and red, pink, or white flowers on spikes that bloom in early summer. The plants grow 16 to 30 inches depending on the individual hybrid. *H. sanguinea* has silvery to variegated leaves. Flower colors include crimson, coral, rose, and white. The leaves of 'Chocolate Ruffles' have brown tops and are a burgundy color underneath. Lavender flowers appear in late spring.

Coreopsis 'Moonbeam'

Coreopsis verticillata 'Moonbeam'

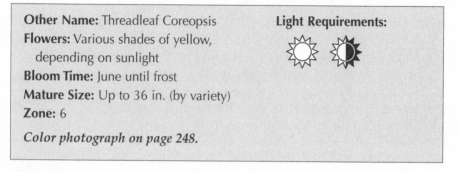

Other Name: Threadleaf Coreopsis

Flowers: Various shades of yellow, depending on sunlight

Bloom Time: June until frost

Mature Size: Up to 36 in. (by variety)

Zone: 6

Color photograph on page 248.

Light Requirements:

The Perennial Plant Association, founded by Dr. Steven Still in Columbus, Ohio, has been naming a Perennial Plant of the Year since 1990. Coreopsis 'Moonbeam' was chosen in 1992. Now here is a perennial that knows how to bloom during the summer. But before we get to the flower, let's look at the plant itself: 'Moonbeam' has very fine, ferny, almost threadlike foliage, and it's a spreading type that grows about 18 inches wide with a height of about 15 inches. Bright-yellow flowers cover the tops of all the foliage. You can maintain the height of 'Moonbeam' by trimming back to 8 inches after each bloom period finishes. Trim back, and more bloom will cover the plant again in three to four weeks. 'Moonbeam' will grow in all kinds of soil as long as the drainage is good. It is also very drought-tolerant—don't worry about watering assistance even during drought periods. 'Moonbeam' will grow and bloom in full to half-day sun. It makes an excellent border plant, or use it to plant around low-growing spring-flowering perennials, like creeping phlox, that tend to disappear when the weather turns hot.

WHEN TO PLANT

Transplant existing 'Moonbeam' when the ferny growth starts to appear in spring. Make each clump at least 6 inches in diameter. Plant new nursery-grown plants in the spring or summer. They will be available in 3-inch, 4-inch, 6-inch, and 1-gallon containers.

WHERE TO PLANT

Plant 'Moonbeam' in any kind of Kentucky soil that drains well. Hot, dry, sunny locations will produce many flowers. 'Moonbeam' will also perform well in half-day shade. Plant in any bed that needs yellow blooms, whether it fills the bed or is used as the front border.

How to Plant

When transplanting existing 'Moonbeam', replant your transplant clumps at the same depth they were growing. For a new planting, loosen the existing soil down to 6 to 8 inches. Dig a hole as deep and twice as wide as the soil clump. Loosen any roots that are wrapped around the soil clump. Backfill, and water-in well to settle the soil.

Care and Maintenance

'Moonbeam' is not susceptible to any bugs or diseases. If left unpruned during the growing season, 'Moonbeam' can reach a mounded height of 3 feet. I keep mine pruned back after each bloom period and it never gets over 15 inches tall. Use a hedge shear to prune. Always deadhead spent blooms to encourage new bloom in a few weeks.

Additional Information

Good companion plants for 'Moonbeam' are purple coneflower, Stokes' aster, gayfeather, and other larger-flowering coreopsis.

Additional Species, Cultivars, or Varieties

'Zagreb' is a plant very, very similar to 'Moonbeam', except it grows lower and has golden-yellow flowers and doesn't bloom as long. *C. verticillata* is another fernleaf coreopsis that grows to 2 to 3 feet and has deep golden-yellow flowers. 'Sunray', a grandiflora-type coreopsis, grows 2 to 3 feet tall and has 2-inch golden-yellow flowers. 'Baby Sun' is a *lanceolata*-type coreopsis that grows 18 to 24 inches tall and has single yellow flowers with orange-red centers.

Did You Know?

All coreopsis should be divided and replanted every three to four years. If you notice that more of the blooms are coming from the outside of the clump, discard the center and replant the outside portions to the inside of the clump.

Daylily

Hemerocallis spp.

Other Name: Hybrid Daylily

Flowers: Everything but pure white

Bloom Time: June until October
(by variety)

Mature Size: 1 to 3 ft. tall (by variety),
spreading

Zone: 6

Color photograph on page 248.

Light Requirements:

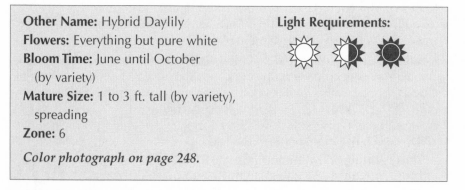

L et's start out with a "Did You Know?" Did you know that daylilies are not lilies at all? They get their common name from the fact that the flowers look like lilies and each individual flower blooms for a day. Daylilies are clumps of roots just like other perennials. Rumor has it that there are over forty thousand named varieties of daylilies (now tell me if you can't find one to please you). There are many colors of flowers that are single or double, some that are ruffled, and some that are fragrant. Talk about low maintenance: daylilies grow in full sun to medium shade to full shade. Most varieties have leaves that grow to about 18 inches tall, with flower stems growing 24 to 30 inches tall. New dwarf varieties have come along over the last dozen years. These shorter-growing plants grow 12 to 18 inches tall. Some of the best of the newer dwarfs are also repeat bloomers. Such varieties as 'Stella de Oro' and 'Happy Returns' will spot-bloom from June to October. All the taller-growing varieties bloom about two to three weeks in June into July. Daylilies make wonderful companion plants for tulips and daffodils; they help conceal the maturing of the bulb leaves and they begin to add new color to the area the bulbs have just left.

WHEN TO PLANT

Install relocated transplants in early spring as the new growth starts to appear. Make sure you transplant daylily clumps at least 6 inches in diameter. For new store-boughts, plant anytime during the growing season. They will be available in spring in 3- and 4-inch pots. Larger 1-gallon sizes will be available all summer. You can plant daylilies anytime the ground is not frozen.

WHERE TO PLANT

Daylilies will grow in any type of well-draining soil. Plant in lots of sun, although my daylilies at home get only four hours of sun each day and bloom very well. Daylilies will grow in full shade; this is especially important when trying to get plants to grow under trees. Don't expect as many flowers, but the foliage will act as a tall ground cover and you can expect some bloom color.

HOW TO PLANT

Loosen the existing soil down 6 to 8 inches. Do not replant any transplants deeper than they were growing in their previous home. With new plantings, dig a hole as deep and twice as wide as the soil clump. Loosen any wrapped roots. Backfill, and water-in well to settle the soil.

CARE AND MAINTENANCE

There isn't a bug or disease that bothers daylilies. They are extremely drought-tolerant. They continue to spread each year, eventually filling their planting area. Divide to thin them in early spring as necessary. Remove a spent flower stem as all the flowers finish on that stem. Fertilize with a balanced plant food following the instructions on the container. Cut back old leaves as they die back in the fall.

ADDITIONAL INFORMATION

To continue to keep the repeat bloomers blooming all summer, you must cut off the flower stalks as the blooms finish. Daylilies make for a beautiful transition between the lawn and woodsy, natural areas. They also look great in massed groups in and among groups of evergreens.

ADDITIONAL SPECIES, CULTIVARS, OR VARIETIES

There are forty thousand large-flowering daylily varieties for you to choose from. 'Stella de Oro' is a repeat bloomer with gold flowers on 12-inch stems. It's fragrant, but keep the old flower stems cut off. 'Happy Returns' is a repeat bloomer with lemon-yellow flowers on 18-inch stems; the flowers are small and ruffled. 'Little Business' is a repeat bloomer with red flowers on 12-inch stems. Keep old or spent flower stems pruned off.

Forget-Me-Not

Myosotis scorpioides

Other Name: Myosotis
Flowers: Bright blue and dark blue
Bloom Time: Late May until fall frost
Mature Size: 6 to 10 in. tall, spreading
  (by variety)
Zone: 6

Color photograph on page 248.

Light Requirements:

Additional Benefit:

As you read about the many cultivars of perennials in this chapter, you will notice one common denominator: all the other perennials mentioned want good soil drainage regardless of soil type. Well, forget-me-nots are the exception to that rule. They want to grow in soil that is well moistened and never dries out, along a stream, pond, or low area that tends to have gravel mixed in with the soil. Most landscapes don't have this kind of situation, but if you have an area that stays wet and other types of plants have not fared well in it, try forget-me-nots. 'Semperflorens' is a great variety to plant; it begins flowering in May and those blooms last into August. When its main blooming season is over, it will still spot-bloom off and on until frost. It's very compact-growing, too. All forget-me-nots grow best in full sun to a half-day of shade. If you have a wet spot in your landscape that needs some low, ground cover–type color, don't forget about forget-me-nots.

WHEN TO PLANT

Transplant existing forget-me-nots in the spring as the new leaves start to appear. Transplant divisions of existing forget-me-nots at least 6 inches in diameter. Plant store-boughts in the spring from plants growing in 3-, 4-, or 6-inch pots.

WHERE TO PLANT

Plant forget-me-nots in a moist woodland setting or in other areas of the landscape that are well watered. Plant among ferns, hostas, or any other perennial that appreciates moist soil. Remember, forget-me-nots grow very low to the ground, bloom for a long period of time, and quickly cover the ground with beautiful blue flowers like a blanket.

How to Plant

Replant existing transplants at the same depth and planting conditions from which they came. Plant new ones that you'll find in 3-, 4-, and 6-inch pots from your garden center in spring. The best selection will be in April to mid-May. Loosen the existing soil to a depth of 6 to 8 inches. Dig a hole as deep and twice as wide as the soil clump. Loosen any wrapped roots around the soil clump, backfill, and water-in well to settle the soil.

Care and Maintenance

Forget-me-nots grow best in a woodland garden near a water source—this could be moisture that you provide through a sprinkler. Apply fertilizer to the plants as they start to grow in the spring. Read the instructions on the container to learn how much to use. If allowed to stress because of insufficient water, mildew and mites could pose a small problem. The best way to attack these problems is to supply sufficient water to keep your forget-me-nots happy.

Additional Information

Forget-me-nots mix well with hardy ferns, hostas, and primrose. Even though they're sun-loving, planting forget-me-nots on the edge of a woodland or in other shady areas with good sky light will give you a beautiful carpet of blue flowers from late May until frost.

Additional Species, Cultivars, or Varieties

M. sylvatica, commonly called woodland forget-me-not, is more tolerant of dry soil conditions; the parent plant may not winter over, but don't worry—it reseeds itself quite readily. 'Victoria' has dark blue flowers on a plant that only grows to 8 inches tall.

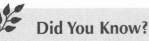 **Did You Know?**

Forget-me-nots could be the perfect plant for that damp-to-wet area in which other perennials fail to grow. When planted in a happy spot, it will grow and prosper for many years.

Garden Mum

Chrysanthemum × morifolium

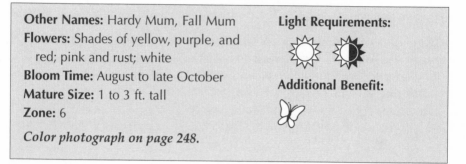

Other Names: Hardy Mum, Fall Mum

Flowers: Shades of yellow, purple, and red; pink and rust; white

Bloom Time: August to late October

Mature Size: 1 to 3 ft. tall

Zone: 6

Color photograph on page 248.

Light Requirements:

Additional Benefit:

True garden mums bloom in the fall, not summer. The common denominator of the whole chrysanthemum group is the fact that all chrysanthemums like full sun, good drainage, and having their spent flowers removed, prolonging the bloom period. Fall mums start blooming in mid- to late August. Their bloom can continue until November. Fall mums are frostproof—don't worry about covering those beautiful flowers when temps dip into the freeze zone. Garden mums look like green veggies in the spring and summer. I recommend growing your fall mums in a sunny, out-of-the-way location in spring and summer—then transplant those plants into a sunny, in-your-face location as they start forming their bloom buds so they can show off all that color in prominent garden spots. Leave in the new location until they start to grow in the spring. Then transplant them back to their out-of-the-way, sunny growing spot until next fall.

WHEN TO PLANT

Transplant existing garden mums in the spring as the new growth appears. Plant nursery-bought new plants in the spring or in late summer to fall.

WHERE TO PLANT

Plant mums in average garden soil that drains well. Choose a site that gets at least morning sun. Full sun is best.

HOW TO PLANT

Plant transplants as deep as they were growing in their previous location; dig transplant clumps that are at least 6 inches in diameter. Plant store-boughts in average to poor garden soil; pre-loosen the existing soil 6 to 8 inches deep. Remove the mums from their container. Loosen any wrapped roots and dig a hole as deep and twice as wide as the soil clump. Backfill, and water-in well to settle the soil.

CARE AND MAINTENANCE

Keep your mums pinched. By that I mean keep them short until the middle of July. If you want your mums to bloom at 18 inches tall, keep them pinched back to 12 inches until mid-July. You can figure them for another 6 inches of growth until they form bloom buds. If you want your mums taller, follow the same math. There are no bugs or diseases that will attack your garden mums. Remember, divide your mums in the spring as they start to grow. Keep your spent flowers pinched off to allow secondary buds beneath the original blooms to further develop and give you more late-fall color.

ADDITIONAL INFORMATION

Great summer companion plants for fall mums are cosmos, black-eyed susans, and Shasta daisies. These summer bloomers will give a mixed bed lots of color until the mums kick in.

ADDITIONAL SPECIES, CULTIVARS, OR VARIETIES

There are many varieties of fall mums. You will see some listed as garden mums, cushion mums, and any other name that a grower puts on the tag. Buying in late summer to fall will allow you to see the bloom size and color of each mum before you buy it.

Did You Know?

Mums from florists, usually called pot mums, have very large blooms and are usually not hardy in Kentucky. These mums, when received in bloom in the spring, can be planted outside and will bloom again in the fall. They are not winter hardy, however, and usually don't winter over. Don't be disappointed.

Gayfeather

Liatris spicata

Flowers: Rosy lavender, lavender, and white
Bloom Time: July to September
Mature Size: 18 to 48 in. (by variety)
Zone: 6

Color photograph on page 248.

Light Requirements:

Additional Benefits:

Gayfeather is a perennial native to the United States. This is a plant that can take very cold winters and very hot summers; it will also give you loads of blooms from July into September. Gayfeather is a compact grower that reaches 24 to 30 inches tall including the flower spikes. It starts to grow in spring with grassy-looking leaves that form short clumps of growth. Then in July a leafy flower spike starts to grow upwards from the center of the plant. When the spike reaches its top height, green buds form and start to open from the top of the flower bud down, producing rosy-purple, fuzzy flowers. In full bloom, the flower spikes resemble a bottlebrush. Gayfeather does best in full sun, although I've seen it grow well in just-morning sun. It will grow in all kinds of soil as long as there's good drainage. All the spent flower stalks should be removed to promote additional bloom. There is no need to separate gayfeather, although if you want to spread the wealth, divide it in the fall. Plant several to an area to make a beautiful color statement.

When to Plant

Divide existing gayfeather in early fall. Divide the corms with a knife and replant on 12- to 15-inch centers. Plant new installs anytime the plants are available. Three- and 4-inch pots will be readily available in early to mid-spring, with larger 1-gallon containers available in mid-spring through the summer.

Where to Plant

Plant gayfeather in well-drained soil. It will tolerate average to poor soil. It grows best in full sun, although you can have nice plants and good bloom on plants receiving five to six hours of morning sun.

How to Plant

Replant your own transplants in their new home at the same depth they were growing in their old home. With new installs, loosen the existing soil to a depth of 6 to 8 inches. Dig a hole as deep and twice as wide as the soil clump. Loosen any wrapped roots, place the soil clump in the hole, backfill, and water-in well to settle the soil.

Care and Maintenance

There are no major pests or disease problems with gayfeather. Mildew can attack during hot, humid weather. When this type of weather exists, be sure to water the soil when dry to eliminate moisture stress. Prune off spent flower spikes to encourage more basal growth and more spikes. Fertilize early each spring as new growth appears with an all-purpose fertilizer, following the instructions on the container. Divide existing clumps of gayfeather in early fall, taking 6-inch clumps.

Additional Information

Gayfeather has quite an impact when planted in groups of nine to twelve plants. It also blends in well with other perennials in a mixed bed. Combine it with plants such as 'Moonbeam' coreopsis, yarrow, *Artemisia* 'Silver Mound', and white-blooming tall phlox. Gayfeather attracts butterflies and makes an excellent cut flower as well as a great flower for drying. Remember, gayfeather is very care-free even in hot, dry, so-so soil.

Additional Species, Cultivars, or Varieties

'Kobold' has rosy lavender-purple spikes of bloom growing 24 inches tall and wide. It blooms July through August and does best in full sun. *L. ligulistylis* is loved by butterflies. And by goldfinches. It has long-lasting lavender flowers that bloom from July into September, and it grows 36 to 60 inches. *L. pycnostachya* is commonly called Kansas gayfeather. It is tall, with 4-foot spikes that produce purple blooms. It makes for a beautiful backdrop for any mixed perennial bed. 'Floristan White' has creamy-white flowers on 36-inch flower spikes.

Hibiscus

Hibiscus moscheutos

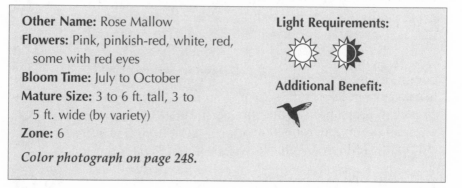

Other Name: Rose Mallow
Flowers: Pink, pinkish-red, white, red,
   some with red eyes
Bloom Time: July to October
Mature Size: 3 to 6 ft. tall, 3 to
   5 ft. wide (by variety)
Zone: 6

Color photograph on page 248.

Light Requirements:

Additional Benefit:

When we see or hear the name hibiscus, most of us think of those tropical plants that have colorful, 3-inch flowers and glossy, green leaves—tropical plants that have to be kept indoors during the winter. But there is another kind of hibiscus. And believe it or not, the hibiscus hybrids I'm going to talk about are even more showy than the tropicals. Here is a hardy perennial that grows to the size of a medium-flowering shrub; the plants' overall size range is 3 to 6 feet tall and 4 to 5 feet wide, by variety. The flower size ranges from 7 to 12 inches in diameter, and that's the size of a dinner plate. The erect flowering stems are stiff and never need staking. The leaves are also attractive, resembling a 6- to 7-inch-long maplelike leaf. Hibiscus starts blooming in July and blooms into October if you deadhead the old flowers. It grows in full sun to a half-day of sun. You may read in other books that hibiscus likes consistently moist soil, but don't worry. I know from personal experience that hibiscus is fairly drought tolerant and will do just fine in ordinary Kentucky garden soil. Do mulch during the summer heat to help retain moisture around the plants.

WHEN TO PLANT
Transplant existing hibiscus in the spring as it starts to grow. Make your divisions at least 6 inches in diameter. Plant nursery-bought plants growing in containers at least 6 inches to 1 gallon in size.

WHERE TO PLANT
Plant hibiscus in good to average soil that has good drainage. It does well in full sun to areas receiving only three to four hours of sun. Plant in areas away from the wind, which can damage those

beautiful large flowers. Plant one as a specimen or several to the rear of a flower bed, and plant where you can see them from both outside and inside the home.

HOW TO PLANT

Plant existing transplants in spring, at the same depth they were growing in their previous home. Plant new nursery-bought hibiscus (growing in 6-inch pots or larger) in mid- to late spring. Loosen the existing soil to a depth of 8 to 10 inches. Dig a hole as deep and twice as wide as the soil clump. Loosen any roots that are wrapped around the soil clump, backfill, and water-in well to settle the soil.

CARE AND MAINTENANCE

After hibiscus loses its leaves in late fall, it looks like a dead bush. To improve the winter look in your landscape, cut back your hibiscus to the ground. Mark the spot where it was so you don't accidentally plant something else next spring on top of its roots. Don't laugh: as far as I know, hibiscus is the last perennial to start to grow the next spring, and you may not see signs of new growth until mid-May. Fertilize your hibiscus with any all-purpose fertilizer.

ADDITIONAL INFORMATION

Use this plant's shrublike appearance to make a real color statement in your landscape. In addition to choosing bloom size, you can choose from bloom colors of red, rose-red, white, and pink (most of which have a red eye in the center of the flower), blooms that have a different color stripe on the edge of each flower, and some that have both stripes and the center eye. Plant several hibiscus in a cluster, and plant variegated maiden grass to the rear. The combination is very rich-looking and colorful.

ADDITIONAL SPECIES, CULTIVARS, OR VARIETIES

'Southern Belle' blooms in white, rose, red, or pink, with most having a red eye in the center of each flower. Plants grow 3 to 5 feet tall and 3 to 4 feet wide. The blooms of 'Lord Baltimore' are a pinkish red and average 7 to 10 inches in diameter; the plants grow 4 to 5 feet wide. 'Mallow Marvels' has red, pink, or white flowers that are 5 inches in diameter and somewhat funnel-shaped.

Hosta

Hosta spp.

Other Names: Plantain Lily, Funkia
Flowers: Lavender, white, purple
 (by variety)
Bloom Time: July into September
 (by variety)
Mature Size: 6 to 48 in. tall
 and wide (by variety)
Zone: 6

Color photograph on page 248.

Light Requirements:

Hostas! They are, in my estimation, the most popular perennial around. This is amazing, considering they are not known for any flower. It's the leaf that is appealing to so many. Hostas come in many combinations of variegated green leaves. Some do have purple flowers in early to late summer, while others have white flowers, some very fragrant, that bloom in August. They have been known in the past as plantain lily and funkia. Hostas come in all growing sizes too, with some growing as small as 6 inches and others growing to 48 inches tall and wide. All hostas do well in shade, with the variegated type tolerating morning sun and green-leaf varieties growing in full sun. Hot summers will cause hostas, especially those getting afternoon sun, to sunscald or leafburn. Hostas like decent soil that stays moist but not wet, especially in the winter.

WHEN TO PLANT

Divide and transplant your hostas in early spring, as the leaves start to grow in early fall. Take clumps that are at least 6 inches in diameter. Plant new hostas from the nursery anytime the plants are available; the best selections will be in spring and summer.

WHERE TO PLANT

All hostas perform well in medium shade to morning sun. Some varieties, especially those that have yellow in their leaves, need some sun for good leaf color, while varieties that have blue leaves prefer less sun. Be sure you buy all your hostas where knowledgeable people are on hand to select the best ones for your home landscape situation.

How to Plant

When moving transplants, replant the clumps no deeper than they were growing in their previous home. With new installs, loosen the existing soil down 6 to 8 inches. Dig a hole as deep and twice as wide as the soil clump. Loosen any wrapped roots, backfill the soil, and water-in well to settle the soil.

Care and Maintenance

Be sure to keep your hostas moist during hot weather. Mulch your hostas 2 inches deep with a high-quality bark mulch. Fertilize hostas with a time-release plant food, following the instructions on the container. Slugs and snails love hosta leaves, especially during wet weather periods. Use organic diotomaceous earth or slug bait to combat them. Deer also find hostas very tasty. Spray your hosta leaves monthly with Bitrex™, a very safe, bitter-tasting substance found in Fertilome's This 1 Works® deer repellent.

Additional Information

Great planting companions for hostas include bleeding hearts and hardy ferns.

Additional Species, Cultivars, or Varieties

'Tiny Tears' is very dwarf, growing only 6 inches tall. 'Gold Standard' has gold leaves with green edges and lavender flowers on plants that grow 24 inches tall and wide. 'Krossa Regal' has blue-green leaves with lavender flowers on a plant that grows 36 inches tall and wide. 'August Moon' has yellowish-green leaves and white flowers on a plant that grows up to 24 inches tall and wide. 'Frances Williams' has bluish-green leaves with gold edges and white flowers on plants growing 24 inches tall and wide. 'Francee', with lavender blooms, has medium-green leaves edged in pure white and is compact, with plants that average 24 inches tall and wide. 'Royal Standard' has solid-green leaves with fragrant white flowers in August; it grows 30 inches tall and wide. 'Aphrodite' has deep-green, large leaves with extremely fragrant flowers that are good for cutting and putting in a vase; this double-flowering hosta is one of my favorites.

Lamb's Ear

Stachys byzantina 'Silver Carpet'

Other Name: Stachys
Flowers: None
Bloom Time: Grown for foliage color
Mature Size: 10 in. tall, 24 in. wide
Zone: 6

Color photograph on page 248.

Light Requirements:

Here is another gorgeous, unusual perennial that's not known for a flower. As the name suggests, the silvery foliage is not only attractive, but soft as a lamb's ear. This plant could have been listed in the ground cover chapter because that's what it does: it covers the ground. Each plant grows to only 10 inches tall and will spread to 24 inches wide. The reason I'm listing lamb's ear with perennials is that it complements so many other perennial plants and shrubs. Plant it where it can separate other varieties of perennials. The silver foliage will bring out the colors of lavender, candytuft, veronica, balloon flower, and mini-flora roses. Some varieties may produce some flowers on 12-inch stems, but pick them off—they detract from the overall beauty of the leaves. And 'Silver Carpet' does not flower at all. Lamb's ear grows so thick that weeds are never a problem. It will grow in all types of Kentucky soil as long as there's good drainage. It is very drought tolerant even though it grows in full sun. It will also grow well in areas receiving only four hours of sun. Lamb's ear will stay mostly evergreen, holding the majority of its leaves. If the leaves do winterburn, just rake up the damaged leaves in early spring and cut back any bare stems. It will look new and fresh in no time.

WHEN TO PLANT

Transplant existing lamb's ear as new growth starts to appear in the spring. Dig up clumps at least 6 inches in diameter. Your plants will start dying out in the center over time; when this happens, discard the old center and transplant a new clump in its place. Plant new lamb's ear in spring, summer, or whenever the plants are available.

WHERE TO PLANT

Plant lamb's ear in full to part sun. It will grow in any type of Kentucky soil as long as there's good drainage. Plant it on or in walkways, pathways, or rock gardens, or up front in a mixed flower bed.

HOW TO PLANT

Plant your transplants at the same depth they were growing in their last home. With new installs, loosen the existing soil to a depth of 6 to 8 inches. Dig a hole as deep and twice as wide as the soil clump. Loosen any wrapped roots around the soil clump, backfill the soil, and water-in well.

CARE AND MAINTENANCE

Low, low maintenance. No bugs or diseases bother lamb's ear. Fertilize once in the spring with a time-release fertilizer like Start-N-Gro®. If you have a variety other than 'Silver Carpet', cut off flower stems as they appear. If the center starts dying out, dig out and remove the old center and transplant some of the newest growth to that spot.

ADDITIONAL INFORMATION

Soft as a baby's skin. That's how to best describe the feel of lamb's ear leaves. Since this plant will grow in any type of well-draining soil, plant it as a ground cover in areas of the landscape where you had difficulty growing other perennials. It makes a beautiful silver-gray ground cover.

ADDITIONAL SPECIES, CULTIVARS, OR VARIETIES

'Big Ears' has large 6- to 7-inch leaves from which it gets its name, and it grows 15 to 18 inches tall. It has the same silver-gray foliage, but the plant grows a little looser, not quite as dense as 'Silver Carpet'.

Did You Know?

Lamb's ear doesn't need to be mulched. It mulches itself with its dense-growing foliage. Water after the dew disappears in the morning to allow the leaves to dry quickly. Do not keep this plant constantly wet. Lamb's ear is very drought tolerant.

Lavender, English

Lavandula angustifolia 'Hidcote'

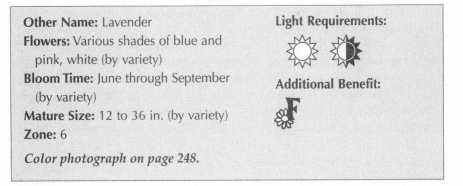

Other Name: Lavender

Flowers: Various shades of blue and pink, white (by variety)

Bloom Time: June through September (by variety)

Mature Size: 12 to 36 in. (by variety)

Zone: 6

Color photograph on page 248.

Light Requirements:

Additional Benefit:

Lavender has been a perennial that, in the past, was known more widely as an herb. Its biggest contribution to the home was in the use of cut flowers and stems with leaves for its fragrance when used in dried arrangements or in sachets and potpourris. But then came 'Hidcote', a summer-blooming variety that gave a new meaning to this great perennial. All lavender has grayish-green foliage and blue to pink flowers during the summer. 'Hidcote', called English lavender, is a compact grower that grows 12 to 15 inches tall. It has slender flower spikes that are always producing deep purple-blue flowers as they grow. 'Hidcote' blooms for about eight weeks. All lavender prefers a sunny location and average soil that drains very well both in the growing season and in winter. English lavender can withstand the heat of summer too. Just don't water it too much during the hot, dry summer.

WHEN TO PLANT

Transplant existing clumps of lavender in early spring as new growth appears, or in early fall. Plant new potted plants from the garden center or greenhouse anytime the plants are available in the spring, summer, or early fall.

WHERE TO PLANT

Lavender is a tough plant that does well in dry soil. Too much moisture, either from rain or from your own irrigation, can be its enemy. If you live in parts of Kentucky that can have lots of winter snow, make sure the soil you plant your lavender in has good drainage. Plant in areas of full sun for best growth and bloom—but it will perform well with only five hours of sun.

How to Plant
Plant your existing transplants as deep as they were growing in their previous home. When installing newly purchased plants, pre-loosen the existing soil to a depth of 6 to 8 inches. Dig a hole as deep and twice as wide as the soil clump. Loosen any wrapped roots, backfill, and water-in well to settle all the backfilled soil.

Care and Maintenance
Always plant 'Hidcote' and other lavenders where there is good drainage that will keep the roots from rotting away, especially during winter weather. Lavender will appear almost as an evergreen, suffering very little dieback in the winter, unlike other perennials. Prune all the stems back in early spring every year or two to promote more compact growth and more flowers. Do not fertilize this plant. It grows very well with the average soil you plant it in.

Additional Information
Lavender grows well in alkaline soil, which is good news for most of us in Kentucky. Lavender's foliage is fragrant, with a clean herbal aroma that will be very pleasing to you and all visitors to its planting site. What a wonderful plant to place near a walkway or patio where you can visit it daily.

Additional Species, Cultivars, or Varieties
'Jean Davis' has light-pink flowers and blue leaves. It grows to 18 inches tall and wide, blooming in summer and again in late fall. *L. angustifolia* is the true English lavender, blooming in June to July with blue-violet flowers on a plant growing to 36 inches tall and 18 inches wide. 'Munstead' is dwarf, growing to 15 inches tall and wide; plant in lots of sun and do not fertilize. It has purple flowers in June to July. 'Rosea' has soft-pink flowers on short 15-inch stems; gray-green leaves on this sun lover.

Did You Know?

Keep your lavender looking young by pruning halfway back every three years in spring—it will always look fresh.

Peony

Paeonia

Other Name: Garden Peony

Flowers: Yellow, white, pink, red, and bicolor

Bloom Time: Late May into June

Mature Size: 2 to 3 ft. tall and wide

Zone: 6

Color photograph on page 248.

Light Requirements:

Additional Benefits:

There are over nine hundred cultivars of peonies offered for sale in the United States. Each plant of each cultivar is capable of living one hundred years or more. How's that for a hardy perennial! To maximize the life and happiness of your peonies, you must dig a ten-dollar hole for a three-dollar plant—peonies want to be planted in a large, over-sized hole located in full sun. They can be planted in beds mixed with other perennials or shrubs, or can be planted by themselves out in the open lawn. Peonies, by cultivar, do not all bloom at the same time. They will, however, all bloom sometime during early midsummer. Many cultivars have large 5- to 7-inch-diameter double flowers that bloom white, pink, red, or bicolor. There are other cultivars of peonies that have large single flowers of the same colors. There is another group called Japanese tree peonies that form a multibranched mini-tree on a very short single trunk. Their flowers, like all peony flowers, are outstanding as well.

WHEN TO PLANT

Divide and replant existing peonies in early fall or in early spring as the new growth starts to appear. Be sure each new division has at least three growing points or eyes. Plant your store-bought peonies from the nursery store in spring or summer. Buy plants growing in 1- or 2-gallon containers.

WHERE TO PLANT

Try to plant peonies in full sun. They will grow and bloom in partial shade as well. Peonies will grow in average soil but will reach their maximum height when placed in an oversized hole and backfilled with soil that's been improved by adding rotted manure, organic peat, compost, and bonemeal.

How to Plant

With relocated transplants, be sure not to replant the clumps any deeper than they were growing in their old home. For new plants, dig a hole 18 inches wide and deep. Amend your existing soil as mentioned before. Please be sure to plant the points or eyes no more than 1 inch deep. Add the backfilled amended soil and water-in well. The single most common reason peonies never bloom is that they're planted too deep. Be sure your planting site has good drainage.

Care and Maintenance

Fertilize your peonies with a balanced fertilizer following label directions. Peonies need support as they get taller and start to bloom. Nothing is more discouraging than waiting all spring for your peonies to flower only to have a rain come along and bend all those beautiful flowers toward the ground. Buy peony rings designed to support those flower stems while being camouflaged by the leaves.

Additional Information

Peonies will not bloom if they don't get enough sun. Many homeowners have planted peonies near a small tree in the sun, failing to realize that when that little tree becomes a big tree, it will take the sun away. Peonies need a minimum of six hours of sun a day.

Additional Species, Cultivars, or Varieties

Each blossom of 'Bowl of Beauty' is bowl-shaped. The fragrant 5- to 7-inch flowers are white in the center and pink on the outer edges. 'Rubra Plena' has double, dark-red flowers with very serrated leaves. There are hybrids galore, so don't be afraid to try any of the peonies you find for sale at your favorite nursery store or greenhouse. Remember, they come with both double and single flowers.

Did You Know?

Ants in your pants can be bothersome, but ants on your peony buds are nothing to worry about. They like the sweet sap that bleeds from the tight flower buds, but they cause no harm.

Phlox, Tall

Phlox paniculata

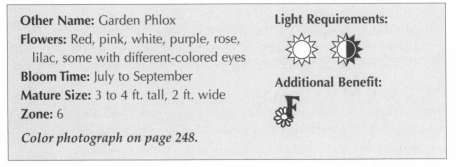

Other Name: Garden Phlox
Flowers: Red, pink, white, purple, rose, lilac, some with different-colored eyes
Bloom Time: July to September
Mature Size: 3 to 4 ft. tall, 2 ft. wide
Zone: 6

Color photograph on page 248.

Light Requirements:

Additional Benefit:

Tall phlox is sometimes referred to as summer phlox because it first starts to bloom in late July. The flowers persist into September. Each flower head is made up of small florets that form a rounded cluster measuring up to 6 inches tall and wide on 3- to 4-foot stems. The flower colors are another beautiful story. Choose tall phlox with blooms of pink, blue, purple, lavender, orange, yellow, red, and combinations of these with dark-colored eyes. You don't get a better choice even when buying ice cream. Many varieties of summer phlox have been around for years. Hybridizers have really done a great job with the *P. paniculata* varieties, making them not only more colorful, but also more disease resistant. When given good air circulation, such varieties as 'David' will be mildew-free. Tall phlox does best in full to half-day sun. It prefers rich, loose soil but will tolerate average soil as long as the drainage is good. Tall phlox works well in a mixed perennial bed with other summer-flowering perennials such as gayfeather, Stokes' asters, and veronica. Be ready to use plant stakes if the phlox gets tall with lots of bloom.

WHEN TO PLANT

Transplant existing tall phlox as new growth appears in early spring. Make your new divisions at least 4 inches in diameter. Plant tall phlox from your nursery store or greenhouse anytime during the growing season. Smaller 3- to 4-inch potted tall phlox will be most widely available in April and May. Larger 6-inch and 1-gallon containers will be available late spring into summer.

WHERE TO PLANT

Tall phlox likes full sun. If such a site is not available, choose morning sun over afternoon sun. Tall phlox will grow in all types of soil as long as there's good drainage.

How to Plant

Replant your transplants at the same depth they were growing previously. With new installs, pre-loosen the existing soil to a depth of 6 to 8 inches. Add a little organic material if your soil is on the clay side. Dig a hole as deep and twice as wide as the soil clump. Loosen any wrapped roots, backfill, and water-in well to settle the soil.

Care and Maintenance

Tall phlox is fairly drought tolerant, but do give it a drink during hot, dry periods of summer. Maintaining even soil moisture and exposing your tall phlox plants to good air movement will reduce the risk of mildew on the leaves. Mildew does not cause serious health problems for the tall phlox, but it sure makes the plant look bad. Feeding your tall phlox with a time-release fertilizer once in spring will get your tall phlox off and growing.

Additional Information

Tall phlox makes quite a colorful statement in the landscape. They don't spread very fast and that's good for air circulation. Plant your new or transplanted tall phlox on 24-inch centers. Tall phlox has a very sweet aroma and is a suitable cut flower, although, when cut, the flowers last but a few days.

Additional Species, Cultivars, or Varieties

'David' is mildew-resistant and has fragrant pure-white flowers growing to 3 feet tall. 'Franz Schubert' has lilac-flavored flowers with dark-purple "eyes" in the flowers' centers; it grows 3 to 4 feet. 'Eva Cullum' has long-lasting blooms of pink with red eyes. The flowers are the size of hydrangeas. 'Bright Eyes' has soft-pink flowers with red eyes on short plants growing 2 to 3 feet. 'Blue Boy' has beautiful powder-blue flowers that bloom on plants growing up to 30 inches. 'Starfire' has a great deep-red, large flower with leaves that are red in spring and turn green when the temps get hot. 'Norah Leigh' has fragrant white flowers with pink eyes, but the prettiest feature of this variety is the green-and-white variegated leaves. Mix this one with other phlox varieties for the contrasting foliage.

Pincushion Flower

Scabiosa caucasica 'Fama'

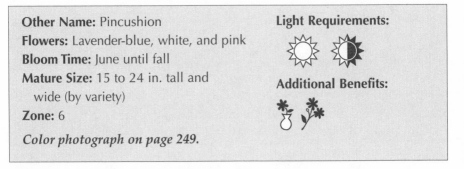

Other Name: Pincushion
Flowers: Lavender-blue, white, and pink
Bloom Time: June until fall
Mature Size: 15 to 24 in. tall and
wide (by variety)
Zone: 6

Color photograph on page 249.

Light Requirements:

Additional Benefits:

I've sold a lot of pincushion but never planted any in my yard until this year. Wow, they are everything that's been said about them. These are trouble-free, easy-to-grow perennials all season long. The only work I had to do was remove spent flowers and water them occasionally during dry weather. No big deal! And did they ever bloom, almost as much as some annuals. 'Fama' has larger flowers than other pincushion varieties. The flowers on 'Fama' are about 3 inches across, a silvery white with just a touch of violet in the center. The centers of all *Scabiosa* have little stems, giving them the appearance of a pincushion, hence the common name. These flowers are made up of many lavender-blue fine petals. Each flower is borne at the top of a tall leafless stem that can grow 15 to 18 inches taller than the leaves. Each plant can have as many as twenty-five of these stems and flowers at one time. 'Fama' and other pincushion varieties grow best in loose, loamy soil. They will tolerate clay soil as long as it's not gumbo clay and the soil drains well.

WHEN TO PLANT

You can divide existing pincushion flowers in early spring when the new growth starts. Transplant clumps that are at least 6 inches in diameter; replant at the same depth they were growing previously. Plant store-bought plants in spring through summer. These plants are mostly available in quart-size and 1-gallon containers. Buy and plant anytime the plants are available.

WHERE TO PLANT

Pincushion flower is easy to grow in any loose garden soil with some fertilizer added. It prefers alkaline soil, so it's perfect for most

Kentucky soil. It blooms best in full sun but will give good bloom production in just a half-day of sun.

How to Plant

Dig and transplant pincushion flower in early spring as the new growth starts to appear. With potted plants of all sizes, dig a hole as deep as the soil clump. Loosen any wrapped roots and place in a hole twice as wide as the soil clump. Backfill, and water-in well to settle the soil.

Care and Maintenance

Little has to be done to keep pincushion flower happy. Cut off spent flowers as they appear. Water during hot, dry periods. There are no bugs or diseases that bother this perennial.

Additional Information

'Fama' looks great in a sunny bed or as a border plant of at least three plants or more. 'Fama' did beautifully in my landscape and it will in yours. Plant this perennial in flower beds of other pastel blooming flowers, or use it as a border plant surrounded with other flowers blooming pink, white, or blue. It is a perennial that blooms like an annual.

Additional Species, Cultivars, or Varieties

'Butterfly Blue' has lilac-blue flowers growing on compact 15- to 18-inch plants. 'Pink Mist' has large orchid-pink 2 1/2-inch-wide flowers on a plant that grows 15 inches tall and blooms until fall. 'Butterfly Blue' has smaller 1 1/2-inch-wide flowers that provide lots of bloom until fall.

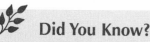

Did You Know?

Pincushion flower, including 'Fama', makes a great cut flower to place in a vase. Cut the flower stems when the flowers are about half open. The cut flowers will last for weeks.

Shasta Daisy

Leucanthemum × superbum

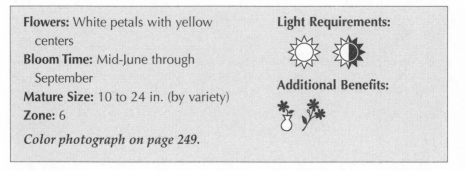

Flowers: White petals with yellow centers

Bloom Time: Mid-June through September

Mature Size: 10 to 24 in. (by variety)

Zone: 6

Color photograph on page 249.

Light Requirements:

Additional Benefits:

Next time you are in the greeting card department, check out the number of friendship cards that have daisies on them. They even decide if she loves you or loves you not. These perennials will bloom and bloom all summer if you deadhead the spent flowers. There are many varieties to choose from. The taller-growing Shasta daisies make for great cutting flowers. All bloom from mid-June through September. Shastas grow best in full sun, although they will grow well in a half-day of sun. Shasta daisy makes a beautiful show in its own bed or when planted with other perennials such as delphiniums, lupines, hardy lilies, and coneflower. This variety of perennial is very easy to grow. They are very drought tolerant but would appreciate a drink of water during hot, dry weather. Plant some and I'll bet she loves you.

WHEN TO PLANT

Plant nursery-grown plants growing in 3- to 4-inch pots or 1-gallon containers in the spring and summer. The smaller sizes will be more plentiful to choose from in April and May. One-gallon and even 2-gallon plants will be available all summer long at area nursery stores. Plant large ones anytime the ground is not frozen.

WHERE TO PLANT

Plant Shasta daisy in good to average garden soil. Make sure your planting location has good drainage. Shastas prefer full sun, but you will get almost as much bloom from plants getting a half-day of sun.

HOW TO PLANT

Transplant existing daisies in the spring as the new growth starts to appear; dig and transplant clumps at least 6 inches in diameter.

Replant at the same depth they were growing. When planting new Shastas from your nursery, dig a hole as deep and twice as wide as the soil clump in pre-loosened soil in your garden. Loosen any roots that are wrapped around the soil clump. Plant, backfill, and water-in well to settle the soil.

CARE AND MAINTENANCE

Fertilize your Shasta daisies with a balanced plant food, following the directions on the container. For larger-growing varieties, cut back all the stems halfway after initial bloom. This will make for shorter and fuller plants that bloom again. If your daisies get a few sucking aphids on them, just use a strong water spray from your hose to remove them. Do water Shasta daisies during hot, dry weather. Don't keep them wet—let them dry out between waterings.

ADDITIONAL INFORMATION

Shasta daisies continue to grow very strong when they are divided every three years. Dig up the clump when the foliage first comes out of the ground in the spring. Discard the center of the clump and replant the younger, outer shoots. The soil moisture you have will dictate the amount of bloom you will enjoy. Remember: moist, not wet.

ADDITIONAL SPECIES, CULTIVARS, OR VARIETIES

'Aglaya' blooms white with a yellow center and grows to a height of 24 inches. It has double, full, 5-inch-diameter blooms. 'Alaska' has white 4-inch-diameter flowers with yellow centers on plants that grow to 24 inches tall. 'Snow Lady' has white flowers with bright-yellow centers. It grows 10 to 12 inches tall and 12 to 18 inches wide; it's a great border plant.

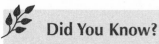

Did You Know?

Shasta daisies make great cut flowers placed in a vase all by themselves, or use in a vase mixed with other cut perennials. Cut the flower stems before the flower is more than half open.

Silver Mound

Artemisia spp.

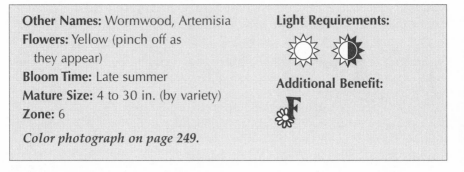

Other Names: Wormwood, Artemisia

Flowers: Yellow (pinch off as they appear)

Bloom Time: Late summer

Mature Size: 4 to 30 in. (by variety)

Zone: 6

Color photograph on page 249.

Light Requirements:

Additional Benefit:

The perennial silver mound is commonly confused with the annual dusty miller, as both have gorgeous silvery foliage that is soft and feathery. The height of silver mound varies according to the variety. 'Silver Bronze' grows 4 to 6 inches tall; true silver mound, *Artemisia schmidtiana*, grows to 15 inches tall; and 'Powis Castle' grows 2 to 3 feet tall. Each of these varieties has its place in the landscape. They all work well in borders, in containers, or mixed in with other perennials for that great splash of silver color. Artemisias are very low-maintenance plants. They are drought tolerant and do not like fertilizer. They grow best in average to poor soil as long as the drainage is good, and also grow best in full sun, although they will tolerate a half-day of shade. They are not known for bloom color; they do produce small yellow flowers in late summer that, like those of the annual coleus, should be picked off. The silver foliage is not only gorgeous but very aromatic as well, and is known to be somewhat medicinal.

WHEN TO PLANT

Divide and transplant existing artemisia in early spring as new growth appears out of the soil. Plant nursery-grown plants in 3- and 4-inch pots in the spring. One-gallon containers will be available from May through summer for your planting pleasure.

WHERE TO PLANT

Artemisia requires at least a half-day to a full day of sun. It will grow in average to poor soil as long as there's good drainage. It grows well when planted as a border plant by itself or in mixed flower beds where the silver foliage will highlight other plantings.

How to Plant

Place your transplanted artemisia in its new home no deeper than it was originally planted, using clumps at least 6 inches in diameter. Plant newly purchased plants in pre-loosened soil. Loosen any wrapped roots and dig a hole as deep and twice as wide as the soil clump. Backfill, and water-in well to settle in the soil.

Care and Maintenance

If your plants start to die out in the center, divide and replant the good parts on 18-inch centers. Be sure to water transplants and newly purchased plants when dry for the first month after planting. After that, they can pretty well "wing it" on their own. Keep any blooms pinched off. Do not fertilize silver mound or keep the plants too wet.

Additional Information

The silver-gray foliage of silver mound is great for separating the green leaves of other perennials. It also highlights and brings out the bloom color of flowering annuals and perennials. Plant silver mound in rock gardens, in borders, or mixed in with other plants.

Additional Species, Cultivars, or Varieties

'Silver Brocade' grows 4 to 6 inches tall and has silver-gray foliage that's deeply divided; it's great for a border planting. 'Powis Castle' grows 24 to 36 inches tall and wide; its silver-gray foliage blends in well with other perennials in the same bed. 'Silver Mound' grows 12 to 15 inches tall and has silvery, fernlike leaves. It does not do as well as 'Silver Brocade' in lots of hot sun—this is a good one for planting in areas receiving only-morning sun.

Did You Know?

Dried artemisia leaves when crushed give off an odor that repels silverfish and moths inside the home. Just place them in areas like a drawer or linen closet.

Stokes' Aster

Stokesia laevis

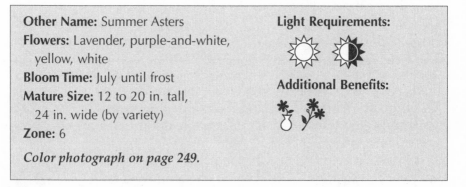

Other Name: Summer Asters
Flowers: Lavender, purple-and-white, yellow, white
Bloom Time: July until frost
Mature Size: 12 to 20 in. tall, 24 in. wide (by variety)
Zone: 6

Color photograph on page 249.

Light Requirements:

Additional Benefits:

How would you like a perennial that thrives in summer heat and is hardy to minus 20 degrees Fahrenheit? Welcome to *Stokesia*, commonly called Stokes' asters. This is a very low-maintenance perennial that blooms from July to frost. Varieties such as 'Blue Danube', 'Purple Palace', 'Mary Gregory', and 'Silver Moon' provide variously colored, 3-inch-diameter flowers. Stokes' asters grow in full sun to a half-day of shade, and they will grow in all types of Kentucky soil as long as the drainage is good. They grow 15 to 18 inches tall and spread, making 18-inch-wide clumps of beautiful summer color. The flowers themselves are unique, having slender, threadlike inner petals with outer petals that are much longer. Don't confuse Stokes' asters with fall asters, which are also listed in this chapter (page 174). Fall asters bloom in the fall and resemble daisies. Stokes' asters bloom from summer until frost. The blooms have to be seen to be appreciated. To me, they're too pretty to describe. Check out their picture and you'll understand.

WHEN TO PLANT

Transplant existing *Stokesia* in the spring as the new growth starts to appear. You can make divisions as small as 3 to 4 inches, and replant them on 15- to 18-inch centers. Plant nursery-grown plants in the spring. Larger-growing Stokes' asters will be available in bloom in 1-gallon containers in mid- to late July; plant these anytime they're available.

WHERE TO PLANT

Plant in any type of Kentucky soil as long as the drainage is good; this is especially important in the winter so crown rot will be avoided. Stokes' asters will grow in full sun to areas receiving only four to five hours of sun. They look great when massed in a bed by themselves or in a mixed bed with other summer bloomers. They also make a great border plant.

How to Plant

Plant existing transplants as deep as they were growing in their last home. For new installs, pre-loosen your existing soil to a depth of 6 to 8 inches. Dig a hole as deep and twice as wide as the soil clump. Loosen any roots that are wrapped around the soil clump, backfill, and water-in well to settle the soil.

Care and Maintenance

As far as bugs and diseases go, there's no problem here. Fertilize with a balanced fertilizer in the spring, following the instructions on the container. Once a week, deadhead the spent flowers to keep the flowers coming on until frost. Give Stokes' asters some water during hot, dry weather.

Additional Information

These plants have incredible flowers, but don't sell the foliage short: Stokes' asters have shiny, narrow leaves. The tops of the stems bear several flowers that open at different time intervals, extending the bloom season until frost, especially when you cut away the spent flowers. *Stokesia* makes an excellent cut flower that has a long lifespan in a vase. In fact, the flowers are among the best for bringing in the house and arranging in a vase all by themselves. As for mixing in the landscape, plant *Stokesia* in combination with pincushion flower, moonbeam coreopsis, baby's breath, and fall asters.

Additional Species, Cultivars, or Varieties

'Blue Danube' grows 12 to 18 inches tall and up to 24 inches wide; its lavender-blue flowers bloom from July until frost. 'Purple Palace' has a bicolor bloom with white inner petals and violet-blue outer petals; it grows up to 18 inches tall. 'Mary Gregory' has yellow flowers on plants that grow to 18 inches tall. 'Silver Moon' has large 4-inch-wide white flowers on plants that grow to 18 inches tall.

Veronica

Veronica spicata

Other Name: Speedwell
Flowers: Blue, pink, or white
Bloom Time: June until September
   (by variety)
Mature Size: 15 to 24 in. tall,
   18 to 24 in. wide (by variety)
Zone: 6

Color photograph on page 249.

Light Requirements:

Additional Benefits:

Veronica is commonly called speedwell. Plant this one and you will see in one season why it was chosen the Perennial Plant Association's plant of the year for 1993. The variety they chose was 'Sunny Border Blue', and it truly deserved the prestigious award. It combines the natural spirit of all veronica varieties with flowers that appear on 18-inch-tall plants that spread to an average of 24 inches across; its flower spikes produce loads of deep-violet blooms in late June. The blooms of all varieties of *spicata* are 4 to 5 inches long. Plant veronica in full sun to partial sun, at least five to six hours. It will tolerate all types of soil as long as the drainage is good. It's a long-lasting perennial that only needs to be divided every five years. This is an excellent plant to use in borders or in mass plantings in landscape beds or on a hillside. *Veronica spicata* is very drought tolerant and rated low-maintenance.

WHEN TO PLANT

Transplant existing veronica in the spring as the new growth starts to grow from the soil. Plant store-bought plants anytime they're available. The best selection of 3- and 4-inch potted plants will be in April and May, with larger 6-inch and 1-gallon sizes available in May through July.

WHERE TO PLANT

Veronica likes full sun but will grow and flower in areas receiving only five to six hours. Less sun will produce fewer blooms, but they will still be very colorful. Veronica will grow in any kind of soil as long as there is good drainage year-round.

How to Plant

With transplants, replant at the same depth they were growing in their previous home. When planting new, loosen the existing soil down to 6 to 8 inches. Dig a hole as deep and twice as wide as the soil clump. Loosen any wrapped roots growing around the outside of the soil clump, backfill, and water-in well to settle the soil.

Care and Maintenance

Veronica is a low-maintenance plant, and there are no bugs or diseases that bother it. Fertilize with a balanced fertilizer just once in the spring, following the instructions on the container. Water first-year installed plants when they become dry. After that, veronica and Mother Nature will work out their own watering schedule. You do need to divide veronica every five years—do it in early spring as it starts to grow.

Additional Information

A solid border of veronica is absolutely gorgeous. Veronicas also complement other perennials such as moonbeam coreopsis, white coneflower, yarrow, and dwarf yellow daylilies. The flowers make great cutting flowers and are easy to air-dry for use in dried arrangements.

Additional Species, Cultivars, or Varieties

'Sunny Border Blue' has deep purple-blue flowers on 4- to 5-inch spikes at the end of 18-inch stems. The plants average 18 to 24 inches tall and wide, and the flowers do not need staking. There's great-looking foliage, too, on this 1993 prize winner. It blooms in late June until September; remove spent flowers to encourage more bloom. 'Red Fox' is not a true red but a deep rosy pink. It has 4- to 5-inch spikes on the ends of 15-inch stems and dark-green leaves (the plants grow 15 inches tall and wide). It grows best in full sun and blooms from late June to early August. Cut off spent flowers to encourage more bloom. 'Icicle' has white flowers on 4-inch flower spikes at the ends of 15- to 18-inch stems. The plants grow 18 inches tall and wide. Remove spent flowers to encourage more bloom. This veronica will do well with just five hours of sun.

Virginia Bluebells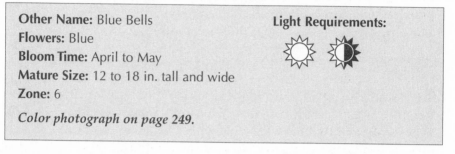

Mertensia virginica

Other Name: Blue Bells **Flowers:** Blue **Bloom Time:** April to May **Mature Size:** 12 to 18 in. tall and wide **Zone:** 6 *Color photograph on page 249.*	**Light Requirements:**

When we think of flowering plants that welcome us to spring, we usually think of spring-flowering bulbs like crocus, hyacinths, early tulips, and daffodils. Well, Virginia bluebells do a colorful job of saying "Welcome to spring," and they do it in partial shade. They begin to appear in April with very attractive gray-blue leaves. Soon after, pinkish-lavender bloom buds appear that then open up to a true-blue flower color. Bluebells average 18 inches in height, and they continue to spread in width. They prefer moist, loamy soil to clay. They do not like to be exposed to hot, late-spring sun; in fact, the entire plant disappears, going dormant in mid- to late June. Bluebells reseed themselves, slowly filling in an entire shady area in a controlled way.

WHEN TO PLANT

Transplant existing bluebells in the spring after they finish blooming; take clumps that are at least 4 to 5 inches in diameter. Install new plants from your garden center in late March to mid-April so you can enjoy their bloom in your landscape right away.

WHERE TO PLANT

Plant bluebells in natural or tree shade—they can tolerate morning sun, but absolutely no hot afternoon sun. Plant them in good, loose soil that stays relatively moist but not wet. Bluebells want to be planted in soil with good drainage. Always surround bluebells with other shade-loving plants that will fill in for the bluebells when they disappear in the summer.

HOW TO PLANT

Replant existing transplants at the same depth they were growing in their last home. For new plantings, loosen the existing soil 6 to

8 inches and dig a hole as deep and twice as wide as the soil clump. Loosen any wrapped roots, backfill, and water-in well to settle the soil. When planting in average soil, add pine bark chips to the existing soil to improve the overall soil condition; do this as you pre-loosen the soil.

CARE AND MAINTENANCE
There are no pests or diseases to bother your Virginia bluebells. Use a plant food for acid-loving plants, following the instructions on the container. During dry springs, add water occasionally to keep the soil moist. Divide your blue-bells in the spring right after they finish blooming.

ADDITIONAL INFORMATION
Use bluebells to underplant small shade-loving plants like 'P.J.M. Rhododendron', bayberry, and abelia. Plant Virginia bluebells with spring-flowering companion peren-nials such as columbine, bleeding heart, hostas, and hardy ferns. You can also plant annuals such as impatiens and caladiums—they will spread and fill in the voids of the bluebells when they go to bed in the summer.

ADDITIONAL SPECIES, CULTIVARS, OR VARIETIES
There are no others that are suitable for Kentucky.

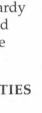

Did You Know?

First-year planted perennials should be mulched their first winter. Most homeowners make the mistake of mulching too soon. You see, the biggest risk to first-year plants is that they might not be fully established and could heave out of the ground with our up-and-down winter temperatures. Wait until the ground freezes and your perennials are firmly in the ground. Then mulch with straw, chopped leaves, or bark to keep the ground frozen and prevent the soil from heaving. This process is called winter mulching.

Whirling Butterflies

Guara lindheimeri

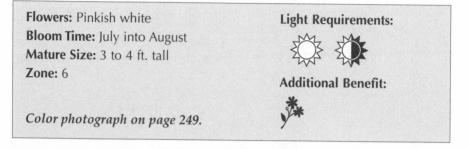

Flowers: Pinkish white
Bloom Time: July into August
Mature Size: 3 to 4 ft. tall
Zone: 6

Color photograph on page 249.

Light Requirements:

Additional Benefit:

I was introduced to this summer-blooming perennial two years ago. I had heard of it, but didn't connect its common name to its appearance. Then I saw it and said, "Wow, it *does* look like small butterflies on top of that plant." It has a long bloom period, about four to six weeks depending on temperature. It is very heat and humidity tolerant and will grow well as a sunny border plant without the need of a water hose. The flowers are pinkish white on a plant that grows 3 to 4 feet. Plant in groups on 3-foot centers. In the wind, it's a real enjoyment for kids of all ages. Keep whirling butterflies blooming longer by cutting off the spent flowers. It's no big deal . . . just do it every couple of weeks. Whirling butterflies is a great plant to use on sunny hillsides that are difficult to water; it will turn such a planting situation into a picture worth taking.

WHEN TO PLANT

Whirling butterflies is available in 3- and 4-inch pots and 1-gallon containers in spring and summer at your favorite plant store. If you are not sure about this one, wait and buy it in 1-gallon containers in July when it's in bloom. If you like its looks, as I do, plant it and enjoy.

WHERE TO PLANT

Plant the whirligigs in full sun to a half-day of sun. This perennial grows in all types of well-drained Kentucky soil. Plant where you can observe it from both outside and inside the house, in a solid bed, or mixed with other perennials.

HOW TO PLANT

Whirling butterflies is available in pots. Dig a hole as deep and twice as wide as the soil clump. Loosen any roots that are attached to the soil clump and plant. Backfill with the existing soil, and water-in well. Use a bark mulch to cover the soil to 2 inches, but don't let the mulch come in contact with the plant stems.

CARE AND MAINTENANCE
Whirling butterflies is free of disease and insects, and is also very drought tolerant. Fertilize when the plant first starts growing in the spring. Read the instructions and fertilize the proper way as directed on the container.

ADDITIONAL INFORMATION
Whirling butterflies is easy to grow. Deadhead the spent flowers as they appear. Plant in groups of at least five plants to get the full effect of this summer-blooming perennial. Whirling butterflies are short-lived, staying around only three to four years.

ADDITIONAL SPECIES, CULTIVARS, OR VARIETIES
There are none known.

Did You Know?
Whirling butterflies is going to be new to many of you. This is a summer-blooming perennial that provides unusual summer blooms on a fairly unknown plant. It's beautiful, and your kids or grandkids will think it is really neat.

Yarrow

Achillea spp.

Other Name: Milfoil
Flowers: Shades of yellow, white, red, pink, copper, and salmon
Bloom Time: June through August
Mature Size: 18 to 36 in. tall, up to 36 in. wide (by variety)
Zone: 6

Color photograph on page 249.

Light Requirements:

Additional Benefits:

This garden book is full of low-maintenance, easy-to-grow plants. Yarrow would certainly qualify for a spot in the top twenty-five. It requires average to poor soil as long as that soil is well drained. Yarrow has large 3- to 4-inch flat-headed flowers that come in many colors. Its height range is from 12 inches to 3 feet. Yarrow has green or grayish-green aromatic foliage that is attractive by itself when yarrow is in-between bloom. By deadheading the spent flowers as they appear, you can keep your yarrow blooming from June until September. The initial bloom in June will be the most plentiful. Cut flower stems back halfway when the flowers finish and your yarrow will continue blooming at a somewhat reduced rate. Yarrow blends in well with other summer-blooming perennials. Because it does best during hot, dry periods, plant in the same bed with your spring-flowering bulbs. Yarrow's foliage will hide the tulip leaves as they mature. It will grow in garden soil where many other perennials would fear to tread. Most yarrow plants spread 24 to 36 inches. A little yarrow goes a long way.

WHEN TO PLANT

Transplant existing yarrow plants in early spring as new growth first appears. Make each divided clump a minimum of 6 inches in diameter. Install nursery-bought plants growing in 3- and 4-inch pots in April and May. Plant 1-gallon potted yarrow anytime the ground is not frozen. Large potted yarrow is best available in late May, June, and July.

WHERE TO PLANT

Plant yarrow in half-day sun to full sun. It will tolerate any type of soil as long as there's good drainage. Don't use bad soil as an excuse not to plant this one.

HOW TO PLANT

Loosen the existing soil 6 to 8 inches deep. With existing transplants, plant no deeper than the yarrow was growing. With nursery-bought plants, dig a hole as deep and twice as wide as the soil clump. Loosen any wrapped roots. Backfill, and water-in well to settle the soil.

CARE AND MAINTENANCE

Remove spent flowers to keep your yarrow blooming all summer. Cut the stems back halfway when removing old flowers. Fertilize following the directions on the container. There are no bugs or diseases that give this plant any trouble. Water yarrow until it's established on newly installed plants in the spring. Now, put the hose away, because the yarrow is very heat and drought tolerant.

ADDITIONAL INFORMATION

Yarrow is excellent for using as cut flowers. Cut the flower stems when each flower cluster is no more than half open. You can also dry yarrow blooms for use in dried arrangements. Thin and divide yarrow every four to five years. Over time, you can create your own meadow of yarrow just from the divisions.

ADDITIONAL SPECIES, CULTIVARS, OR VARIETIES

'Appleblossom' has rosy-pink flowers on a plant growing to 24 inches. 'Red Beauty' has dark-red flowers and grows to 24 inches. 'Moonshine' has dull-yellow, early-blooming, silvery-green foliage that's fernlike. Early-blooming 'Coronation Gold' has golden-yellow flowers and grows to 36 inches. 'Anthea' has cherry-red flowers with gold centers. It is low-growing, to 18 inches, and its flowers fade to pink as they finish blooming. 'Summer Pastels' offers many colors and grows to 36 inches tall.

The gardener who

plans reaps the greatest

reward . . .

Ageratum
Ageratum houstonianum

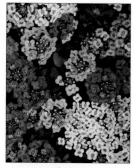

Alyssum
Lobularia maritima

Asparagus
Asparagus spp.

Blue Salvia
Salvia farinacea

Browallia
Browallia speciosa

Celosia
Celosia plumosa

Cobbitty Daisies
Argyranthemum frutescens

Coleus
Coleus × *hybridus*

Cosmos
Cosmos bipinnatus

Dianthus
Dianthus hybrids

Dusty Miller
Senecio cineraria

Flowering Tobacco
Nicotiana alata

241

Geranium
Pelargonium × hortorum

Globe Amaranth
Gomphrena globosa

Hypoestes
Hypoestes phyllostachya

Impatiens
Impatiens wallerana

Lobelia
Lobelia erinus

Marigold
Tagetes spp. and hybrids

Melampodium
Melampodium paludosum

Million Bells®
Calibrachoa hybrids

Nemesia
Nemesia cultivars

Ornamental Cabbage and Kale
Brassica oleracea

Pansy
Viola × wittrockiana

Pentas
Pentas lanceolata

Petunia
Petunia × hybrida

Portulaca
Portulaca grandiflora

Primrose
Primula × polyantha

Salvia
Salvia splendens

Scaevola 'New Wonder'
Scaevola aemula

Snapdragon
Antirrhinum majus

Spider Plant
Cleome hassleriana

Sunflower
Helianthus hybrids and cultivars

Torenia
Torenia fournieri

Verbena
Verbena × hybrida

Vinca
Catharanthus roseus

Wax-Leaf Begonia
Begonia semperflorens-cultorum

Zinnia
Zinnia elegans

Allium
Allium spp.

Bearded Iris
Iris germanica hybrids

Caladium
Caladium × hortulanum

Canna
Canna × generalis

Crocus
Crocus vernus

Crown Imperial
Fritillaria imperialis

Daffodil
Narcissus species and cultivars

Dahlia
Dahlia spp.

Gladiolus
Gladiolus × hortulanus

Grape Hyacinth
Muscari spp.

Hyacinth
Hyacinthus orientalis

Lily
Lilium spp.

Scilla
Scilla siberica

Snowdrops
Galanthus nivalis

Tuberous Begonia
Begonia × *tuberhybrida*

Tulip
Tulipa spp.

Winter Aconite
Eranthis hyemalis

Ajuga
Ajuga reptans

Chameleon Plant
Houttuynia cordata

Creeping Juniper
Juniperus spp.

Creeping Phlox
Phlox subulata

English Ivy
Hedera helix

Lily-of-the-Valley
Convallaria majalis

Lily Turf
Liriope muscari

Myrtle
Vinca minor

Pachysandra
Pachysandra terminalis

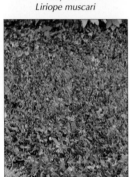

Wintercreeper
Euonymus fortunei 'Coloratus'

Blue Fescue
Festuca ovina 'Glauca'

Feather Reed Grass
Calamagrostis acutiflora 'Overdam'

Fountain Grass
Pennisetum alopecuroides 'Hameln'

Hardy Pampas Grass
Erianthus ravennae

Japanese Blood Grass
Imperata cylindrica var. *rubra*

Maiden Grass
Miscanthus sinensis 'Gracillimus'

Ribbon Grass
Phalaris arundinacea var. *picta*

Aster
Aster novae-angliae

Astilbe
Astilbe × arendsii

'Autumn Joy' Sedum
Sedum 'Autumn Joy'

Baby's Breath
Gypsophila paniculata 'Bristol Fairy'

Balloon Flower
Platycodon grandiflorus

Beebalm
Monarda didyma

Black-Eyed Susan
Rudbeckia fulgida var. *sullivantii* 'Goldsturm'

Blanket Flower
Gaillardia × grandiflora 'Goblin'

Bleeding Heart
Dicentra formosa 'Luxuriant'

Candytuft
Iberis sempervirens 'Snowflake'

Cardinal Flower
Lobelia cardinalis

Columbine
Aquilegia

Coneflower
Echinacea purpurea

Coral Bells
Heuchera 'Palace Purple'

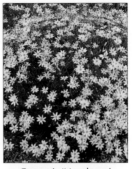

Coreopsis 'Moonbeam'
Coreopsis verticillata 'Moonbeam'

Daylily
Hemerocallis spp.

Forget-Me-Not
Myosotis scorpioides

Garden Mum
Chrysanthemum × *morifolium*

Gayfeather
Liatris spicata

Hibiscus
Hibiscus moscheutos

Hosta
Hosta spp.

Lamb's Ear
Stachys byzantina 'Silver Carpet'

Lavender, English
Lavandula angustifolia 'Hidcote'

Peony
Paeonia

Phlox, Tall
Phlox paniculata

Pincushion Flower
Scabiosa caucasica 'Fama'

Shasta Daisy
Leucanthemum × superbum

Silver Mound
Artemisia spp.

Stokes' Aster
Stokesia laevis

Veronica
Veronica spicata

Virginia Bluebells
Mertensia virginica

Whirling Butterflies
Guara lindheimeri

Yarrow
Achillea spp.

'Bonica' Meidiland™
Rosa Meidiland

'Chrysler Imperial'
Rosa 'Chrysler Imperial'

'Fame'
Rosa 'Fame'

'Golden Showers'
Rosa 'Golden Showers'

'Knockout'
Rosa 'Knockout'

'Lady Sunblaze'
Rosa 'Lady Sunblaze'

'Show Biz'
Rosa 'Show Biz'

'The Fairy'
Rosa 'The Fairy'

Abelia
Abelia × *grandiflora*

Azalea
Rhododendron spp.

Bayberry
Myrica pensylvanica

Blue Holly
Ilex × *meserveae*

Blue Mist Shrub
Caryopteris × *clandonensis*

Bottlebrush Buckeye
Aesculus parviflora

Butterfly Bush
Buddleia davidii

Crapemyrtle
Lagerstroemia indica

Crimson Pygmy Barberry
Berberis thunbergii var. *atropurpurea*

Dwarf Burning Bush
Euonymus alatus 'Compactus'

Dwarf Spirea
Spiraea spp.

Falsecypress
Chamaecyparis obtusa 'Nana Gracilis'

Forsythia
Forsythia × *intermedia*

Fothergilla
Fothergilla gardenii

Juniper
Juniperus spp.

Korean Boxwood
Buxus microphylla var. *koreana*

Korean Lilac
Syringa meyeri 'Palibin'

Nandina
Nandina domestica

Oakleaf Hydrangea
Hydrangea quercifolia

Scarlet Firethorn
Pyracantha coccinea

St. Johns Wort
Hypericum patulum 'Sungold'

Summersweet
Clethra alnifolia

Viburnum 'Alleghany'
Viburnum × rhytidophylloides

Virginia Sweetspire
Itea virginica 'Henry's Garnet'

Weigela 'Java Red'
Weigela florida

Yew, Spreading
Taxus spp.

Yew, Upright
Taxus cultivars

American Holly
Ilex opaca

American Yellowwood
Cladrastis kentukea

Bald Cypress
Taxodium distichum

Carolina Silver Bell
Halesia tetraptera

Common Thornless Honeylocust
Gleditsia triacanthos inermis

Dogwood
Cornus florida

Flowering Crabapple
Malus spp.

Hemlock
Tsuga canadensis

'Heritage' River Birch
Betula nigra 'Heritage'

Japanese Maple
Acer palmatum

Japanese Zelkova
Zelkova serrata

Kentucky Coffee Tree
Gymnocladus dioicus

Norway Spruce
Picea abies

Ornamental Pear
Pyrus calleryana

Redbud
Cercis canadensis

Red Maple
Acer rubrum

Red Oak
Quercus rubra

Serviceberry
Amelanchier arborea

Silver Linden
Tilia tomentosa

Sweetbay Magnolia
Magnolia virginiana

Sweetgum
Liquidambar styraciflua

Weeping Cherry
Prunus subhirtella 'Pendula'

Weeping Willow
Salix babylonica

White Ash
Fraxinus americana

White Fringetree
Chionanthus virginicus

White Pine
Pinus strobus

'Winter King' Hawthorn
Crataegus virdis 'Winter King'

Boston Ivy
Parthenocissus tricuspidata

Clematis
Clematis hybrids

Climbing Hydrangea
Hydrangea anomala ssp. *petiolaris*

Mandevilla
Mandevilla × amabilis

Moonflower
Ipomea alba

Morning Glory
Ipomoea purpurea

Silver Lace Vine
Polygonum aubertii

Trumpet Vine
Campsis radicans

Virginia Creeper
Parthenocissus quinquefolia

Wisteria
Wisteria floribunda

Kentucky
USDA HARDINESS ZONE MAP

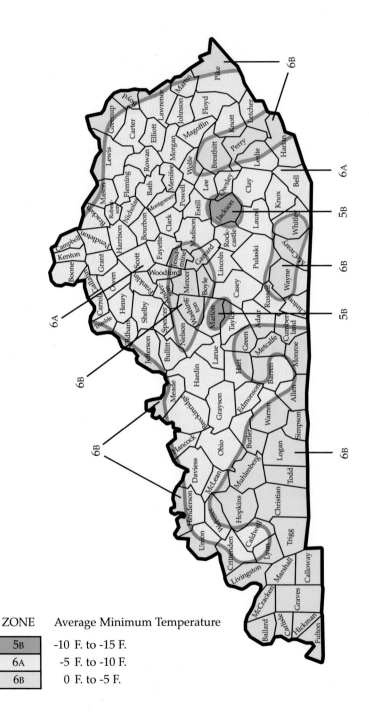

ZONE	Average Minimum Temperature
5B	-10 F. to -15 F.
6A	-5 F. to -10 F.
6B	0 F. to -5 F.

Gardening

is a journey, not a

destination . . .

CHAPTER SIX

Roses

OUR NATIONAL FLOWER, that's what it is, and it deserves to be—but the rose group has been a very challenging group of plants to grow successfully in Kentucky. Fortunately, it's getting a lot easier. Many, many new varieties have been produced over the last twenty years, especially in the last ten. For many years, hybrid teas, floribundas, grandifloras, and climbing roses have been available. Add to the original list of four Meidiland™ landscape roses, shrub roses of all colors and mini-flora, a cross between a floribunda and a miniature. I will list some of each in this chapter and explain their growing habits.

SUNSHINE

Yes, roses do best in full-day sun. If you don't have this type of exposure, morning sun is the better half to have. Morning sun dries the dew off the plants, and that's important in reducing diseases like blackspot and mildew.

LOTS OF ROOM

Roses like to be planted in an open area where they get good air movement among the individual plants. Plant your roses 5 feet apart to give each plant good growing and wind space.

A LITTLE T.L.C.

Many of the newer rose varieties are more disease- and insect-tolerant, but certain groups, especially hybrid teas and grandifloras, need a little assistance. There are spray products that can be used to protect roses from disease and insect attack.

SOIL FOR ROSES

Roses in general would love good, loamy soil. But roses will tolerate clay soil as long as the soil drains well.

How Many Rose Varieties Are There?

Thousands . . . more than we could count. Most garden centers and nursery stores try to sell roses that come from some of the best growers, nurseries like Conard-Pyle's Star Roses, Weeks, and Jackson and Perkins. Buying roses grown at these great nurseries gives you greater assurance that you are buying high-quality plants representing high-quality varieties.

How to Buy a Rose

Roses are available three different ways: 1) Bare-root plants have roots packed in moist packing material and wrapped in a plastic or foil-type bag. 2) "Boxed" potted roses are available in early spring. These are basically bare-root plants packed in a peat-type material. We hope our retail nurseries will quit handling these types—they have a short shelf life because the roots are difficult to water. My advice when you select this type is "Buyer Beware." 3) The best way to buy a rosebush is to buy one potted in a soil medium in which the roots are actually growing. These roses are usually potted during the winter and are well established by the time they're available for you to buy. They'll cost more, but the value is much greater.

Remember, as is true of any living plant that you want to purchase, it won't get any better-looking during the ride home. Always buy healthy, vigorous-growing plants, including roses.

How Will My Rose Stay Warm for the Winter?

Many roses need to be protected from cold Kentucky winters. The base of each plant known as the bud union is the most vulnerable part. Leave the rose canes long, at least 3 feet tall. Do not prune climbers at all. Buy or make rose collars to encircle the base of each plant; you can use any material that will hold together for the winter. Fill the collar with well-draining material like pine bark chips or oak leaves.

'Bonica' Meidiland™

Rosa Meidiland

Flowers: Large, 3-in. pastel-pink double flowers
Bloom Time: May until frost
Height × Width: 3 to 5 ft. by 4 to 5 ft.
Type: Hedge rose
Zone: 6

Color photograph on page 249.

Light Requirements:

Additional Benefits:

'Bonica' is just one of many great new hedge roses. The Meidiland™ roses offer a series of rose plants that are low-maintenance, pest-resistant, and disease-tolerant. 'Bonica', as well as other Meidiland varieties, offers care-free solutions for the landscapes of the millennium. 'Bonica' has pastel-pink flowers that are 3 inches in diameter and fully double. You will enjoy those pink flowers in late spring, all summer, and fall until the cold weather settles in. 'Bonica' grows up to 4^1/$_2$ to 5 feet wide. You can trim this rose to keep it contained to your growing space. All Meidiland roses want a sunny location, or at least a half-day of full morning sun. These plants have self-cleaning flowers all season. The rose hips (seedheads) form in the fall and give you late-fall and winter color because they remain on the plant all winter long.

WHEN TO PLANT
'Bonica' Meidiland roses are available potted in the spring; they should be available from early May through June. You can plant 'Bonica' anytime the ground is not frozen, but the best selection will be in the spring and early summer.

WHERE TO PLANT
Plant these roses in a sunny location. All roses want to be planted in well-drained soil. 'Bonica', like other Meidiland varieties, is very winter hardy. Plant enough for a hedge that will literally stop a tennis ball from going through after it is well established. Plant 'Bonica' in a location that you can see from both outdoors and indoors.

HOW TO PLANT
Select your sunny location. Dig a hole as deep as the soil clump and twice as wide. Use existing soil and break up all soil clumps

to the size of golf balls. Backfill and water-in to settle the soil.

CARE AND MAINTENANCE

'Bonica' and other Meidilands are care-free. They are also resistant to disease and insects. They don't even need much winterizing because they survive very cold temperatures. Prune them back in the spring if you want to maintain a certain growing height. If they end the year at 4 feet high and that's where you want them to remain, prune them back to 2 feet in early spring as they start to leaf out.

LANDSCAPE MERIT

'Bonica' makes a a tight, blooming hedge that produces lots of yard color. This rose is low-maintenance and even provides beautiful winter color with its red rose hips.

ADDITIONAL INFORMATION

There have been other varieties of shrub roses in the past, but most of them have been disappointing. Some didn't bloom like the picture, while others had lots of disease problems. Stick with 'Bonica' or other Meidilands, and you will be very pleased.

ADDITIONAL SPECIES, CULTIVARS, OR VARIETIES

'Cherry' Meidiland has bright, cherry-red, 2 1/2-inch flowers; the plant itself grows 3 to 4 feet and blooms continuously. 'Coral' Meidiland has deep-coral 2 1/2 inch-wide flowers with white centers; it grows 4 feet high by 3 feet wide. 'Ice' Meidiland is a low-growing ground cover type with white blooms that is great for slopes and banks. 'Red' Meidiland produces red flowers with white centers; it is also a great, low ground cover, growing only to 2 1/2 feet high.

 Did You Know?

Meidiland roses are not only great hedge roses, but some varieties make great, low-maintenance ground covers. Think of these when you are trying to landscape a sunny hillside that can't be mowed.

'Chrysler Imperial'

Rosa 'Chrysler Imperial'

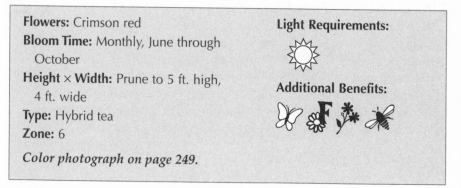

Flowers: Crimson red

Bloom Time: Monthly, June through October

Height × Width: Prune to 5 ft. high, 4 ft. wide

Type: Hybrid tea

Zone: 6

Color photograph on page 249.

Light Requirements:

Additional Benefits:

'Chrysler Imperial' is an old-time favorite. A prizewinner back in 1953, it remains one of the most popular hybrid tea roses. 'Chrysler Imperial' is richly fragrant and produces an abundance of full flowers that are a dark-crimson red. The flowers average 4 inches in diameter when in full bloom. This variety is excellent for cutting and putting in a bud vase as a flower starts to open. Hybrid teas are sometimes called "monthly roses" because it takes a new stem on a hybrid tea approximately one month to grow and produce a new flower. Hybrid teas are all single-stem bloomers—one flower to each stem. To keep your hybrids producing large blooms every month, cut back each single stem to the second or third set of leaf stems that are growing away from the center of the plant. This will encourage the next month's bloom and stem to be about the same size as the previous month's.

WHEN TO PLANT

It is best to buy roses already growing in their own pots. The best selection will be from May 1 through June 30. You can plant potted roses anytime the ground is not frozen and the plants are available.

WHERE TO PLANT

Plant hybrid tea roses in full sun. Select a planting site that's large enough to hold the number of rose plants you intend to plant. Remember, hybrid teas should be planted 5 feet apart for good air circulation. Don't cheat, or you will pay a high-maintenance price. If you can give your hybrids only a half-day of sun, make it morning sun.

How to Plant

Hybrid tea roses are as easy to plant as any tree or shrub. Make sure your planting site is well drained, then dig a hole as deep as the soil clump and twice as wide. Backfill, using the existing soil that you've chopped up to the size of golf balls. Water-in well to settle the soil.

Care and Maintenance

All hybrid teas need a maintenance schedule. Roses are heavy feeders, which means that you feed them as often as the package of rose food directs. In Kentucky, stop feeding your roses in mid-September. There are several companies that combine a systemic insecticide with rose food. Follow the instructions and pour it on the soil around each individual plant. Blackspot can be a problem sometimes, especially if you haven't planted your roses in a rose-friendly location. There are fungicides that you can apply on a weekly basis to combat this leaf disease. Manually remove any infected leaves.

Landscape Merit

'Chrysler Imperial' has great flower color and fragrance. Nothing makes a homeowner feel more accomplished than growing hybrid tea roses successfully.

Additional Information

Do not cut off any more rose blossoms after mid-September. Let the flowers finish on the plant and go to seed (called rose hips). When the rose hips form, they send a signal to the roots to shut down for the season. Hybrid teas get winter damage most often when they are allowed to continue active growth, causing them to remain soft when the real cold weather sets in.

Additional Species, Cultivars, or Varieties

'Brandy' has dark-green foliage and golden-bronze buds that open to fragrant apricot blooms. 'Friendship' is a great cutting rose with flowers that range in color from rich pink to salmon and coral. 'Honor' has white flowers on a plant that's handsome and winter hardy and grows rather tall. 'Miss All-American Beauty' has extra-large flowers that are pink and fragrant.

'Fame'

Rosa 'Fame'

Flowers: Large, 4-in., deep-pink blooms
Bloom Time: Memorial Day through
  the fall
Height × Width: 4 to 6 ft. by 3 to 4 ft.
  (by variety)
Type: Grandiflora
Zone: 6

Color photograph on page 249.

Light Requirements:

Additional Benefits:

'Fame'—a great name for a great rose. This 1998 All-America Rose Selection earned the award for several reasons. 'Fame' has large, glossy green leaves; its deep-pink blooms measure 4½ inches across and have a nice fragrance. Grandifloras as a group have large blooms, just like the hybrid teas. But they differ from hybrid teas in their bloom stems, which have two or three blooms on a long stem, and overall height, which averages 5 to 6 feet. Because of the extra height, they should always be planted to the back of a rose bed in which you're mixing grandifloras with hybrid teas and floribundas. When it comes to hardiness, grandifloras are the same as hybrid teas. There are many varieties of grandifloras. Don't be afraid to use them in any sunny landscape situation.

WHEN TO PLANT

It is best to buy roses already growing in their own pots. The best selection will be from May 1 through June 30. You can plant potted roses anytime the ground is not frozen and the plants are available.

WHERE TO PLANT

Plant grandiflora roses in full sun. Select a planting site that's large enough to hold the number of roses you intend to plant. Grandifloras should be planted 5 feet apart for good air circulation. Don't cheat, or you will pay a high-maintenance price. If you can give your grandifloras only a half-day of sun, make it morning sun.

How to Plant

Potted grandiflora roses are as easy to plant as any tree or shrub. Make sure your planting site is well drained, then dig a hole as deep as the soil clump and twice as wide. Backfill, using the existing soil that you've chopped up to the size of golf balls. Water-in well to settle the soil.

Care and Maintenance

All grandifloras need a maintenance schedule. Roses are heavy feeders, which means that you feed your monthly roses as often as the package of rose food directs. In Kentucky, stop feeding your roses in mid-September. There are several companies that combine a systemic insecticide with rose food. It's easy to apply. Just follow the instructions, and pour it on the soil around each individual plant. Blackspot leaf disease can be a problem sometimes, especially if you haven't planted your roses in a rose-friendly location. There are fungicides available to spray on the rose leaves and remove any yellow infected leaves from the plant.

Landscape Merit

The tall-growing 'Fame' grandiflora, as well as other grandifloras, makes an excellent color show in the landscape. Because of their size, they have many landscape uses. If you plant this rose, one thing is for sure: you will get plenty of compliments from neighbors.

Additional Information

Grandiflora roses grow tall enough to use as a screen-type hedge to hide a bad, low view or to keep people and objects in. Each plant can grow to 6 feet high and up to 4 to 5 feet wide.

Additional Species, Cultivars, or Varieties

'Gypsy Carnival' has a beautiful combination of large, orange-red to yellow blooms that give lots of color. 'Love's Promise' is a fragrant, red-blooming grandiflora with cup-like flowers and dense, glossy green leaves. 'Sonia' has peach-pink, fragrant large flowers and glossy green leaves that are great for cutting.

'Golden Showers'

Rosa 'Golden Showers'

Flowers: Large, bright-yellow
double flowers
Bloom Time: From late May
until fall
Height × Width: 7 to 8 ft. by 5 ft.
Type: Climbing rose
Zone: 6

Color photograph on page 249.

Light Requirements:

Additional Benefits:

'Golden Showers', an older rose variety that's making an all-new showing for the millennium, was recognized back in 1956 as the climber of the year by the All-America Rose Selection (AARS) committee. 'Golden Showers' produces medium to large double-flowering blossoms that have a honey-scented aroma. When you hear the name "climbing rose," most of you think of climbers that give lots of color around Memorial Day, but none after that. Not so with 'Golden Showers'— it blooms from spring until fall. 'Golden Showers' also has beautiful, glossy green leaves that add to its overall beauty. This variety is quite resistant to insects and disease, just like other varieties that I'll list later. All climbing roses want at least a half-day of sun, preferably in the morning, but full sun is best. Climbing roses need support to grow on, such as a wooden fence, an arbor, or a trellis. Climbing roses bloom on second-year wood. That is why you do little to no pruning of them in the fall or early spring. Climbers bloom best on canes growing horizontally or downward. As your climber reaches the top of its support, train it back down toward the ground or weave it left to right, right to left.

When to Plant

As I do with all roses, I recommend you buy only potted climbing roses—but I don't mean those roses that have their roots covered in a paper box with a picture on it. The roots of real potted roses are growing in a soil medium. The best selection of all climbing roses will be from May 1 through June 30.

WHERE TO PLANT

Climbing roses want full-day sun—but they will grow and bloom as long as they have full-morning sun. Remember, climbing roses need the support of a structure to grow on.

HOW TO PLANT

Potted climbing roses are easy to plant. Before planting your climber, have its support in place. Next, dig a hole as deep and twice as wide as the soil clump. Make sure your planting site has good drainage. Backfill with existing soil, breaking up all soil particles to the size of golf balls. Water-in well to settle the soil.

CARE AND MAINTENANCE

'Golden Showers' and other climbing roses require a lot less care than hybrid teas and grandifloras. As long as they get good sun and timely rose food, your climber will be fairly bug- and disease-free.

LANDSCAPE MERIT

'Golden Showers' is a continuously blooming climber with beautiful foliage color.

ADDITIONAL INFORMATION

'Golden Showers' and other climbers do not self-cling. You can weave the canes as they grow through wooden lattice or take jute twine and loosely tie those canes to their support. Remember that climbers bloom better on canes that are growing horizontally or downward. Climbing roses can be great as a screen planted on sunny property lines. Their growth can be maintained on ten-gauge galvanized wire supported with 4-by-4 pressure-treated posts. Use three rows of wire, 2 feet apart in height.

ADDITIONAL SPECIES, CULTIVARS, OR VARIETIES

'Don Juan' has deep crimson red, fragrant flowers that repeat their bloom. 'New Dawn' produces showy, pale-pink flowers on fast-growing canes that repeat-bloom all season. 'White Dawn', a cousin of 'New Dawn', gives beautiful white repeat flowers on a fast-growing vine.

'Knockout'

Rosa 'Knockout'

Flowers: Cherry red	**Light Requirements:**
Bloom Time: Late spring through late fall	
Height × Width: 3 ft. by 3 ft.	
Type: Deciduous	**Added Benefits:**
Zone: 6	
Color photograph on page 250.	

'Knockout' is a new introduction from Star Roses that has been named a winner for 2000 by the All-America Rose Selection (AARS) committee. Rosarians have described this plant as one of the best flowering shrub roses to hit the market. 'Knockout' has deep, almost fluorescent, cherry red blossoms and dark moss-green leaves. Talk about low maintenance, 'Knockout' is drought tolerant, surviving and even thriving during any summer drought. You will also be hard-pressed to find a speck of blackspot on this vigorously growing plant. Nothing keeps 'Knockout' from blooming. You can expect lots of 3½-inch blooms every day throughout the summer for a show of color well into late fall and early winter. Plant 'Knockout' with other shrub roses, or plant a bed of the plants by themselves.

WHEN TO PLANT

Buy shrub roses that are already growing in a soil mix in their own pots. Don't bother with any roses that aren't sold that way. Plant shrub roses anytime the ground is not frozen.

WHERE TO PLANT

Plant 'Knockout' and other shrub roses where they can receive lots of sun, at least a half-day. Make sure the soil drains well. Plant 'Knockout' in an area where you can see and enjoy the blooms whether you are outside in the yard or inside the house on rainy days.

HOW TO PLANT

Buy shrub roses growing in their own pots. Stay away from 'Knockouts' that are sold bare root or in cardboard boxes in early April. Dig a planting hole as deep as the pot and twice as wide.

Chop up the soil to the size of golf balls, backfill, and water-in well to settle the soil.

CARE AND MAINTENANCE

'Knockout' and other shrub roses have low-maintenance needs. They can have a few bugs or a little blackspot during the rainy seasons or as a result of poor planting sites. But don't let either problem intimidate you. This plant may need to be fertilized occasionally with rose food. 'Knockout' is self-cleaning.

LANDSCAPE MERIT

One of the most carefree varieties of roses you can grow, 'Knockout' gives high color through several late-fall frosts.

ADDITIONAL INFORMATION

'Knockout' and other shrub roses have small individual flowers, 1 to 3 1/2 inches in diameter by variety, but each plant can have as many as five hundred blooms at one time. Bigger is not always better! This rose will give you great yard color and a lot of it, too.

ADDITIONAL SPECIES, CULTIVARS, OR VARIETIES

'Bonica', a 1987 AARS winner, presents you with plenty of 2-inch shell-pink flowers. 'Carefree Beauty' is another great pink variety that constantly blooms on a disease-resistant plant. 'Topaz Jewel' features bright-yellow single-type flowers and a weeping growth habit. 'Sea Foam' is known for upright, white flowers; it is a very winter-hardy plant with a mild flower fragrance. 'The Fairy' is a pink-flowering, winter-hardy shrub rose that produces thousands of 1-inch blooms.

Did You Know?

All-America Rose Selection (AARS) is an organization of rose producers who evaluate new rose varieties across the United States. This two-year process of evaluation in all climatic conditions brings you only the top performers.

'Lady Sunblaze'

Rosa 'Lady Sunblaze'

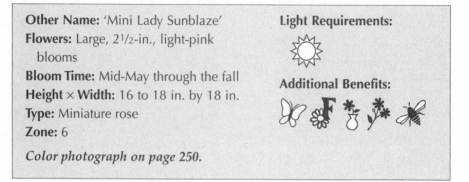

Other Name: 'Mini Lady Sunblaze'

Flowers: Large, 2½-in., light-pink blooms

Bloom Time: Mid-May through the fall

Height × Width: 16 to 18 in. by 18 in.

Type: Miniature rose

Zone: 6

Color photograph on page 250.

Light Requirements:

Additional Benefits:

The 'Sunblaze' group of miniature roses are great small-growing roses that are extremely hardy, easy to grow, and give you great color all summer long. These are compact-growing plants that produce loads of bloom all summer and return year after year. 'Lady Sunblaze', like all 'Sunblaze' miniature roses, grows from 16 to 18 inches tall and wide with 1½- to 2½-inch-wide blooms. 'Lady Sunblaze' makes a great low, rose-blooming hedge around a bed of hybrid teas and grandifloras. 'Sunblaze' roses do well in patio pots or wall planters. Just make sure that 'Lady Sunblaze' gets lots of sun. To produce many more blooms, prune off the spent flowers as they finish. These miniatures are quite resistant to insects and disease. The blooms appear in clusters of three to five flowers. Each flower is a full bloom in miniature of its larger-flowering cousins. 'Lady Sunblaze' miniature roses make a great Mother's Day gift from a child to a grandparent.

WHEN TO PLANT

'Lady Sunblaze' and other 'Sunblaze' roses are available in the spring in 1-gallon containers. The best shopping selection will be from May 1 through June 30. Plant anytime the plants are available.

WHERE TO PLANT

'Lady Sunblaze' miniature roses are just like all the other members of the rose family—they want to grow in sun. If full-day sun is not available, give them at least all of the morning sun. These miniatures will grow in all types of well-draining soil. They can also go in patio pots and other planters. If this is the method you choose, you must put those pots and planters in an unheated garage for the winter, remembering to water them once a month. If you leave them in containers outside during the winter, the roots stand a good chance of freezing and the plant could die.

How to Plant

If you choose to plant these in soil, dig a hole as deep, and twice as wide, as the soil clump. Loosen any roots wrapped around the soil clump. Break up all existing soil clumps to the size of golf balls. Backfill the soil and water-in well.

Care and Maintenance

Miniature 'Sunblaze' roses are resistant to insects and disease. Just be sure they're getting lots of sun. 'Sunblaze' roses, like all roses, want to be fertilized with rose food. But be sure to reduce the amount recommended on the rose food container by 50 percent. You can assist these miniatures for winter by putting 6 to 10 inches of mulch or shredded leaves on their stems in late fall. Do not cut off any spent flowers after mid-September.

Landscape Merit

'Lady Sunblaze' is low-maintenance but produces lots of color on short, bushy plants. It is great for planters and pots on a sunny deck or patio.

Additional Information

It's hard to describe to you just how much color you will get from these small growing plants. There are many colors of 'Sunblaze' to choose from. You can mix up the colors or plant a low rose hedge of all the same variety.

Additional Species, Cultivars, or Varieties

'Sweet Sunblaze' has bright-pink blooms measuring 2 inches across and dark-green glossy leaves. 'Orange Sunblaze' has deep-orange flowers that do not fade in hot weather, each bloom lasting about two weeks. 'Bridal Sunblaze' produces soft white, double flowers that are extremely long-lasting; these are the best of the whites. 'Golden Sunblaze' has bright, golden-yellow flowers with glossy green leaves. 'Red Sunblaze' produces crimson-red, long-lasting blooms; this plant grows vigorously and makes a great hedge.

'Show Biz'

Rosa 'Show Biz'

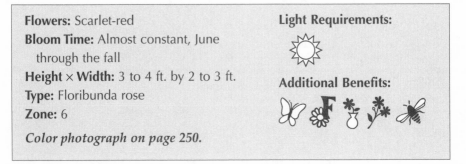

Flowers: Scarlet-red
Bloom Time: Almost constant, June
  through the fall
Height × Width: 3 to 4 ft. by 2 to 3 ft.
Type: Floribunda rose
Zone: 6

Color photograph on page 250.

Light Requirements:

Additional Benefits:

Floribunda roses are derived and refined from hybrid teas. Floribundas, as a group, make excellent landscape plants. They grow shorter than the hybrid teas but produce loads of flowers borne in clusters rather than one bloom per stem like the tea roses. Their habit of growth and bloom qualifies them to be used as a low-blooming hedge, a great border plant, or for planting in their own bed for fantastic yard color. Floribunda 'Show Biz', a 1985 prizewinner, produces showy clusters of scarlet-red blooms on vigorous-growing, but compact plants. Its blooms are lightly scented. 'Show Biz', like most other floribundas, produces almost constant blooms from Memorial Day until the fall. Floribundas, like all roses, want full sun if possible. If not, plant 'Show Biz' in all-morning sun.

WHEN TO PLANT
As I do with all roses, I recommend you buy only potted floribunda roses. The roots of real potted roses are growing in their own soil medium. The best selection of all floribunda roses will be from May 1 through June 30.

WHERE TO PLANT
Plant 'Show Biz' and other floribundas in full sun. If that's not possible, at least try to give them morning sun. Floribundas will grow in all types of well-drained soil. Make sure that you plant your floribundas where you can see and enjoy all their color.

HOW TO PLANT
Floribunda roses are as easy to plant as any tree or shrub. Make sure your planting site is well drained, then dig a hole as deep as the soil

clump and twice as wide. Backfill using the existing soil that you've chopped up to the size of golf balls. Water-in well to settle the soil.

CARE AND MAINTENANCE

All floribundas need a maintenance schedule. Roses are heavy feeders, which means that you should feed your roses as often as the package of rose food directs. In Kentucky, stop feeding your roses in mid-September There are several companies that combine a systemic insecticide with rose food. It's easy to apply. Just follow the instructions and pour it on the soil around each individual plant. Blackspot leaf disease can be a problem sometimes, especially if you haven't planted your roses in a rose-friendly location. There are fungicides that you can spray to reduce this problem. Hand-remove and discard any yellow infected leaves.

LANDSCAPE MERIT

'Show Biz' produces great landscape color. Its stems and flowers make a great, short bouquet. It is also not as prone to blackspot disease as are some other varieties.

ADDITIONAL INFORMATION

Do not cut off any more rose blossoms after mid-September. Let the flowers finish on the plant and go to seed (called rose hips). When these rose hips form, they send a signal to the roots to shut down for the season. Most winter damage to roses comes when the plants are still soft and actively growing when the real cold weather hits.

ADDITIONAL SPECIES, CULTIVARS, OR VARIETIES

'Brass Band' has beautiful, blooming clusters in unique shades from apricot to pink. 'French Lace' has classic white blooms with a mild fragrance. 'Sun Sprite' produces bright-yellow cluster blooms with glossy green leaves. 'Sweet Inspiration' has beautiful deep-pink flowers so full of bloom that one branch makes a full bouquet.

'The Fairy'

Rosa 'The Fairy'

Flowers: Small and light-pink
Bloom Time: Late spring through the fall
Height × Width: 3 ft. by 3 ft.
Type: Shrub rose
Zone: 6

Color photograph on page 250.

Light Requirements:

Additional Benefits:

/ T he Fairy' rose starts blooming in late May and never goes out of bloom until December. This variety is easy to grow and hardy. 'The Fairy' has small, polyantha-type blooms of light pink that will give any homeowner constant color. Shrub roses in general need lots of sun to prosper—at least a half-day of morning sun. In exchange, you will get flowers that never stop. They come in all colors and bloom on plants that are short in stature but high in bloom count. Plant shrub roses as a low hedge, use as a border for a hybrid tea and grandiflora rose bed, or mix them in with other true perennials for extended summer color; none will outbloom a shrub rose.

WHEN TO PLANT

Buy shrub roses that are already growing in a soil mix in their own pots. Don't bother with any roses that aren't sold that way. Plant shrub roses anytime the ground is not frozen.

WHERE TO PLANT

Plant 'The Fairy' and any other shrub rose where there is lots of sun. Make sure there is good soil drainage. Plant shrub roses in any area that's visible. You'll want to be able to enjoy all the blooms, whether from the yard or from inside the house.

HOW TO PLANT

Buy your shrub roses growing in a soil mix in their own pots. Stay away from those that are bare-root or in cardboard boxes in early April. Dig a hole as deep as the pot and twice as wide. Chop up the dug-out soil to the size of golf balls, backfill, and water-in well to settle the soil.

CARE AND MAINTENANCE

'The Fairy' and other shrub roses are low-maintenance. They can have a few bugs or a little blackspot during the rainy seasons or as a result of poor planting sites. But don't let that intimidate you. They still do not require much maintenance other than some occasional rose food.

LANDSCAPE MERIT

'The Fairy' is one of the most care-free varieties of roses you can grow. 'The Fairy' is also low-maintenance yet gives high color.

ADDITIONAL INFORMATION

'The Fairy' and other shrub roses have small individual flowers, about 1 to 2 inches in diameter, but each plant can have as many as 500 blooms at one time. Bigger is not always better! This rose will give you great yard color and a lot of it, too.

ADDITIONAL SPECIES, CULTIVARS, OR VARIETIES

'Bonica', a 1987 AARS winner, gives you plenty of 2-inch, shell-pink flowers. 'Carefree Beauty' is another great pink variety that constantly blooms and is disease-resistant. 'Topaz Jewel' has single flowers of bright yellow and a weeping growth habit. 'Sea Foam', a winter-hardy rose, is more upright and has white flowers with a mild fragrance.

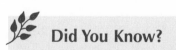 **Did You Know?**

Like the family of Meidiland roses, true shrub roses produce as much yard color as annual impatiens, and they don't have to be replanted each year.

CHAPTER SEVEN

Shrubs

Shrubs, or bushes, are woody perennials and make up the large group of plants most often purchased and installed by homeowners. They can be needled evergreens, broadleaf evergreens, or deciduous plants that drop their leaves in fall. Even builders who consider landscaping a nuisance will take the trouble to install ten or twelve shrubs in front of a newly built home, a message for prospective buyers that says, "Hey, this house is ready for you to move into."

Shrubs: Landscape Basics

For years, the front of every home was framed with evergreen, needle-type shrubs. There were junipers and yews and yews and junipers, with an occasional arborvitae. Within the last twenty years, landscape designers as well as homeowners have realized: "Hey, I don't look at my shrubs in the winter, does anyone else?" The answer of course is "NO, I'm too cold to worry about whether the shrubs in front of my house are evergreen." This discovery has opened up an all-new type of landscape design that allows front plantings to be a mixture of evergreen and deciduous shrubs. Deciduous shrubs offer much more seasonal color during the growing season than do simple mixes of evergreen needles and leaves. Deciduous shrubs have many different leaf colors, and blooms to boot. A mixture of deciduous and evergreen shrubs makes for a very colorful attractive landscape. Deciduous shrubs also have an interesting leafless winter attraction. Go ahead, mix them up.

Purchasing the Plants

In January and February in Kentucky, we're eager for any sign of spring. The mail-order catalogs begin to arrive, and our minds shift into planting gear. Be careful, though, and don't be taken in by prices that seem too good to be true, descriptions of unfamiliar plant varieties, and pictures of plants that are artist's illustrations instead of actual photos. Many of these plants may be small enough to fit through a slide-in mailbox themselves! It's always best to buy locally so you can see what you're buying before the wallet opens.

PLANTING PRACTICES

You will note that I give the same advice throughout this chapter: you can plant anytime the ground is not frozen, springtime offers the best selection at nurseries, and you should make sure the plant is dry before watering. Timely watering during hot, dry weather helps any plant, but use a trowel and check the soil down 5 inches first. You will read about shrubs that do well in different types of soil, from great organic soil to clay soil.

Abelia

Abelia × grandiflora

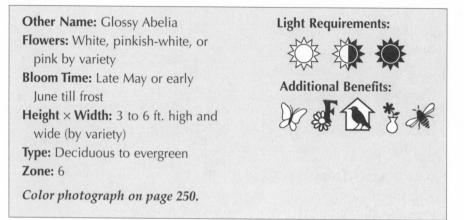

Other Name: Glossy Abelia

Flowers: White, pinkish-white, or pink by variety

Bloom Time: Late May or early June till frost

Height × Width: 3 to 6 ft. high and wide (by variety)

Type: Deciduous to evergreen

Zone: 6

Color photograph on page 250.

Light Requirements:

Additional Benefits:

Abelia is a great flowering shrub for Kentucky. This shrub in the northern parts of the state will lose its leaves in late fall whereas abelia in the southern and western parts of the state will hold on to its leaves throughout most winters. Abelia has glossy-green leaves in summer, turning bronze-green to bronze-red in late fall and into winter. Its whitish-pink, funnel-shaped flowers bloom in clusters. Each flower is about 3/4 inch long and 1/2 inch wide. Abelia starts to bloom in late May or early June and continues to bloom till frost. In the fall, the flowers turn a light purplish-white after a hard freeze and can remain on the plant all winter. The shrub itself grows and can be maintained at 3 to 6 feet high and wide. Abelia has a natural rounded, spreading growth habit with multiple stems producing arching branches. This plant adds texture to any landscape. It looks great as a one-of-a-kind plant, or it can become a wonderful-looking hedge. Also consider abelia as a backdrop for a color bed of annuals and perennials.

WHEN TO PLANT

Abelia is available balled and burlapped or in containers. If you buy abelia in early spring, you might think you're buying a bunch of sticks. Fear not. This flowering shrub can be planted anytime the ground is not frozen.

WHERE TO PLANT

Abelia will grow in sun to shade. It tends to bloom better if it receives at least three to four hours of daily sun. The plant likes well-drained soil and will tolerate clay soil with good drainage. Plant in areas of the landscape where you can enjoy the flowers all summer long.

HOW TO PLANT

Dig a hole as deep as the soil clump and twice as wide. Break up any heavy clay particles to the size of golf balls. Backfill and water-in well to settle the soil. Mulch to a depth of 2 inches, especially during the heat of summer.

CARE AND MAINTENANCE

This trouble-free shrub has no serious bug or disease problems. Young plants may require pruning in early spring to encourage fuller growth. This pruning will not affect this year's bloom because abelia blooms on new wood.

ADDITIONAL INFORMATION

Abelia prefers acidic, well-drained, moist soil. Since most of Kentucky tends to be on the alkaline side, you may want to acidify your soil with Ironite® by following the directions on the box. Give abelia an occasional drink of water during the heat of summer.

ADDITIONAL SPECIES, CULTIVARS, OR VARIETIES

'Compacta' grows 3 to 4 feet high and wide with pinkish-white flowers. 'Francis Mason' is a low-growing, densely branched shrub that has glossy, variegated leaves with light-pink flowers. 'Prostrata' is low growing, 1½ to 2 feet high. This plant with fragrant white flowers can be used as a ground cover or a bank planting. This one does best in full sun.

Azalea

Rhododendron spp.

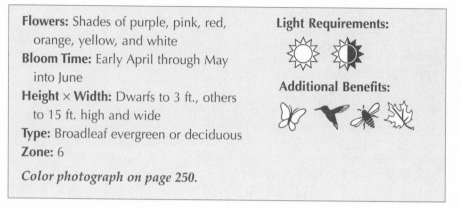

Flowers: Shades of purple, pink, red, orange, yellow, and white

Bloom Time: Early April through May into June

Height × Width: Dwarfs to 3 ft., others to 15 ft. high and wide

Type: Broadleaf evergreen or deciduous

Zone: 6

Color photograph on page 250.

Light Requirements:

Additional Benefits:

A "Did You Know?" for azaleas is that they are all rhododendrons. The large-leaf varieties have a difficult time growing successfully in much of Kentucky because rhodos have been known to get smaller rather than larger in heavy alkaline soil. The best way to grow large-leaf rhodos in Kentucky is to set them on top of the existing soil, bring in new, rich soil to form a mound, and plant in the mound. Azaleas, on the other hand, adjust much better to our Kentucky soils. Although there are hundreds of varieties, some grow here much better than others. Most azaleas, as this chapter suggests, are listed as evergreens, but they truly are not. Most are deciduous. The confusion comes from the fact that azalea leaves turn orange-red in the fall and hold that color through winter. The leaves are forced off the plant in spring as new green leaves appear. There are other varieties that do drop their leaves in the fall, and you will find these varieties listed as true deciduous plants.

WHEN TO PLANT

Most azaleas and other rhododendrons are container-grown and available for purchase in spring. There are still some nurseries that grow true rhododendrons as field-grown plants, and these are available balled and burlapped. All plants do best when they are planted from spring to early fall (mid-September).

WHERE TO PLANT

A big misconception is that rhododendrons and azaleas like shade. What they don't want in Kentucky is total exposure to the northwest winter wind. Locate these plants in an area of good natural light or sun where they are blocked from the wind. My azaleas do best on the southeast side of my house. Avoid planting them where they would get summer tree shade and winter sun.

How to Plant

Rhododendrons and azaleas have fine-textured root systems. They produce hundreds of roots that need to be placed in decent, acidic soil. Good drainage is also a must. Plant no deeper than the existing grade. And if the soil consists of heavy clay, seriously consider mound-planting.

Care and Maintenance

There are many soil acidifiers that can be added to the alkaline planting beds. Feed the plants with a higher-middle-number plant food (such as 6-12-8) in spring as new growth appears, and again in early summer. Few insect problems threaten this group, but root rot caused by poor drainage can be a serious problem.

Additional Information

Most true rhododendrons are evergreen, while azaleas are deciduous. True rhododendron flowers are bell-shaped and have ten stamens, while azaleas flowers are funnel-shaped and have five stamens. Stay away from varieties that have been grown in Oregon—Kentucky-grown plants are best.

Additional Species, Cultivars, or Varieties

Three of my favorite rhododendron are 'English Roseum', which has light-rose flowers and is very cold hardy; 'Scintillation', a compact-growing plant with light-pink flowers; and 'Nova Zembla', which has bright-red flowers and is cold-tolerant and heat-resistant. 'Karens' is a lavender azalea and a landscaper's favorite. 'Girard' is available in various colors and is a very hardy azalea. 'Northern Lights' is a great group of deciduous azaleas.

Bayberry

Myrica pensylvanica

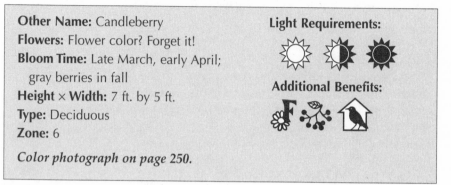

Other Name: Candleberry
Flowers: Flower color? Forget it!
Bloom Time: Late March, early April;
  gray berries in fall
Height × Width: 7 ft. by 5 ft.
Type: Deciduous
Zone: 6

Color photograph on page 250.

Light Requirements:

Additional Benefits:

Bayberry is a hardy shrub that can withstand any urban stresses it might face. It grows well in poor soil, in sun to shade, and in spaces that many other plants will not tolerate. A vigorously growing plant, its size can be controlled by pruning; in fact, if you can cut it back to within 12 inches of the ground, it will respond like a brand-new shrub. Bayberry has flowers, but they are insignificant. The female produces lovely gray berries in fall. A mild winter will allow the leaves to remain on this plant. Mass bayberry along property lines, use as a screen, or mix with true evergreens. Bayberry more than makes up for lack of bloom, providing you with a very trouble-free plant that will make you wonder why you didn't plant it sooner.

WHEN TO PLANT

You can plant bayberry anytime the ground is not frozen. At the nursery, you will find bayberry growing in containers. Because there is no phenomenon known as "fall fever," most homeowners do the majority of their plantings, including bayberry, in spring. You may have difficulty finding this plant in the fall, but if you do, go ahead and plant.

WHERE TO PLANT

Bayberry will adapt to just about any area of your landscape. They will tolerate hot, dry areas as well as moist, shady ones. If you have a trouble spot where no other shrub wants to grow, try bayberry—you only need to avoid soil that is in low areas where water stands after a heavy rain. This plant is also very salt tolerant.

HOW TO PLANT

Dig a hole no deeper than the soil clump and twice as wide. Break up any heavy clay particles to the size of golf balls. Backfill, and water-in well to settle the soil. Mulch to a depth of 2 inches, especially in dry soils.

CARE AND MAINTENANCE

Bayberry is a trouble-free shrub. There are no known bugs or diseases that will threaten its health and well-being. Bayberry can put on quite a lot of new growth annually. Don't be afraid to prune this shrub at any time to keep it contained in the space you've allowed for it.

ADDITIONAL INFORMATION

Bayberry is dioecious, which means that if you want the fragrant berries on the girl plants, you will need at least one boy plant. One boy bayberry can pollinate many girl bayberries. Unfortunately, plants are not marked or labeled by sex, so buy several and you're bound to have some berries on the female plants.

ADDITIONAL SPECIES, CULTIVARS, OR VARIETIES

There are none known at this time and this one would be hard to beat.

Did You Know?

One of the most popular holiday candles is the bayberry candle. To put that great scent in those candles, manufacturers use the scent from the berries of the bayberry. Bayberry shrubs offer the same scent when growing in the landscape, especially when you brush by the leaves.

Blue Holly

Ilex × meserveae

Other Name: Meserve Holly

Flowers: White flowers eventually form bright-red to yellow fruit

Bloom Time: Late spring to summer

Height × Width: Spreaders grow to 5 by 5 ft.; uprights 6 by 3 ft.

Type: Evergreen

Zone: 6

Color photograph on page 250.

Light Requirements:

Additional Benefits:

This is a wonderful plant family that gives you, the homeowner, a great group of shrubs, both spreading and upright, with which to landscape your home. For years, taxus and junipers have been the main choices for the front of the home. Now you can plant broadleaf evergreens that have glossy leaves, are extremely winter hardy, and have females with red berries. The foliage is quite dark, blue-green to shiny green. You can install them close together, to form a hedge, or space them apart to grow as individual plants. The upright varieties give you an evergreen holly that's easy to keep under 6 feet.

WHEN TO PLANT

Blue hollies can be planted anytime the ground is not frozen. They are mostly container grown, but you will find upright varieties that are field-grown and available balled and burlapped.

WHERE TO PLANT

These cold-hardy hollies make wonderful foundation plants. They also work well to close in a patio or low deck. They do best in full sun to natural shade. They will not do as well in summer shade from trees that allow winter sun when the trees' leaves fall. Blue hollies like acidic soil that has good drainage. For those of you in Kentucky who have alkaline clay soil, acidifiers can be added to keep the plants happy.

How to Plant

Dig a hole no deeper than but twice as wide as the soil clump. If your soil is heavy clay, add a little organic material to amend it. Make sure the backfill soil is no larger than golf balls. Water-in well to settle the soil and eliminate air pockets.

Care and Maintenance

Blue hollies are trouble-free when it comes to bugs and diseases. Yellow leaves can be the result of alkaline soil, but you can acidify with Holly Tone® or Ironite®. Do not overwater or the green leaves will turn black.

Additional Information

Female hollies need to be pollinated by a male holly. A male holly within a city block will do the trick, and one male can pollinate thousands of females. There are also deciduous hollies that are a great addition to any landscape. Check them out for great winter berry color. They can be considered a tall shrub or a small, ornamental tree. Trim the plant to suit the form and shape you desire.

Additional Species, Cultivars, or Varieties

'Berri-Magic' is a spreading plant that has both a male and a female plant growing together in one container; it has lots of berries and is evergreen. Other cultivars are 'Blue Maid' (compact), 'Blue Stallion' (a great male match for 'Blue Maid'), 'Blue Girl' (loose growing, good fruit), 'China Girl' (glossy leaves, good fruit), 'China Girl Upright' (pyramidal, prune to desired size), and 'China Boy' (could be considered the mate of 'China Girl'). Winter Berry, which is deciduous, has many great cultivars. 'Golden Girl' is identical to 'Blue Maid' except it has yellow berries. The Japanese holly, *Ilex crenata*, is hardy to Kentucky. It comes in both spreading and upright forms. Check with your local garden center to see which variety is best for you.

Blue Mist Shrub

Caryopteris × clandonensis

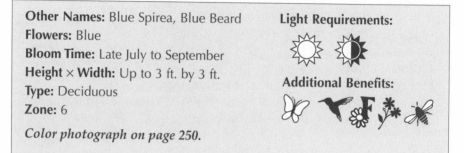

Other Names: Blue Spirea, Blue Beard
Flowers: Blue
Bloom Time: Late July to September
Height × Width: Up to 3 ft. by 3 ft.
Type: Deciduous
Zone: 6

Color photograph on page 250.

Light Requirements:

Additional Benefits:

This shrub is almost considered a herbaceous perennial rather than a shrub. In Kentucky, the plant dies back to the ground each winter. This is a benefit because you know your blue mist shrub will never grow bigger than 3 feet high and 3 feet wide. It provides lovely, bright-blue flowers in late summer. The bloom period lasts over a month; the blue flowers appear up and down all of the plant stems. The leaves are gray-green, adding more ornamental beauty. Blue mist does best in full sun but will provide good entertainment even when receiving only a half-day. It is a great, small-growing shrub for late-summer color that lasts into fall.

WHEN TO PLANT

Container-grown blue mist shrubs can be planted anytime the ground is not frozen. Try to plant in spring or early summer to enjoy color the first year of planting. Some garden stores don't stock this plant until midsummer as the plants get ready to flower.

WHERE TO PLANT

Blue mist shrub prefers full sun to very light shade to maximize the number of blooms. It grows uniformly, making it perfect for a low hedge. It also works well in existing perennial beds to assure that the beds generate late-summer color. In mixed color beds, plant blue mist with black-eyed susans or yellow butterfly bush.

HOW TO PLANT

Dig a hole no deeper than but twice as wide as the soil clump. Loosen any wrapped roots, and backfill the hole with the existing soil. Make sure no backfilled clay particle is larger than a golf ball. Water-in well to settle the soil.

CARE AND MAINTENANCE

Blue mist shrub is resistant to bugs and disease. Fertilize it with an all-purpose fertilizer in spring. Spring is also the time to cut back all the dead branches to the ground. The first spring after planting will be scary. "Where's my plant?" you'll ask. Be patient, it will be there; it doesn't show new growth until May. Give blue mist an occasional drink of water during hot, dry weather.

ADDITIONAL INFORMATION

Blue mist shrub has been known to attract hummingbirds. All of its flowers bloom on the new growth that appears each spring season. It is an outstanding addition to any landscape. Plant in areas that you can enjoy from both outside and inside the home.

ADDITIONAL SPECIES, CULTIVARS, OR VARIETIES

'Heavenly Blue' produces bright-blue flowers that start blooming in late July and last well into September. 'Kew Blue' is a very dark-blue variety that grows 4 ft. high by 4 ft. wide and blooms from August into September.

Did You Know?

Blue mist shrub and butterfly bush are two of the last shrubs to leaf out in the spring. Don't panic and think they're dead when all your other shrubs have spring leaves. These two varieties will leaf out eventually—they are just late bloomers.

Bottlebrush Buckeye

Aesculus parviflora

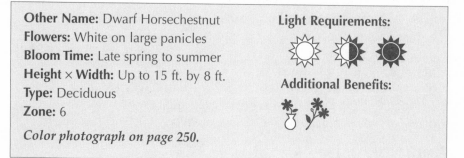

Other Name: Dwarf Horsechestnut
Flowers: White on large panicles
Bloom Time: Late spring to summer
Height × Width: Up to 15 ft. by 8 ft.
Type: Deciduous
Zone: 6

Color photograph on page 250.

Light Requirements:

Additional Benefits:

Bottlebrush buckeye is not a tree, but a shrub. It shows off well in a mass planting, planted as a shrub border, or used as a one-of-a-kind planting; it also does well as a screening along a 4- to 8-foot-high deck. The white flowers appear in late May to early June and last four to six weeks. The bloom clusters look like a bottlebrush, hence its common name. This buckeye tends to be wide-spreading with multiple stems, but it can easily be controlled by pruning. Bright-yellow, fall-colored leaves add to its landscape value. Look around—I'll bet you'll find a home for at least one, maybe more.

WHEN TO PLANT

Bottlebrush buckeye is best planted in spring, and is available either balled and burlapped or in containers. It prefers acid soil but also adapts to alkaline clay. You can plant container-grown buckeyes during the summer and fall.

WHERE TO PLANT

Buckeye averages 8 to 12 feet high and 8 to 15 feet wide, but it can be pruned to a desired size. The bottlebrush buckeye is usually listed as needing full sun to part shade, but I have seen it do exceptionally well when planted underneath shade trees with no direct sun at all.

HOW TO PLANT

Dig a hole no deeper than the soil clump and twice as wide. For container-grown plants, loosen any roots that are wrapped around the soil clump. For plants that are balled and burlapped, loosen the top of the burlap and pull the burlap down over the ball after you set it

in the hole. Backfill the hole. If you are planting in clay, add some organic material to the existing soil. Water-in well.

CARE AND MAINTENANCE
Bottlebrush buckeye has virtually no problems with disease or insects. Some beetles will pick on a few leaves in early summer, but it's no problem—a few holes won't affect any plants. It will continue to be a great, care-free shrub. You may experience some oak scorch in hot weather.

ADDITIONAL INFORMATION
This plant variety is underused. Basically, not many people are aware of it, so many garden centers and nursery stores don't stock it. There are special nurseries, though, that will have it in stock. Don't be afraid to ask for it.

ADDITIONAL SPECIES, CULTIVARS, OR VARIETIES
'Walter' is the most popular of these shrubs available. 'Rogers' blooms around July; *A. parviflora* var. *serotina* also blooms fairly late but doesn't have as many flowers.

 Did You Know?

Aesculus glabra is the true Ohio buckeye, and the Ohio state tree. It is a tree that grows 20 to 40 feet in height and width. It produces greenish-yellow panicles of flowers that are 4 to 7 inches long and 2 to 3 inches wide in mid-May. Also, all horsechestnut trees are cousins to the buckeye family. If the University of Kentucky and Ohio State were to decide to play each other in basketball, the playing site could have a Kentucky coffee tree and a buckeye tree at center court to jump over.

Butterfly Bush

Buddleia davidii

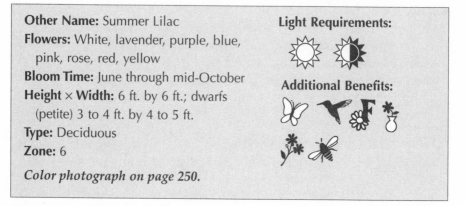

Other Name: Summer Lilac

Flowers: White, lavender, purple, blue, pink, rose, red, yellow

Bloom Time: June through mid-October

Height × Width: 6 ft. by 6 ft.; dwarfs (petite) 3 to 4 ft. by 4 to 5 ft.

Type: Deciduous

Zone: 6

Color photograph on page 250.

Light Requirements:

Additional Benefits:

B utterfly bush does just what its name suggests: it attracts butterflies in summer. It is sometimes referred to as summer lilac because of its long, upright panicles of flowers. It is fast-growing, yet it grows to the same size every year. That is because most of each year's growth will die back to within a foot of the ground by the next spring. Butterfly bush grows upright, and its flowers sit on the branch tips. It is available in several colors, usually in shades of lilac from purple to black—white, pink, or yellow ones are available, too. Some varieties have been known to bloom from July into early October. The average size is 6 feet tall and 6 feet wide for standard varieties and 4 to 5 feet tall for dwarfs.

WHEN TO PLANT

The best selection of butterfly bushes will be found in spring, growing in containers. Technically, you can plant them anytime the ground is not frozen. Do yourself and the butterfly bush a favor: plant in spring to early summer so you can enjoy the blooms the first year and give the plant a chance to get established before its first winter. Most garden centers will have a good selection of butterfly bushes when they are in bloom so you can see which color best pleases your eye.

WHERE TO PLANT

Butterfly bushes grow best in full sun but will do okay if they are given at least a half-day of sun. Avoid planting them in lots of shade because they will be disappointing. This is a shrub to plant in a spot where kids of all ages can enjoy it from inside or outside the house.

If you live in a naturally windy area, plant the shrubs out of the breeze to encourage butterflies.

How to Plant

Dig a hole no deeper than but twice as wide as the soil clump. Loosen any roots that are wrapped around the clump. Use the existing soil to backfill, making sure none of the returned soil clumps are larger than a golf ball. Water-in well to eliminate air pockets.

Care and Maintenance

In Kentucky, most winters will cause the butterfly bush to die back to within one foot of the ground. When new growth starts to appear near the ground in spring, prune back all the branches to within a foot of the ground. After each stem blooms, cut back halfway to encourage additional blooms. There are no known bugs or diseases that bother the butterfly bush.

Landscape Merit

The butterfly bush has lilac-shaped flowers that attract butterflies and other beneficial insects.

Additional Information

Young children love to watch the butterflies feed off the lilac-shaped flowers. The blooms also make for good cut flowers for table arrangements.

Additional Species, Cultivars, or Varieties

'Black Knight' has dark-purple blooms. 'Nanho White' produces lilac-colored flowers. 'Pink Delight' has fragrant, lilac-pink flowers. 'Royal Red' blooms in bright-red flowers. 'Honeycomb' has fragrant yellow flowers. 'White Profusion' is a great variety with white flowers.

Did You Know?

There are many varieties of butterfly bush whose names begin with "Petite." These varieties tend to stay smaller in size and produce summer flowers. They are great for smaller landscapes because their average size is 4 feet tall by 4 feet wide.

Crapemyrtle

Lagerstroemia indica

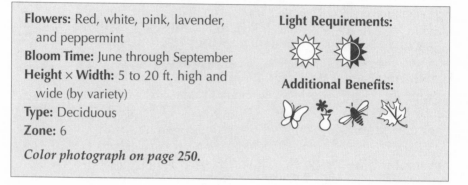

Flowers: Red, white, pink, lavender, and peppermint

Bloom Time: June through September

Height × Width: 5 to 20 ft. high and wide (by variety)

Type: Deciduous

Zone: 6

Color photograph on page 250.

Light Requirements:

Additional Benefits:

Crapemyrtle can be considered a small- to medium-growing, upright-flowering shrub or a small ornamental tree. The leaves tend to be heaviest toward the top of the plant, and that's good. You see, crapemyrtle also has very good-looking bark. There are many cultivars, and all of them bloom. The flowers resemble the bloom clusters of lilac. They come in white, shades of pink, peppermint-striped, lavender, and red. The flowers appear on the ends of the current year's growth, and the blooms, which start to appear by variety in June, continue to bloom off and on all summer. Fall leaf color is another asset; most varieties have leaf colors of orange-red, yellow-orange, red, and maroon by cultivar. Crapemyrtle cultivars can be grouped into three growing sizes: semidwarf, which averages 5 to 10 feet high; intermediate, which averages 10 to 20 feet high; and tree type, which can and will grow in excess of 20 feet high. Crapemyrtle can provide lots of great color and interest to any landscape year-round.

WHEN TO PLANT

Plant crapemyrtle anytime the ground is not frozen. The best selections from the garden center will be offered in the spring. They will be available growing in containers of various sizes, and some may be balled and burlapped.

WHERE TO PLANT

Crapemyrtle prefers to be planted in moist, well-drained soil that receives full sun. It will tolerate a half-day of sun and clay soil as long as the soil drains well. Plant in the landscape where you have the opportunity to view the summer flowers daily.

How to Plant

Dig a hole as deep as and twice as wide as the soil clump or ball of earth. If you choose container-grown plants, loosen any wrapped roots around the soil clump. Backfill the hole with the soil, leaving no soil particle bigger than a golf ball, and water-in well.

Care and Maintenance

Prune any dead wood that appears in the spring. Do not prune any growth from August into early December because pruning encourages winter cold damage and dieback. Failing to plant in a location with enough sun can promote mildew growth on the leaves. This plant is considered trouble-free overall.

Additional Information

Crapemyrtle is an attractive summer-flowering shrub or tree. The maturing bark peels away to expose various-colored underbark, adding to this plant's overall beauty. Some varieties grow much taller than others. Choose the variety that fits your landscape.

Additional Species, Cultivars, or Varieties

'Acoma' has pure-white blooms. This weeping plant, which can be maintained at 6 to 7 feet high and wide, is mildew resistant. Large pink bloom clusters with great fall leaf color characterize 'Pecos'. Maintain it at 8 feet tall and 6 feet wide. It, too, is mildew resistant. 'Zuni' is known for its large lavender flowers with striking fall leaf color of orange-red to maroon. It grows to 9 feet tall by 8 feet wide, and it is mildew resistant.

Crimson Pygmy Barberry

Berberis thunbergii var. *atropurpurea*

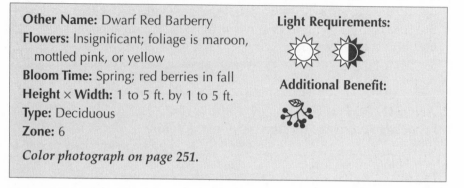

Other Name: Dwarf Red Barberry

Flowers: Insignificant; foliage is maroon, mottled pink, or yellow

Bloom Time: Spring; red berries in fall

Height × Width: 1 to 5 ft. by 1 to 5 ft.

Type: Deciduous

Zone: 6

Color photograph on page 251.

Light Requirements:

Additional Benefit:

Barberry may be thorny, but the pygmies in my landscape are some of my favorites. In fact, I have lined my front walk with them. During the growing season they have beautiful red dwarf leaves; the foliage is either maroon, mottled pink, or yellow. Even in the winter they look great with their leafless red twigs. Add snow and you have a holiday card. They can take heavy shearing, which will allow you, like me, to have a barberry hedge 12 inches high by 10 inches wide. You can even plant a sunny hillside with these, making an outstanding landscape site. To maximize the maroon leaf color, plant these shrubs in lots of sun. Another value of barberry is its thorns, which make it a great barrier plant.

WHEN TO PLANT

Most if not all barberries are nursery-grown in containers. Plant them anytime the ground is not frozen.

WHERE TO PLANT

To maximize leaf color, plant barberry in as much sun as possible, at least a half-day or more. Barberries are drought tolerant. Avoid planting them in areas with poor drainage. For hedging, plant them on 24-inch centers.

HOW TO PLANT

Dig a hole no deeper than but twice as wide as the soil clump. Container-grown plants should have their roots loosened before you place them in the planting hole. These plants adapt well to clay soil. Be sure not to overwater them during dry periods.

CARE AND MAINTENANCE

Barberries are self-sustaining—they grow very well in what could be described as terrible soil as long as it drains well. No bugs or diseases bother the plants. In fact, bunnies don't even like to run through them. To shape barberries, prune them anytime you like. Pruning shears are best, but hedge shears go faster as long as you can control the bigger blades.

LANDSCAPE MERIT

Barberries provide great spring and fall color.

ADDITIONAL INFORMATION

Pygmy barberries give leaf color to any landscape during the entire growing season. Pygmy is very slow growing. Wear gloves when pruning; these plants are quite prickly. They excel both as individual plants and as dwarf hedging. This plant also does well as underplanting for an upright-growing foundation tree such as a river birch.

ADDITIONAL SPECIES, CULTIVARS, OR VARIETIES

'Bagatelle' barberry is very dwarf and has red leaves and great fall color. 'Atropurpurea' grows larger than a pygmy. 'Crimson Velvet' is also a dwarf plant, with smoky maroon leaves. 'Gold Nugget' has gold leaves on a compact body. 'Bonanza Gold' is a semidwarf with golden-yellow leaves. 'Rose Glow' has a combination of pink and red leaves and is a very good variety for Kentucky.

Did You Know?

Barberry varieties come with red, pink, or gold leaves. Plant some of each in the same general area and the color contrast will be fantastic.

Dwarf Burning Bush

Euonymus alatus 'Compactus'

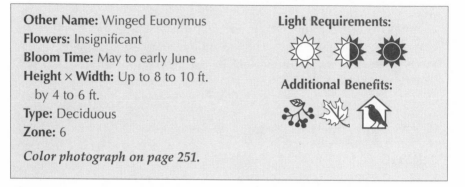

Other Name: Winged Euonymus
Flowers: Insignificant
Bloom Time: May to early June
Height × Width: Up to 8 to 10 ft.
  by 4 to 6 ft.
Type: Deciduous
Zone: 6

Light Requirements:

Additional Benefits:

Color photograph on page 251.

Dwarf burning bush is a popular plant, not because of its bloom but because it will fill in any spot in the landscape. It can be used anywhere as a specimen plant or grouped for a great screen hedge. Burning bush has insignificant white flowers in spring, but it has lush, dark-green leaves during the growing season that turn a brilliant red in the fall. Like any shrub, it wants good drainage but will tolerate heavy clay soil. This plant will grow in full sun to full shade. Those that are planted in shady areas tend to turn red later in the fall than those that have been exposed to sun. Burning bush is considered to be a dwarf not because it grows slowly, but because it will tolerate heavy pruning. Some think this plant has been overused, but if you want a low-maintenance shrub, it is perfect. Oh, and yes, sometimes the plants will have red berries in the fall.

WHEN TO PLANT

You can buy dwarf burning bush either balled and burlapped or container-grown. It is easily transplanted anytime the ground is not frozen. This plant will also spread through the soil; transplant any of those underground shoots in early spring to other areas that you want to have dwarf burning bushes.

WHERE TO PLANT

Burning bush fits many landscape situations. Plant many of them to screen out an unsightly view. Plant it to hide the foundation of a home. The nice thing is knowing that it will grow well in sun or shade and anywhere in-between. It's great to use around a basketball backboard or the sides of a tennis court to help keep a ball within easy reach when it wants to go out of bounds.

How to Plant

Dig a hole no deeper than but twice as wide as the soil clump. In clay soil, make sure none of the backfill is larger than a golf ball. Water-in well to settle the backfill. Make sure none of the burlap remains above the hole; if it does, cut it away. Before planting container-grown plants, loosen any roots that are wrapped around the soil clump.

Care and Maintenance

This is another of my recommended low-maintenance plants. There are no problematic bugs or diseases that plague this variety. Prune it as often as necessary to the size and shape you prefer. If you forget and don't prune for years, you can literally cut the plants back to the ground in the spring and *voila*, they're brand-new. This type of pruning will cause a lot of new shoots to grow from the soil; leave them in place to add thickness, or transplant to other areas.

Landscape Merit

This bush has ridged, somewhat square twigs and dark-green leaves that turn red in fall and give it a great look in the winter landscape.

Additional Information

Dwarf burning bushes are not known for flowering. Pay close attention and you will notice a few white flowers in spring that can produce some small red berries in the fall. Dwarf burning bush growing in tree shade will not turn red until the leaves fall off the shade-producing tree.

Additional Species, Cultivars, or Varieties

'Chicago Fire' is compact, with rich red fall color. 'Compactus' also has great fall color, and is the most common variety available. 'Angelica Compactus' is up to twice as dense and compact as the others listed here. 'Rudy Haag' is probably the best dwarf variety, growing to 4 to 5 ft. high and wide with red fall color. It is a Kentucky introduction. Check out the ones at Bernheim Arboretum.

Dwarf Spirea

Spiraea spp.

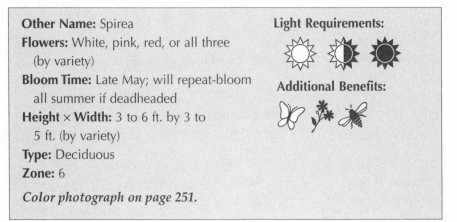

Other Name: Spirea

Flowers: White, pink, red, or all three (by variety)

Bloom Time: Late May; will repeat-bloom all summer if deadheaded

Height × Width: 3 to 6 ft. by 3 to 5 ft. (by variety)

Type: Deciduous

Zone: 6

Color photograph on page 251.

Light Requirements:

Additional Benefits:

Spirea is one of the oldest shrubs in the landscape. In the early fifties, a dwarf variety was beginning to make a name for itself. *Spirea* 'Anthony Waterer' started showing up in garden centers . . . much smaller-growing than the then-popular "bridal wreath spirea," this plant was known to grow to an average size of only 4 feet high by 5 feet wide. Since then, many new varieties of dwarf spirea have been introduced. Some have golden leaves, some green, some green-and-red, and some yellow-and-red. All have great orange-red fall color. They bloom in late spring to summer. Some of the dwarf spirea plants bloom in white, some pink, and some red, and one variety blooms in all of those colors at the same time. That one is called 'Shibori', and it is perfect for homeowners who can't make up their minds on color.

WHEN TO PLANT

Spireas are grown in containers and can be planted anytime the ground is not frozen. You will find them available all season long in 1-, 2-, and 3-gallon containers.

WHERE TO PLANT

Dwarf spireas do great in any type of soil. Just make sure there's good drainage. They bloom best in full sun but will tolerate a half-day of shade. Dwarf spireas make a great low hedge or an underplanting around a high-branched tree. They also have a nice winter appearance, with bare twigs that say, "Hey, I'm part of this landscape even in winter." Every landscape has room for them.

How to Plant

Most spireas are container-grown. Dig a hole no deeper than the soil clump and twice as wide. If you have clay soil, break up the existing soil so that no particle is larger than a golf ball. Backfill and water-in well.

Care and Maintenance

These spireas are free of bugs and diseases. They have their first—and I mean their first—bloom period in late May. After the bloom is finished, take a pair of hedge shears and remove all the spent flowers. Stand back and wait a month, and they will bloom again. Then remove those spent flowers. Repeat this process all summer, and this plant will remind you of a monthly rose. The pruning will also keep the shrubs at a suitable growing size.

Additional Information

Prune off spent blooms and the plants will keep blooming all summer.

Additional Species, Cultivars, or Varieties

'Dolchia' has red flowers and crispy foliage. 'Limemound' has pink flowers and lemon-yellow leaves. 'Gold Princess' has pink flowers and golden-yellow leaves. 'Snow Mound' blooms in white. 'Shibori' produces pink, red, and white flowers, all on the same plant. 'Little Princess' is a great variety with pink flowers and attractive green foliage. It is a good repeat bloomer. The average size is 2 ft. high and wide.

Did You Know?

For best landscape effect and color, always plant three of the same variety. If you would like more than three plants, use several varieties in three-plant clusters.

Falsecypress

Chamaecyparis obtusa 'Nana Gracilis'

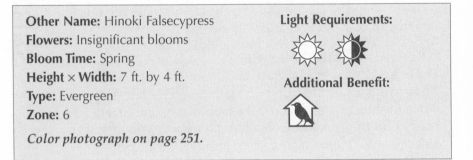

Other Name: Hinoki Falsecypress
Flowers: Insignificant blooms
Bloom Time: Spring
Height × Width: 7 ft. by 4 ft.
Type: Evergreen
Zone: 6

Color photograph on page 251.

Light Requirements:

Additional Benefit:

This beautiful dwarf-growing evergreen is one of the most prized plants in my landscape. It has dark-green needles with new growth that offers just a tinge of light-green color, beautiful rare color that visitors sometimes think is unreal. It is strictly a specimen plant that you will want to place in a prominent viewing area that can be appreciated from both inside and outside the home. Plant it in an area that provides good drainage and some protection from the prevailing northwest winds of winter. A native of Japan and Formosa, *C. obtusa* 'Nana Gracilis' brings a little bit of the Orient to Kentucky. There are many cousins of this variety, which I've listed below.

WHEN TO PLANT

Most falsecypress are grown in containers. A few may be grown in the Pacific Northwest, field-dug during the months of February and March, and balled and burlapped. Both types are shipped to Kentucky nurseries beginning in March and can be planted anytime. Remember, frozen ground is the only deterrent to planting any tree, shrub, or evergreen here.

WHERE TO PLANT

Plant falsecypress in full sun to a half-day of shade. Make sure your planting site has decent soil (no heavy clay) that will provide good drainage. Place falsecypress where you can visually enjoy it year-round. Plant as a centerpiece in a dwarf conifer bed, or use it as the anchor plant in a bed full of annuals and perennials. This plant needs protection from cold winter wind.

HOW TO PLANT

Dig your planting hole 50 percent wider than the rootball or soil clump, and no deeper than the depth of the roots. Make sure the planting site is not made up of heavy clay soil. Break up your soil into particles no larger than golf balls. Backfill, and water-in thoroughly.

CARE AND MAINTENANCE

Be sure to keep this plant moist but *not* wet during hot, dry summers. It does well in nonacidic soil, soil that is typical for most of Kentucky. This plant is definitely considered low-maintenance and has no known bugs or diseases.

ADDITIONAL INFORMATION

All falsecypress shed inner needles in spring and in fall; please don't overreact and think your plant is in trouble. This plant has a wonderful, natural, upright-growing shape. Don't prune it to be uniform and stiff-looking; let it establish its own shape.

ADDITIONAL SPECIES, CULTIVARS, OR VARIETIES

C. nootkatensis has arching branches and is another great specimen plant. *C. pisifera* 'Golden Mop' cypress has a spreading habit. *C. pisifera* 'Filifera Aurea' has drooping branches on a spreading plant.

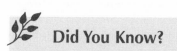 **Did You Know?**

There are many other cultivated varieties of falsecypress. If you find one you like, just be sure it's cold hardy enough for Kentucky winters.

Forsythia

Forsythia × intermedia

Other Names: Border Forsythia, Golden Bells
Flowers: Yellow
Bloom Time: March to April
Height × Width: Up to 8 to 10 ft. by 10 to 12 ft.; trim to desired size
Type: Deciduous
Zone: 6

Color photograph on page 251.

Light Requirements:

Forsythia is one of the oldest shrubs used in landscapes. It is what I call the "Spring Breaker"—when forsythia starts to bloom, spring is in the air. It is an upright-growing shrub; some varieties sweep their branches to the ground. Forsythia blooms in early spring, making its yellow flowers vulnerable to late frosts. Those same flowers form bloom buds beginning in late August. Prune them back, if necessary, right after they bloom (within thirty days) so as not to prune off the flower-producing wood. In fact, all spring-flowering shrubs form their buds in late summer, so the same pruning rule applies to them as well. One forsythia makes a great shrub for spring color, or plant several for a fantastic screen hedge that will screen your neighbor's property (that's not being mean, either, as both you and your neighbor gain both privacy and gorgeous color).

WHEN TO PLANT
Plant forsythia anytime the plants are available and the ground is not frozen. The best selection is in spring. Since forsythia comes in different shades of yellow, buy your plants when they are in bloom at your favorite garden center or nursery store so you can select the color.

WHERE TO PLANT
One half-day of sun or more is necessary for good bloom color. Forsythia likes good, rich soil (don't all plants?) but will adapt to heavy clay soil if that is its only option. Good drainage is a must. Plant in groups or mix with other spring-flowering shrubs like weigela and honeysuckle.

How to Plant

Forsythia plants come from the nursery either balled and burlapped or growing in containers. Container-grown plants should have their roots loosened. Dig a hole as deep as the soil clump and twice as wide. Cover the top burlap of balled-and-burlapped plants with soil or mulch. Backfill with existing soil, making sure each soil clump is no bigger than a golf ball. Water-in well.

Care and Maintenance

Forsythia is low-maintenance and drought tolerant. This fast-growing plant will eventually have to be trimmed to keep it contained. That's easy to do—just do it within a month after the forsythia blooms. Give forsythia a drink of water if the summer is hot and dry.

Additional Information

After your forsythia has been planted for eight to ten years, start pruning off one-third of the oldest growth back to within 12 inches of the ground every year or so after they bloom. To start an all-new plant, you can prune back the entire plant to 12 inches from the ground right after it blooms.

Additional Species, Cultivars, or Varieties

'Lynwood Gold' has bright-yellow flowers. For the amount of bloom color on a single plant, 'Spectabilis' has set the standard for all other varieties. *F. viridissima* 'Bronxensis' is a dwarf-growing variety that acts as a ground cover. Many other varieties will produce favorable results. 'Gold Tide' is another great compact dwarf variety. With lots of yellow blooms and graceful, arching branches, it grows 1 1/2 ft. high and 5 ft. wide.

Did You Know?

Make spring happen early indoors. You can go outside in January and February and cut end branches off your forsythia, bring them in, and put them in a vase of water. Within two weeks, you will have beautiful yellow blossoms for your dining room table.

Fothergilla

Fothergilla gardenii

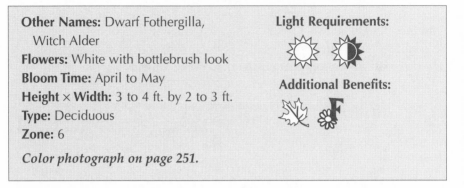

Other Names: Dwarf Fothergilla, Witch Alder

Flowers: White with bottlebrush look

Bloom Time: April to May

Height × Width: 3 to 4 ft. by 2 to 3 ft.

Type: Deciduous

Zone: 6

Color photograph on page 251.

Light Requirements:

Additional Benefits:

A great American dwarf shrub, fothergilla has beautiful white flowers in late April to May. It blooms for about two weeks with flowers that resemble bottlebrushes. Its bluish-green leaves are quite attractive and the fall color is spectacular: the leaves on each plant will vary from bright-yellow to orange to red. You may have all three leaf colors on the same plant at the same time. Use this plant in foundation plantings or in borders, or plant several in one area to give you that mass-planting look. It works well with other dwarf shrubs like azalea, hypericum, and dwarf spirea, and looks good planted in front of bottle-brush buckeye.

WHEN TO PLANT

You will find fothergillas in 1-, 2-, and 3-gallon containers at garden centers. You can plant them anytime the ground is not frozen, but the best selection will be in spring. If my description of this plant and its flowers has not painted a clear picture, stop into your favorite nursery store when the plant's in bloom and check it out for yourself.

WHERE TO PLANT

Plant fothergillas on the east to southeast side of the house where they can get good spring sun but some relief from the hot summer afternoon sun. They prefer good, loose, acidic soil that is well drained. You can amend the soil to suit this plant's needs. I've had good luck with this durable plant in many landscapes, and it will do well in Kentucky.

How to Plant

Dig a hole no deeper than the soil clump. Loosen any roots that are wrapped around the soil clump when you remove the container. Backfill, making sure that no soil particle is bigger than a golf ball. Water-in well.

Care and Maintenance

Fothergilla is trouble free. Hey, if it weren't, I would not be listing a plant that most people have never heard of. This plant will give your landscape added interest in both spring and fall. It requires very little pruning to keep it in bounds. If you find it getting spindly after a few years, prune it back to within 6 inches of the ground after it blooms and it will come back like brand-new.

Landscape Merit

Fothergilla provides both spring flowers and great fall color.

Additional Information

Trouble-free fothergilla makes a great Father's Day gift.

Additional Species, Cultivars, or Varieties

'Blue Mist' definitely wants summer shade. It has beautiful blue-green foliage and fragrant flowers. 'Mt. Airy', which was selected out of Mt. Airy Arboretum in Cincinnati, Ohio, is known for its consistent great fall color; it also has lots of flowers and grows a little taller (5 to 6 feet).

🌿 Did You Know?

Fothergillas are native to the United States. The plant was named after a doctor, John Fothergill (1712–1780), who cultivated many American plants in Essex, England, and many great varieties have come from the initial discovery.

Juniper

Juniperus spp.

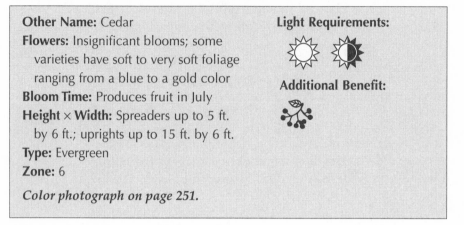

Other Name: Cedar

Flowers: Insignificant blooms; some varieties have soft to very soft foliage ranging from a blue to a gold color

Bloom Time: Produces fruit in July

Height × Width: Spreaders up to 5 ft. by 6 ft.; uprights up to 15 ft. by 6 ft.

Type: Evergreen

Zone: 6

Color photograph on page 251.

Light Requirements:

Additional Benefit:

Juniper is a hardy shrub that has thirteen varieties native to the United States. In Kentucky we have a native species with the name *Juniperus virginiana,* often called Eastern Red Cedar. The wood of this native juniper, which grows along our interstates, is used in making furniture, paneling, and even pencils. Junipers are available to home landscapes as both spreaders and uprights. As spreaders, some junipers grow very low to the ground, which makes them excellent ground covers (see page 140). Others grow to an average height of 4 feet, and they grow best in sunny locations. Uprights can become large, pyramidal trees if they are allowed to. Many of the new varieties of juniper are soft to the touch, easy to trim, and work in well with any landscape. I have room to name only a few of those I consider the great varieties, but keep in mind that new varieties are constantly being introduced.

WHEN TO PLANT

Most junipers are available in containers. Plant any variety whenever the ground is not frozen.

WHERE TO PLANT

Junipers are sun lovers. Give them at least a half-day of sun, whether west or east. These plants are also drought tolerant. Keep them out of the mist of a sprinkler system. Before you buy a particular juniper variety, ask a nursery employee at what height and spread you can maintain it.

How to Plant

Most juniper varieties come from the nursery in containers. Loosen any roots that are wrapped around the outside of the soil clump. Backfill the hole with the soil you dig out. Water-in well. With varieties that spread over the top of the hole, be sure that the backfill goes completely around the soil clump as you fill in so there will not be air pockets exposing the roots. Take your hand and feel around the backfill to make sure the planting hole is filled with soil.

Care and Maintenance

Junipers need a sunny, well-drained site to thrive—any area where rainwater doesn't stand after 1/2 inch of rain. The new varieties listed are quite resistant to bugs and diseases. Problems usually result from planting a juniper in an inappropriate area.

Landscape Merit

Junipers produce berries that attract songbirds.

Additional Information

There is no limit to the use of junipers in the home landscape. Several species are native to the United States. Those used in the Kentucky area are *J. chinensis*, *J. communis*, *J. conferta*, *J. horizontalis*, *J. virginiana*, and *J. squamata*.

Additional Species, Cultivars, or Varieties

The following varieties, listed by type, are my favorites: juniper 'Gold Coast', juniper 'Gold Lace', and juniper 'Mint Julep' are all 3-by-4-foot spreaders; juniper 'Hetzii Columnaris' and juniper 'Robusta Green' are uprights that grow 10 to 15 feet high by 5 feet wide; juniper 'Wichita Blue' grows upright 10 to 15 feet high by 5 to 8 feet wide; juniper 'Welchii' grows upright to 8 feet.

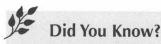 **Did You Know?**

The fruit of the juniper is used to flavor gin.

Korean Boxwood

Buxus microphylla var. *koreana*

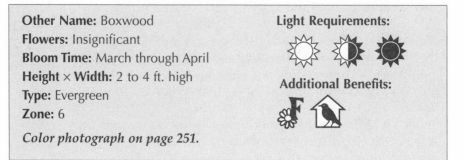

Other Name: Boxwood
Flowers: Insignificant
Bloom Time: March through April
Height × Width: 2 to 4 ft. high
Type: Evergreen
Zone: 6

Color photograph on page 251.

Light Requirements:

Additional Benefits:

For many years, homeowners and landscapers alike have tried to incorporate common English boxwood into home landscapes in Kentucky. Too often, our cold winters can wreak havoc on these tender evergreens, causing the leaves to turn brown and dieback to occur. But then along came the Korean boxwood, whose hardiness and compactness allow homeowners in Kentucky to use boxwoods in almost any exposure. Most Korean boxwoods hold their dark, sometimes glossy, green leaf color year-round and really live up to the term "low-maintenance." This plant comes in many varieties, both spreading and upright. It works well as a hedge, an individual foundation plant, an underplanting for an ornamental tree, or a replacement plant for those who want an Alberta spruce but don't want to continually spray for mites.

WHEN TO PLANT
Korean boxwood plants are field-grown (balled and burlapped) or container-grown. Both types can be planted from early spring to late fall, anytime the ground is not frozen.

WHERE TO PLANT
Korean boxwood prefers moist but well-drained soil. The plants will tolerate clay soil as long as it has good drainage. A location that has summer shade that becomes winter sun when the shade tree's leaves come down in fall may result in some leaf burn during a cold winter. Avoid such a location if possible.

HOW TO PLANT
Dig a hole no deeper than, but twice as wide as the rootball or soil clump. Amend heavy clay soil by adding up to 20 percent organic

material to the backfill. Chop up all soil particles so that each one is no larger than a golf ball. Water-in well. For plants that are balled and burlapped, pull back the top burlap after placing the ball of earth into the hole.

CARE AND MAINTENANCE

Korean boxwoods are low-maintenance plants. Spring aphids can cause some leaf curl, but it is not a serious problem. It's best to prune boxwood with pruning shears; since they grow slowly, this is not a big chore. Check for moisture during hot, dry periods. Water as necessary, and keep a 2-inch mulch layer under each plant.

LANDSCAPE MERIT

Korean boxwood is cold hardy and makes a great evergreen hedge.

ADDITIONAL INFORMATION

Some varieties grow naturally smaller than others. Check with a nursery employee to make sure you get the right variety for your landscape needs. Some varieties have bluer leaves than others, and that may be what you're looking for.

ADDITIONAL SPECIES, CULTIVARS, OR VARIETIES

'Green Gem' and 'Green Velvet' are spreading, and each grows like a round ball. 'Green Mountain' forms a perfect pyramidal upright form. 'Winter Gem' is also spreading, but grows more quickly; it has glossy, green leaves. 'Wintergreen' is compact and spreading. This one can winterburn from cold wind and dry soil.

Did You Know?

If you need a number of plants of a boxwood variety, buy them all at one time so you get a matching set.

Korean Lilac

Syringa meyeri 'Palibin'

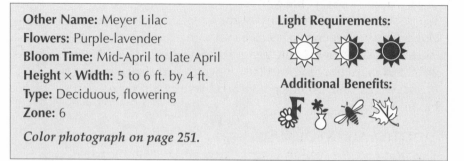

Other Name: Meyer Lilac
Flowers: Purple-lavender
Bloom Time: Mid-April to late April
Height × Width: 5 to 6 ft. by 4 ft.
Type: Deciduous, flowering
Zone: 6

Color photograph on page 251.

Light Requirements:

Additional Benefits:

For many years, homeowners have bought common and French lilacs, thinking they were buying a true shrub. The truth is, they were buying a plant that they couldn't trim if they wanted to keep future bloom. Finally a true lilac shrub has come along. *S. meyeri* is described as a true dwarf. The common and French lilacs should have been described as ornamental trees—that's how big they grow. Meyer lilac is a plant that can be kept small and will tolerate shade. It does not mildew in hot, humid weather and will repeat some blooms during the summer. *S. meyeri* will also give you fantastic orange-red fall leaf color. Now this is a lilac you can learn to love.

WHEN TO PLANT

This plant variety is available balled and burlapped or growing in containers. You can plant anytime the ground is not frozen, but if you plant in the early spring, you can enjoy your first blooms this year.

WHERE TO PLANT

For the best blooms, plant Korean lilac in full sun to part shade. This plant will grow in any type of soil that has decent drainage and will also produce flowers even when it is a very young plant. The more sun it gets, the better the fall leaf color it will have. I have planted meyeri in areas of no sun but good natural light, and they have bloomed and provided fall color anyway.

HOW TO PLANT

Dig a hole as deep as the soil clump and twice as wide. If you have clay soil, break up the clumps to the size of golf balls. Water-in the backfill to remove any air pockets. Mulch to preserve summer moisture.

CARE AND MAINTENANCE

In spring, prune off as many of the finished flowers as possible. This will encourage more spot-bloom of lilac flowers during the summer. There are no bug or disease problems with this plant. Give your lilac an occasional drink during hot, dry weather. Do not prune after July 4 to assure good bloom next year.

ADDITIONAL INFORMATION

This plant works well in your landscape by itself, or use it in a grouping. Plant it in front of larger evergreens, and the flowers of your lilac will be more pronounced. It makes a great gift for mom on Mother's Day.

ADDITIONAL SPECIES, CULTIVARS, OR VARIETIES

'Miss Kim' is another good dwarf variety. *S. vulgaris* is a popular purple or white lilac. French has large flowers. 'Meyeri Standard' is the tree form of the Korean.

Did You Know?

There are many other members of the lilac family. The common and French lilacs (Syringa vulgaris)*, the Persian lilacs* (Syringa × persica)*, and the Preston lilacs* (Syringa × prestoniae) *should be planted in full sun with lots of room so they can grow as flowering trees rather than shrubs. To keep any of these in the 6 ft. to 7 ft. range would take much pruning that will discourage some blooms.*

Nandina

Nandina domestica

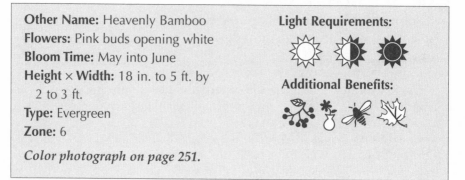

Other Name: Heavenly Bamboo
Flowers: Pink buds opening white
Bloom Time: May into June
Height × Width: 18 in. to 5 ft. by
  2 to 3 ft.
Type: Evergreen
Zone: 6

Color photograph on page 251.

Light Requirements:

Additional Benefits:

Nandina's common name is heavenly bamboo, but it's not in the grass family at all. Nandina is considered evergreen, although in certain parts of Kentucky during really cold winters, it has lost its leaves and the wood has suffered dieback. Even under these conditions, all plants responded well the following spring. There are different cultivars that grow to different heights, but all are upright growing. Nandina's new spring growth is coppery to purplish red and turns a bluish green as leaves mature. The red leaf color returns in the winter in sunny locations. Nandina blooms in May to June with pink flower buds opening to white. The flowers form clusters 1/2 inch wide and 8 to 15 inches long. From the flowers come beautiful clusters of berries that turn red in September and remain until winter. Nandina's berries are showier than the berries of most hollies because nandina's berries are not hidden by the leaves. This plant deserves serious consideration as an addition to your landscape.

WHEN TO PLANT

The best selection will be plants growing in containers in the spring. They will come in 1- to 5-gallon containers. You can plant nandina anytime the ground is not frozen.

WHERE TO PLANT

Nandina prefers moist, fertile soil where it will respond with great growth. It's nice to know, though, that the plant will grow in sun to shade and is adaptable to most types of well-draining soil. It can handle the extremes of temperature and wind exposure that we can have in many parts of Kentucky. Nandina also has good drought tolerance.

How to Plant

Dig a hole as deep as and twice as wide as the soil clump. Loosen any roots that are wrapped around the outside of the soil clump. Break up all soil particles so that each one is no bigger than a golf ball. Backfill, and water-in well to settle the soil.

Care and Maintenance

There are no bugs or disease to seriously threaten this trouble-free plant. After a very cold winter, you can expect some twig dieback. If you notice this, prune back the branches to the green, healthy wood or stems.

Additional Information

There are many uses for nandina in your landscape. Use it as a feature plant in a flower bed or as an unusual, colorful hedge along the deck or patio. Remember, nandina does well in sun or shade, even underneath a large shade tree. It competes well with tree roots.

Additional Species, Cultivars, or Varieties

'Firepower' is one of the best coloring nandinas with crimson leaves from fall through winter. Great for borders, it grows 2 feet high and 2 feet wide. 'Compacta', known for its good fall color, grows 4 to 5 feet high and 3 feet wide. Use it in mass plantings. 'Plum Passion'™ is a new cultivar with the best leaf color of all nandinas. Plant it in full to half-day sun; it grows 4 to 5 feet high and 3 feet wide.

Oakleaf Hydrangea

Hydrangea quercifolia

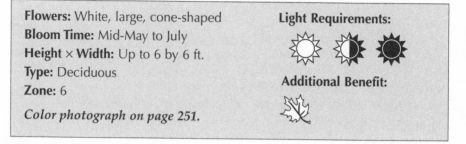

Flowers: White, large, cone-shaped
Bloom Time: Mid-May to July
Height × Width: Up to 6 by 6 ft.
Type: Deciduous
Zone: 6

Color photograph on page 251.

Light Requirements:

Additional Benefit:

This is a great flowering shrub for many landscape situations. It will do well in total shade to full sun. As its name indicates, oakleaf hydrangea has large, oak-shaped leaves. It produces large, cone-shaped, white blooms that size out at 8 inches long and 3 to 4 inches wide and begin to appear in mid-May into July. Leave the flowers on the plant because they dry to a pinkish-purple that lasts into the fall. Oakleafs will brighten shady or sunny areas and make for a great, showy group planting and for shrub borders. Only room for one? That will look good, too, and the fall color is outstanding.

WHEN TO PLANT

Oakleaf hydrangeas are best planted in spring to maximize the time these plants will have to get their roots established. You will find them available both balled and burlapped and in containers. Both types will transplant very easily.

WHERE TO PLANT

Oakleaf hydrangeas prefer fairly decent soil that is on the acidic side and has good drainage. They will, however, adapt to clay or alkaline soil. Feed with a soil acidifier every spring.

HOW TO PLANT

If you have clay soil, dig a hole no deeper than the soil clump but about three times as wide. Add some organic material to the existing soil, and break up clay soil particles so that none are larger than a golf ball. Mix in some organic material and backfill. Water-in well.

CARE AND MAINTENANCE

Oakleafs can really look stressed the first year they're installed. Try not to overwater and overfertilize when you first plant. Be patient, they'll get a lot better looking. Be sure to keep your hydrangea mulched to 2 inches deep, and check for water during hot, dry periods. Always prune away any dead stems as they appear, and don't do any tip-pruning to your hydrangea more than sixty days after it blooms. If any branches fail to leaf out in spring, remove them with pruners.

LANDSCAPE MERIT

Oakleaf hydrangea produces a good bloom and great fall color.

ADDITIONAL INFORMATION

Oakleaf hydrangeas set their bloom buds in the fall for the next season, so don't do any pruning after May 1. The large, oak-shaped leaves turn a crimson red, giving you great fall leaf color.

ADDITIONAL SPECIES, CULTIVARS, OR VARIETIES

'Snow Queen' has bigger flowers than oakleaf hydrangea. *H.* 'Peegee' has similar flowers but blooms in August. *H.* 'Annabelle' is a great white flowering hydrangea, as is *H.* 'Tardiva'. This is a late bloomer, flowering in late August into September. *H.* 'Dooley' is a macrophylla type with blue flowers. It is very cold hardy and named for Coach Vince Dooley of the University of Georgia.

Did You Know?

Hydrangea macrophylla *has blue or pink blooms and needs winter protection from cold wind in northern Kentucky. If you want the blooms to be blue, acidify the soil.* Hydrangea macrophylla *will never flower if it is located in an area with a northern exposure. Tuck it away in a corner of the foundation on the east or southeast side of the house.*

Scarlet Firethorn

Pyracantha coccinea

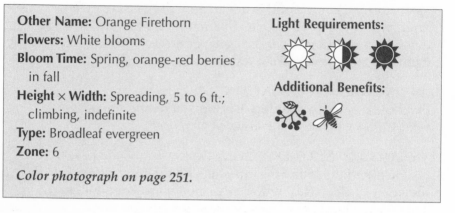

Other Name: Orange Firethorn
Flowers: White blooms
Bloom Time: Spring, orange-red berries in fall
Height × Width: Spreading, 5 to 6 ft.; climbing, indefinite
Type: Broadleaf evergreen
Zone: 6

Color photograph on page 251.

Light Requirements:

Additional Benefits:

Firethorn is a plant that can be used as a shrub, an informal hedge, or a great barrier plant, an excellent plant to consider if you want a true living fence between "good" neighbors. It produces sharp thorns that grow from 1/2 to 3/4 inches long. It is also excellent for planting close to a high wall as an espalier. It can be trained to grow up a trellis or arbor. Select from the winter-hardy varieties that I have listed below. It has small, showy, white flowers in spring that form beautiful orange-red berries in fall.

WHEN TO PLANT

Firethorn should be planted in spring to give the plant plenty of time to get established before its first winter. Do not transplant to another part of your landscape after it's been planted one year.

WHERE TO PLANT

Plant firethorn in well-drained soil. It does well in hot, dry summer locations, and does best in soil that ranges from a little acidic to a little alkaline. Plant it where you can enjoy the fall and winter berries.

HOW TO PLANT

Plant firethorn from a container in spring. Make sure the planting location does not hold water after a heavy rain. Dig a hole no deeper than the soil clump and twice as wide, loosening any roots attached to the soil clump. Backfill with existing soil and water-in well.

CARE AND MAINTENANCE

Firethorn, when planted in stressful sites, can attract fire-blight and a disease called "scab" that turns the berries a dark, musty color. Plant this one in well-drained soil in a location that has good air circulation. Extremely cold winters can cause branches of certain varieties to die back, but the varieties I list below are resistant to this.

ADDITIONAL INFORMATION

Pyracantha spines can induce reactions in humans. Always wear gloves when pruning and handling.

ADDITIONAL SPECIES, CULTIVARS, OR VARIETIES

I recommend the following varieties for all of Kentucky. 'Chadwicki' is a hardy, prolific fruiter; trim to your delight. 'Lalandei', a hardy, vigorous grower, has large berries. 'Wyattii' and 'Yukon' are both cold hardy and produce great berries. 'Gnome' is densely branched with a spreading growth habit. It is very hardy with lots of berries. 'Mohave' is upright growing and produces large masses of bright orange-red berries.

Did You Know?

If you want to keep the neighbor's cat or dog out of your yard, you can plant firethorn as a living hedge. Be sure to leave a way for your favorite neighbors to come into your yard to visit.

St. Johns Wort

Hypericum patulum 'Sungold'

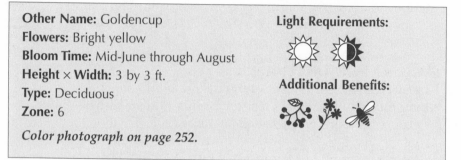

Other Name: Goldencup
Flowers: Bright yellow
Bloom Time: Mid-June through August
Height × Width: 3 by 3 ft.
Type: Deciduous
Zone: 6

Color photograph on page 252.

Light Requirements:

Additional Benefits:

This is one summer-blooming shrub that I really love. It can be called semievergreen because most of the leaves remain on the plant in zone 6. The common name that I have given this hypericum is "the yellow daffodil bush," because the blooms look like and are the color of yellow daffodils. I have a grouping of five in my front landscape right outside the picture window in my living room. They bloom some in June, then in all of July and August, and I get to enjoy them both from outside and from inside my picture window. These plants maintain a size of 3 feet high and 3 feet wide. As they continue to grow taller they will continue to have yellow blooms on the tips of their many branches. The leaves are an attractive gray-green color.

WHEN TO PLANT

St. Johns wort is available from the garden store in early spring. You won't be impressed yet because it will look like a pot of sticks and some leaves. Since you can plant St. Johns wort anytime the ground is not frozen, wait, if you like, until they start to bloom. If you have taste like mine, you'll buy three to five of them. They are so easy to grow and enjoy.

WHERE TO PLANT

This plant has flowers that produce best in full sun. It will, however, tolerate a few hours of daily shade. St. Johns wort appreciates good, loose soil but will tolerate clay. Make sure the planting site has good drainage. If you want just one, plant it in your perennial bed.

How to Plant

Since all these plants are grown in containers, remove the soil clump from the pot and loosen any wrapped roots. Dig a hole no deeper than but twice as wide as the soil clump. Break up clay particles to the size of golf balls, and water-in well.

Care and Maintenance

In early spring, prune back all twigs to within 8 inches of the ground. This plant is resistant to insects and disease. Because St. Johns wort is shallow-rooted, protect those roots with a 2-inch covering of mulch. This plant is drought tolerant, but appreciates a drink in dry, hot weather. Keep the mulch off the stems of the plants.

Additional Information

From the flowers on hypericum come the fruit. The fruit will remind you of black olives, and the birds like them too. Hypericum does extremely well in heavy clay soils compared to many other shrubs. You will find their persistent bloom a welcome addition to your landscape.

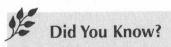

Additional Species, Cultivars, or Varieties

Hypericum frondosum 'Sunburst' has characteristics similar to those of 'Sungold', but it grows a little taller and wider.

Did You Know?

St. Johns wort is an herb that is considered to be nature's anti-depressant.

Summersweet

Clethra alnifolia

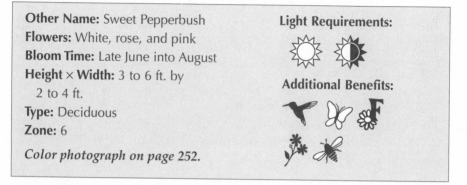

Other Name: Sweet Pepperbush
Flowers: White, rose, and pink
Bloom Time: Late June into August
Height × Width: 3 to 6 ft. by
  2 to 4 ft.
Type: Deciduous
Zone: 6

Color photograph on page 252.

Light Requirements:

Additional Benefits:

Summersweet is loved for its summer flowers, attractive dark-green leaves, and wonderful fragrance. It makes a good, narrow-growing shrub border (great for small yards) and an excellent plant for shade and poorly drained areas. Dwarf varieties like 'Hummingbird' have white flowers and grow to an average size of 30 to 40 inches, while 'Rosea' has pink flowers and will average a height of around 6 feet. There are many varieties to choose from, and they are all great landscape additions.

WHEN TO PLANT

Plant summersweet anytime the ground is not frozen. If you have a choice, choose spring, and you will be able to enjoy those great blooms the very first year.

WHERE TO PLANT

With the exception of deep shade, summersweet will grow in any exposure. The fact that it will tolerate poor, slow-draining soil should make this plant a must for homeowners who have those conditions. Plant summersweet where you can stop and smell the blossoms. Plant to form a narrow hedge along your property line or in a narrow bed between the house and the sidewalk. Plant summersweet in an area where you can enjoy the hummingbirds without disturbing them.

HOW TO PLANT

Most if not all summersweet comes in containers. Dig a hole no deeper than the soil clump and twice as wide. Loosen any roots that are wrapped around the outside of the soil clump. Backfill the hole with the existing soil, making sure no particle of soil is larger than a golf ball. Water-in well to settle the back-filled soil.

CARE AND MAINTENANCE
Be sure to give summersweet an occasional drink of water during hot, dry weather. Do any necessary pruning in spring.

ADDITIONAL INFORMATION
The flowers of summersweet are long-lasting and very fragrant. The fall color is yellow; if the plant is growing in acidic soil, the fall color is a golden-yellow.

ADDITIONAL SPECIES, CULTIVARS, OR VARIETIES
'Hummingbird' is dwarf-growing and has large 6- to 7-inch white flowers. 'Rosea' has dark-pink flowers. 'Pink Spire' has light-pink flowers. 'Ruby Spice' has deep-pink flowers.

Did You Know?
This plant is underused by landscape designers. If you are having professional landscape help and this plant is not suggested, bring it to your designer's attention. 'Hummingbird' is considered by many to be the finest plant available to gardeners.

Viburnum 'Alleghany'

Viburnum × rhytidophylloides

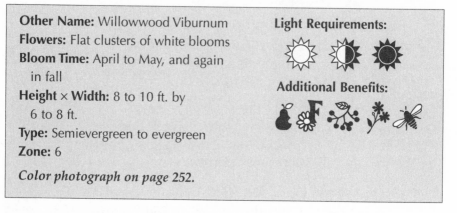

Other Name: Willowwood Viburnum
Flowers: Flat clusters of white blooms
Bloom Time: April to May, and again in fall
Height × Width: 8 to 10 ft. by 6 to 8 ft.
Type: Semievergreen to evergreen
Zone: 6

Color photograph on page 252.

Light Requirements:

Additional Benefits:

This mostly evergreen shrub has dark, leathery, green leaves with light gray-brown undersides. The leaves appear coarse, almost leather-like, which makes them quite attractive. In zone 6, the leaves hold on for most if not all of the winter; they may drop in zone 5, but there is no twig dieback, and all-new leaves appear in spring. 'Alleghany' blooms in mid-April to May with white cluster flowers that are 3 to 4 inches in diameter. It has reddish fruit in summer that turns black in the fall. The plant does well in full sun to full shade and has many landscape uses: you can plant several around foundations as a tall screen, or use it in tree shade where you were thinking of planting a hemlock or white pine. It grows to an average of 8 feet tall, but can be pruned and kept smaller.

WHEN TO PLANT

'Alleghany' is available in spring at area garden centers. Smaller sizes are usually available in containers and larger sizes, 4 feet and up, are mostly available balled and burlapped (B&B). You can plant either anytime the ground is not frozen.

WHERE TO PLANT

Viburnum 'Alleghany' has many landscape uses, especially screening. It does well in full sun to partial shade. It will tolerate summer shade and winter sun, but such conditions will cause the leaves to fall off in late November. In southern Kentucky, the leaves should stay on all winter.

How to Plant

Dig a hole no deeper than the soil clump and twice as wide. Break up the soil to particles the size of golf balls. Water-in well to settle the backfill.

Care and Maintenance

No bugs or diseases bother this plant. Be sure to water during hot, dry periods, especially if it is growing in the root zones of surrounding trees.

Additional Information

This variety is much improved over the true leatherleaf viburnum. It can take heavy pruning to keep the plants controlled.

Additional Species, Cultivars, or Varieties

Viburnum rhytidophylloides 'Willowwood' is a faster-growing cultivar similar to 'Alleghany'. *Viburnum × juddii* is a deciduous species that has sweet spring aroma and great fall color. *Viburnum plicatum tomentosum* 'Shasta' is a deciduous variety with white blooms in spring and black berries in fall. *Viburnum plicatum* is a deciduous variety that is called "Japanese snowball" for its white flower clusters. *Viburnum nudum* 'Winterthur' has glossy leaves, abundant white flowers in sprays, and very large clusters of purple-black fruit in the fall.

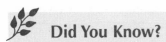

🌿 Did You Know?

From the flowers to the fruit to the fall leaf color, the deciduous types of the viburnum family are a wonderful group of ornamental shrubs. Always prune right after bloom so as not to affect the next season's bloom. There are many other varieties not listed because of space. In my opinion, this is the finest family of flowering shrubs available.

Virginia Sweetspire

Itea virginica 'Henry's Garnet'

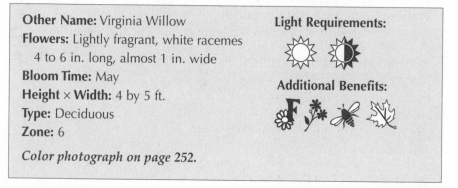

Other Name: Virginia Willow
Flowers: Lightly fragrant, white racemes
   4 to 6 in. long, almost 1 in. wide
Bloom Time: May
Height × Width: 4 by 5 ft.
Type: Deciduous
Zone: 6

Color photograph on page 252.

Light Requirements:

Additional Benefits:

If you think I like hypericum, wait until you read how much I like this shrub. Virginia sweetspire is a very interesting shrub that has fragrant flowers in May. It is basically a spreading plant, growing a lot wider than tall. Sweetspire is largely unknown to homeowners and many nursery employees. It blooms for about three weeks. In fall, its leaves turn a burgundy red and stay on the plant well into December. In fact, in mild Kentucky winters, sweetspire holds its beautiful leaves throughout the winter. This plant does best in moist or wet areas, but it also does well in dry clay soils. Sweetspire plants make a great group, whether grown as a low hedge or as an underplanting around a flowering tree.

WHEN TO PLANT

Sweetspire is available in containers. You can plant this beauty anytime the ground is not frozen. Don't wait until fall; if you plant sweetspire in spring, you can enjoy its flowers the very first year you own it. The best selection of sizes is in April or May.

WHERE TO PLANT

This plant can adapt to many different pH levels. It prefers moist, acidic areas but will grow in full sun to half-day sun. Water sweetspire occasionally during hot, dry weather. Plant it where you can enjoy its burgundy leaves from inside the house in late fall and winter. If planting in heavy clay, add some compost or pine bark chips to the existing soil as you backfill.

How to Plant

Container-grown sweetspire needs a hole that's no deeper than the depth of the soil clump, and twice as wide. Loosen any roots wrapped around the soil clump. Backfill with existing soil, and water-in well to remove any air pockets.

Care and Maintenance

Sweetspire is a plant that spreads by sending up new stems from the soil clump. Prune away any unwanted growth anytime you see it. Sweetspire blooms off old growth, so trim it back right after it blooms to the height you desire.

Additional Information

This plant can make more new plants in your landscape if you divide the root clump with a spade in early spring. Sweetspire's great winter color makes it a great plant for all seasons.

Additional Species, Cultivars, or Varieties

'Little Henry' is a Kentucky introduction and a more compact variety that has 3- to 4-inch-long flowers on a shorter-growing shrub; it also has great fall color.

Did You Know?

Dwarf-growing shrubs like Itea *need to be pruned annually to be kept at your desired height and width. Remember, no shrub stops growing until the day it dies.*

Weigela 'Java Red'

Weigela florida

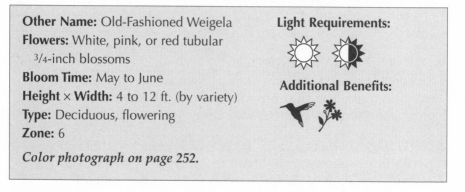

Other Name: Old-Fashioned Weigela
Flowers: White, pink, or red tubular
3/4-inch blossoms
Bloom Time: May to June
Height × Width: 4 to 12 ft. (by variety)
Type: Deciduous, flowering
Zone: 6

Color photograph on page 252.

Light Requirements:

Additional Benefits:

This group of flowering shrubs dates way back. There are varieties that grow 8 to 10 feet wide, with some blooming in pink and some blooming in red. Their trumpet-shaped flowers appear in early May to June and have been known to spot-bloom during the summer. 'Java Red' is a variety that can be used in many ways. Its average size is 3 to 4 feet high and 4 to 5 feet wide. The flowers start as carmine-red buds that open to rose-pink in full bloom. The leaves are ornamental as well. They're deep-green with a reddish-purple overcast, and need a half-day or more of sun for best leaf color. This is a great shrub for low hedges or group plantings.

WHEN TO PLANT
'Java Red' is available in containers all season long. Most home-owners plant in spring. Plant anytime the ground is not frozen.

WHERE TO PLANT
Plant weigela in an area that gets at least a half-day of sun. This plant has landscape beauty even when it's not in bloom. In a group, weigela makes an excellent low hedge. It also looks great planted in clusters of five to seven plants. All weigela plants do well in clay soil but would appreciate good drainage.

HOW TO PLANT
Dig a hole no deeper than the soil clump and twice as wide. Loosen any attached roots. Chop up all soil clumps to the size of golf balls, backfill, and water-in well to settle the soil.

CARE AND MAINTENANCE

Weigela forms most of its bloom buds in the fall. Do not prune until after they bloom. If you want to keep this plant at a certain size, always prune back one-third of the older growth. Weigela is free from bug or disease problems.

ADDITIONAL INFORMATION

Remember, just because the nursery sign says "Weigela," that does not mean they are all 'Java Red'. Be sure to get plenty of information about the variety you plan to buy.

ADDITIONAL SPECIES, CULTIVARS, OR VARIETIES

'Bristol Ruby' grows upright, up to 7 feet, and has ruby-red flowers. 'Variegata' has deep-rose flowers and green-and-white leaves. 'White Knight' is a white-blooming weigela that grows to 6 feet. Wine and Roses™ has burgundy leaves and hot-pink flowers, and grows from 4 to 5 feet. 'Minuet' is very dwarf growing with deep-red flowers and purple-tinged, dark green leaves.

Did You Know?

Although weigela is one of the oldest shrubs available, new cultivars make this plant, especially the dwarf, excellent for modern-day landscapes. They do attract hummingbirds but not bees.

Yew, Spreading

Taxus spp.

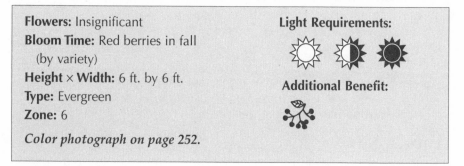

Flowers: Insignificant
Bloom Time: Red berries in fall
(by variety)
Height × Width: 6 ft. by 6 ft.
Type: Evergreen
Zone: 6

Color photograph on page 252.

Light Requirements:

Additional Benefit:

Spreading taxus or yews have been the most popular plant in home foundation plantings for years. They grow in full sun to full shade. One thing all spreading yews require is good drainage. They do not want to be planted in low areas that collect water after a heavy rain. Some, like *Taxus cuspidata*, grow much faster than the cultivar *Taxus × media* 'Brownii'. Some female varieties have red berries in the fall that add to their ornamental beauty. One of the worst exposures you can have for almost any evergreen is summer tree shade that becomes winter sun when those trees drop their leaves. But Japanese yews can tolerate those drastic light changes and remain great plants in your landscape. Grow as a hedge or space to leave each plant in a row as an individual plant. Trim to the size and shape you wish your yews to attain.

WHEN TO PLANT

You can plant spreading yews anytime the ground is not frozen. Most Japanese yews are available at your local garden center as balled and burlapped; some are field-potted and available in containers. However the taxus is available, it will transplant very easily.

WHERE TO PLANT

Good drainage is a must. Even in clay soil, the planting area must drain after heavy rains. This plant will do well on the north side of the house where other evergreens might fail or look ugly because of lack of sun. Do not plant under a downspout.

How to Plant
Plant your yew in a hole half again as wide as the soil clump. In clay soil, chop up the soil so that no clump is larger than a golf ball. Plant at a depth no deeper than the rootball.

Care and Maintenance
Japanese yew spreaders have few insect and disease problems. Deer, on the other hand, can be a problem for those of you who have deer in your neighborhood. Sprays are available to make your yews less desirable to deer. Ferti-lome makes a product called This 1 Works® that really does, and it remains on the plant for up to six months.

Landscape Merit
Spreading yews are easy to maintain, green in sun to shade.

Additional Information
Spreading Japanese yews make great individual plants, or a great low hedge when they are allowed to grow together. For hedges, plant on 3-foot centers. You can trim spreading yews and keep them as small as 12 by 12 inches, or prune to another desired size. Yews are best trimmed with hand-pruners. In 1942, to help with identification, a collection of *Taxus* was begun at the Ohio Agricultural Research and Development Center in Wooster, Ohio, and there are many large specimens around the University of Kentucky.

Additional Species, Cultivars, or Varieties
The following yew species are all basically spreading in habit: *Taxus cuspidata*, *Taxus × media* 'Brownii', 'Densiformis', 'Dark Green Spreader', 'Runyan', 'Wardii', 'Andersonii', 'Natorpiana', 'Everlow', and 'Broad Beauty'. Some will appeal more to your eye than others. Go with the one that will grow the way you like.

Yew, Upright

Taxus cultivars

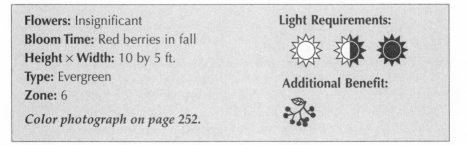

Flowers: Insignificant
Bloom Time: Red berries in fall
Height × Width: 10 by 5 ft.
Type: Evergreen
Zone: 6

Color photograph on page 252.

Light Requirements:

Additional Benefit:

Every landscape that was installed as recently as ten years ago, either by the homeowner or by a landscape contractor, is likely to have some upright yews. These plants grow at a slow to medium pace, are resistant to bugs and disease, and grow well in sun or shade. The most popular cultivar is *Taxus × media* 'Hicksii'. It is a columnar or upright evergreen that makes a great hedge for screening purposes and works well for a home with a high foundation. Most of the plants have red berries in the fall, loved by the birds. Japanese yews are among the oldest plants known to humankind. They have great longevity under good growing conditions and, once established, literally take care of themselves.

WHEN TO PLANT

Plant upright yews, whether balled and burlapped or in a container, anytime the ground is not frozen. Supply and demand have kept upright yews at the same price they were fifteen years ago.

WHERE TO PLANT

Upright yews will grow in sun or shade. Sun growth is a bright green, while shade growth will be more bluish-green. Yews must have well-drained soil. Although they will adapt to heavy clay, make sure the planting area does not hold water for several hours after a heavy rain. Plant these upright evergreens wherever you need some height and green foliage year-round.

HOW TO PLANT

Plant yews the same way you would other evergreens: one-half again the width of the soil clump and no deeper. Break up all the soil clumps to the size of a golf ball before backfilling the hole. Water-in well as you backfill with the soil.

CARE AND MAINTENANCE

Japanese yew uprights have few insect and disease problems. Deer, on the other hand, can be a problem if you have them in your neighborhood. Sprays are available to make your yews less desirable to them. Ferti-lome makes a product called This 1 Works® that really does, and it remains on the plant for up to six months; it's a very bitter-tasting substance that the deer will shy away from.

ADDITIONAL INFORMATION

Upright yews can be trimmed and kept at any size, most easily accomplished by handpruning and keeping the hedge shears in the garage. It may look like lots of work, but believe me, the plants will stay a lot more attractive by handpruning.

ADDITIONAL SPECIES, CULTIVARS, OR VARIETIES

In addition to the columnar *Taxus* × *media* 'Hicksii', there's *Taxus* × *media* 'Capitata', a pyramidal evergreen that shows up well on the corner of the foundation or wherever you want a pointed evergreen. It will grow up to 40 feet unpruned but can be kept to 6 to 10 feet if pruned once a year. 'Hatfieldii' is another good columnar upright; although somewhat vase-shaped in form, it makes a good hedge cultivar like 'Hicksii'.

Did You Know?

As their name indicates, Japanese yews are native to Japan. They have been known to grow for over a hundred years when given a suitable environment.

CHAPTER EIGHT

Trees

ALL LIVING PLANTS give us the oxygen we breathe; a large amount of that oxygen is given to us by trees. And that's just the beginning of the benefits we can gain from trees. A well-placed shade tree on the south or west side of our home can replace a very large air-conditioner that costs many dollars to cool our house in the summer. That same tree drops its leaves in the fall, allowing the winter sun to help warm the house during the cold months and again saving us many utility dollars. Ornamental trees do the same thing, especially in smaller yards where there just isn't enough room for a large shade tree. They also provide seasonal color. And don't forget about fall color—trees can give the artist's touch to any autumn landscape. Some ornamental trees give us fall fruit, which adds to our landscape color and also provides fruit for us and our feathered friends. Not only can trees of all types make the home landscape complete, they can make the whole neighborhood beautiful.

HOW BIG WILL THAT TREE GROW?

No living tree or shrub stops growing until the day it dies. But don't be intimidated by the mature sizes of the trees listed in this chapter. A tree that you buy at 8 feet might take thirty years before it reaches a height of 40 feet. The average time a family lives in one home is about ten years. Many of you will not see a tree you have planted reach mature height. Still, you don't want to plant a tree that you know will grow 40 feet wide any closer than 25 feet from the house. One other thing: evergreen trees grow much wider at the bottom than they do at the top. Make sure you've got the yard space to give up to this spread. As grandma used to say, "Look up, look down, look all around."

STAKING

To stake or not to stake? Actually, the staking of trees has been proven to be unnecessary in almost all situations. Trees do best when not secured by a piece of wire attached to a stake. Make sure that you backfill all planting holes with the soil you've dug out. Backfill, breaking up all soil particles to the size of golf balls. Water-in well, and as the soil-filled hole is filling with water, take your spade or shovel and work the backfilled soil up and down to settle it. This practice will cause the soil clump to become locked in place.

MULCH: IS IT IMPORTANT?

Mulching freshly planted trees is very important. Mulch rings not only look good, frustrate weeds, and retain moisture, but they serve another great function—keeping the lawn mower from nicking or bruising the trunk. Remember that 2 inches of mulch is enough, but don't put any of the 2 inches on the trunk itself.

DID YOU KNOW?

It's a good idea to determine just what function you want a tree to serve in your landscape, and then select a tree that is known to be good for that function. A few suggestions follow. Many trees may be grown as shrubs—those marked with an asterisk (*) are described in the Shrubs chapter.

Trees that make fast-growing screens:	Trees for formal shearing:	Deer-resistant trees:
Arborvitae	Amur Maple	American Holly
Canadian Hemlock	Arborvitae	Eastern White Pine
Eastern White Pine	Columnar Red Maple	Falsecypress*
Hinoki Falsecypress*	Eastern White Pine	Norway Spruce
Norway Spruce	Juniper Uprights*	Redbud
Red Maple	Washington Hawthorn	
Serviceberry		
White Willow		

American Holly

Ilex opaca

Other Name: Holly Tree
Flowers/Foliage: Small white blooms/
dark-green, dense leaves
Bloom Time: April to early May
Height × Width: 20 to 30 ft. high
by 10 to 20 ft. wide
Type: Broadleaf evergreen
Zone: 6

Color photograph on page 252.

Light Requirements:

Additional Benefits:

American holly is a native broadleafed evergreen tree. It was largely ignored as a landscaping plant during the frigid winters of the 1970s. Extreme low temperatures burned the leaves severely in most home landscapes. Most hollies did not die, but the damage to branches left most reduced to half their size. Homeowners tended to shy away from planting new hollies for several years. In the meantime, new varieties were developed, with improved cold hardiness. Now these new, hardier varieties should be included in many landscapes. To have red berries, the female hollies require a male holly nearby, although the male does not have to be in the same yard. Any male holly within two city blocks will pollinate a female, resulting in beautiful red berries. There are many varieties of holly to choose from, but I recommend the varieties listed in this book.

WHEN TO PLANT

Plant hollies that are balled and burlapped in the spring or fall. Container-grown hollies can be planted anytime the ground is not frozen.

WHERE TO PLANT

Ideally, holly would like to be in fertile, moist, loose, acidic, well-drained soil in partial shade to full sun—in Kentucky, just make sure the planting location is well drained. Stay away from dry areas with exposure to northwest winter wind.

How to Plant

Dig your planting hole as deep as the soil clump and twice as wide. Trees grown in containers should have their roots loosened from the sides of soil clump. Backfill, breaking up any clay clumps, and water-in well.

Care and Maintenance

A few insect problems such as holly leaf miner can occur occasionally, but it is never life-threatening. This problem and any other insect problems can be handled by using a soil-drench systemic pesticide. Carefully follow label instructions.

Landscape Merit

Holly makes an excellent specimen plant or group planting.

Additional Information

This plant does poorly in shady conditions that are caused by surrounding trees. Always give the holly its own root space. These hollies grow in a pyramidal shape with dark- green, densely grown leaves. To shape your holly, prune it anytime; save some pruning for the holidays to have fresh-cut holly boughs for December. Visit Bernheim Forest for a look at some great specimens.

Additional Species, Cultivars, or Varieties

'Greenleaf' is strong-growing with glossy leaves and has bright red berries when it is young. 'Jersey Princess' has dark-green leaves, lots of berries, and is cold hardy. 'Jersey Knight' is the male version of 'Jersey Princess'; the males do not have berries. Foster holly (*Ilex fosteri*) is a great plant for Kentucky.

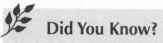 **Did You Know?**

The great holly varieties listed here are hardy to minus 20 degrees Fahrenheit.

American Yellowwood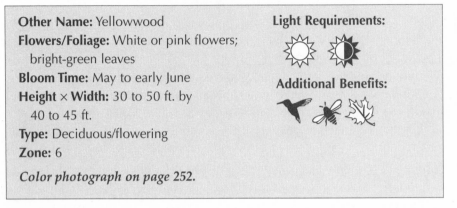

Cladrastis kentukea

Other Name: Yellowwood
Flowers/Foliage: White or pink flowers;
   bright-green leaves
Bloom Time: May to early June
Height × Width: 30 to 50 ft. by
   40 to 45 ft.
Type: Deciduous/flowering
Zone: 6

Color photograph on page 252.

Light Requirements:

Additional Benefits:

Yellowwood grows equally well in high pH soils and in acidic soils that have good drainage. It reaches 30 to 50 feet in height, growing a little more than a foot per year, and 40 to 45 feet wide. It is usually low branched with multiple stems. Its white flowers bloom in May to early June. The flowers tend to be plentiful every other year, and even for the years in between, yellowwood is colorful. Very young trees start producing flowers, much to the delight of the bees that seek the flower nectar. The leaves open in the spring with a bright-yellowish-green turning green for the summer. Yellowwood has excellent yellow fall leaf color. Growing on limestone cliffs and ridges, this tree is native to Kentucky. Many garden centers don't stock this tree because they don't know about it or you don't ask for it. Let's inform everyone about it so that more Kentuckians can enjoy this native tree.

WHEN TO PLANT

Plant yellowwood balled and burlapped or from containers anytime the ground is not frozen and the plants are available. You may want to make a few calls to local nurseries to make sure they have these trees before making a trip.

WHERE TO PLANT

Yellowwood is a relatively slow-growing ornamental tree, which makes it a desirable shade/flowering tree for a small yard. Plant it in an area that receives full sun to a half-day of sun. Plant in any type of Kentucky soil as long as the drainage is good.

How to Plant

Dig a hole as deep as and twice as wide as the soil clump or rootball. If you are planting from a container, loosen any roots that are wrapped around the soil clump. Place the roots in the hole, and backfill the soil, making sure all soil particles are no bigger than a golf ball. Water-in well to settle the soil.

Care and Maintenance

Prune yellowwood only during the summer because the tree bleeds profusely if it is pruned in winter or spring. Insects and disease present almost no problems for this tree. Water during the hot, dry periods of summer for a couple of years after planting.

Additional Information

This ornamental tree is known for both its foliage and its bloom color. Plant one as a yard specimen or several to create a group planting or screen.

Additional Species, Cultivars, or Varieties

'Virgilia' is a white-flowering, medium-growing tree with good-looking leaves that turn bright yellow in the fall. 'Rosea', a pink-flowering tree with fragrant flowers, could have a new name soon—'Perkins Pink'.

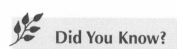 **Did You Know?**

Yellowwood gets its common name from the color of the freshly cut heartwood, which is yellow.

Bald Cypress

Taxodium distichum

Flowers/Foliage: Inconspicuous
flowers/needles drop in fall
Bloom Time: Late March to April
Height × Width: 50 ft. by 20 ft.
Type: Deciduous conifer
Zone: 6

Color photograph on page 252.

Light Requirements:

Additional Benefits:

How about this! A conifer, which we usually think of as evergreen, may not be evergreen at all. Bald cypress has needles, but in the fall those needles turn to an orangey brown and fall off. Bald cypress is a stately upright tree that will tolerate many site conditions, including clay soil and wet soil. Let me warn you, though, that in wet areas, the roots form knobby knees (sections of the root growing aboveground as high as 8 inches) that can be real trippers. These knees, roots that need to be aboveground to get oxygen, can occur 10 to 15 feet beyond the spread of the plant. Plant bald cypress in well-drained soil and you won't have to worry about those knobby knees. This tree makes a great specimen planted out in the open yard. This deciduous conifer also offers small, 1-inch cones that are purple in July, brown in the fall. The bark of the tree is interesting as well, somewhat resembling that of a redwood. It's reddish brown and very fibrous.

WHEN TO PLANT

Most of the bald cypress I've seen in garden centers are grown in containers. If you find any that are balled and burlapped (B&B), make sure they were dug in late winter. Container-grown plants can be planted anytime during the growing season, which is early spring to late fall. If you buy B&B trees, make sure you get at least a one-year guarantee.

WHERE TO PLANT

Bald cypress is flexible about its planting site, but remember that well-drained soils keep the knees from occurring. Bald cypress trees grow best in their own place in the sun and will do well in open areas in a half-day of sun. They make a great screen when they are planted in a group. You can plant bald cypress within 15 feet of a house.

HOW TO PLANT

Whether your cypress is container-grown or balled and burlapped, dig a hole as deep as the soil clump and twice as wide. In wet areas, elevate about 25 percent of the soil clump above the ground and mound-plant. Backfill using existing soil, and break up soil particles to the size of golf balls. Water-in well. No staking is required.

CARE AND MAINTENANCE

As with most plants in this chapter, bald cypress is low maintenance, unbothered by bugs or diseases. Give bald cypress an occasional drink of water when it is planted in hot, dry locations. Do cosmetic pruning anytime it is needed. It will continue to grow in a pyramidal shape for the rest of its life.

LANDSCAPE MERIT

Bald cypress grows quickly, 2 feet per year, and produces great fall color. It is a needle-bearing plant that drops its needles in the fall.

ADDITIONAL INFORMATION

Bald cypress grows upright and somewhat pyramidal without your pruning help. This plant does not take up the ground space as do its evergreen relatives (spruce and pine). It is an interesting tree for many landscapes.

ADDITIONAL SPECIES, CULTIVARS, OR VARIETIES

'Monarch' grows much wider, spreading up to 60 feet wide. Not many people will have enough yard space for this one, in which case the bald cypress is the better choice. 'Shawnee Brave' grows more narrow, 75 feet high and only 18 feet wide. It could be used as a street tree or a single specimen plant in a small yard.

Carolina Silver Bell

Halesia tetraptera

Other Names: Silver Bells, Opossumwood

Flowers/Foliage: Flowers in white to various shades of pink

Bloom Time: April to early May, for 10 to 14 days

Height × Width: 10 to 15 ft. by 10 to 15 ft.

Type: Deciduous/flowering

Zone: 6

Color photograph on page 252.

Light Requirements:

Many of you may have never heard of Carolina silver bell. Well, let's introduce it. Though a native of the South, it is a very cold-hardy plant. Most ornamental trees need at least a half-day of sun, but silver bell will bloom profusely even in shady areas. The white or pink flowers are bell-shaped, borne in clusters that bloom in mid-April to early May. This tree grows about 12 inches a year, more upright than spreading, and has light-green leaves in the summer that turn to a yellowish-green in the fall. Even though silver bell is a native of Kentucky, many people don't know about it; your garden store may have to order it.

WHEN TO PLANT

Spring is the best time to plant balled-and-burlapped silver bells. Container-grown plants can be installed anytime the ground is not frozen.

WHERE TO PLANT

Even though silver bell grows best in sun, it will grow well and bloom beautifully in those shady areas where other ornamental trees will not. This tree will do well in all types of Kentucky soil as long as the drainage is good.

HOW TO PLANT

Whether your silver bell is balled and burlapped or container-grown, dig a hole no deeper than the soil clump but twice as wide. In clay soil, break up all soil particles to the size of golf balls. Backfill with existing soil and water-in well.

CARE AND MAINTENANCE

If you want to grow a very low-maintenance plant, silver bell is the one. It has no bug or disease problems, and is drought and shade tolerant.

LANDSCAPE MERIT

Carolina silver bell is a small ornamental tree that makes a great-looking lawn tree.

ADDITIONAL INFORMATION

Even though there are several cultivars that I will list, you may have problems finding these trees. If your nursery store or garden store does not know where to find it, have them check with their University of Kentucky Extension Service to see where a particular plant can be located.

ADDITIONAL SPECIES, CULTIVARS, OR VARIETIES

'Arnold Pink' has rose-pink flowers. 'Rosea' blooms a rich pink when planted in alkaline soil; in acidic soil, the blooms will be a bluish-pink color. 'Wedding Bells', which was discovered in Ohio, has beautiful white flowers. *H. diptera* is another great one that has white bell-shaped flowers and is a native of Kentucky.

Did You Know?

There are many great trees, shrubs, and evergreens that you may not even be aware of. Don't be afraid to try a new plant variety in your landscape. Make sure your garden center will guarantee these new ones for at least a year.

Common Thornless Honeylocust

Gleditsia triacanthos inermis

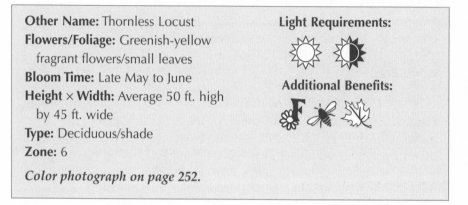

Other Name: Thornless Locust

Flowers/Foliage: Greenish-yellow fragrant flowers/small leaves

Bloom Time: Late May to June

Height × Width: Average 50 ft. high by 45 ft. wide

Type: Deciduous/shade

Zone: 6

Color photograph on page 252.

Light Requirements:

Additional Benefits:

Some plant experts think this tree is overused. On the contrary, it's the *cousin*, the black locust, that lines the highways and interstates of Kentucky. The thornless honeylocust is seldom planted in home landscapes. Garden centers say they don't have them for sale because nobody buys them. Homeowners, on the other hand, say that nurseries don't carry them so they can't buy them. This could be a case of "the chicken or the egg." Well, let's see if we can help both groups. To begin with, honeylocust is a fast grower (as much as 2 feet or more per year). This tree will tolerate all types of soil as long as the drainage is good; it will tolerate clay soil and dry soil, has a great tolerance for salt, and grows well in urban or dusty locations. It also produces fragrant, greenish-yellow flowers in late May to June. It provides filtered shade that allows grass to grow right up to the trunk, and when the leaves come off in the fall, they are small enough that no raking or gutter cleaning is necessary.

WHEN TO PLANT

Smaller sizes of honeylocust are available in containers; larger varieties are available balled and burlapped. Plant either type in the spring or summer. Stay away from field-grown trees that are freshly dug in the fall. Plant trees that have been dug in late winter anytime the ground is not frozen.

WHERE TO PLANT

Give honeylocust some yard space to grow in. Don't plant them within 20 feet of the house. They provide excellent shade for a deck or patio.

HOW TO PLANT

Dig a hole no deeper than and twice as wide as the soil clump. Backfill with existing soil, breaking up all soil clumps to the size of golf balls. Water-in well. No staking is required.

CARE AND MAINTENANCE

Honeylocusts can attract webworm, which builds a nest up in some of the branches and eats the leaves. Use a bamboo pole or a strong water jet to break up the nests.

LANDSCAPE MERIT

The honeylocust is fast-growing and extremely hardy, and will grow in average to heavy clay soil.

ADDITIONAL INFORMATION

Don't be afraid to be the first home on the block to plant a honeylocust. They provide great shade without inhibiting other vegetation from growing under the tree. Honeylocust produces good, yellow fall color.

ADDITIONAL SPECIES, CULTIVARS, OR VARIETIES

'Shademaster' is a strong grower with deep-green leaves; it grows 45 feet tall by 45 feet wide. 'Skyline' grows upright, in a pyramidal shape, and has great fall color; it grows 45 feet tall by 35 feet wide. 'Halka' is a good grower with a large, oval, rounded top; it grows 40 feet tall by 40 feet wide.

Did You Know?

Black locusts with thorns are one of the most naturalized trees on our interstates. You definitely know when they bloom, as they have very fragrant white flowers.

Dogwood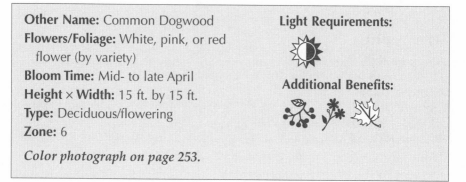

Cornus florida

Other Name: Common Dogwood
Flowers/Foliage: White, pink, or red
 flower (by variety)
Bloom Time: Mid- to late April
Height × Width: 15 ft. by 15 ft.
Type: Deciduous/flowering
Zone: 6

Color photograph on page 253.

Light Requirements:

Additional Benefits:

Even though this tree grows wild in the eastern part of the United States, in Kentucky it can be considered the most disappointing flowering tree around. I say this because in most of Kentucky in the last few years, we've had wet springs and very dry summers. Planting these trees in open, sunny locations where summer moisture is limited has caused many of the *Cornus florida* varieties to decline and die. Dogwoods like an acidic, well-drained soil and a location that is in partial, but not total, shade. Many people who are buying new homes with heavy clay soil have a *Cornus florida* dogwood. All dogwoods have a natural wilt because of the hot sun, and many homeowners, thinking these trees are dry, start watering and watering and watering, until the trees die from overwatering. If you have soil that isn't the best and you want a dogwood, plant *Cornus kousa,* commonly called Chinese dogwood. It blooms later in June but will withstand those planting sites that are not suitable for *C. florida* varieties. Both types have great fall color.

WHEN TO PLANT

When to plant? The bigger question is "When to dig?" Dogwoods are best dug from Kentucky nurseries in February and March. They can be delivered and healed-in at local nurseries and garden centers in early spring, and you can then plant them anytime the ground is not frozen. The same holds true for container-grown plants.

WHERE TO PLANT

Dogwoods grow best where they get overhead protection from hot, summer sun, but are not planted in total shade. Native dogwoods are always seen on the front edge of woody areas where there is good natural light and not a lot of competing tree roots. Do not plant dogwoods in a sunny, heavy-clay location. If dogwoods won't work on your site, there are many other varieties of flowering trees listed in this chapter to choose from.

How to Plant

Dogwoods come either balled and burlapped or container-grown. For container-grown trees, loosen any roots that are wrapped around the soil clump. Dig a hole no deeper than but twice as wide as the ball or soil clump. Break up the soil particles to the size of golf balls, and water-in well.

Care and Maintenance

No matter how pretty the dogwood was where you grew up, don't plant one in clay soil. Choose a redbud instead. There won't be much of a problem with bugs or disease unless you have planted in a poor location. If so, these trees can suffer from mildew, anthracnose, and borers.

Landscape Merit

Dogwoods offer great fall leaf color, berries, and beautiful blooms.

Additional Species, Cultivars, or Varieties

Florida cultivars: *C. florida* has white flowers, but it can take years to bloom. 'Cherokee Chief' has deep-pink, almost red flowers. 'Cloud Nine' blooms with many white flowers. 'Rubra' has pink blossoms. 'Cherokee Princess' has large white flowers. **Kousa cultivars:** *C. kousa* is stress-hardy and produces white flowers in June. 'Rutger's Hybrids' offers different colors of the Chinese strain.

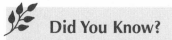

Did You Know?

Dogwoods produce red berries along with their great red fall leaf color. The berries on the Chinese varieties look like strawberries.

Flowering Crabapple

Malus spp.

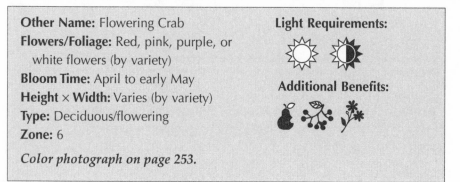

Other Name: Flowering Crab

Flowers/Foliage: Red, pink, purple, or white flowers (by variety)

Bloom Time: April to early May

Height × Width: Varies (by variety)

Type: Deciduous/flowering

Zone: 6

Light Requirements:

Additional Benefits:

Color photograph on page 253.

Crabapples have been in the home landscape for many years. Most of the varieties that were available in the sixties and seventies presented problems for the homeowner. Many varieties were susceptible to leaf scab, which caused early leaf drop in the spring and sometimes in the summer. The crabapples that produced fruit would drop that fruit in August and it would attract yellow jackets. But over the last twenty years, many new varieties, both upright and weeping, have been introduced. These new varieties grow to all different shapes and, most important, hold their fruit until the birds clean the tree in late winter. The blossoms of the flowering crab come basically in red, pink, and white with single, semidouble, and double blossoms. Crabapples are one of the showiest-blooming ornamental trees that you can have in your landscape. I will list some varieties that are dwarf, some that weep, some that are upright, and some that really spread. Get ready to learn about a family of ornamental trees that will fit into any landscape.

WHEN TO PLANT

Plant crabapples anytime the ground is not frozen. To shop for your favorite bloom color, go to the garden store in early spring when the crabs start to bloom. Then you will know before you buy exactly what the bloom will look like.

WHERE TO PLANT

To plant your crabapple, pick any spot in the yard that has good drainage. Crabapples bloom best in full sun but will also give lots of color with a half-day of sun. These trees grow well in all types of

Kentucky soil. Since there are many varieties with different mature sizes, pick a variety that will fit your spot.

How to Plant

Larger-sized crabapple trees are available balled and burlapped. Younger trees are container-grown. With both types, dig a hole no deeper than the soil clump and twice as wide. Loosen roots attached to the soil clump on container-grown trees, and cut away any twine wrapped around the trunks of trees that are balled and burlapped. Break up soil clumps, backfill, and water-in well.

Care and Maintenance

Assuming that your selection is a newer, disease-resistant variety, no fungicide needs to be applied during wet seasons. As with any newly planted tree, water your crabapple when needed during its first year in your yard, especially during hot, dry weather.

Landscape Merit

The flowering crabapple is a medium- to fast-growing and cold-hardy tree. It produces gorgeous flowers and great-looking fruit.

Additional Information

Flowering crabs always have a deeper color when in bud than when in full bloom. Varieties described as "red" will be red in bud, then pink in full bloom. "Pink" varieties will be pink in bud and almost white in full bloom.

Additional Species, Cultivars, or Varieties

'Baskatong' is an upright-growing tree with reddish-purple flowers; it produces purple fruit in the fall. 'Red Jade' is a weeping variety, with pink buds opening to white; it grows well in limited space and produces great fruit. 'Sargent' is a dwarf-growing, upright variety; it produces pink buds that open white, and small, red fruit. 'Harvest Gold' grows upright and into a rounded shape. It has pink flowers in the spring and golden apples in the fall. 'Donald Wyman' has rounded, spreading growth; it has white flowers with red fruit. 'Prairifire' has rounded, spreading growth with red flowers and purple fruit. 'Tina' is dwarf growing with white flowers.

Hemlock

Tsuga canadensis

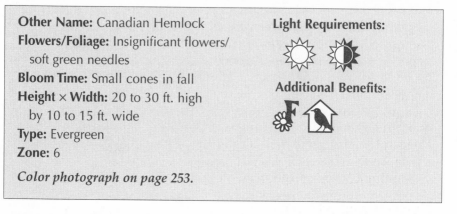

Other Name: Canadian Hemlock

Flowers/Foliage: Insignificant flowers/ soft green needles

Bloom Time: Small cones in fall

Height × Width: 20 to 30 ft. high by 10 to 15 ft. wide

Type: Evergreen

Zone: 6

Color photograph on page 253.

Light Requirements:

Additional Benefits:

Without a doubt, hemlock is one of the easiest evergreens to sell. Everyone loves the looks of hemlock with its soft, pendulous, weeping branches. You can control its height and width by pruning away new growth as it appears in late spring. Hemlocks do best in *moist*, well-drained, acidic soils. This plant has problems in strong, drying winds. Although hemlock tolerates shade, it does not do well in tree shade where it is planted among competing tree roots. It has no tolerance for urban conditions, and, even in the suburbs, this plant does not appreciate heavy clay soil. You should be realistic about your planting site if you want to install a hemlock. If not, you'll be disappointed.

WHEN TO PLANT

Hemlocks do best when planted in the spring, while we still have a lot of natural moisture. If a hemlock that's been dug from the nursery is allowed to dry out just once, it will never be a good plant again. You can also plant hemlock other times of the growing season as long as the nursery has taken good care of it.

WHERE TO PLANT

Hemlock prefers moist and well-drained soil. It's best if your soil is slightly acidic. Hemlocks will tolerate heavy clay if the drainage is good and you add organic material to the backfill.

How to Plant

Make sure the hemlock you're about to buy looks good. It won't get better than it looks today when you take it home tomorrow. Dig a hole no deeper than the rootball and twice as wide. Add organic material—up to 25 percent—to the soil, backfill, and water-in well to settle the soil. Break up clay particles to the size of golf balls.

Care and Maintenance

Avoid planting in shady locations that are surrounded by competing roots from other trees. Hemlocks can tolerate natural shade, but avoid summer tree shade that exposes them to winter sun and wind. In alkaline areas, acidify the soil with Ironite® or other soil acidifiers.

Landscape Merit

Hemlock stands out by itself as a beautiful specimen evergreen, or as an extremely graceful hedge or screen. It also works well as a foundation.

Additional Information

When hemlocks are allowed to grow with sufficient room, they can get quite tall. You can trim to keep them smaller for awhile, but eventually they'll need new growth to maintain their soft look. *Tsuga canadensis* are native to the northeast and mountains of Kentucky and Tennessee. The hotter your summer temps are, the more unhappy your hemlocks will be.

Additional Species, Cultivars, or Varieties

'Jeddeloh' is a low-growing, soft-needled evergreen that grows to 2 feet tall and 3 feet wide. It is great for rock gardens.

Did You Know?

When planting any tree, dig the hole at least half again as wide as the soil clump. If it's practical to dig the hole twice as wide, that's even better. Always use the soil you dug out to backfill around the soil clump or ball of earth.

'Heritage' River Birch

Betula nigra 'Heritage'

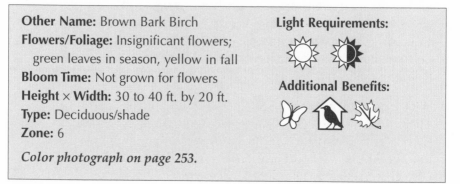

Other Name: Brown Bark Birch

Flowers/Foliage: Insignificant flowers; green leaves in season, yellow in fall

Bloom Time: Not grown for flowers

Height × Width: 30 to 40 ft. by 20 ft.

Type: Deciduous/shade

Zone: 6

Color photograph on page 253.

Light Requirements:

Additional Benefits:

*B*etula nigra 'Heritage' is a refined, light-brown cultivar of river birch. All birches love cool summers and good, loamy soil, so you may wonder how a birch made it into the *Kentucky Gardener's Guide.* It is true that white birches don't live very long; they grow under constant stress, and soon the birch borer finds them and finishes them off. The river birch, while it doesn't like the climate any better than the white birch, will tolerate Kentucky soil much better and will grow and even thrive here. Never plant a 'Heritage' birch near a pool, especially a swimming pool; during hot, dry summers, it will shed leaves and make for a nasty maintenance problem. 'Heritage' river birch has good yellow fall color. It is great as a yard tree or as a corner tree for a two-story house. With its many stems, it is a fine ornamental tree for many locations, and it is also available with single trunks.

WHEN TO PLANT

River birch trees are available in many sizes. Smaller 4- to 6-foot plants are available in containers. You will find larger trees, 12 to 16 feet in height, available balled and burlapped; request one that was dug in the winter. Plant river birch trees anytime the ground is not frozen.

WHERE TO PLANT

River birch trees love full sun and slightly acidic soil. If you have mostly alkaline soil, which is common in Kentucky, acidify it. This tree does well in dry to moist soil, but needs the acidity to keep the leaves dark-green instead of yellow-green.

HOW TO PLANT

If planting trees in containers, loosen any roots that are wrapped around the soil clump. For trees that are balled and burlapped, remove any twine that wraps around the trunks. Dig a hole no deeper than but twice as wide as the soil clump. Break up soil particles so they're no bigger than golf balls. Backfill and water-in well to settle the soil. No staking is required.

CARE AND MAINTENANCE

There are few bugs or diseases that bother this plant. Water it occasionally during hot, dry summers to keep leaf drop to a minimum. Trim off any growth that does not please you. Don't let early leaf drop concern you—it goes with the variety.

LANDSCAPE MERIT

The peeling bark of the river birch and its fall leaf color add beauty to any landscape.

ADDITIONAL INFORMATION

Heritage birch trees are available as single-trunk or multi-stem trees. Both types make for a great landscape specimen.

ADDITIONAL SPECIES, CULTIVARS, OR VARIETIES

Betula nigra is the straight species with darker-brown bark than 'Heritage'. Both *nigra* and 'Heritage' are great birch trees in Kentucky.

Did You Know?

There are many varieties of birch. The white-bark ones seem to be the prettiest, but a healthy brown-bark birch will grow best. You can always spray white paint on the 'Heritage' to make the bark more white.

TREES

Japanese Maple

Acer palmatum

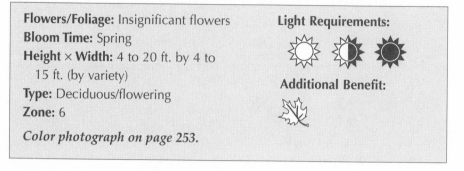

Flowers/Foliage: Insignificant flowers
Bloom Time: Spring
Height × Width: 4 to 20 ft. by 4 to
   15 ft. (by variety)
Type: Deciduous/flowering
Zone: 6

Color photograph on page 253.

Light Requirements:

Additional Benefit:

W hat a wonderful family of plants. Japanese maples have many landscape uses. There are varieties that grow best in full sun, some in full shade, and many that will grow and color well in just a half-day of sun. Japanese maple makes a wonderful accent plant or a one-of-a-kind specimen, the larger-growing varieties can give shade to a patio, and all will add great leaf color to accent any landscape. Japanese maples, depending on the variety, have either crimson-red leaves, green leaves, green leaves with a tinge of red, or variegated green-and-white leaves. The size of this tree at maturity can vary widely, so it can be confusing when you go to shop for them. Here is where plant buyers get in trouble. *How big will this variety grow?* When you go to the garden center, you will see several varieties that are all about the same size, let's say 2 feet tall. Some will be priced at $18.95, while others are priced at $99.50. You say, "Boy, somebody made a mistake with that $99.50, so I'll be a wise shopper and buy the cheaper one." But different varieties of Japanese maple grow at different rates, and prices will reflect this. Ask nursery personnel about the growth qualities of the maple.

WHEN TO PLANT

Japanese maples are available both balled and burlapped and container-grown. You can plant any Japanese maple anytime the ground is not frozen.

WHERE TO PLANT

This is a family of plants that you should purchase from a qualified nursery store or garden center. Nursery technicians can recommend the best variety for your location, giving you information on how big it will grow.

How to Plant

Japanese maples are available balled and burlapped or in containers. After you've picked a planting site suitable for the variety you have purchased, dig a hole to the depth of the soil clump and twice as wide. With plants that are balled and burlapped, set the ball of earth into the hole and remove the top of the burlap, laying it back alongside the ball of earth. For a container-grown plant, remove it from the container and loosen any roots that are wrapped around the soil clump. Backfill with existing soil, making sure no soil particle is larger than a golf ball. Water-in well.

Care and Maintenance

You can trim or prune a Japanese maple anytime. Never use a hedge shear or chain-saw. Use handpruners instead, and prune entire unwanted branches. You can also tip-prune uneven growth anytime it appears. This group of plants is bug and disease free. Don't be concerned if you notice small pinholes on some of the leaves during the summer. These are called "sun spots" and are caused by water droplets on the leaves in hot sun.

Landscape Merit

There are many varieties for sun or shade. Most Japanese maples are slow-growing; their small size can be maintained by pruning.

Additional Information

The leaves of most varieties of red-leaf Japanese maples will turn greenish-red in hot, summer weather. Don't be concerned. This is normal, and the new growth in late summer will have deep-red leaves.

Additional Species, Cultivars, or Varieties

'Bloodgood' has reddish-purple leaf color and grows to an average of 15 to 20 feet high and wide; in the fall it has great color. 'Crimson Queen' is a red-leaf variety with serrated edges; some are low-growing, 2 to 3 feet, and others grow up to 6 to 8 feet. 'Inaba Shidare', with its large, red leaves, is a dwarf cultivar that grows faster than other serrated-edged cultivars. 'Viride' has green, serrated leaves with a touch of white; it is a great tree for shade.

Japanese Zelkova

Zelkova serrata

Other Names: Zelkova, Saw-Leaf Zelkova

Flowers/Foliage: Insignificant flowers/ dark-green foliage

Bloom Time: April

Height × Width: 50 ft. high by 30 ft. wide

Type: Deciduous

Zone: 6

Color photograph on page 253.

Light Requirements:

Additional Benefit:

Japanese zelkova—have you heard of it? Probably not. If I said American elm, would you know that one? Probably so. We all know that the American elm has been on the decline for many years due to the Dutch elm disease. Some nursery persons have referred to zelkova as the replacement for the American elm. It definitely is not that, but many say the resemblance is there. To begin with, Japanese zelkova has leaves that are 1 1/2 inches long with serrated edges. The bark on older trees resembles that of the Chinese elm. Zelkova grows 50 to 80 feet tall with a spread of about one-half to two-thirds its height. Zelkova is a great-looking tree because of its good-looking foliage, attractive bark, and an interesting, upright growth habit that qualifies it as a wonderful street tree. Unfortunately, many urban foresters are not familiar with this tree, and not many are planted in urban situations. The leaves are dark green during the growing season, yellow to orange to brown in the fall. Some cultivars will even give you deep red to purplish-red leaf color in the fall, depending on the weather.

WHEN TO PLANT

Most zelkovas are available balled and burlapped, after they have been dug during February and March from nurseries. Spring will give you the best selections. These trees are very easy to transplant.

WHERE TO PLANT

Zelkovas do best in full sun, but they will also grow in a half-day of sun. Zelkovas will grow in all types of soils, including clay, as long as there is good drainage—that is why this tree is very suitable for urban areas, including street plantings.

How to Plant

Most zelkovas are available balled and burlapped; some are available in containers. With either type, dig a hole no deeper than the soil clump and twice as wide. Backfill, using the existing soil and breaking up all soil clumps to the size of golf balls. Water-in well. No staking is required.

Care and Maintenance

This tree is resistant to Dutch elm disease. No other major problems exist. To ward off bugs and disease, just make sure that timely water is provided the first couple of years during hot, dry weather. Mulching all trees keeps moisture in the soil longer, especially important when the rains are not plentiful.

Landscape Merit

Japanese zelkova is a beautiful, elm-like tree that adapts well to urban conditions. It is fast-growing, up to 2 feet per year.

Additional Information

Do any major pruning in the fall. Young zelkovas might need to be pruned at an early age to eliminate rubbing branches. Zelkovas start off very slowly after their initial transplanting but will grow 2 feet a year after they are established.

Additional Species, Cultivars, or Varieties

'Green Vase,' as the name implies, is a cultivar that grows in a vase shape. It is a tall-growing plant that has dark-green leaves and orange to red-bronze fall color. This plant grows twice as fast as 'Village Green'. 'Village Green' is a great cultivar with a straight trunk whose leaves turn brownish-red in the fall. This cultivar is highly resistant to Dutch elm disease, and to leaf-chewing beetles.

Kentucky Coffee Tree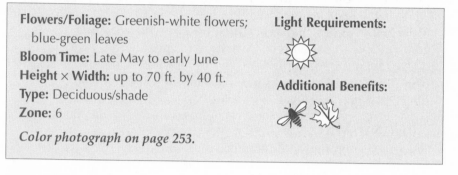

Gymnocladus dioicus

Flowers/Foliage: Greenish-white flowers; blue-green leaves

Bloom Time: Late May to early June

Height × Width: up to 70 ft. by 40 ft.

Type: Deciduous/shade

Zone: 6

Color photograph on page 253.

Light Requirements:

Additional Benefits:

This is the state tree of the great state of Kentucky. The national champion of this tree, which is located in West Liberty, Kentucky, is 90 feet tall and 89 feet wide. Its name comes from a practice of the early settlers of Kentucky; they used the seeds from the pods of the female trees as a coffee substitute. Kentucky coffee tree is upright growing in general, but no two trees grow alike. Its growth rate is considered slow to medium, at a little more than 1 foot per year. The fruit on the female comes from the brownish-black seedpod that can be 10 inches long and 2 inches wide. This tree adapts well to urban settings and is a great choice for golf courses, parks, and other large areas. Nursery growers are being encouraged to grow only the male varieties of this tree since most homeowners aren't looking for a coffee substitute and don't appreciate the pods hanging on the trees all winter and dropping to the ground the following spring. Overall, Kentucky coffee tree is a great tree for a great state.

WHEN TO PLANT

Kentucky coffee tree is available balled and burlapped and growing in containers. The best selection will be in the spring, but you can plant one anytime the ground is not frozen.

WHERE TO PLANT

Plant this tree in rich, moist soil in full sun for best growth. You may protest, "But I don't have great soil." Relax. This tree will adapt to a wide range of soil types, including clay, and to drought conditions. Just provide it with good drainage. It will do well in urban areas where some trees do not thrive.

How to Plant

Dig a hole as deep as and twice as wide as the rootball or soil clump. Break up all soil particles so that none is bigger than a golf ball. Water-in well to settle the soil. Finish with 2 inches of mulch, but keep the mulch off the trunk.

Care and Maintenance

Perform any pruning in the winter or early spring. Like any transplanted tree, it will require water during the hot, dry periods of summer the first couple of years after planting. There are no known bug or disease problems with Kentucky coffee tree.

Additional Information

Kentucky coffee tree has unusual, ornamental bark. The tree is also one of the latest trees to leaf out in the spring, getting its new leaves around the second week of May. New leaves have a pinkish tinge at first, changing to dark green as the leaves mature. Fall leaf color is yellow.

Additional Species, Cultivars, or Varieties

Upright-growing and vase-shaped like an elm, 'Espresso' grows 50 feet high and 30 feet wide; it is fruitless. 'Prairie Titan'™ is a fruitless, male tree that is upright growing to 60 feet high by 30 to 40 feet wide; it has blue-green summer leaves. 'Stately Manor' is a more upright, narrow-growing male tree, which reaches 50 feet high and 20 feet wide.

Norway Spruce

Picea abies

Flowers/Foliage: Insignificant flowers; dark-green needles

Bloom Time: Not grown for flowers

Height × Width: 30 to 50 ft. by 15 to 25 ft.

Type: Evergreen

Zone: 6

Color photograph on page 253.

Light Requirements:

Additional Benefits:

Mike Dirr, the master of good plant varieties, wrote in his *Manual of Woody Landscape Plants* (my bible, by the way) that Norway spruce is much overplanted. But any homeowners who have white pine in their landscape may wish that they had Norway spruce instead. Norway spruce is a stately, pyramidal, dark-green plant that performs best in sandy, acidic, well-drained soils but will tolerate heavy clay or somewhat alkaline soil as long as the planting site has good drainage. The Norway grows more slowly than the white pine, but in the long run, it grows well and lasts for many years. Norway spruce trees make a great tall screen and windbreak, some growing taller than others. You will find the entire spruce group to be very landscape-friendly. There is even a cultivar called 'Bird's Nest' that is a low spreader suitable for foundation planting. And don't forget *Picea pungens,* the blue spruce—it's gorgeous.

WHEN TO PLANT

Look for balled-and-burlapped spruce trees in the spring to fall. If you are buying a Norway that has been pre-dug and is healed-in at your garden store, be sure to plant it at your home right away. Don't leave the ball of earth sitting around out of the ground for more than a day.

WHERE TO PLANT

Norway spruce prefers full sun to half-day shade; spruce tend to grow weakly in lots of shade. Make sure the planting site has good drainage. Remember, it might be a cute little tree today, but in twenty years it will be 20 feet wide. Don't plant close to sidewalks or drives, or near your house.

How to Plant

Dig a hole no deeper than the ball of earth and half again as wide as the ball's diameter. Backfill, breaking up all soil particles to the size of golf balls. Water-in well.

Care and Maintenance

This plant is susceptible to a few bugs; keep it mulched and water during hot, dry weather. Bad bugs tend to stay away from healthy trees.

Landscape Merit

Norway spruce is great as a windscreen, giving privacy year-round. It produces cones and gives shelter to wildlife.

Additional Information

If you want to slow down the overall growth of your spruce, shear off new growth during its "new growth stage" in late spring. This will also assist in making your spruce much fuller.

Additional Species, Cultivars, or Varieties

Green-needle: *Picea abies* 'Bird's Nest' spruce is a low-growing, spreading tree. 'Pumila' is globular and low-growing. 'Serbian' is tall and pyramidal, with needles that are silver on the underside. **Blue-needle:** Colorado blue (*Picea pungens*) is tall-growing and has bluish new growth. *P.* 'Hoopsi' is slow-growing and pyramidal, with silver-blue needles. 'Montgomery' spreads to a rounded shape and has a great blue color. 'Globosa' also spreads, though it is more rounded than 'Montgomery'; it also has great blue color.

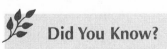 **Did You Know?**

Horticulture oil is an environmentally safe bugkiller, but never spray this oil on blue spruce because it will remove the blue color.

Ornamental Pear

Pyrus calleryana

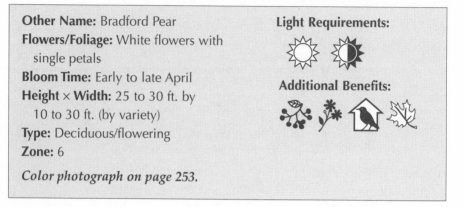

Other Name: Bradford Pear

Flowers/Foliage: White flowers with single petals

Bloom Time: Early to late April

Height × Width: 25 to 30 ft. by 10 to 30 ft. (by variety)

Type: Deciduous/flowering

Zone: 6

Color photograph on page 253.

Light Requirements:

Additional Benefits:

Ornamental pears (the most popular of which is the Bradford pear) were first introduced to me in the early sixties—beautiful trees that grow in a fan shape. Twenty years later, the industry discovered that the early Bradfords grew narrow-crotched, lateral branches that caused the trees to split during high winds. Well, now there's good news for Bradford lovers. There is an improved Bradford available that, so far, has shown tremendous improvement over its older namesake. All ornamental pears have glossy green leaves, beautiful white flowers that introduce us to spring in April, and tremendous red fall leaf color. Pears stand out in the landscape, being the last trees to produce fall color. Ornamental pears are relatively fast-growing, but there are many varieties that grow to different widths. I'll point out those varieties later, but one thing you can say about them all is that they make a great flowering tree or street tree, tolerating some not-so-great plant locations. 'Chanticleer', also known as 'Cleveland Select', is probably my favorite. It is narrow-growing, making it suitable for planting close to the house.

WHEN TO PLANT

Ornamental pears are available in the spring as balled-and-burlapped trees or in containers. You can plant flowering pear trees anytime the ground is not frozen. You may want to put this one in the ground early so you can enjoy the first-year blooms in your yard.

WHERE TO PLANT

This tree will perform best in full sun or will grow well on the east or west side of your home (half-day shade). Don't plant it too close to other trees where its overall shape could be negatively affected. Ornamental pears will do well in all types of Kentucky soil as long as the planting location is well drained.

How to Plant

Pears come either balled and burlapped or container-grown. For container-grown plants, loosen any roots that are wrapped around the soil clump. Dig a hole no deeper than but twice as wide as the soil clump. Place the rootball in the hole. Make sure the backfill is chopped up so no particle is larger than a golf ball. Water-in well. Do not stake.

Care and Maintenance

There are no problems with the pear varieties in this book— no bugs or disease will give your pear any trouble. Some varieties can have a viral problem, but if you go with the ones recommended here, you will have no trouble.

Landscape Merit

The ornamental pear is fast-growing and cold hardy with great spring blooms and fall leaf color.

Additional Information

Because of their glossy leaves, white spring flowers, and relatively fast growth rate, flowering pears are the most popular ornamental tree sold at the garden center. There are also many new varieties that I have not listed here because I personally have not seen them grow. Check with your local nursery.

Additional Species, Cultivars, or Varieties

'Improved Bradford' has shiny leaves, and its branches are wider-crotched, making them less vulnerable to breaking. 'Cleveland' is a narrow-growing variety that makes a great street tree or a tree you can plant within 15 feet of your house. 'Aristocrat' is pyramidal-growing, with great spring bloom and fall color. It's a Kentucky introduction by William Straw. 'Redspire' is pyramidal-growing, and grows more slowly, yet still has great bloom and leaf color.

Redbud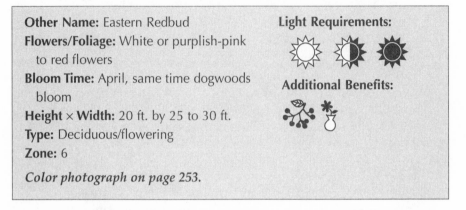

Cercis canadensis

Other Name: Eastern Redbud

Flowers/Foliage: White or purplish-pink to red flowers

Bloom Time: April, same time dogwoods bloom

Height × Width: 20 ft. by 25 to 30 ft.

Type: Deciduous/flowering

Zone: 6

Color photograph on page 253.

Light Requirements:

Additional Benefits:

This is a tree that should have a spot in anyone's landscape. Redbud is a native of the eastern part of the United States. It is considered a small tree, and has multiple trunks at the ground (clump form) or a short single trunk that branches out close to the ground. Redbud is a handsome tree that produces ascending branches from the top of the canopy. The common redbud has flowers that are reddish-purple in bud, opening to a rosy pink. The flowers, which appear in April, sit up on the individual branches. The blooms follow the silhouette of the tree. From the flowers come seedpods that resemble pea pods and add to the tree's winter look. Dry autumns produce golden-yellow leaf color. Redbud is an excellent tree to plant in a sunny area where you were considering planting a dogwood because it is much more hardy. Redbud will also tolerate shade, which gives you more planting options. There is a variety that blooms white and one that has purple-red leaves during the growing season.

WHEN TO PLANT
Plant redbuds that are balled and burlapped or container-grown anytime the ground is not frozen. An ideal planting site would have moist, well-drained soil. But this tree will do exceptionally well in any type of soil—clay, sandy, acidic, or alkaline—as long as the planting site has good drainage, which means no standing water.

WHERE TO PLANT
Redbuds will adapt to sun or shade. The more sun it gets, the more blooms it will produce. Large, heart-shaped leaves along with the

tree's low-branching habit make it a great tree to use as a screen.

How to Plant

Dig the hole as deep as the soil clump, and twice as wide. For container-grown trees, loosen any roots wrapped around the soil clump. For trees that are balled and burlapped, peel back the top of the burlap after placing the ball in the hole. Break up any clay clumps, backfill, and water-in well. No staking is required.

Care and Maintenance

As long as you have planted your redbud in a well-drained site, you're trouble free. Redbud will appreciate a good drink of water occasionally during hot, dry weather. As the tree matures, trim off bottom branches to suit your lawn-mowing needs.

Landscape Merit

Redbud is a hardy, handsome tree with beautiful white or red blooms and large, heart-shaped leaves.

Additional Information

As your redbud gets larger, prune off a few branches in February, bring them inside, set them in a vase of water, and in ten days, enjoy some spring color indoors. This tree flowers before its leaves appear.

Additional Species, Cultivars, or Varieties

'Appalachian Red' has reddish- to deep-purple flowers. 'Forest Pansy' has purple leaves and reddish-purple flowers. 'Alba' is a cold-hardy variety that produces white flowers.

Did You Know?

Redbud will not even look alive if you buy one when it is dormant (leafless). But believe me, it will become a very beautiful specimen tree in a few short years after planting.

Red Maple

Acer rubrum

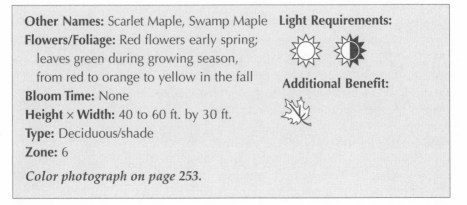

Other Names: Scarlet Maple, Swamp Maple

Flowers/Foliage: Red flowers early spring; leaves green during growing season, from red to orange to yellow in the fall

Bloom Time: None

Height × Width: 40 to 60 ft. by 30 ft.

Type: Deciduous/shade

Zone: 6

Color photograph on page 253.

Light Requirements:

Additional Benefit:

Red maple is one of the most popular shade trees in Kentucky. The basic *Acer rubrum* is a seedling-grown tree that can have fall color ranging from yellow-green, to yellow, to orange, to red. Now that can be very disappointing to the homeowner who thinks he or she is buying a tree that has green leaves during the growing season (they all do) but then turns red in the fall as the name implies. *Wrong.* Seedling red maples can be *many* colors in the fall, not necessarily red. But plant researchers have now produced varieties on which you can go to the bank and say, "Hey, my red maple has red leaves in the fall." All red maples are considered fast-growing for a maple. They are very shapely, growing in an upright, pyramidal shape. Red maples, like all maples, have red flowers before they leaf out in spring. From these flowers come helicopter-type seeds that fall to the ground in late May. Be sure to use a weed seed germination preventer (Preen®) in your planting beds so you don't wind up with many new baby maple trees. Any seedlings that start to grow in lawn areas can be eliminated by mowing.

WHEN TO PLANT

Red maples can be planted anytime the ground is not frozen. They will be available in smaller sizes growing in containers; larger specimens are available balled and burlapped (B&B).

WHERE TO PLANT

Red maples do best in full sun as a specimen tree. They will grow well when surrounded by other trees but will produce their best fall color in lots of sun. Plant at least 20 feet from the house.

How to Plant

Dig a hole no deeper than the soil clump but twice as wide. Backfill, using existing soil with particles no larger than a golf ball. Water-in well to settle the new soil. Staking should not be necessary.

Care and Maintenance

All maple trees have shown stress during the last few years. Maples, under good growing conditions, put on at least a foot of growth per year. Please water them when Mother Nature does not. Always check the soil around newly transplanted maples with a trowel during dry, hot weather, digging down 5 to 6 inches. If the soil is dry, you need to water it. If moisture is found, leave the hose alone until the soil does dry; don't overwater.

Additional Information

Red maples have really been improved over the last twenty years. Always buy trees from a reputable garden center or landscape firm that will ensure you are getting a variety that's true to the name on the tag.

Additional Species, Cultivars, or Varieties

'Autumn Flame' has great early red fall color and grows to an average size of 60 feet high and 50 feet wide. 'Autumn Blaze' is a fast-growing red maple, oval in form, with fall color that persists longer than others. 'Red Sunset' has been around for many years and is popular for its deep-red fall leaf color. 'Autumn Glory' is more upright-growing than spreading. It is a great shade tree for planting close to a patio or deck.

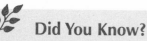 **Did You Know?**

Many older sugar and Norway maples have been showing signs of stress due to wet springs and dry summers. Red maples are proving to be durable during those same times.

Red Oak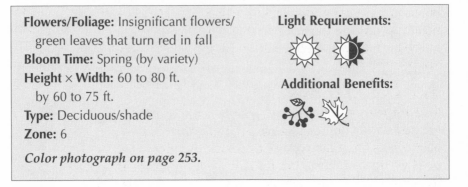

Quercus rubra

Flowers/Foliage: Insignificant flowers/ green leaves that turn red in fall

Bloom Time: Spring (by variety)

Height × Width: 60 to 80 ft. by 60 to 75 ft.

Type: Deciduous/shade

Zone: 6

Color photograph on page 253.

Light Requirements:

Additional Benefits:

Red oak is a very misunderstood tree. Most people think all oaks are slow growing. While this may be true of some varieties of oak, it is definitely not true of red oak. Red oaks can grow up to 2 feet per year once they've gotten established in their planting sites, and they can get quite large because of their long lifespan. When planted in a good location, they can easily live 100 years and grow to 80 feet tall. Their acorns take two years to mature, but it can take up to twenty-five years to even start producing the acorns. Red oaks are best planted as yard trees rather than as street trees. The fall leaf color of red oaks is just as their name suggests: they have green leaves during the growing season that turn reddish-brown in the fall. A first cousin, scarlet oak, has a little brighter red fall color. Red oaks prefer slightly acidic soil but can adapt to alkaline clay soil.

WHEN TO PLANT

Most red oaks are dug from the nursery in late fall to late winter. Trees that you will inspect at your local garden center will already have been dug. This means you can plant a red oak anytime the ground is not frozen. Small sizes will be available in containers; plant these anytime also.

WHERE TO PLANT

Plant oaks in full sun with lots of room to grow. Plant no closer than 25 feet from the house. Red oaks prefer loose, well-drained soil, but as long as the planting site has good drainage, they will adapt to heavier soil.

How to Plant

When selecting your oak, choose one that has a trunk diameter of 3 inches or less. Dig a hole as deep as the soil ball and twice as wide. Backfill using the existing soil, and break up the soil particles so that none is bigger than a golf ball. Water-in well to settle the soil. Staking should not be necessary.

Care and Maintenance

Mulch the tree ring with a 2-inch layer of mulch. There are no serious bug or disease problems that bother red oaks. Oaks have the type of tree bark that deer love to use to remove their antler fuzz. Protect young trees with tree wrap in the fall. Remove it after spring for the rest of the year.

Landscape Merit

Red oak is a handsome tree for any landscape. It is fast-growing, provides lots of shade, and does not retard grass growth underneath.

Additional Information

Once planted, all oak trees dislike having their roots disturbed. If you are building on a lot that has oak trees, keep the bulldozer and trencher away from them. The same holds true if you want to widen an existing driveway at home. Stay away from the root zone of the tree or the tree could be seriously damaged.

Additional Species, Cultivars, or Varieties

Willow oak (*Quercus phellos*) has good overall texture and form with leaves like a willow tree. It's a good tree for central and western Kentucky. Pin oak (*Q. palustris*) is probably the most popular variety and does best in acidic, well-drained soil. It holds its leaves over winter and drops them in spring. White oak (*Q. alba*) has leaves with rounded lobes and is another great member of the oaks. Shumard oak (*Q. shumardii*) is pyramidal-growing with great red leaf color in the fall. It is very drought tolerant.

Serviceberry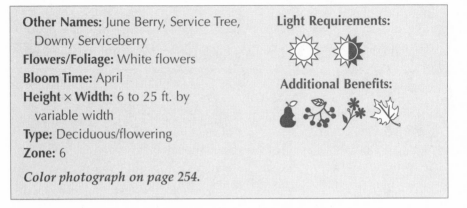

Amelanchier arborea

Other Names: June Berry, Service Tree, Downy Serviceberry

Flowers/Foliage: White flowers

Bloom Time: April

Height × Width: 6 to 25 ft. by variable width

Type: Deciduous/flowering

Zone: 6

Color photograph on page 254.

Light Requirements:

Additional Benefits:

Even though this ornamental tree is not known to many people, it is one of the great ornamental trees of the future. Serviceberry is an upright-growing tree with some varieties that have multiple leaders similar to those of a birch, and other varieties that have a single trunk. All varieties are known for beautiful white clumps of blooms (they kind of look like the Jacks that you collect in the game of Jacks) that bloom in April. From the flowers grow round, edible fruits, 1/3 inch in diameter, that first appear green, then turn to red, and finish up a purplish-black—slightly sweet and very tasty. Just ask the birds. The fruit ripens in June, and the birds know it. In fact, you will have to fight the birds to get your portion. Fall color can vary from year to year depending on temperatures and rainfall, but you can always expect leaf color to vary from yellow, to orange, to red. Sometimes all colors appear the same fall on the same tree. You can use serviceberry in many landscape situations in Kentucky.

WHEN TO PLANT

Plant serviceberry trees that are balled and burlapped in the spring or fall. Container-grown plants can be installed anytime the ground is not frozen.

WHERE TO PLANT

Serviceberry grows best in full sun to half-day shade; it will tolerate more shade, but too much could affect the amount of bloom and the fall color. Serviceberry prefers acidic soil but will adjust to less-than-perfect soil. Make sure the planting site has good drainage.

How to Plant

Dig a hole no deeper than but twice as wide as the soil clump. When working with clay soil, be sure to break up all soil particles to the size of golf balls. Backfill, and water-in well to settle the soil. No staking is necessary.

Care and Maintenance

Most of the new varieties remain free of any bugs or disease. To shape your serviceberry, prune anytime. Be sure to water this tree occasionally during its first couple of summers when it's hot and dry.

Landscape Merit

Serviceberry offers beautiful white blooms, edible fruits, and fall leaf color.

Additional Information

Some varieties of serviceberry are listed as true shrubs. Those varieties grow smaller and bushier than those I'm talking about. If you see serviceberry listed in a catalog as a shrub, remember that there are tall-growing ones too.

Additional Species, Cultivars, or Varieties

'Autumn Brilliance' is a grandiflora type that grows up to 25 feet at maturity; it is cold hardy, even to 35 degrees below zero Fahrenheit. 'Princess Diana' is another grandiflora that has large fruit, and great, red fall leaf color; it also can withstand temperatures to 35 degrees below zero. 'Lamarki' is an *A. canadensis* variety that is cold hardy; it grows like a small tree to a shrub with multistems.

Did You Know?

Mike Dirr puts this as one of his top pie-desserts. He states that the ripe fruit from serviceberry is better than highbush blueberries. Try it yourself, and let Martha Stewart know what you think.

Silver Linden

Tilia tomentosa

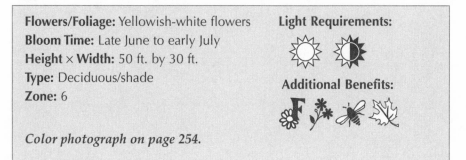

Flowers/Foliage: Yellowish-white flowers
Bloom Time: Late June to early July
Height × Width: 50 ft. by 30 ft.
Type: Deciduous/shade
Zone: 6

Color photograph on page 254.

Light Requirements:

Additional Benefits:

Lindens are an underused shade tree. They are slower growing than some of the other popular shade trees. Because growth rate regulates price and because linden is slower growing, its price per size of tree will be higher than others. But read on. This tree does a lot more than many other shade trees. To begin with, it has yellowish-white and very fragrant flowers in late June to early July. Some linden varieties attract Japanese beetles, but not the silver linden. It also makes a great street tree because it tolerates heat and drought much better than other trees. Its branching habit is compact, and it can be planted closer to the home or other structures than can most other shade trees. The leaves during the growing season have a shiny, dark-green cast on the top of the leaf with a silvery cast on the underside. Add wind and you have a beautiful sight. Silver linden grows pyramidal in shape at a young age and more oval as it matures. This is a great ornamental shade tree with beautiful, golden-yellow fall color. You might have to call around to a few garden centers to locate silver linden. You can also view planted ones in public areas such as your local arboretum.

WHEN TO PLANT

You will find most lindens at the nursery balled and burlapped. You might find very young trees in containers. Both types can be planted anytime the ground is not frozen.

WHERE TO PLANT

Easy to transplant, silver linden, like all lindens, would prefer moist, well-drained, and good soil (wouldn't all trees!). The nice thing about lindens is that they will adapt well to different types of alkaline and acidic soil and they are tolerant of polluted conditions.

Silver linden makes a great street tree. It does best in full sun to half-day shade.

How to Plant
Dig a hole no deeper than, but twice as wide as, the soil clump. Always use the existing soil to backfill. Break up the soil clumps so that they're no larger than golf balls. Water-in well to settle the soil. Staking should not be necessary.

Care and Maintenance
Even though silver linden is drought resistant, an occasional drink of water during hot, dry weather is appreciated the first few years your linden is planted. Littleleaf varieties of linden may attract some Japanese beetles for a few weeks, but the beetles don't seem to enjoy the silver linden variety.

Landscape Merit
Silver linden has fragrant flowers, showy foliage, and good fall color. It is drought tolerant and adapts to most planting sites.

Additional Information
This tree grows very shapely on its own with little or no pruning on your part. And seldom will you find a shade tree with such showy, fragrant flowers.

Additional Species, Cultivars, or Varieties
'Sterling Silver' makes a great street tree with its broad, pyramidal shape. It has gorgeous, deep-green leaves with silver undersides. 'Green Mountain' is very similar to 'Sterling Silver' but has an improved and more rapidly growing form. *Tilia cordata* 'Greenspire' is a variety of littleleaf linden, but it has smaller leaves and is slower growing; it produces great fall color.

Sweetbay Magnolia

Magnolia virginiana

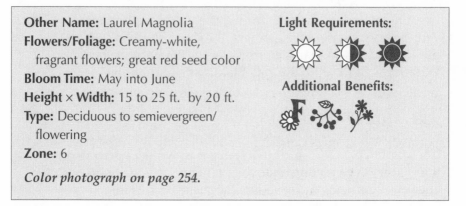

Other Name: Laurel Magnolia

Flowers/Foliage: Creamy-white, fragrant flowers; great red seed color

Bloom Time: May into June

Height × Width: 15 to 25 ft. by 20 ft.

Type: Deciduous to semievergreen/ flowering

Zone: 6

Color photograph on page 254.

Light Requirements:

Additional Benefits:

Sweetbay magnolia is another plant that should be in every landscape. It's considered a smaller-growing patio or specimen tree. Sweetbay blooms in early to late June, so its flowers are never threatened by spring frost. Other spring-flowering magnolias cannot make that claim. You and your neighbors will know when sweetbay is in bloom. The creamy-white flowers look and smell like gardenias. The lemon-scented 2- to 3-inch flowers are not overwhelming, just wonderful. Now, as for the tree itself: the leaves are a shiny green on the top side and silvery underneath. In the wind, they make a beautiful contrast. You can plant sweetbay off the corner of a house, plant it out in the yard as a specimen tree, or plant several in groups to screen off an unpleasant view. This tree will grow under many circumstances. Sweetbay will tolerate heavy clay soil, sun or shade, and will sustain itself in extremely dry to somewhat wet areas. You can prune this tree to confine it to most areas of the landscape.

WHEN TO PLANT

Magnolias as a family are slow to generate new roots after transplanting. You will see more growth the first year from balled-and-burlapped trees that are planted in March to late fall. But you can plant any magnolia—balled and burlapped or container-grown—anytime, and do it successfully.

WHERE TO PLANT

Some will tell you that sweetbay magnolias love wet areas. While they will tolerate a wet location, sweetbays also appreciate good drainage along with decent soil. This is definitely a tree for all locations. If you have alkaline soil, add an acidifier each spring. You will know if the soil is too sweet by the yellowish-green color of the leaves.

How to Plant

Dig a hole as deep as the soil clump, but twice as wide. In poorly drained soils, leave 25 percent of the rootball above grade level. For container-grown plants, loosen any roots that are wrapped around the soil clump. Backfill with existing soil, leaving no soil particles bigger than a golf ball. Water-in well to settle the backfill.

Care and Maintenance

Sweetbay is an easy tree to care for. It grows in all types of soil, even wet soil, and has no problems with bugs or disease. Prune it to get the shape you want. You can keep this tree within your bounds—remember, you control the shears.

Landscape Merit

Sweetbay grows in just about any soil condition. It is fast-growing with very fragrant blooms.

Additional Information

To keep the size you want, prune off new growth right after the trees bloom. All magnolias form their bloom buds in the fall. Never prune any variety after July 15 so you do not negatively affect the next year's bloom.

Additional Species, Cultivars, or Varieties

'Henry Hicks' has been known to keep its leaves even at temperatures below zero. *Magnolia stellata* is called the "star magnolia" and produces white flowers in early spring; it can be damaged by frost. *Magnolia × soulangeana* is also known as "saucer magnolia" and grows into a large, ornamental tree; the flowers of this species are especially susceptible to spring frost. *Magnolia grandiflora* is an evergreen variety whose common name is "southern magnolia." 'Bracken's Brown Beauty' is one of the best grandifloras. It is a great tree for Kentucky, growing 30 to 40 feet high by 15 to 20 feet wide with 5- to 6-inch-wide fragrant white flowers.

Sweetgum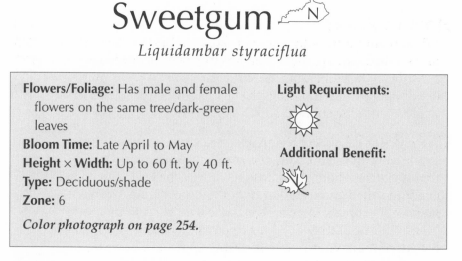

Liquidambar styraciflua

Flowers/Foliage: Has male and female flowers on the same tree/dark-green leaves

Bloom Time: Late April to May

Height × Width: Up to 60 ft. by 40 ft.

Type: Deciduous/shade

Zone: 6

Color photograph on page 254.

Light Requirements:

Additional Benefit:

Sweetgum is a shade tree that's known for dark, glossy-green leaves during the spring and summer. It's also known for its beautiful fall colors—all the colors of the fall rainbow. Unfortunately, it is also known for its gum balls, seedpods that are very spiny, 1 to 1½ inches in diameter, and can really hurt when they press into your skin. There are many varieties of sweetgum, some of which are much more cold hardy than others. As for the shape of the tree, young sweetgums are quite pyramidal. As the tree grows toward maturity, the head rounds out. In rich, moist soil, sweetgum will grow 2 to 3 feet per year. Even in soil that is not ideal, sweetgum still will grow 12 to 18 inches per year. It has a mature height of 60 feet and a width of 40 feet. This tree makes an excellent yard tree for shade.

WHEN TO PLANT

If you plant a sweetgum tree that is balled and burlapped, it's best to plant in the spring. A lot of smaller, 6- to 8-foot sweetgums are available in containers; you can plant this type anytime the ground is not frozen. Sweetgum's roots are very fleshy and can take one year or more to get established. So be patient.

WHERE TO PLANT

Sweetgum prefers full sun with its own root area to enjoy, so don't plant sweetgums close to other trees. They prefer good, moist soil that's slightly on the acidic side. Sweetgums do adapt well to lesser soil quality as is seen in some beautiful specimens in Lexington and Louisville. Good drainage, though, is a must.

How to Plant

When planting trees that are either balled and burlapped or container-grown, dig a hole no deeper than but twice as wide as the soil clump. Backfill with existing soil, and break up all soil particles to the size of golf balls. Water-in well to settle the soil. No staking is required.

Care and Maintenance

When you first plant your sweetgum, you might notice that it just sits there, with little or no new growth. You may even find the leaves smaller than they should be. This is normal. The tree's roots are getting established in their new home, and until they do, your tree won't grow. Once established, though, your tree will start to grow and do what you planted it for. Any heavy pruning should be done during the winter. Be sure to water during hot, dry periods of the growing season.

Landscape Merit

Sweetgums provide shade without discouraging grass growth under the canopy.

Additional Information

Many homeowners are finding that with the 'Moraine' and 'Rotundiloba' sweetgums, not many, *if any*, gum balls will be found.

Additional Species, Cultivars, or Varieties

'Moraine' grows fast and uniformly. It is cold hardy, and its glossy green leaves give excellent fall color; it is a sweetgum that has few, if any, gum balls. 'Rotundiloba' grows 40 feet high by 25 feet wide. It is more upright-growing with mostly yellow to red fall leaf color. This is another variety with very few, if any, gum balls.

Weeping Cherry

Prunus subhirtella 'Pendula'

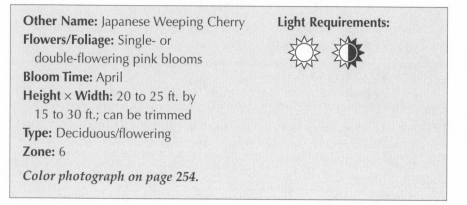
Ornamental cherries come in two basic types. The first is the upright-growing tree that has beautiful white or pink flowers. These are the trees that prompt the cherry blossom festival in Washington, D.C. One problem with this type of cherry: it is short-lived. The lifespan of trees grown in Kentucky is eight to twelve years. In eastern Kentucky you can expect them to live twelve to eighteen years. This is not long when compared to the lifespans of other flowering trees. The second type is the Japanese weeping cherry, which can be purchased with single or double pink blossoms. It lives much longer, with an average lifespan in Kentucky of thirty to forty years. Weeping cherry is a broad-growing tree with long, weeping branches. The most common mistake homeowners make when planting this tree is buying one with a small, weeping top and then planting it within 10 feet of the house. Give this tree lots of room, and it will become a gorgeous specimen tree in your landscape.

WHEN TO PLANT

Most weeping cherry trees are planted in the spring. That's when we see these beautiful trees in bloom and we just plain want to have one. You can really plant these trees anytime the ground is not frozen.

WHERE TO PLANT

Weeping cherry likes lots of sun, a half-day or more. Well-drained soil is a must. (If you have heavy clay soil, you might consider planting a weeping crabapple tree instead.) Do not plant a weeping cherry within 15 feet of the house, walkway, or drive.

How to Plant

Weeping cherries are available both balled and burlapped or container-grown. Dig a hole no deeper than but twice as wide as the soil clump. Break up the soil particles to the size of golf balls, backfill, and water-in well to settle the soil.

Care and Maintenance

Other than a few bug holes in some leaves, weeping cherries have no real problems with bugs and disease. Trim off excess weeping growth anytime you want.

Landscape Merit

As the name implies, the weeping cherry has a weeping growth habit. This tree is ornamental year-round. Young trees look beautiful at holiday time if you dress them with miniature lights.

Additional Information

Japanese weeping cherries are grown two ways. The natural weeping cherry is seed-grown and weeps from the ground up. The most popular way to grow them is by grafting weeping branches to the top of a 6-foot seedling cherry trunk. At a young age, they look like an umbrella tree. Sometimes, growth off the wild trunk will branch out and provide upright growth to go along with the budded, weeping growth. If this occurs, trim off the upright growth.

Additional Species, Cultivars, or Varieties

'Snow Fountain' has pinkish-white flowers on a narrow-growing tree. It grows 10 feet tall but only 6 feet wide. This variety can be planted close to the house as part of the foundation planting. 'Pendula' has pink flowers on weeping branches.

Did You Know?

Most ornamental flowering trees just look like any other tree after they flower. But weeping cherries continue to accent the landscape even after they bloom because of their soft, weeping branches.

Weeping Willow

Salix babylonica

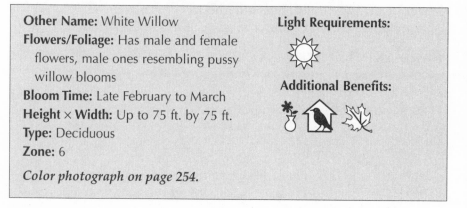

Other Name: White Willow

Flowers/Foliage: Has male and female flowers, male ones resembling pussy willow blooms

Bloom Time: Late February to March

Height × Width: Up to 75 ft. by 75 ft.

Type: Deciduous

Zone: 6

Color photograph on page 254.

Light Requirements:

Additional Benefits:

I wasn't sure I was going to include the weeping willow in this book because there are so many that are misplanted and misunderstood. Then I thought, "Denny, maybe that's why it should be included." First of all, weeping willow will tolerate poorly drained soil—although that doesn't mean it will look forward to such a planting experience. If you've ever seen a white weeping willow in a wetland environment, you probably noticed that it is hardy—but there's lots of dead wood on this tree that looks sick the older it gets. You will constantly see older branches dropping their leaves. Though they are replaced with young, new growth, it is still a constant mess. If you have lots of yard space and good soil drainage, the white willow will make a nice-looking tree. But compared to the other, larger-growing shade trees listed in this chapter, white willow, even under the best growing conditions, is shorter-lived.

WHEN TO PLANT

Most weeping willows are nursery-grown in containers; they are usually available from garden centers and nursery stores in early spring. Because most are container-grown, you can plant them anytime the ground is not frozen.

WHERE TO PLANT

Weeping willows need lots of room. If planted in good conditions, these trees will grow 75 to 100 feet tall and 50 to 75 feet wide. In other words, they need a lot of space. Plant them in full sun, and avoid very heavy clay soil.

How to Plant

Slide the root clump out of the pot and loosen any wrapped roots. Dig a hole as deep as the soil clump and twice as wide. Backfill with existing soil, breaking up all soil clumps to the size of golf balls, and water-in well.

Care and Maintenance

When planted in wet areas, some willows' stems will die back. Trim off dead wood anytime it appears. Happy willows don't present any serious problems. Keep in mind that willows grow large; if you try to dwarf them by pruning, you'll soon realize you have the wrong plant in the wrong place.

Landscape Merit

The white willow makes a nice-looking tree in a big yard with good soil drainage.

Additional Information

If you decide to plant your willow in an area where other trees are growing, you will soon discover that this tree's growth and roots will dominate. The willow's surface roots will always outcompete other plant species. They can also wreak havoc on sidewalks and other man-made structures.

Additional Species, Cultivars, or Varieties

'Babylon' is a smaller variety that grows 30 to 40 feet high and wide. 'Sericea' grows up to 40 to 50 feet high and wide; it has silvery leaf color and will tolerate hard pruning. 'Tristis' is called the "golden weeping willow" because the bark of new growth has a yellowish color; the older growth of this tree often becomes messy and windblown.

White Ash

Fraxinus americana

Other Name: White Seedless Ash
Flowers/Foliage: Inconspicuous flowers
Bloom Time: April
Height × Width: Varies (by variety)
Type: Deciduous/shade
Zone: 6

Color photograph on page 254.

Light Requirements:

Additional Benefit:

White ash is a great shade tree for Kentucky. The best ones to plant are selected clone varieties. White ash trees are seedless, grow relatively fast, and have great fall leaf color. There have been some problems with well-established ash trees over the last few years. Wet springs have caused some of them to contract a disease called anthracnose. This problem does not cause permanent damage, but it does cause some early leaf drop. The leaves become distorted and a few black edges show up on the sides of the leaves. Even so, I have seen both white and green ash varieties do well in Kentucky. Many landscape architects have designed seedless ash trees into traffic island plantings in parking lots. This is probably the worst environment you can place any living plant, but those property managers that arrange for watering during hot, dry weather have seen their ash trees do very well. As with any plant in Kentucky over the last few years, the better you assist Mom Nature, the better your plants will respond.

WHEN TO PLANT

Most white ash and green ash (*F. pennsylvanica*) are available for planting in the spring. Most nurseries dig these trees during late winter to early spring. Once the nursery store or garden center gets theirs in, they are healed-in so that they can be planted anytime the ground is not frozen.

WHERE TO PLANT

White ash, like its cousin green ash, can get rather big. Unlike green ash, though, white ash trees tend to grow more tall than they do wide, so plant them at least 20 feet from the house. One white or green ash tree can produce a lot of shade, especially on the hot side of the house. Seedless ash trees grow well in all types of soil, but they do prefer good drainage.

How to Plant

Dig a hole no deeper than the soil clump but half again as wide. In clay soil, break up each soil particle to the size of a golf ball. Backfill with the existing soil and water-in well to settle the soil. No staking is required.

Care and Maintenance

All seedless ash trees can have problems if they are forced to grow under stressful conditions. The solution is to keep them happy, and they will reward you with fast growth, good shade, and great fall color. That includes timely summer watering during dry periods and keeping them out of poorly drained soil.

Landscape Merit

White ash is fast-growing and its leaves do not inhibit lawn growth under the tree. It also produces great fall color.

Additional Information

All varieties of seedless white ash trees turn purplish-red in the fall. Seedless green ash trees turn yellow. They've proven to be great, large-growing shade trees when given some tender, loving care as young trees.

Additional Species, Cultivars, or Varieties

White Ash: 'Autumn Purple' has deep-green leaves during the growing season that turn purplish-red in the fall; this tree has an oval form, and grows quickly to 60 feet tall by 45 feet wide. 'Autumn Blaze' has the same characteristics as 'Autumn Purple' but grows only to 50 feet tall by 25 feet wide. **Green Ash:** 'Marshall Seedless' has great fall yellow color; it grows to a rounded form that is 60 feet tall and 50 feet wide. 'Patmore' is an upright, large-growing seedless green ash; though it grows more slowly than 'Marshall', it will grow up to 60 feet tall and 50 feet wide.

White Fringetree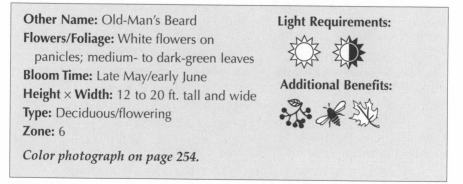

Chionanthus virginicus

Other Name: Old-Man's Beard

Flowers/Foliage: White flowers on panicles; medium- to dark-green leaves

Bloom Time: Late May/early June

Height × Width: 12 to 20 ft. tall and wide

Type: Deciduous/flowering

Zone: 6

Color photograph on page 254.

Light Requirements:

Additional Benefits:

Fringetree can be classified as a large shrub or a small ornamental tree. I prefer to see this plant as the latter. Fringetree is similar in size and shape to a Florida dogwood. This tree grows best in full sun to a half-day of shade. The leaf color is very similar to that of a sweet-bay magnolia. The white flowers bloom in late May and are dioecious, which means there are boy trees and girl trees with the girl trees producing dark-blue, fleshy, egg-shaped berries from August through September. The fruit is not very showy from the street because the leaves hide most of it. But don't worry. The birds love the fruit and will clean the tree by fall. This tree prefers fertile, acidic soil but will adapt to almost any planting situation as long as the spot has good drainage. Fringetree reaches an average size of 12 to 20 feet tall and wide. It is a great tree for a small yard or an area where you need a summer screen off your deck or patio. It would be a wonderful substitute for a Florida dogwood if you want a carefree ornamental tree with lots of showy color.

WHEN TO PLANT

Plant balled-and-burlapped or container-grown plants in the spring. They can be planted anytime the ground is not frozen as long as the balled-and-burlapped trees were dug in late winter to early spring.

WHERE TO PLANT

Fringetree prefers to be planted in fertile, acidic soil. This tree will adapt to almost any location with decent drainage, however. Choose a location that receives full sun to half-day of shade.

How to Plant

Dig a hole as deep as and twice as wide as the soil clump or rootball. If you have the energy, dig the hole twice as wide with container-grown trees, too. Loosen any roots that are wrapped around the outside of the soil clump. Break up all soil particles so they're no larger than golf balls. Backfill, and water-in well to settle the soil.

Care and Maintenance

No known serious bug or disease problems affect this tree. Borers can bother trees that are suffering stress because of weather conditions or a poor planting site. Pruning is rarely required. Give fringetree an occasional drink of water during hot, dry weather for the first couple of years after planting.

Additional Information

Fringetree is a very beautiful large shrub or ornamental tree. Plant several in a group, plant them near large buildings, or use one as the main tree in a small yard. With its outstanding yard color, this tree adapts well to urban conditions.

Additional Species, Cultivars, or Varieties

'Floyd', the only American clone, is known for its upright growth habit and large white flower panicles; it is predominantly male, which means there is no fruit. *Chionanthus retusus* is the Chinese version of fringetree, which grows 15 to 25 feet high and wide with snow-white flowers.

White Pine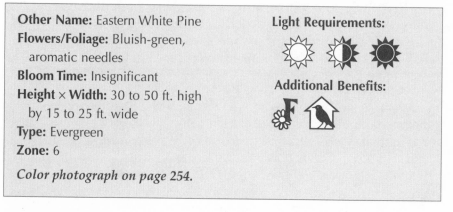

Pinus strobus

Other Name: Eastern White Pine
Flowers/Foliage: Bluish-green, aromatic needles
Bloom Time: Insignificant
Height × Width: 30 to 50 ft. high by 15 to 25 ft. wide
Type: Evergreen
Zone: 6

Color photograph on page 254.

Light Requirements:

Additional Benefits:

White pine has done very well throughout Kentucky for forty of the last fifty years. But for the last ten years, white pine has been on the decline throughout most of the state. Recently I asked an area extension agent what was going on. His reply was, "Denny, that's why they're called Eastern pine." He's right—we're in Kentucky, and we don't always have the soil loved by this tree. There are areas of Kentucky where the soil is loose and on the acidic side, and if you have this kind of soil, you will love this plant. It is fast-growing with 5-inch-long soft needles of bluish-green. It makes a fast-growing screen or windbreak or both. But please, before you plant, be sure to check out how other white pines are growing in your neighborhood.

WHEN TO PLANT

You will find the best selection of white pines in spring and fall, and they can be planted anytime from spring through fall. Make sure that the white pines you're thinking of buying are Kentucky-grown. Also make sure that the tree has a decent-sized ball of earth and that the nursery or garden center will guarantee the tree for at *least* one year. Cones take two years to mature.

WHERE TO PLANT

White pine trees want good, loamy soil that is on the acidic side. Lots of new housing communities have lots of clay soil, and that's not good. At least make sure the drainage is good. White pines will tolerate natural shade, but they don't do well when they are planted among shade trees because there is too much root competition.

How to Plant

Dig a hole no deeper than the rootball and twice as wide. In clay soil, leave 25 percent of the rootball above ground and mound-plant. Break up soil particles to the size of golf balls, and water-in well. No staking is required.

Care and Maintenance

If you plant white pines in good soil, they will take care of themselves. Plants that grow under the stress of poor planting sites will give you all kinds of problems from bugs to needle chlorosis.

Landscape Merit

The white pine provides shelter for birds, and cones for holiday decorations.

Additional Information

White pines have been popular because of their fast growth, and because of this they cost up to 50 percent less than their cousins, the spruce. If you have poor planting sites such as I've described, consider planting the spruce described in this chapter, even if it costs more per size.

Additional Species, Cultivars, or Varieties

'Pendula' is a weeping variety of white pine. 'Nana' is dwarf and spreading.

Did You Know?

Realize that as any conical-shaped evergreen tree grows larger, it gets wider at the ground. Make sure you have the yard space to spare.

'Winter King' Hawthorn

Crataegus virdis 'Winter King'

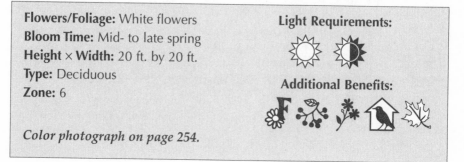

Flowers/Foliage: White flowers
Bloom Time: Mid- to late spring
Height × Width: 20 ft. by 20 ft.
Type: Deciduous
Zone: 6

Color photograph on page 254.

Light Requirements:

Additional Benefits:

'Winter King' is the most attractive variety of hawthorn and has year-round appeal. In the spring, this tree has loads of beautiful, single, white flowers. Soon the spent flowers begin to form loads of small green berries that turn to a beautiful orange-red color by mid- to late summer. The berries remain on the tree until the birds feast on them in early winter. The silver-tinted bark in the winter makes for additional landscape appeal. It's a great tree for a small yard. The 'Winter King' grows best in full sun, but will also accept up to a half-day of shade. Because of the thorns, don't land your Frisbee or kite in this tree.

WHEN TO PLANT

Most field-grown trees, which are balled and burlapped, are dug during late winter and early spring before leaf-bud break. Container-grown trees are always ready for planting; plant anytime the ground is not frozen.

WHERE TO PLANT

Any hawthorn requires at least a half-day of sun. Consider using this tree as part of the corner foundation planting or as a specimen out in the yard. Because of its thorns, do not plant it near a sidewalk.

HOW TO PLANT

Dig your planting hole 50 percent wider than the rootball or soil clump. Leave the hole 10 percent shallower than the depth of the roots. Backfill with the existing soil, breaking up any clumps to no larger than a golf ball. Backfill and water-in well. To eliminate air pockets, use a spade to work the backfill as you're adding water. No staking should be required.

CARE AND MAINTENANCE

Check the need for additional watering during hot or dry periods. Place the hose near the trunk, and let the water run slowly for fifteen minutes or so. Check the surrounding soil with a garden trowel to see if there's moisture around the root clump before adding additional water. Little other care, either spraying or pruning, is necessary.

LANDSCAPE MERIT

Birds love the berries produced by the 'Winter King' hawthorn; and you will love its great landscape color.

ADDITIONAL INFORMATION

This tree is really low maintenance. Just be sure that you don't plant it in a place where kids are tempted to climb it. This tree has 2-inch thorns that could pose a hazard. But if you want to keep robins near your home year-round, plant a 'Winter King'.

ADDITIONAL SPECIES, CULTIVARS, OR VARIETIES

The Washington hawthorn, *Crataegus phaenopyrum*, is very susceptible to cedar hawthorn rust and is especially vulnerable during cool, wet springs. This disease causes "outer-space" lesions on the fruit, which ruin the fruit for the season (the fruit becomes spiny and then turns black).

🌿 Did You Know?

This tree provides a natural bird sanctuary during the winter. A picture of the 'Winter King' with fruit and snow cover would make a beautiful holiday card.

CHAPTER NINE

Turfgrasses

G RASS IS THE NUMBER ONE PLANT (if you are counting actual numbers of plants!) that we have in our landscapes. And if we are talking about drive-by appearance, we judge the beauty of many a home by the looks of that home's lawn. I've often said that if a lawn appears green from the street, it's perfectly okay. How many times have you said, "My neighbor across the street doesn't do half the yard work I do, and his lawn looks better than mine"? Well, that's because we're not picking up our neighbor's newspaper every morning as we do our own. Every morning we walk out on our lawn and say to ourselves, "Look, I have this weed, this brown 3-inch spot, and oh, what's that?" We can become lawn fanatics. We view our neighbor's yard from afar, where his lawn looks better. Want to feel better? Go pick up your neighbor's paper and you will see the same things or worse in his lawn than you see in your own.

Lawns can be very challenging, but don't become a "lawn nut." In this chapter I have listed several varieties of lawn grass. Read carefully and find the one that fits your growing situation, from soil type to exposure to ease of growing. Don't argue with yourself, hoping to get the grass you thought you wanted and finding it doesn't fit your growing environment. The following is information that I want you to study and understand before reading about individual grass varieties.

WHAT'S IN THE SEED I'M BUYING?

All grass seed sold in Kentucky is tested by the Kentucky Department of Agriculture. All seed that you buy has to have a label that tells you the following.

Variety: the correct name(s) of the grass seed you're buying. No common names such as "super blend" are allowed.

Seed Purity: the percentage of pure grass seed that you're buying. This percentage should always be above 95 percent.

Other Crop Seed: the percentage by weight of unlisted grass seed varieties that are in your seed. This percentage should always be 1 percent or less.

Inert Matter: the non-seed count or other non-seed material that you are buying. It, too, should be 1 percent or less.

Weed Seed: the percentage of bad, weed-causing seed that's in your seed. It should be less than .05 percent. Remember, just 1 percent of weed seed can amount to one million chickweed seeds.

Noxious Weeds: should read "none found." You never want to buy any grass seed with noxious weed seed in it.

Lot Number: the number that was assigned to a particular crop of seed that came from the same harvest and the same growing field.

Germination: the percentage of the seed you're buying that you can expect to grow. It should be 80 to 90 percent.

Origin: the state where the seed was grown.

Test Date: the date that the seed from your particular lot was tested. Your grass seed should be good for two-and-a-half years after the testing date shown if it is kept cool and dry.

The above information is actually gathered by people working in a lab. They count all the seed and other matter by hand and test that seed for germination. Always check the label, especially if comparing prices.

How Much to Pay for Seed

Not all grass seed is equal. Grass seed is sold by the pound, but the price per pound should not be the determining factor in buying decisions. The number of seeds in an actual pound of grass seed varies with the type of seed you're buying. Example: Kentucky bluegrass has approximately one million seeds to a pound, while turf-type rye and turf fescue have 200,000 seeds to a pound. That means bluegrass will cover five times the soil area as the other two. Buy grass seed by the coverage, not by the pound.

Lawn Food: What the Numbers Mean

Let's go to the garden center to buy some fertilizer for the lawn. What should we buy? It's important to know that all established grass needs one pound of nitrogen for every 1,000 square feet of lawn. You will see three numbers on a bag of fertilizer. The numbers (sometimes called the "analysis") show the amounts by weight of the nitrogen (N), phosphate (P), and potash (K), always in that order. A fertilizer with an analysis of 10-6-4 contains 10 percent nitrogen, 6 percent phosphate, and 4 percent potash. You may see an 18-pound bag of lawn food whose analysis is 20-4-6 and whose directions say it covers 5,000 square feet. Well, let's do some math. Take 20 percent of 18 pounds (multiply by .20) and we come up with 3.6 pounds of nitrogen per 5,000 square feet. Not enough. We might find a 50-pound bag of 10-6-4 fertilizer that will cover 5,000 square feet of lawn. Using the same math, 10 percent of 50 pounds is 5 pounds of nitrogen per 5,000 square feet, which is the right amount. Just looking at the numbers on the bag without factoring in the coverage information might have you believe that 20 is more than 10. Do the math.

How Sharp Is My Mower Blade?

The easiest and cheapest way to have a good-looking lawn is to sharpen the lawnmower blade at least twice a season. Have it done professionally (it's cheap) so the blade remains balanced (weighs the same on both sides of the center hole). Grass does not like to be cut. It's a plant designed to grow to maturity and then produce seed. (Boy, wouldn't our neighbors love that . . .) We must mow to keep our lawns looking neat. Every time we cut the grass, we injure the blade tissue, which is a water and nutrient reservoir. When we cut our grass with a dull blade, moisture and nutrients escape. A sharp mower blade allows the cut blade to reseal immediately.

Grass Clippings: To Leave or to Collect?

Grass clippings do not cause thatch. Thatch is caused by the natural growing habits of bluegrass and creeping fescues. These plants create thatch as part of their normal growth process. So what to do about clippings? Just leave them. That's right. A full season of grass clippings returned to the soil is the equivalent of one full feeding of lawn food. If the grass gets extra-long between mowings due to rain, re-mow the lawn after the wet clumps dry to blow the grass clippings uniformly over the lawn.

When Is the Best Time to Put Down Grass Seed?

Fall seeding (mid-August to the end of September) is best. During this period soil temperatures are high, which promotes quick germination. Annual weeds are less likely to be a concern; irrigation may be necessary, however, if natural rains are not available.

Dormant seeding (1 January to 15 March) is second best. Soils are usually freezing and thawing during this time, which works the seed into the soil. Naturally, seed will not germinate until soil temperatures reach at least 55 degrees Fahrenheit, but having seed in the soil before then can give desirable grasses a head start on spring-germinating weeds.

Spring seeding (15 March to 15 June) is third best. Germination can be obtained during these months, but weed competition will be at its highest. Tupersan® should be applied to prevent crabgrass infestation from crowding out desirable grasses. Broadleaf weeds should be ignored until desirable grasses have matured (or have been mowed 2 to 3 times). At that time weeds should be treated.

Summer seeding (15 June to 15 August) is fourth best. With irrigation, germination will be fast during these summer months, but the high day and night temperatures may result in diseases such as damping-off, pythium, and brown patch. Crabgrass is also likely to be present.

Late-fall seeding (mid-October to 1 January) is the least desirable. It is likely that seed will germinate during this period, but it will not have enough time to develop an adequate root system for winter heaving and thawing. In most cases this seeding will result in seedlings being "popped" out of the ground and just drying out (desiccating).

LAWN SEEDING CARE

Grass, like any other living plant, will thrive when planted properly in the right location. Many of us think grass seed will grow if we simply throw it on the lawn and walk away. For winter seeding, this is mostly true. But for fall or spring seeding—not so. Here are some step-by-step ways to successfully seed your lawn.

Spot-seeding bare spots:

1. Take a steel rake and loosen the soil.

2. Apply seed with an applicator or by hand at the rate of 4 to 5 seeds per inch (freeze grass seed overnight for faster germination). Not necessary for winter seeding.

3. Dampen down daily until the seed germinates (a light application of straw is optional).

4. After germination, deep-water the new grass once a week (an equivalent of 1 inch of water minus any rainfall that occurs).

5. Mow as soon as the new grass reaches 2¼ inches or more. Cut to a height of 2 inches. Raise the mower ½ inch after four cuttings of the new grass.

Seeding new or re-seeding an existing lawn:

Let's discuss some DON'Ts before we cover the DOs.

Don't rototill the soil. This process causes the soil to settle unevenly and wakes up thousands of weed seeds that will compete with the new grass (and it's a lot of unnecessary work).

Don't apply topsoil to the overall area unless you spread it to a depth of 4 to 6 inches to the entire area. Use topsoil to fill in any low areas. Settle the new topsoil with irrigation or rain before putting down your seed. Re-loosen the top soil with a steel rake to break up the crust. Then put down your seed.

Don't even read any further unless you can keep new seed dampened down daily until germination (assuming no rain on a given day). Try the winter seed method if this seems like too much trouble!

Now for the DOs—please read carefully:

Do kill all existing vegetation in the area to be reseeded. Weeds and other vegetation should be watered well before the application of the herbicide (healthy weeds die faster). In the fall, allow 3 to 4 weeks to retreat some weeds that regrow after initial treatment. The old lawn should be between 2 to 3 inches tall when treating; this is especially true with nut grass. Great vegetation killers that are safe to use are Roundup® and Finale®.

Do rent a seed-slitter or verti-slicer. Set the blade to cut a 1/2-inch-deep slit. Run the machine east to west and north to south (a checkerboard pattern). Most machines come with a seed box. If so, set the seeder to drop 4 to 5 seeds per inch of soil. For turf fescue and turf rye, make another couple of passes northeast to southwest and southeast to northwest.

Do freeze your seed overnight. It can even stay frozen until you're ready to apply it. Do it now before you forget. (This is not necessary when winter seeding.)

Do fertilize with a starter-type fertilizer like a 9-18-18. Do not mix seed and fertilizer together in the same applicator hopper. Apply the fertilizer first.

Do lightly water grass seed daily (assuming rainless days) to keep the seed moist until germination. Then water once weekly with the equivalent of 1 inch of water and/or rain. Continue to water as above during hot, dry weather.

Do mow your grass as soon as it reaches 2¼ inches. Mow to 2 inches and mow often. The more cuttings, the quicker the new grass will mature. You will get a few new broadleaf weeds. Do not apply a broadleaf weedkiller until you've given the new grass three mowings. Raise the mower 1/2 inch after three cuttings.

Do use good grass seed. If you're going to do all the above steps, don't mess everything up with so-called bargain seeds. Check the seed label for purity, weed seed content, and inert ingredients.

Lawn Notes

1. The best feeding times for all types of lawns are early September (with a high-nitrogen fertilizer), to late November (high nitrogen), and spring (¹/₂ rate nitrogen).

2. Leave grass clippings. They will continue to feed the lawn. (An exception is the tall clippings due to rainy periods. Collect those that would clump and smother grass plants or wait until the clumps dry and mow again.)

3. Choose grass varieties that fit your maintenance schedule.

   Bluegrass: high maintenance
   Perennial grass: medium to high maintenance
   Turf-type fescue: low maintenance

4. Winter seeding is a great way to go if you can't seed in fall. In late January or early February, go out and remove any fallen leaves and twigs from the areas to be reseeded. Apply your seed to those areas (4 to 5 per inch) and go back inside and watch TV. Freezing and thawing will occur, causing the seed to have a natural seedbed. The seed will germinate in spring when the soil warms to the proper germination temperature.

5. For spring and fall seedings, straw helps to hold moisture around the seed—but straw does not replace the moisture. You will have to water daily. If you decide to use straw, a bale should cover 2,000 square feet. This is a very light application. If done this way, no straw removal will be necessary, as the straw will decompose.

Do I feed first or seed first? An easy question to ask, an even easier question to answer. When putting down lawn food and grass seed the same day, always put down the fertilizer first so you're not walking on your grass seed any more than is necessary.

INSECTS AND DISEASE

Bluegrass offers the biggest challenge here. Bluegrass lawns are wonderful for attracting chinch bugs, grubs, and other insects. Grubs do not cause spring damage to lawns, but new grubs returning into the soil in the fall can be quite damaging. Two new, low-toxic products have been introduced to get the grubs and other harmful lawn insects without killing the good guys like earthworms. These products, Grub X® and Grub-b-gone®, can be applied from 15 May to 15 August. Please read the instructions, guys. Turf disease is more difficult to control. Environmental conditions along with natural drought stress and other negative factors can cause many diseases that, for the most part, only do temporary damage. You will find more turf disease problems with bluegrass and turf-rye than with turf-fescue. When in doubt about a turf problem, take a 12-by-12-inch sample that has both good grass and bad grass on it to your garden center or cooperative extension office for an analysis.

DID YOU KNOW?

One acre of grass gives off 2,400 gallons of water every hot summer day. This has the cooling effect of a 140,000-pound air conditioner—a 70-ton machine.

Theodore Roosevelt once stated, "Grass is what saves and holds the water that keeps life good and going. It keeps the falling rain from flushing away. Blades of grass take water from the air and transfer it into the ground. That works the other way around, too. Because grass blades help put water back into the air so that rain can fall again." Here are ten ways to conserve water on established lawns during hot, dry weather—save water and money by following these ten methods:

1. *Mow as infrequently as possible.* Mowing puts the grass plant under additional stress and it will use more water.

2. *Mow higher than normal.* Larger leaf surfaces hold plant liquids and shade the root zone. Never remove more than one-third of the leaf blade in one mowing. Longer blades usually mean deeper, more efficient roots.

3. *Water and mow in the early evening or morning.* Less wind and heat reduce stress on the plant and allow for greater penetration and less runoff or evaporation.

4. *Water for deep penetration.* Interrupt watering when puddles or runoff occur, allowing the water to penetrate into the soil before restarting. Light, infrequent sprinkling may actually bring roots to the surface and do more harm than good.

5. *Spot-water.* Drier areas near buildings and on slopes require more water than flat areas where water doesn't run off.

6. *Aerify or verti-cut turf.* Increased penetration of water and air will place the water where it can be used by the grass plant.

7. *Use a soil probe.* Test the soil moisture with a probe or screwdriver. Water only when the soil is dry or the probe is difficult to push into the ground.

8. *Match fertilizer to plant requirements.* Extension agents or agronomists can recommend timing and amounts of fertilizer needed by each grass variety. This reduces waste and mowing needs and diminishes overly succulent, water-wasting growth.

9. *Increase disease and insect control, with care.* Drought-stressed turf is more susceptible to pest problems, but too much pesticide will also increase plant stress.

10. *Accept a little-less-than-lush lawn.* Grass will naturally go dormant during periods of drought, but it will readily regenerate when water becomes available. Reduce traffic on these areas if possible.

Bermudagrass

Cynodon dactylon

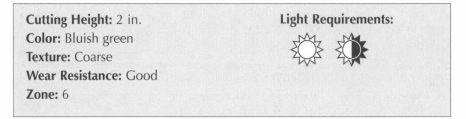

Cutting Height: 2 in.
Color: Bluish green
Texture: Coarse
Wear Resistance: Good
Zone: 6

Light Requirements:

Now here's a variety of grass that does well in Bermuda where it's tropical and never gets cold. So why is it in a Kentucky gardening book? Well, many of you in western Kentucky have found this grass variety acceptable. Like zoysia, it's definitely a southern grass that is durable in our soil and hot, sunny locations during our summers. Unfortunately, it also goes dormant (brown) after a fall killing frost. Bermudagrass will tolerate very light shade, but will not grow into areas that receive medium to mostly shade. It's considered low maintenance during its growing season here because of its low-growing height and its heat and drought tolerance. If you don't mind that the grass is green six months and brown six months, the best varieties to plant from plugs or sod are Tufcote, U-3, and Midiron. These varieties have been developed for lawn use, and Midiron has proven to be the most winter hardy. Planting common bermudagrass from seed has not been successful because it is not winter hardy.

WHEN TO PLANT

Plant bermudagrass when it's actively growing. In Kentucky, that would be from late May to mid-August. Because of the state's tendency to be hot and dry during the summer, plant bermudagrass from mid- to late May.

WHERE TO PLANT

Bermudagrass is not shade tolerant. Plant your plugs or sod in areas that receive full sun to a half-day of shade. The grass will dictate how much shade it will tolerate by growing only in the areas of your lawn where it has enough sun to thrive.

How to Plant

Plant bermudagrass from plugs or sod. Common bermudagrass, which is available from seed, is not winter hardy.
At ground level, plant the plugs on 1-foot centers, or
plant from sprigs on 6-inch centers in rows that are
12 inches apart.

Care and Maintenance

Keep your newly planted bermudagrass watered during
the hot, dry periods of its first summer. After planting,
fertilize the grass with a starter-type fertilizer, one that's
high in the middle number (for example, 9-18-18).
Minimize foot traffic throughout the first year (no touch
football playing).

Landscape Merit

This tough-growing, heat-tolerant grass does better in
southern and western Kentucky than in other parts of the
state. Because it can be very invasive to planting beds,
keep bermudagrass under control by trimming it or treating it with a nonselective herbicide such as Finale.

Additional Information

Planting common bermudagrass from seed may seem to be
the most cost-effective method, but remember, common
bermudagrass is not always winter hardy in Kentucky. The
best way is to plant plugs, which can take up to four years
to form a solid turf. If you want to try the common seed
anyway, seed at the rate of 2 pounds per 1000 square feet
(if it is hulled), or 5 to 10 pounds per 1000 square feet (if
the seed is unhulled, that is, the seed shell is intact).

Additional Species, Cultivars, or Varieties

Tufcote, U-3, and Midiron are considered to be the most
cold-hardy varieties.

Fine-Leaf Fescue

Festuca

Other Name: Fine-textured Fescue
Cutting Height: 2 to 3½ in. (by season)
Color: Soft, medium-green
Texture: Fine, somewhat wiry
Wear Resistance: Good in spring and fall;
   weak in summer because of extra
   foot traffic, summer heat and drought
Zone: 6

Light Requirements:

Fine-leaf fescues are just that—fine- or thin-bladed varieties of turf-grass that will grow in sun or shade. The two most popular types are chewing fescues, which grow in clump form, and creeping red fescue, which spreads through underground rhizomes. Like bluegrass, creeping red fescue makes its own thatch with those rhizomes. Fine-textured chewing fescues grow like their wider-bladed cousins, the turf fescues. Fine-leaf fescues are more drought- and shade-tolerant than bluegrass. They grow much better in shade to semi-shade where the grass does not get the hot afternoon summer sun. You can make your turf more durable by mixing your fine-leaf fescue varieties with a variety or two, or even three, of Kentucky bluegrass. In semi-shade situations, mix with bluegrass at the rate of 50 percent fine fescue, 50 percent bluegrass.

WHEN TO PLANT

The best time to plant any grass seed in Kentucky is in the fall, between mid-August and the end of September. The second-best time is in the winter, spring is third, summer is fourth, and late fall is the worst.

WHERE TO PLANT

Plant creeping red and chewing fescues in natural or tree shade. These varieties will tolerate shady and dry sites better than perennial rye or bluegrass.

HOW TO PLANT

Never rototill any area to prepare for grass seed. Rototilled soil will settle unevenly and will bring thousands of buried weed seed to the surface. Loosen the existing soil with a steel rake in small areas, and rent a seed-slitter for larger areas. Refer to page 393 for complete instructions. Seed fine-leaf fescue at the proper rate: 2 to 3 pounds of seed per 1000 square feet for bare areas.

CARE AND MAINTENANCE

When using a seed mix of fine-leaf fescue and bluegrass, mow both types at 2½ inches in the spring and fall, and 3 inches during the summer. If you are seeding straight varieties of fine-leaf fescue, reduce those cutting heights by ½ inch. Fertilize with a high-first-number lawn food in September and November. You can also give the fescue a light feeding of lawn food in mid- to late May. Even though it is somewhat drought-tolerant, make sure that fine-leaf fescue receives 1 inch of water per week in hot, dry weather.

LANDSCAPE MERIT

Fine-leaf fescue is fine-textured and easy to mow. It is shade- and somewhat drought-tolerant and grows best in semi-shaded areas of your lawn.

ADDITIONAL INFORMATION

Fine-leaf fescues are vigorous growers in the spring and fall. They'll grow and stay greener in the late summer with supplemental watering, when Mother Nature gets chintzy with the rain. Wet springs can cause some fungus diseases, none of which is fatal.

ADDITIONAL SPECIES, CULTIVARS, OR VARIETIES

Improved, newer varieties of creeping red fescue are 'Pennlawn' and 'Dawson', both known for their tolerance of shade. 'Banner III' and 'Checker' are good varieties of chewing fescue. Employees at your favorite garden store will direct you to other good varieties as well.

Kentucky Bluegrass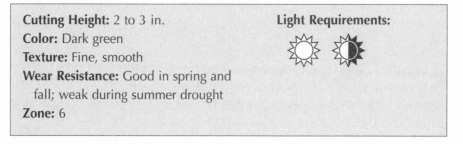

Poa pratensis

Cutting Height: 2 to 3 in.
Color: Dark green
Texture: Fine, smooth
Wear Resistance: Good in spring and
fall; weak during summer drought
Zone: 6

Light Requirements:

Ah, Kentucky bluegrass. For many years, it has been the grass of choice. We got used to fertilizing it four or five times a year if we wanted a lawn to look like the one on the box of seed. There were not a lot of other choices. Over the last twenty years, agronomists have discovered that bluegrass doesn't do well under certain environmental conditions. To begin with, it likes the decent soil you are most likely not to have, and it doesn't tolerate the heat of summer experienced in most of Kentucky, and it stresses during the dry periods of the growing season. Weakened by stress, bluegrass becomes vulnerable to insects and disease. Ken Blue is a variety of bluegrass that was developed in Kentucky and is very persistent when maintained at 2 to 2½ inches in cutting height and not fed too often with high nitrogen. Other summer quality bluegrasses are Adelphi, Vantage, and Glade.

WHEN TO PLANT

The best time to plant any grass seed in Kentucky is during the fall, between mid-August and the end of September. The second-best time is in the winter, spring is third, and summer is fourth.

WHERE TO PLANT

Bluegrass does best in full sun, although it will tolerate up to a half-day of shade. If your planting area has partial shade, you would be better off adding some creeping red fescue to your seed mix. Bluegrass does not do well in heavy clay soil. If you have this soil type, stick to the turf fescue.

HOW TO PLANT

Never rototill any area to prepare it for grass seed. Rototilled soil will settle unevenly and will bring thousands of buried weed seeds to the surface. Loosen existing soil with a steel rake in small areas, and rent a seed-slitter for larger areas. Refer to pages 393–394 in this chapter for complete instructions. Seed at the rate of 1 to 2 pounds per 1000 square feet. If mixing with other seed varieties, cut the amount of your bluegrass seed in half.

CARE AND MAINTENANCE

Thatch is the number one problem with bluegrass—not the clippings, but the growth habit itself. Thatch layers are caused by the rhizomes that bluegrass grows to make new plants. Thatch can be controlled by aerating your lawn twice a year. Mow bluegrass to a height of 2 to 2½ inches in the spring and fall. Raise the mower ½ inch for summer mowing. Bluegrass will have to be watched constantly for soil insects and disease. Timing is everything for these problems. Check your lawn weekly during cool, wet periods in the spring and again during the months of July, August, and September. If you see areas of your bluegrass lawn turning brown, seek professional help.

LANDSCAPE MERIT

Kentucky bluegrass is the Cadillac of grasses. When it is growing well, its looks are unmatched by other grass varieties. The challenge is to keep it looking as good in the summer as it does in the spring. Bluegrass is constantly making new plants. This means that bare spots of 6 to 8 inches will fill in by themselves. Bluegrass sod is always available to give you an instant, green-blue grass carpet.

ADDITIONAL INFORMATION

Kentucky bluegrass can become dormant when the weather causes summer heat and drought. In layman's terms, that means it turns brown. Be sure to give your bluegrass lawn at least ¼ inch of water during this period, minus any rainfall. That will keep the roots alive so that when the weather cools down and more natural rainfall occurs, your bluegrass will turn green and start to grow again.

Perennial Rye

Lolium spp.

Cutting Height: 2 to 3½ inches
Color: Medium to dark green
Texture: Medium to fine
Wear Resistance: Good
Zone: 6

Light Requirements:

Perennial rye is a turfgrass that is quick to germinate and begin growing. It is most often mixed with bluegrass and/or fine-textured fescue to act as a starter grass to get your newly seeded area off to a fast start. Some, like my neighbor, have planted 100 percent perennial rye. Perennial rye grows like turf fescue in that it grows in clump form. Many new varieties of perennial rye have come along over the last ten years. These varieties are much improved over their ancestors. Yet one common problem still exists with all perennial ryes: they are susceptible to turf disease when the weather doesn't cooperate. The newer varieties are more resistant, but not as resistant as the turf fescues. You can plant perennial rye in sun or in shade—just make sure the shady area has good natural light. When mixing with bluegrass, never have more than 20 percent rye to 80 percent bluegrass.

WHEN TO PLANT

The best time to plant any grass seed in Kentucky is fall, between mid-August and the end of September. The second-best time is the winter, spring is third, and summer is fourth.

WHERE TO PLANT

Perennial turf-type rye grows best in full sun. The more shade, the more problems you can have. Turf-type rye prefers moist areas; it does not fare well in heavy clay soils. This grass does not perform well in soil types that dry out quickly.

HOW TO PLANT

Never rototill any area to prepare for grass seed. Rototilled soil will settle unevenly and will bring thousands of buried weed seed to the surface. Loosen existing soil with a steel rake in small areas, and rent a seed-slitter for larger areas. Refer to pages 393–394 in this chapter for complete instructions. Seed at the rate of 6 to 8 pounds per 1000 square feet of area. If mixing with other seed varieties, cut the amount of turf-type rye so it is no more than 50 percent of the mix.

CARE AND MAINTENANCE

Always use a lawn food that has a seed-starter formula. This will help the new grass seedlings get established faster. Mow turf-type rye to 2½ to 3 inches in the spring and fall, and raise the mower ½ inch for summer cutting. Make sure your turf-type rye receives 1 inch of water per week during the hot summer months. You also need to watch for disease problems, which usually occur during cool, rainy periods. Treat for weeds anytime they rear their ugly heads. Fertilize rye in mid-spring and twice in the fall, in early September and early to late November.

LANDSCAPE MERIT

Perennial rye germinates quickly, usually within a week or less. It works great as a starter grass when mixed with Kentucky bluegrass or fine-textured fescues.

ADDITIONAL INFORMATION

Lots of improvements have come about with turf-type rye varieties. You will get best results by mixing together two to three of the better varieties.

ADDITIONAL SPECIES, CULTIVARS, OR VARIETIES

Improved varieties include 'Pennant II', ' Premier II', 'All Star', 'Citation II', and 'Fiesta II'. 'Fiesta II' and 'Citation II' are both reported to have better shade tolerance than other turf-type rye.

Turf-Type Tall Fescue

Festuca spp.

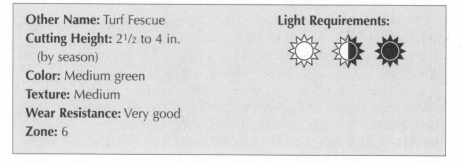

Other Name: Turf Fescue
Cutting Height: 2¹/₂ to 4 in.
  (by season)
Color: Medium green
Texture: Medium
Wear Resistance: Very good
Zone: 6

Light Requirements:

You know that grass that grows in the median strips of interstates and on many sports fields? That's Kentucky 31 fescue, a tall, coarse-growing grass that grows in clumps and gets mowed at 4 to 5 inches. Well, it has a new relative that I am absolutely sold on. I'm talking about turf-type fescue. The first cultivars were introduced over twenty years ago, and many improved varieties have been introduced since. This will be *the* grass for most of Kentucky. Seed hybridization has improved turf fescue so much that the newest cultivars have the blade texture of bluegrass. Add to that the deep-root characteristics of coarse fescue and the shade tolerance of fine-leaf fescue, and you have a good-looking, drought-resistant, disease-, insect-, and shade-tolerant grass. Not bad for one of the newest kids on the seed block. If you decide to plant this grass in your lawn, you really should get rid of all the others before making the switch.

WHEN TO PLANT
The best time to plant any grass seed in Kentucky is in the fall, between mid-August and the end of September. The second-best time is in the winter, spring is the third, and summer is fourth.

WHERE TO PLANT
Plant turf-type fescue in sun to shade. This grass is drought-tolerant in sunny areas and shade-tolerant where no sun exists. Turf-type fescue will do well in all the soil types we find in Kentucky. It's also a great grass for heavy traffic areas, where kids of all ages like to play.

HOW TO PLANT
Never rototill any area to prepare for grass seed. Rototilled soil will settle unevenly and will bring thousands of buried weed seed to the

surface. Loosen existing soil with a steel rake in small areas. Refer to pages 393 to 394 in this chapter for complete instructions. Seed turf-type fescue at the rate of 5 to 7 pounds per 1000 square feet.

CARE AND MAINTENANCE

Mow turf-type fescue at a height of 2½ to 3 inches in the spring and fall, and raise the cutting height by ½ inch for the summer. Because of this grass's vast deep-root system, grubs aren't much of a problem. Turf-type fescues also contain endophytes, a natural ingredient that top-feeding insects, such as bill bugs, do not like. Brown patch is the only disease problem I've seen, and that problem is not terminal. Turf-type fescue is a lot more drought-tolerant, so there's not much to worry about during dry periods. It's a low-maintenance grass—unless you consider mowing turf-type fescue in the summer, when other grasses have gone dormant and turned brown, to be a high-maintenance chore.

LANDSCAPE MERIT

Turf-type tall fescue grows in all types of soil and works great for either sun or shade. Add to that drought tolerance and resistance to insects or disease, and you can't beat this type of lawn.

ADDITIONAL INFORMATION

Turf-type fescue will do just fine with two fall applications of lawn food put down at the rate of 1 pound of nitrogen per 1000 square feet in September, and 1½ pounds of nitrogen per 1000 square feet in November. That November feeding will also take care of the needed spring nutrients. If your lawn winterburns, you may want to put down ½ pound of nitrogen per 1000 square feet in mid-May.

ADDITIONAL SPECIES, CULTIVARS, OR VARIETIES

'Finelawn 5 GL', 'Finelawn Petite', 'Cross Fire II', 'Southern Choice', and 'Rebel III' are some of the newest varieties. There are others of equal quality. To find out which one grows best in your area of Kentucky, check with your local seed or garden store.

Zoysia

Zoysia spp.

Cutting Height: 1¹/₂ to 2 in.
Color: Medium to dark green
Texture: Medium, wiry
Wear Resistance: Great in summer, poor
  in winter
Zone: 6

Light Requirements:

It is important to remember that you are reading the Kentucky book, not the Georgia book. Zoysia is a southern grass. So what's it doing this far north? Well, for people who don't like to cut grass, it's okay, even though it's only green about five months a year. You don't have to mow it much, as it stays rather low. It will only grow in sunny areas, and its biggest problem is neighbors. That's right. You might want zoysia in your yard, but it's impossible to keep out of your neighbor's yard, and that can cause serious problems between you and the person who lives next door. Another problem with zoysia comes when your lawn is brown or dormant. When zoysia is asleep, it is very intolerant to wear. Just check the path the mailman makes when he walks over the same area of brown zoysia each day during the winter. You'll find a bare path. Same damage occurs with kids playing on it during zoysia's dormancy period. This grass is better appreciated in western Kentucky.

WHEN TO PLANT

Zoysia is best planted from sod or plugs. Since zoysia is expensive to plant by the yard, make up to one hundred plugs or pieces from each cut yard and plant them into your existing sunny lawn when it's green, which will be sometime between mid-May through mid-August.

WHERE TO PLANT

Plant in sunny areas of your lawn. Make sure the areas where you plant your zoysia are well drained.

HOW TO PLANT

Tear plugs out of a yard roll of zoysia, and plant them on 12-inch centers into your existing lawn, using a garden trowel or a bulb planter. Plant to the same depth as the zoysia sod is thick. You don't have to kill other existing grasses because the zoysia will take over. Water freshly planted plugs as often as required to keep moisture around the new transplants. Once the new zoysia starts to grow, you can reduce the watering so the other grasses become weak, and that is when the zoysia will take over.

CARE AND MAINTENANCE

Feed your newly planted zoysia with a starter type of plant food when you first plant. Fertilize every other summer after that. There are no known bugs or diseases to worry about, but check the label on any selective herbicide you may choose to use if weeds are present when your zoysia first starts growing—some herbicides may not work with zoysia. Remember, this grass stays green only about five months. Stay off it when it's asleep (brown).

LANDSCAPE MERIT

When zoysia is green, you don't even have to mow. In full sun, it dominates all other grasses. It will not tolerate any shade and will not stay out of your neighbor's yard.

ADDITIONAL INFORMATION

Remember, this is a southern grass, and we live in Kentucky. So you really need good justification to plant zoysia in your lawn. Please keep the neighbors in mind as you make your decision. You still have to mow zoysia with a sharp mower blade every ten to fourteen days to keep it really short.

ADDITIONAL SPECIES, CULTIVARS, OR VARIETIES

'Meyer' is available in 2-inch-by-2-inch plugs or as sod that's 18 inches wide by 6 feet long. 'Zenith' can be planted by seed if you can locate the seed, and it requires a little fertilizer. With 'Emerald' you should plant plugs or sod, and mow every seven to ten days to keep at $1^{1}/_{2}$ inches.

CHAPTER TEN

Vines

VINES HOLD A VERY SPECIAL PLACE in a well-designed landscape. I say well-designed because some homeowners who design their own landscapes are either fearful of vines or just plain don't understand them. Many might not even know about them. Hence this chapter.

Vines serve many purposes. To begin with, a properly placed vine growing against the home on the south or west side is like adding room air-conditioners to those windows in those exposures. Using vines that drop their leaves in the fall allows winter sun to help warm the home on cold winter days. Vines by their nature are vertical. They take up very little yard space. A vine can also be a beautiful, blooming shade provider for an outdoor people area. Lattice over a deck or patio can be made into a Garden of Eden by planting vines to cover the lattice. And what looks more inviting in a yard than an arbor covered with blooming vines? Even without flowers, the leaves add landscape beauty.

How to Hold On . . .

Different vines have different ways to cling. Some vines have their own methods for attaching themselves to a structure; others need our assistance to remain upright. In this chapter I will explain what each vine needs or doesn't need to stay upright. Vines do not grow vertically in thin air. Whether a vine is self-clinging or not, a structure is needed. That structure could be the side of your house or a wooden or plastic trellis or arbor. It could be soft jute twine attached to something at both ends. It could even be a chain-link fence that you know could use some landscape help.

. . . or Not to Hold On

All vines will make a ground cover when they are not furnished with support. When some plants can't stand up, they lie down and, in the case of vines, they cover the ground. Unsupported vines will continue to grow in a very horizontal way. There may be situations in which you would prefer to have a vine grow as a ground cover.

I'M THE BOSS!

Yes, you are the boss. Control the height and spread of vines by pruning. Do that pruning anytime a particular vine starts growing out of *your* bounds. Remember, annual vines die in late fall. Remove all of their old growth to the ground when you're in the mood.

A BIG NO-NO

Never plant self-attaching vines to painted wood or the siding on your home. The vines hold moisture and can cause quick deterioration of painted wood; they can cause permanent stains on siding. If the wall is brick or stone, go ahead and plant the vines.

Boston Ivy

Parthenocissus tricuspidata

Other Name: Japanese Creeper
Flowers: Insignificant
Height × Width: It's a vine, keeps growing
Bloom Time: Mid-June
Type: Deciduous vine
Zone: 6

Color photograph on page 254.

Light Requirements:

Additional Benefits:

It's called Boston ivy, so what's it doing in Chicago on the outfield walls of Wrigley Field? What it's doing is growing very well and, in some cases, hiding the ball from the outfielder. This is a wonderful vine that has beautiful three-lobed leaves that are a dark, glossy green during the growing season. These same leaves turn scarlet red in the fall, then drop to the ground. When first planted, the leaves of Boston ivy are very small. The next few years find them expanding to become 4- to 6-inch leaves. The vine is self-clinging and can really hide an ugly wall. It also does one heck of an air-conditioning and heating job. Plant Boston ivy against the west or south side of a house where it will shade that side during the growing season. After beautiful fall color, the leaves will fall, allowing those same walls to receive the warmth of the sun. (Your utility company will not be happy.)

WHEN TO PLANT

Boston ivy is available in containers from garden centers and nursery stores. You will find it for sale in spring and summer. Plant it anytime the ground is not frozen.

WHERE TO PLANT

Boston ivy can certainly handle hot sun to shade (check out Wrigley Field's outfield). You will get the best fall color where Boston ivy gets sun; it's nice to know, though, that it does well in all exposures.

HOW TO PLANT

You will find most if not all Boston ivy plants available in 1-gallon containers. Dig the hole no deeper than the soil clump but twice as wide. Plant the soil clump as close to its "wall to climb" as possible.

Loosen any wrapped roots around the soil clump, and backfill using the existing soil, first breaking up all soil clumps to the size of golf balls. Water-in well.

CARE AND MAINTENANCE

Boston ivy never stops growing, but it needs something to grow on. Don't be afraid to prune this plant to keep it contained. It will also adapt to any soil condition as long as the soil is well drained. There are no major bugs or diseases that can wreak havoc on Boston ivy. It may be called Boston ivy, but it grows well in every part of Kentucky.

LANDSCAPE MERIT

Boston ivy is fast growing, has beautiful fall color, and does a great job screening an ugly sight.

ADDITIONAL INFORMATION

This plant makes a wonderful screen. If you don't have a natural wall for it to grow against, use an arbor or trellis to give you privacy. Just remember, you're the boss. Keep it contained by pruning it to the space you've allotted it.

ADDITIONAL SPECIES, CULTIVARS, OR VARIETIES

'Fenway Park': now that's in Boston. This variety has good green foliage that starts off yellow in spring, then has great red fall color. 'Green Showers' has fresh green leaves, large in size; the fall color is burgundy. 'Purpurea' has reddish-purple leaves throughout the summer. 'Robusta' is gorgeous; its leaves are green during the growing season, turning an orange-red fall color.

Clematis

Clematis hybrids

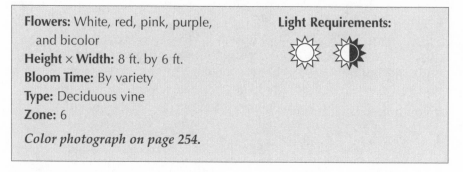

Flowers: White, red, pink, purple, and bicolor
Height × Width: 8 ft. by 6 ft.
Bloom Time: By variety
Type: Deciduous vine
Zone: 6

Color photograph on page 254.

Light Requirements:

What a beautiful vine! No, they don't self-cling—they need a trellis or at least twine to grow on. But the flowers are absolutely gorgeous, and they bloom in many colors, from white to blue to purple to red. You will see them on lampposts, on mailbox posts, even growing against tree trunks. Clematis is one of the most popular vines, as well it should be. It has flowers that range from 3 to 7 inches in diameter. It blooms from May until frost, some varieties blooming for three weeks, while others bloom off and on all summer long. It is a vine that blooms under less-sunny conditions. In a sunny location it likes shade over the lower 12 inches of the plant. Clematis wants to have its cake and eat it too: it likes sun on the vine, but shade on the roots. Always surround it with low-growing plants.

WHEN TO PLANT
Clematis is sold in containers; buy the 1-gallon size when possible. The best selection is always in the spring. Don't be disappointed if your clematis sits and doesn't grow the first year. This is common. You'll be very pleased with second-year growth.

WHERE TO PLANT
Clematis appreciates good, well-drained soil.

HOW TO PLANT
Dig a hole no deeper but up to three times as wide as the soil clump. If you have heavy clay soil, you might decide against planting clematis. But if you think your soil is okay, backfill with existing soil and water-in well. Geraniums, dwarf spirea, or other 12-inch plants should be planted around the base to keep the roots cool.

CARE AND MAINTENANCE

Clematis will cling to any wood- or string-type trellis; young plants might need some guidance to get them started. Clematis blooms on new growth to old growth, by variety. To prune it at the proper time, you will have to know the name of the variety you have. You don't want to prune off the old growth in the fall or spring if you have a variety that blooms on old wood. Same thing goes for varieties that only bloom on new wood that needs to be pruned. Check before you buy to find out when to prune your new purchase.

LANDSCAPE MERIT

Clematis is fast growing and has beautiful blooms.

ADDITIONAL INFORMATION

Chain-link fences would seem to be natural planting spots for clematis. Unfortunately, clematis vines do not like the heat reflected off a metal fence located in the sun. They cook! Grow on a wood- or string-type trellis.

ADDITIONAL SPECIES, CULTIVARS, OR VARIETIES

Florida Group: These vines flower in late spring on last-year's wood. Double-flowered 'Belle of Woking' is pale mauve. 'Kathleen Dunford' has semi-double, rosy-purple flowers. Prune after flowering. **Jackmanii Group:** These plants flower in July to August on new growth. 'Comptesse de Bouchard', pink and lavender, blooms June to August. 'Jackmani' has purple flowers that bloom June through August. 'Victoria' has light blue 4- to 5-inch-diameter flowers that bloom all season. **Lanuginosa Group:** These vines flower in June on last-year's wood. 'Candida' has large white flowers. Beautiful 'Nelly Moser' has large, mauve-pink flowers. 'Henryi' has 4- to 5-inch white flowers. 'Crimson King' has large, double, red flowers. **Patens Group:** Vines in this group bloom on old wood. 'Daniel Deronda' has large violet-blue flowers. 'Miss Bateman' has white flowers with brown centers. 'The President' has 6-inch deep-violet flowers. **Viticella Group:** This group blooms on new and old wood. 'Ernest Mackham' has reddish purple flowers 3 to 4 inches in diameter. 'Mrs. Spencer Castle' has large, double, lavender flowers; it blooms May into June and again in the fall. 'Huldine' has bright, white, 3- to 4-inch-diameter flowers.

Climbing Hydrangea

Hydrangea anomala ssp. *petiolaris*

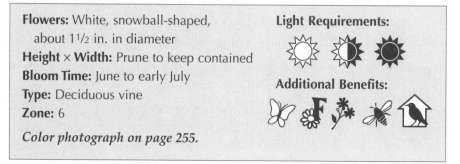

Flowers: White, snowball-shaped, about 1½ in. in diameter
Height × Width: Prune to keep contained
Bloom Time: June to early July
Type: Deciduous vine
Zone: 6

Color photograph on page 255.

Light Requirements:

Additional Benefits:

You will soon read and understand why this is my favorite vine. It would be yours, too, unless *a)* you've never heard of it, or *b)* you've never seen it growing. Climbing hydrangea is a vine that is slow in getting established the first couple of years it's planted, but then it takes off and does a beautiful job of covering walls, arbors, trees, or any free-standing structure. It's self-clinging, too. It does require decent soil that's well drained. Give it that, and it will grow in full sun to shade, providing you with small, white, snowball-like flowers in June to early July. The flowers have a good fragrance—when this vine is in bloom, it's outstanding. Even when not in bloom during the growing season, its leaves are attractive—2 to 4 inches long with a glossy, dark-green luster. The leaves remain on the vine into late fall to early winter. There is not much of a fall color, although some varieties will turn yellow. Most just drop those green leaves. Look around your landscape. You've got to have room for at least one.

WHEN TO PLANT

Always buy your climbing hydrangea growing in containers. The best selection at the garden store or nursery center will be in spring. You can plant this vine anytime the ground is not frozen.

WHERE TO PLANT

Hydrangeas will have the most blooms where they get the most sun, although I have seen some good blooming specimens growing with only four hours of sun. Climbing hydrangeas would appreciate being shielded from strong northwest winter winds. Remember, hydrangea appreciates moist but well-drained soil.

How to Plant

Dig a hole as deep as the soil clump and twice as wide, even wider if you have clay soil. Loosen any wrapped roots around the soil clump. Break up all existing soil to the size of golf balls. If you're working with clay soil, mix in several shovelfuls of organic material. Backfill, and water-in well.

Care and Maintenance

Climbing hydrangeas are slow to start growing after they are transplanted into your landscape. Be patient. Don't overfertilize and don't overwater. These plants will certainly kick in by the third year and start to put on some serious growth. There are no known bugs or diseases that threaten this plant's health, growth, and vigor.

Landscape Merit

Once established, climbing hydrangea is a fast grower, offering fragrant blooms on a plant that has shiny leaves.

Additional Information

This plant does a great job of clinging in any situation it's exposed to. During the winter months, it still looks great, adding great winter interest with its peeling, shaggy bark, especially nice when planted near entryways.

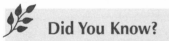 **Did You Know?**

This plant is a native of Japan and China, like so many other plants, and was first introduced in 1865. They're definitely something old, something new.

Mandevilla

Mandevilla × amabilis

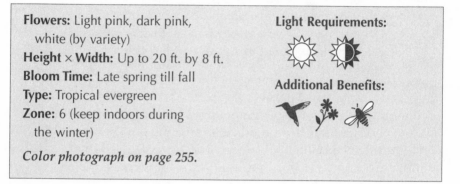

Flowers: Light pink, dark pink, white (by variety)
Height × Width: Up to 20 ft. by 8 ft.
Bloom Time: Late spring till fall
Type: Tropical evergreen
Zone: 6 (keep indoors during the winter)

Color photograph on page 255.

Light Requirements:

Additional Benefits:

Mandevilla is a tropical vine. That translates into a plant that will not survive the winter weather here in Kentucky. So what's it doing in this book? Well, let me tell you. This is a vine that will bloom all summer. "So what?" you say. "I'll have to plant it new each year." No, you won't. Listen up. Mandevilla is a vine that's available from the garden center in spring. It comes in 1- or 5-gallon containers. If you buy a 1-gallon size, repot it immediately into a 5-gallon container. Plant your mandevilla, pot and all, into the ground close to the structure it's to grow on. Why do you want to go to this trouble? No other vine, in this chapter or otherwise, will bloom as much as mandevilla. It has trumpet-shaped flowers, some pink, some white, some the size of a morning glory, and they bloom all summer long. The reason you plant the mandevilla pot and all is so you can lift the pot out of the ground in mid-September and cut away all but the first 18 inches of the vine. Bring it inside your home and treat it like any other indoor tropical plant over the winter. Then wait until late May, take it back outside, and repeat the whole process.

WHEN TO PLANT

Mandevilla is a tropical plant; a late-spring frost will damage it severely. Wait until the danger of frost is over in your area of Kentucky.

WHERE TO PLANT

Mandevilla will grow in full sun to a half-day of sun. In southern and western Kentucky, 'Alice du Pont' mandevilla prefers a location that offers a little relief from the hottest part of the day. Remember, mandevilla is a vine that has some varieties that grow 15 to 20 feet in one season. They need support to grow on. You can use arbors, trellis, latticework, or even soft jute twine for that support.

How to Plant

If your plant is in a 1-gallon container, repot it into a 5-gallon container. You can probably get it free at the nursery where you bought your 1-gallon. Dig a hole close to your vine support. Dig the hole as deep as the pot and wide enough for the pot to fit into the ground. When planted, the top edge of the pot should be level with the top of your soil.

Landscape Merit

Mandevilla is a fast-growing vine that blooms profusely. For the little bit of work you have to perform—taking your mandevilla outside each spring, then reversing the procedure in early fall—you will get a vine that will bloom and bloom all summer long. It can be treated like any other houseplant when you protect it inside your home during the winter.

Additional Information

A variety called 'Red Riding Hood' is more compact-growing, suitable for hanging baskets and wall planters.

Additional Species, Cultivars, or Varieties

'Alice du Pont', a twining tropical evergreen, has ice-pink flowers and a darker-pink throat; it grows 15 to 20 feet long and 4 to 5 feet wide. 'Monte', with pure-white flowers, grows 15 to 20 feet; protect it from hot summer sun. 'Red Riding Hood' is compact, growing to 6 to 8 feet; it has deep-pink flowers with yellow throats.

Moonflower

Ipomea alba

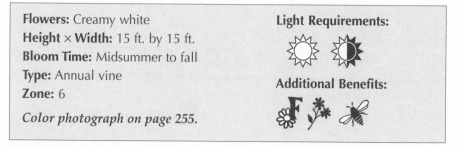

Flowers: Creamy white
Height × Width: 15 ft. by 15 ft.
Bloom Time: Midsummer to fall
Type: Annual vine
Zone: 6

Color photograph on page 255.

Light Requirements:

Additional Benefits:

No vine chapter would be complete without an annual vine that you can plant from seed. In fact, you *have* to plant moonflower from seed because it is not available in plant form. Moonflower grows very readily from seed, and you can get approximately thirty plants for under one dollar. Now, whether you have room for thirty plants is another story. Figure on one plant per seed—better yet, plant three seeds per planting spot to make for a fuller-growing vine. Moonflower has large flowers that measure up to 6 inches across; it is a first cousin to morning glory, and starts blooming in midsummer. As its name implies, the vine blooms each day at sundown (you will see blooms earlier in the day if the sky is cloudy). It's a wonderful plant for any homeowner who wants a fast-growing vine that needs special support (the support could come from that ugly chain-link fence that's starting to rust). Being an annual, it does die with a fall killing frost, but it is certainly easy to replant the following spring.

WHEN TO PLANT
Don't try to start moonflower seeds early indoors. Wait until the middle of May to early June to plant the seed directly in the ground where you want the vines to grow.

WHERE TO PLANT
Plant the seeds in a sunny location, at least a half-day of sun. The seeds will germinate in average soil, nothing special. Make sure you have a structure for moonflower to grow up on.

HOW TO PLANT
Loosen the soil over a 6-inch-diameter area to a depth of 6 inches. Place three seeds about 2 inches apart and about 1 inch deep. Water-

in and be patient. It can take up to two weeks for the seed to germinate.

CARE AND MAINTENANCE

Moonflower doesn't need to be "mothered." In fact, many homeowners cause serious harm to this vine by being too kind. It doesn't need to be fertilized, and it should be watered only during hot, dry summers if the leaves are drooping. Prune away any growth that you do not want; you can do this anytime.

LANDSCAPE MERIT

Moonflower blooms each day at sundown with large flowers. It is good for hiding unsightly structures.

ADDITIONAL SPECIES, CULTIVARS, OR VARIETIES

Moonflower is a first cousin of common morning glory. If you want more color, mix moonflower with morning glory. Other vines that are first cousins are cypress vine and cardinal climber.

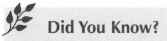 **Did You Know?**

Moonflower, an annual, gets all its flowers in one season. Plant off a deck or patio where you sit at night so you can enjoy the evening blooms.

Morning Glory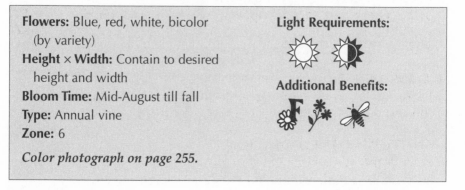

Ipomoea purpurea

Flowers: Blue, red, white, bicolor
(by variety)

Height × Width: Contain to desired
height and width

Bloom Time: Mid-August till fall

Type: Annual vine

Zone: 6

Color photograph on page 255.

Light Requirements:

Additional Benefits:

This rapid-growing annual vine is one of the oldest known plants in the home landscape. Morning glory can be traced back to the settlers who moved in, built homes, and wanted some summer color. I've never seen morning glory available at the garden center as a pregrown plant. It's like its cousin, the moonflower: it should be planted from seed—and yes, be patient, because it won't start blooming until late summer. That's really not a bad time, though, because most color areas of Kentucky landscapes are looking a little tired by mid-August. But at that time, morning-glory vines are just beginning to bloom, and bloom. They do so in colors of blue, violet, white, pink, and bicolor (more than one color to a flower). Morning glory also does a great job of concealing a chain-link fence or an arbor that you want full-looking every summer.

WHEN TO PLANT

Plant morning glory from seed. Place the seeds directly into the ground around the middle to the end of May. You can even plant the seeds by mid-June and get great results.

WHERE TO PLANT

Plant morning glory seeds in a sunny to half-sunny location. Morning glory will tolerate any type of soil as long as there's good drainage. You can also grow it in hanging baskets and wall planters; just be sure to plant quicker-blooming annuals with them for full-season color.

How to Plant

Dig a 6- to 12-inch-diameter hole about 6 inches deep. Loosen the existing soil, backfill, and place three seeds ¹/₂ inch deep and 3 inches apart. It will take up to four weeks for the seeds to germinate and start to grow; make sure they have a structure to grow on.

Landscape Merit

Fast-growing morning glory will screen lots of ugly sights. It offers fresh flowers when other vines are getting tired.

Additional Information

Once planted, morning glory does not like to be moved. Make sure you plant the seed where you want the vine to grow. Do not fertilize as you do other flowers; to do so would cause too many leaves and not enough color. Morning glory is the perfect summer remedy for ugly, rusty chain-link fences. The hotter, the better for these vines.

Additional Species, Cultivars, or Varieties

'Heavenly Blue' is light blue with 3- to 4-inch-diameter flowers. 'Pearly Gates' has white, large-blooming flowers. An All-America Selection, 'Scarlet O'Hara', has good bloom in deep red.

Silver Lace Vine

Polygonum aubertii

Other Names: Fleece Flower, Russian Vine

Flowers: White to greenish-white

Height × Width: Trim and contain to desired size

Bloom Time: July, August into September

Type: Deciduous vine

Zone: 6

Color photograph on page 255.

Light Requirements:

Additional Benefits:

This is another vine for those of you who need a vine but just don't have very good soil for most vines. Silver lace vine does not care what kind of soil it has to grow in, and for many of you Kentucky gardeners who have basically rotten soil, this could be the vine for you. Silver lace grows in sunny to shady locations. It is easily transplantable, and it rapidly spreads by means of underground stems. Never be afraid to cut or spray with a nonselective vegetation killer to keep this vine contained. But for those of you who say, "Hey, it's a vine that will grow in my lousy soil," you will receive white flowers, sometimes pinkish white that are fragrant. They are small flowers, only about 1/4 inch in diameter, but there are many clinging close together, giving you lots of color in July, August, and much of September. Because of its rapid growth, there may be a few weeks in-between bloom. Be patient. More flowers are coming.

WHEN TO PLANT

Silver lace vine will be available from your favorite garden center or nursery store in the spring. If they don't have it, tell them to get you one. Most major cities have Horticultural Plant Centers that are located within a few miles of the city, and these retail outlets can order you one. You can plant this vine anytime the ground is not frozen.

WHERE TO PLANT

Silver lace vine will grow in sun to shade, but you will get more bloom with more sun. This vine will grow in any kind of soil type, but it does not like poor-draining soil that holds water after a rain.

How to Plant

Dig a hole no deeper than the soil clump but twice as wide. Loosen any roots that are wrapped around the clump. Backfill with existing soil, breaking up all soil clumps so the pieces are no bigger than golf balls. Water-in well.

Care and Maintenance

There are no bad bugs or diseases that attack this vigorous, fast-growing vine. The plant makes a good quick cover, but prune to keep within the area you've allowed it—prune anytime the plant needs it.

Landscape Merit

This fast-growing perennial tolerates poor soil as long as the soil drains well.

Additional Information

Silver lace vine needs support—a trellis, lattice, or arbor— to grow on. It grows quickly; if it dares to grow out-of-bounds, trim off the excess anytime.

Additional Species, Cultivars, or Varieties

I know of none for sure. Other varieties might be listed, but as far as I know, they're not registered.

Trumpet Vine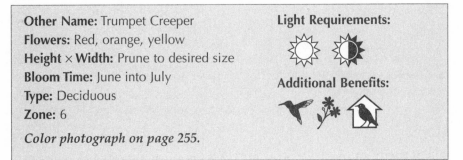

Campsis radicans

Other Name: Trumpet Creeper
Flowers: Red, orange, yellow
Height × Width: Prune to desired size
Bloom Time: June into July
Type: Deciduous
Zone: 6

Color photograph on page 255.

Light Requirements:

Additional Benefits:

This is a vine that is extremely hardy, if not aggressive. Very fast growing, trumpet vine does well in full sun to half-day sun, growing best on some type of lattice, trellis, fence, or arbor. The flowers range in color from yellowish-orange to orange to red, depending on the variety. The trumpet-shaped flowers are 3 inches long, grow in clusters of four to twelve, and flower in June into July. Trumpet vine attaches itself by means of aerial roots that hold the vine to its support. It blooms on new wood, so you can prune way back in early spring if it's getting bigger than the space you've allocated for it. Prune off the seedpods as they start to form after flowering, and you'll be able to extend the blooming period into fall. Trumpet vine's fall color is a yellowish green. Soil types are not important, as trumpet vine will tolerate most conditions. If you cannot grow this vine, stay out of the garden.

WHEN TO PLANT

Trumpet vine is container-grown. You can plant it anytime the ground is not frozen. The best selection at the garden store will be in May to early June.

WHERE TO PLANT

Trumpet vine performs best in full sun but will give you satisfactory results in a half-day of sun. This vine will take all types of soil conditions as long as water doesn't stand after a rain.

HOW TO PLANT

Dig a hole as deep as but twice as wide as the soil clump. Use existing soil to backfill, breaking up all soil particles to the size of golf balls. Water-in well.

CARE AND MAINTENANCE

Don't let this plant get any bigger than the space you've allowed. After five years, start pruning back some of the oldest growth to within 12 inches of the ground—do this in early spring. Wait until bloom appears before pruning new growth.

LANDSCAPE MERIT

Fast-growing trumpet vine has great bloom colors and makes a wonderful screen plant for hiding an undesirable view.

ADDITIONAL SPECIES, CULTIVARS, OR VARIETIES

'Flava' has large yellow to orange-yellow flowers; it is, in my opinion, the best of the trumpet vines. 'Crimson Trumpet' has large-flowering, velvet-red blooms; it's a strong-growing variety. 'University Hybrids' are relatively new, and offer a mixed bag of colors on different varieties. These could really cause more homeowners to plant trumpet vine.

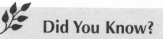

Did You Know?

Want hummingbirds? They love trumpet vine and they will find yours if they're in the neighborhood.

Virginia Creeper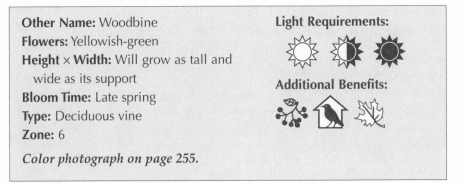

Parthenocissus quinquefolia

Other Name: Woodbine

Flowers: Yellowish-green

Height × Width: Will grow as tall and wide as its support

Bloom Time: Late spring

Type: Deciduous vine

Zone: 6

Color photograph on page 255.

Light Requirements:

Additional Benefits:

Wait! Is that poison ivy growing in my landscape? No, it has five leaflets for each leaf stem (petiole). You are looking at Virginia creeper! This first cousin to Boston ivy has beautiful, glossy green leaves that when first developed are a bright, waxy bronze to red. This deciduous vine grows very fast and is self-clinging—that means it needs no support. It is good for growing up southern- or western-exposed walls of the house. It will also grow up on a tree, which does not hurt the tree, and can be used as a ground cover, trailing over the top of any bed area. As for attaching it to the house, be sure to keep it off painted surfaces, as it can help these surfaces deteriorate. This vine will do well in full sun to full shade. It will tolerate extreme cold, windy conditions, and just about any type of soil. Remember, it drops its leaves in the fall after giving you a "fall color spectacular" with its purplish-red fall leaf color. Because it drops its leaves, it exposes the sunny, winter sides of your house to a nice warming during the day. That saves on utility bills.

WHEN TO PLANT

Plant Virginia creeper from containers anytime the ground is not frozen. Your best selection will be in the spring.

WHERE TO PLANT

Virginia creeper grows well in sun or shade. It will grow well in any soil type as long as there is decent drainage.

How to Plant

Dig a hole no deeper than but twice as wide as the soil clump. Loosen any roots that are wrapped around the clump. Always backfill with the existing soil, breaking up all soil clumps to the size of golf balls. Water-in well.

Care and Maintenance

Guide this vine in its young stages so it grows where you want it to. Trim away all unwanted growth. No bugs or diseases bother this vine.

Landscape Merit

Self-attaching Virginia creeper is fast-growing and offers great spring and fall leaf color.

Additional Information

This tough, low-maintenance vine will cover walls, trellises, and the ground. It provides clusters of black berries that show through after leaf drop.

Additional Species, Cultivars, or Varieties

'Engelmannii' has smaller leaves that grow more dense than those of the species. 'Dark Green Ice' has shiny, dark-green leaves that tend to be more yellowish in the fall when planted in shade.

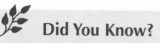 **Did You Know?**

You will find lots of Virginia creeper in natural woodland areas. This plant readily reseeds itself and makes for a natural forest floor.

Wisteria

Wisteria floribunda

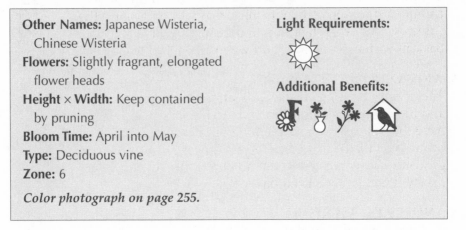

Other Names: Japanese Wisteria, Chinese Wisteria

Flowers: Slightly fragrant, elongated flower heads

Height × Width: Keep contained by pruning

Bloom Time: April into May

Type: Deciduous vine

Zone: 6

Color photograph on page 255.

Light Requirements:

Additional Benefits:

One of the most-often-asked questions I get on radio is "Why won't my wisteria bloom?" A lot of homeowners plant American wisteria, but this variety has one problem in Kentucky: it is sometimes too stubborn to bloom because it can't tolerate certain very cold winters. You see, all wisteria form their bloom buds in the fall along with their vegetative buds. What that means is all homeowners who have planted wisteria in cold-exposed areas will see the bloom buds freeze before spring. Add to that the fact that many wisteria are seed-grown, and seed-grown plants can take up to twelve years to produce flowers. Disappointment can be the name of the wisteria game. But even with difficult bloom, wisteria is an excellent vine to cover patios, decks, and any other wood structure that allows the wisteria to grow. Chinese varieties tend to be more winter hardy and tend to bloom at an earlier age.

WHEN TO PLANT

Wisterias are available container-grown, with the best selection in spring. Technically, you can plant wisteria vine anytime the ground is not frozen.

WHERE TO PLANT

Plant in sun to part shade. Wisteria blooms best where it has protection from the prevailing northwest wind in winter. The vines will grow in all types of soil as long as the soil is well drained; this is a hardy vine that covers a lot of ground.

How to Plant

Plant wisteria as close to its climbing structure as possible. Dig the hole twice as wide as and no deeper than the soil clump, and loosen any roots that are wrapped around the clump. Chop up each clump to the size of golf balls. Backfill with existing soil, and water-in well.

Care and Maintenance

These vines become very woody after only a few years, and they need a support structure to climb. Make sure you have the structure before planting your wisteria. You can prune the vine from summer to fall to keep it within your growing allowance. There are no bug or disease problems that will hassle your wisteria.

Landscape Merit

Fast-growing wisteria provides lots of shade when used on wood structures built over patios and decks.

Additional Information

If you have a wisteria that has never bloomed, you may have bought a seedling. To try to get this plant to bloom, take a spade and make a circular cut 1 foot from the main trunk. Make the cut the depth of the spade and continue around the plant. This practice could shock the wisteria into bloom.

Additional Species, Cultivars, or Varieties

'Violacea Plena' has double violet-blue flowers on 10- to 12-inch racemes, or flower heads. 'Alba' has 11-inch flower heads of fragrant white flowers. Pale rose/purple 'Rosea' has very fragrant 18-inch flower heads.

Did You Know?

The only difference between a wisteria vine and a wisteria tree is the way it is trained . . . either "end result" can come from the same plant.

Resources

LENGTH OF GROWING SEASON AND FREEZE DATA

	Average Date Last Spring 32°	Average Date First Fall 32°	Average Length of Growing Season
Ashland	Apr. 24	Oct. 24	177
Bowling Green	Apr. 15	Oct. 20	180
Covington	Apr. 26	Oct. 17	181
Greensburg	Apr. 16	Oct. 17	180
Heidelberg	May 2	Oct. 16	169
Henderson	Apr. 8	Oct. 25	200
Hopkinsville	Apr. 10	Oct. 25	199
Lexington	Apr. 22	Oct. 26	185
Louisville	Apr. 20	Oct. 18	182
Paducah	Apr. 5	Oct. 24	200
Pikeville	Apr. 18	Oct. 25	181
Williamsburg	Apr. 25	Oct. 20	171

1. Exercise caution in using these dates because local site characteristics can make the date vary by as much as a couple of weeks; low-lying areas, in particular, will experience the first freezing morning of fall much earlier and the last freeze of spring much later.

2. The length of the growing season is not equal to the number of days between the average date of the first and last freezing temperatures because these dates occur independently.

3. The shortest growing seasons in the Bluegrass State are found in the mountainous parts of eastern Kentucky where cold air drains off the high ridges and pools in the deep valleys. The longest growing seasons are found in the low, humid areas of the far west along the Mississippi River.

GROWING SEASON DATA

MEAN NUMBER OF DAYS WITH A LOW TEMPERATURE OF 32° F OR COLDER

January – June

	JAN	FEB	MAR	APR	MAY	JUN
Ashland	23	20	16	5	1	0
Bowling Green	22	19	14	3	0	0
Covington	26	22	16	5	*	0
Greensburg	23	20	16	4	0	0
Heidelberg	22	20	17	6	1	0
Henderson	22	19	14	2	0	0
Hopkinsville	24	20	14	2	0	0
Lexington	22	20	15	4	0	0
Louisville	22	19	14	2	0	0
Paducah	23	18	13	2	0	0
Pikeville	19	17	11	3	0	0
Williamsburg	22	22	16	5	1	0

July – December

	JUL	AUG	SEP	OCT	NOV	DEC	YR
Ashland	0	0	0	3	14	22	104
Bowling Green	0	0	0	2	13	21	94
Covington	0	0	*	3	13	22	106
Greensburg	0	0	0	5	15	22	105
Heidelberg	0	0	0	5	16	22	109
Henderson	0	0	0	2	12	21	92
Hopkinsville	0	0	0	2	14	22	98
Lexington	0	0	0	2	13	21	97
Louisville	0	0	0	2	11	21	91
Paducah	0	0	0	2	12	20	90
Pikeville	0	0	0	2	12	19	83
Williamsburg	0	0	0	5	13	20	104

*=Less than one; only occasionally during an exceptional spell of weather will the temperature drop to freezing during these months.

MAIL-ORDER
SEED SOURCES

Alberta Nursery & Seeds
P.O.Box 20
Bowden, AV TOM, Canada
Phone: 403-224-3544
Fax: 403-224-2455

W. Atlee Burpee Co.
300 Park Ave.
Warminster, PA 18974
Phone: 215-674-4900
Fax: 215-674-0838

E & R Seed Co.
1356 E. 200 S.
Monroe, IN 46772
(No phone—Amish—write
for catalog.)

Ferry-Morse Seeds
P.O. Box 488
Fulton, KY 42041
Phone: 800-283-3400

Gurney Seed & Nursery
Gurney Building
Yankton, SD 57078
Phone: 605-665-4451
Fax: 605-665-6435

Harris Seeds
60 Saginaw Drive
Rochester, NY 14623
Phone: 716-442-0410
Fax: 605-442-9387

Holmes Seed Co.
P.O. Box 9087
Canton, OH 44709
Phone: 330-492-0123
Fax: 330-492-0167

Ed Hume Seeds, Inc.
1819 S. Central Ave., Bay 33
Kent, WA 98032
Phone: 253-859-1110
Fax: 253-859-0694

J. W. Jung Seed Co.
335 S. High Street
Randolph, WI 53956
Phone: 920-326-3121
Fax: 920-326-5769

Lindenberg Seeds Ltd.
803 Princess Ave.
Brandon, MB, R7A 0P5, Canada
Phone: 204-727-0575
Fax: 204-727-2832

McFayden Seeds
(c/o A.E. McKensie)
P. O. Box 1060
Brandon, MB, R7A 6E1, Canada
Phone: 204-725-7333
Fax: 204-571-7538

Nichols Garden Nursery
1190 North Pacific Hwy.
Albany, OR 97321
Phone: 541-928-9280
Fax: 541-967-8406

George W. Park Seed Co.
Hwy. 254 N.
Greenwood, SC 29657
Phone: 864-223-8555
Fax: 864-941-4206
Toll-free: 800-845-3369

Mail-Order Seed Sources

Seed Saver's Exchange
3076 North Winn Road
Decorah, IA 52101
Heirloom Vegetable and Flower Seeds

Seeds of Change
P. O. Box 15700
Santa Fe, NM 87506
*Organically Grown Vegetable and
    Flower Seeds*

R. H. Shumway
P. O. Box 1
Graniteville, SC 29828
Phone: 803-663-9771
Fax: 803-663-9772

T & T Seeds Ltd.
P. O. Box 1710
Winnipeg, MB, R3C 3P6, Canada
Phone: 204-895-9962
Fax: 204-895-9967

Tomato Growers Supply
P. O. Box 720
Fort Meyers, FL 33902
Phone: 888-478-7333
Fax: 888-768-3476

Totally Tomatoes
P. O. Box 1626
Augusta, GA 30903
Phone: 803-663-0016
Fax: 888-477-7333

Vermont Bean Seed Co.
Garden Lane
Fair Haven, VT
Phone: 803-273-3400

West Coast Seeds, Ltd.
Unit 206-84 Ontario St.
Vancouver, BC, V5X 3E8, Canada
Phone: 604-482-8800
Fax: 604-482-8822

THE KENTUCKY STATE UNIVERSITY EXTENSION SERVICE

The Kentucky State University Extension Service is a wonderful resource for all Kentucky gardeners. The service continually brings current research-based information to you through classes, workshops, newspaper articles, and master gardener programs. It also provides a bimonthly newsletter to hundreds of us in the industry. It has printed Bulletin sheets available on the Internet at **www.ca.UKY.edu.** The Bulletins cover hundreds of topics from bugs to disease to many "how to" tips on growing many plants in Kentucky. The printed sheets are also available at your county extension office and are a good local resource for gardeners and landscape professionals alike. Always feel free to contact your local county office for a list of publications, soil test information, and other resources available in your county.

Adair: PO Box 309, Columbia, KY 42728-0309; (270) 384-2317/5864

Allen: PO Box 355, Scottsville, KY 42164-0355; (270) 237-3146

Anderson: 300 Lincoln St. Center, Lawrenceburg, KY 40342-1235; (502) 839-7271/6806

Ballard: PO Box 237, LaCenter, KY 42056-0237; (270) 665-9118

Barren: 936 Happy Valley Rd., Glasgow, KY 42141; (270) 651-3818

Bath: 85 Miller Dr., Owingsville, KY 40360-2212; (606) 674-6121

Bell: 101 Courthouse Square, Pineville, KY 40977-1635; (606) 337-2376

Boone: PO Box 676, Burlington, KY 41005-0876; (606) 586-6101

Bourbon: 603 Millersburg, Paris, KY 40361-2044; (888) 317-2555 or (606) 984-1895

Boyd: PO Box 556, Catlettsburg, KY 41129-0556; (606) 739-5184/5

Boyle: PO Box 1487, Danville, KY 40423-1487; (606) 236-4484

Bracken: PO Box 66, Brooksville, KY 41004-0066; (606) 735-2141/2

Breathitt: PO Box 612, Jackson, KY 41339-1191; (606) 666-8812

Breckenridge: Rt 3 Box 203A, Hardensburg, KY 40143; (270) 756-2182

Bullitt: 1470 Hwy. 44 East., Shepherdsville, KY 41065-6125; (502) 543-2257

Butler: PO Box 170, Morgantown, KY 42261-0370; (270) 526-3767

Calloway: George H. Weaks Community Center, 607 Poplar, Murray, KY 42071-2587; (270) 753-1452/6

Campbell: 3500 Alexandria Pike, Highland Heights, KY 41076-1705; (606) 572-2600

Carlisle: PO Box 518, Bardwell, KY 42023-0518; (270) 628-5458/3722

Carroll: County Extension Office 440, Main Suite 6, Carrollton, KY 41008-1060; (502) 732-7030

Carter: 300 W. Main St., Grayson, KY 41143; (606) 474-6686 or 474-6687

Casey: 1517 S. Wallace Wilkinson Blvd. Liberty, KY 42539-9805; (606) 787-7384/5803

Chalon: PO Box 207, Albany, KY 42602-0207; (606) 387-5404

Christian: 509 1/2 West Ninth St., Hopkinsville, KY 42240-2133; (270) 886-6328

Clark: 34 S. Main St., Room 8, Winchester, KY 40391-2600; (606) 744-4682

Clay: PO Box 421, Manchester, KY 4092-0421; (606) 598-2789

Coldwell: 100 E. Market St., RM1 Courthouse, Princeton, KY 42445-1600; (270) 365-2787

Crittendon: 107 South Main - Ste. 101, Marion, KY 42064-1500; (270) 965-5236

Cumberland: PO Box 39, Burkesville, KY 42717-0039; (270) 864-2681

Daviess: 4800A New Hartford Rd., Owensboro, KY 42303; (270) 685-3276

Edmonson: 227 Mammoth Cave Rd., Brownsville, KY 42210-9003; (270) 597-3628

Elizabethtown Area Farm Analysis: Commonwealth Bldg. Suite 205, 615 N. Mulberry St., Elizabethtown, KY 42701-1927; (270) 737-4799

Elliott: PO Box 709, Sandy Hook, KY 41171-0709; (606) 738-9700

Estill: 149 Richmond Rd., Irvine, KY 40336-9316; (606) 723-4557

Fayette: 1140 Red Mile Place, Lexington, KY 40504-7772; (606) 257-5582

Fleming: PO Box 192, Flemingsburg, KY 41041-0192; (606) 845-4641

Floyd: 921 South Lake Dr., Prestonsburg, KY 41653; (606) 886-2668

Franklin: 101 Lakeview Ct., Frankfort, KY 40607-8750; (502) 695-9035

Fulton: Extension Office, 2006 South Seventh, Hickman, KY 42050-1842; (270) 236-2351/2404

Gallatin: PO Box 805, Warsaw, KY 41095-0805; (606) 567-5481

Garrard: PO Box 648, Lancaster, KY 40444-1238; (606) 792-3026

Grant: 224 South Main St., Williamstown, KY 41097-1220; (606) 824-3355

Graves: 251 Housman Street, Mayfield, KY 42066-1165; (270) 247-2334

Grayson: 123 Commerce Dr., Leitchfield, KY 42754-9148; (270) 259-3492/6342

Green: PO Box 371, Greensburg, KY 42743-0377; (270) 932-5311/3949

Greenup: 226 W. Main St., Greenup, KY 41144; (606) 473-9881/2/3

Hancock: PO Box 10, Havesville, KY 42348-0070; (270) 927-6618

Hardin: 201 Peterson Dr., Elizabethtown, KY 42701-9370; (270) 765-4721

Harrison: Rt 7 Box 153, Cynthiana, KY 41031-0153; (606) 234-5510

Hart: PO Box 367, Munfordville, KY 42765-0367; (270) 524-2453

Hartan: 579 S. Main St., Harlan, KY 40831-1191; (606) 573-4464

Henderson Area Farm Analysis: 409 S. Green St., Henderson, KY 42420-3577; (502) 827-1395

Henderson: 3341 Hwy 351 East., Henderson, KY 42420-9202; (270) 826-8387/8

Henry: PO Box 246, Highway 421, New Castle, KY 40050-0246; (502) 845-2811

Hickman: PO Box 198, Clinton, KY 42031-0198; (270) 653-2231

Hopkins: PO Box 450, Madisonville, KY 42431-0450; (270) 821-3650

Jackson: PO Box 188, McKee, KY 40977-1635; (606) 337-2376

Jefferson: Jefferson Co. Ext Office Suite 1, 8012 Vinecrest Ave., Louisville, KY 40222-4690; (502) 425-4482/48

Jessamine: 206 South First St., Nicholasville, KY 40356-1527; (606) 885-4811

Johnson: PO Box 806, Painesville, KY 41240-0806; (606) 789-8108

Kenton: 10990 Marshall Rd., Covington, KY 41015-9326; (606) 356-3755

Kentucky Leadership Center: 17500 Hwy 196, Nancy, KY 42544; (270) 866-4215

Kentucky State University: Cooperative Extension Programs, Kentucky State University, Campus Box 196, 400 E. Main St., Frankfort, KY 40601-0196; (502) 227-5905

Kentucky State University: National Center for Diversity, Kentucky State University, Campus Box 196, 400 E. Main St., Frankfort, KY 40601-0196; (502) 227-5904

Knott: PO Box 462, Handman, KY 41822-0462; (606) 785-5329

Knox: HC84 Box 518, Barbourville, KY 40906-8910; (606) 546-3447

Larue: PO Box 210, Hodgersville, KY 42748-0210; (270) 358-3401/9464

Laurel: 200 County Extension Rd., London, KY 40741-9008; (606) 864-4767

Lawrence: 310 E. Main St., Louisa, KY 41230; (606) 638-9695/6

Lee: PO Box 546, Beattyville, KY 41311-0546; (606) 464-2759

Leslie: PO Box 788, Hyden, KY 41749-0788; (606) 672-2754

Letcher: PO Box 784, Whitesburg, KY 41858-0784; (606) 633-2362/94

Lewis: 806 East Second St., Vanceburg, KY 41179-1104; (606) 796-2732

Lexington Area Farm Analysis: 640 South Broadway, Ste. 210, Lexington, KY 40508; (606) 252-3673

Lincoln: PO Box 326, Stanford, KY 40484-0326; (606) 365-2458/47

Livingston: PO Box 189, Smithland, KY; (270) 928-2168

Logan: PO Box 660, Russellville, KY 42276-0660; (270) 726-6323

Lyon: PO Box 36, Eddyville, KY 42038-0036; (270) 388-2341

Madison: PO Box 270, Richmond, KY 40475; (606) 623-4072

Magoffin: PO Box 349, Salyersville, KY 41465-0349; (606) 349-3216/1236

Marion: 135 E. Water St., Labanoa, KY 40033-7550; (270) 692-2421

Marshall: 905 Joe Creason Dr., Benton, KY 42025-1460; (270) 527-3285

Martin: PO Box 325, Inez, KY 41224-0325; (606) 298-7742/3

Mason: 800 US 68, Maysville, KY 41056-1141; (606) 564-6808/9

McCracken: 2705 Olivet Church Rd., Paducah, KY 42001-9755; (270) 554-9520/2

McCreary: PO Box 278, Whitley City, KY 42653-0278;
(606) 376-2524/3037

McLean: PO Box 265, Calhoun, KY 42327-0265; (270) 273-3690/21

Mearle: PO Box 539, Brandenburg, KY 40108-1002; (270) 422-4958

Melcalfe: PO Box 55, Edmonion, KY 42129-0055; (270) 432-3561

Menifee: PO Box 85, Frenchburg, KY 40322-0085; (606) 768-3866

Mercer: PO Box 324, Harrodsburg, KY 40330-0324; (606) 734-4378

Monroe: 1194 Columbia Ave., Tompkinsville, KY 42167-1246;
(270) 487-5504

Montgomery: 158 Civic Center, Mt. Sterling, KY 40353-1400;
(606) 498-8741/2

Morgan: PO Box 35, West Liberty, KY 41472-0035; (606) 743-3292/484

Muhlenberg: PO Box 199, Greenville, KY 42345-0199; (270) 338-3124

Nelson: 317 S. Third St., Bardstown, KY 40004-1032; (502) 348-9204

Nicholas: 368 East Main St., Carlisle, KY 40311-1158; (606) 289-2312

North Central 4-H Center: (606) 289-5308

Ohio: PO Box 66. Hanford, KY 42347-0066; (270) 293-7441

Oldhain: 7815 North Highway 393, LaGrange, KY 40031-8632;
(502) 222-9453

Owen: 265 Ellis Hwy., Owenton, KY 40359-9300; (502) 484-5703

Owsley: PO Box 186, Booneville, KY 41314-0184; (606) 593-5109

Paducah Area Farm Analysis: PO Box 8028, Paducah, KY 42002;
(270) 443-6634

Pendleton: 604 Ridgeway Ave., Falmouth, KY 41040; (606) 654-3395

Perry: 933 Perry Park Rd., Hazard, KY 41701-5322; (606) 436-2044 or
439-2665

Pike: 148 Trivette Dr., Pikeville, KY 41501-1271; (606) 432-2534

Powell: PO Box 38, Stanton, KY 40380-0038; (606) 663-6404/5

Pulaski: PO Box 720, Somerset, KY 42502-0720; (606) 679-6361

Robertson: PO Box 283, Mt. Olivet, KY 41064-0203; (606) 724-5796/900

Robinson Experiment Station: Robinson Substation, 130 Robinson
Rd., Jackson, KY 41339-9081; (606) 666-2438, from Lexington 257-9511

Rockcastle: PO Box 900, Mt. Vernon, KY 40456-0900; (606) 256-7403;
256-9652

Rowan: PO Box 848, Morehead, KY 40351-0848; (606) 784-5457/8416

Russell: 2340-8 S. Hwy. 127, Russell Springs, KY 42642-4013; (270) 866-4477

Scott: 1130 Cincinnati Rd., Georgetown, KY 40324-8931; (502) 863-0984

Shelby: 1201 Mt. Eden Rd., Suite 200, Shelbyville, KY 40065-8822; (502) 633-4593

Shelbyville Area Farm Analysis: PO Box 108, Shelbyville, KY 40066-0108; (502) 633-5513

Simpson: PO Box 446, Franklin, KY 42135-0446; (270) 586-4484

Somerset Area Extension Programs: The Center for Rural Development, 2292 South Highway 27, Suite 200, Somerset, KY 42501; (606) 679-6361

Spencer: PO Box 368, Taylorsville, KY 40071-0368; (502) 477-2247

Taylor: 1712 E. Broadway, Campbellsville, KY 42718-9231; (270) 465-4511

Todd: PO Box 97, Elkton, KY 42220-0097; (270) 265-5659

Trigg: PO Box 271, Carliz, KY 42211-0271; (270) 522-3269

Trimble: PO Box 244, 43 High County Rd., Bedford, KY 40006-0244; (502) 255-7188

Union: 1938 US Hwy 60 West, Morganfield, KY 42437-6246; (270) 389-1400

Warren: 3132 Nashville Rd., Bowling Green, KY 42101; (270) 842-1681

Warren: PO Box 2280, Bowling Green, KY 42102-2280; (270) 842-5823/3633

Washington: 211 Progress Ave., Springfield, KY 40069-1435; (606) 336-7741/2

Wayne: 1820 N. Main St., Ste. B, Monticello, KY 42633-2048; (606) 348-8453

Webster: PO Box 229, Dixon, KY 42409-0229; (270) 639-9011

Whitley: 428 Main St., Williamsburg, KY 40769-1126; (606) 549-1430

Wolfe: PO Box 146, Campion, KY 41301-0146; (606) 668-3712

Woodford: 184 Beasley Rd., Versailles, KY 40383-9558; (606) 873-4600

GLOSSARY

Acidic soil: soil with a pH lower than 7.0.

Acidifier: one of different types of materials that will help to lower the pH of alkaline soil.

Alkaline soil: soil with a pH higher than 7.0. Most of the Kentucky clay soil is derived from limestone, which naturally has a high pH.

All-purpose fertilizer: granular, liquid, or powdered fertilizer that contains all the necessary nutrients to help your plant grow. A higher first number (nitrogen) will promote growth, while a high middle number (phosphorus) will promote new roots and bloom. The last number (potash) promotes strong stems; its presence in the soil helps to keep plant cells from freezing (just like anti-freeze in our cars).

Annual: any plant that completes its entire life cycle in just one growing season.

Balled and burlapped: describes any plant that is field-grown in a nursery and dug up, forming a rootball that is then covered with burlap. Such plants are often referred to as B&B.

Bare-root: describes plants that are sold not growing in soil. The roots are packed in peat or sawdust. This is not the best way to buy any living plant.

Barrier plant: any thick-growing plant that is placed in a given area to stop foot traffic of either man or beast.

Beneficial insects: the good bugs that destroy lots of bad bugs. Ladybugs, yellow jackets in the spring and summer, and praying mantids are good examples.

Biennial: a plant that lives for two years. The first year it just grows leaves, and the second year it flowers, seeds, and then dies. Most biennials reseed themselves, so they might appear to be perennial.

Bract: a modified leaf structure on a plant stem near its flower that resembles a petal. Often it is more colorful and visible than the actual flower, as in dogwood.

Bud or graft union: the place where the top of a plant was grafted to the rootstock; usually refers to roses, and ornamental crabs and pears.

Canopy: the total spread (diameter) of the lower tree branches that tells you how much of your yard a tree is covering.

Glossary

Cell-pack: container that resembles an ice cube tray and holds small plants growing in a planting mix. Each pack can contain one, two, three, four, six, or twelve cells. This is the most common way annuals are sold.

Cold hardiness: the ability of a herbaceous perennial or woody ornamental to survive the winter cold. All plants listed in cold-hardy plants in this book are cold hardy for zone 6.

Composite: a flower that is actually composed of many tiny flowers. Typically, they are flat clusters of tiny, tight florets, sometimes surrounded by wider-petaled florets. Composite flowers are highly attractive to bees and beneficial insects.

Compost: organic material that has decomposed over time until it turns into a black, peat-like material that makes for a great soil conditioner.

Container grown: describes any plant that has been grown in a pot. No roots have been cut prior to your buying it. Always loosen any wrapped roots before planting a container-grown plant.

Crown: the base of the plant where the roots go down and the stems or blades go up, or the upper portion of a tree.

Cultivar: a cultivated variety. It is a naturally occurring form of a plant that has been identified as special or superior and is purposely selected for propagation and production.

Deadhead: to remove faded flower heads from plants to improve their appearance, abort seed production, and stimulate further flowering (a pruning technique).

Deciduous plants: trees and shrubs that lose their leaves in the fall.

Drainage: the ability of the soil to drain away water. Good drainage (which almost all plants need) means there is no standing water around the roots after 1/2 inch of rain.

Division: the practice of splitting apart perennials to make more plants for you to enjoy, or to control the size of your existing perennials. It is also required to keep certain perennials blooming.

Dormancy: that period of time when a given plant takes a rest. Most plants sleep during the winter, while certain bulbs sleep during the summer. Everyone needs some rest.

Glossary

Established: a stage of plant growth that can be said to begin when the roots start to grow in their new home. A newly transplanted plant will not grow until it becomes established.

Evergreen: any plant that keeps its needles or leaves over winter. Evergreens do lose some needles or leaves every fall, but the majority of the foliage remains on the plant.

Field grown: describes any woody or perennial plant that is grown in nursery soil. These plants are dug and then the rootball is wrapped in burlap (B&B) or placed in pots.

Field potted: describes a plant that is field grown in a nursery and whose rootball is placed in a pot whose size is determined by the size of the dug root clump.

Foliage: the leaves or needles of any plant.

Germinate: to sprout and start to grow. Germination is a seed's first step in developing a plant.

Group planting: three or more of a particular variety of plant placed in a certain area of your landscape. Always plant groups in odd numbers if possible.

Growing season: those months of the year that a plant, including leaves, flowers, and roots, is putting on new growth.

Healed-in: describes a balled-and-burlapped plant whose rootball is covered with leaves, sawdust, or other organic material. The organic material helps to keep moisture around the rootball while the plant is being offered for sale at a nursery or garden center.

Herbaceous: describes any soft-stemmed plant that dies back to the ground after a killing frost.

Hybrid: a plant that results from the cross-pollination of two or more plant varieties of the same species or genus.

Installs (plural noun): informal term—"garden materials (shrubs, trees, groups, etc.) to be arranged and planted in a landscape."

Mass planting: using many plants of the same variety in a given area where you want to make a large planting statement.

Glossary

Mound planting: taking extra soil and piling it to form a raised mound on top of the existing soil. The plants will be installed in the soil that forms the mound.

Mulch: a thin layer of any organic or inorganic material that helps retain soil moisture and discourage weeds, and just plain looks nice. Such materials as wood chips, bark, pine needles, and gravel are the most popular. Never have more than a 2- or 3-inch layer around any plant at any time. Keep the mulch from touching any part of the plant.

Natural light: describes the light in an area of your landscape that does not receive any direct sunlight but does have good sky light. This is an area that is bright enough that you could read this book in it without adding a flashlight.

Natural shade: describes the shade that is caused by nearby plants and shifting light. It is not as dark and dense as the shade caused by a large, leafy tree.

Naturalize: to plant seed, bulbs, or ornamental plants in a scattered, informal way as they might appear if growing from windblown seed. In other words: to plant some here, there, and everywhere.

Organic matter: once-living plant material that has been accumulated and piled up, allowing for its breakdown. Once composted, this organic material makes a great soil amendment for clay soil.

Part shade: a location in your landscape that receives up to 6 hours of shade per day. Part sun would be any area receiving up to 6 hours of sun per day.

Perennial: a plant that returns for more than two years. The tops of herbaceous perennials die every fall, but the roots remain alive to generate new growth the next spring. Trees and shrubs are also considered perennials.

pH: the measurement of the soil's acidity (low pH) or alkalinity (high pH) on a scale of 1 to 14, with 7 being neutral. Most of Kentucky soil tends to be on the alkaline side. Soil acidifiers are sometimes required to assist acid-loving plants.

Pinching back: removing soft tissue growth for the purpose of creating a shorter and bushier plant.

Glossary

Pruning: removing unwanted growth from any plant to control height, spread, and width. This can be done with handpruners, pruning saw, and hedge shears.

Reseeding: describes the tendency of some plants to sow their seeds in various parts of the landscape and have those create new seedlings the next season. This could be rewarding . . . or "weedy."

Root flare: the transition at the base of a tree trunk where the bark ends and the roots begin to form just prior to entering the soil. Do not cover the flare with soil or mulch.

Screen plant: any tree, shrub, or evergreen that will naturally grow in such a way as to screen or hide a view, or to give us privacy from neighbors.

Semievergreen: describes a broadleaf evergreen that holds its leaves all winter under normal temperatures. Extreme winter temps could cause leaves to drop, but they should return in the spring.

Sky light: describes the light received by a fairly bright area of your landscape that does not have a lot of direct sunlight but is not shaded.

Soil amendment: organic material such as compost, peat moss, and pine bark chips that can be added to heavy clay soil to improve that soil's porosity and drainage.

Soil preparation: the process of improving existing soil to make better growing conditions for our plants. Just loosening the existing soil before planting allows the new plants to get off to a good growing start. You may also need to add soil amendments under certain conditions.

Sucker: fast-growing stems coming up from the roots under the soil or growing off the lower part of the trunk. They can also grow off main branches when trees have been improperly pruned. Keep suckers pruned off whenever they appear.

Time-release fertilizer: capsulated fertilizer prills that contain all the nutrients a plant will need. Small amounts of nutrients are released every time the plant is watered or it rains. One application in spring feeds the plant for the entire growing season.

Glossary

Tree shade: the fairly dark, dense shade caused by a large, leafy tree.

Variegated: having various colors or color patterns on a plant's leaves or needles. The term usually refers to plant foliage that is streaked, edged, blotched, or mottled with a contrasting color, often green with yellow, cream, or white.

Water soluble: describes a powdered fertilizer that is mixed according to the instructions on the container with water and applied to the leaves and/or roots of plants.

Woody ornamental: describes plants with trunks, stems, and branches that stay alive during the winter and grow new growth from that wood each spring.

INFORMATION RESOURCES FOR THIS BOOK

BOOKS

Cox, Jeff, *Perennial All Stars*, Emmaus, PA: Rodale Press, 1988.

Dirr, Michael A., *Manual of Woody Landscape Plants*, Champaign, IL: Stipes Publishing, 1998.

OTHER RESOURCES

Ball Seed Co., 622 Town Road, West Chicago, IL 60185-2688

Conard-Pyle Co., 372 Rose Hill Road, West Grove, PA 19390-0904

Four Star Greenhouse, 1015 Indian Trails, Carleton, MI 48117

Horstmeyer, Steve, Meteorologist, WKRC TV, 1906 Highland Ave., Cincinnati, OH 45219

Imperial Nurseries, 11245 Mosteller Road, Cincinnati, OH 45241-1825

Monrovia Nursery, 18331 E. Foothill Blvd., Azusa, CA 91702-2638

Ohio Nursery and Landscape Association, 72 Dorchester St., Westerville, OH 43081-3350

OSU Extension Adm., 3 Agriculture Adm. Bldg., 2120 Fyffe Rd., Columbus, OH 43210-1084

Proven Winners North America, 426 West Second St., Rochester, MI 48307

Sakata Seed America, Inc., 18095 Serene Drive, Morgan Hill, CA 95037

White Flower Farm, P. O. Box 50, Litchfield, CT 06759-9988

Willoway Nurseries, Inc., 4534 Center Road, Avon, OH 44011

Wood, James, Denny McKeown Landscape, Cincinnati, OH

INDEX

Index

Index

Index

Index

Index

Index

Index

Index

Index

Index

Index

Denny McKeown

*D*ENNY MCKEOWN has been in the nursery business for thirty-eight years, twenty-nine of them with Natorp's, where he retired as Vice-President of Marketing. In January 1992, McKeown started The Bloomin' Garden Centre, a year-round retail garden sales business. Denny McKeown Landscape is a full-service landscape division featuring design and installation for residential and commercial properties.

In 1990, the author received The Jack Schneider Award, from the Garden Centers of America, a division of the American Nursery and Landscape Association—it is the highest award given to anyone in the retail nursery business. In 1992, The American Nursery and Landscape Association presented McKeown with The Garden Communicators Award, which is given to the person who has done the most to promote gardening and planting across America.

The author has been involved in radio broadcasting for 20 years. His syndicated gardening radio show is heard throughout Ohio and Kentucky, every Saturday from 6 AM to 9 AM and Sundays from 9 AM till noon.

The author has served as President of The Garden Centers of America and has created a complete set of seasonal gardening videos. Previous works include *Denny McKeown's Complete Guide to Midwest Gardening,* a book now in its fifth printing. The author's first book for Cool Springs Press, *The Gardening Book for Ohio,* was released in early 2000 and is in its second printing. The *Kentucky Gardener's Guide* is the author's newest book for Cool Springs Press.

OTHER GARDENING TITLES
from Cool Springs Press: